TRAVELER

argentina

NATIONAL GEOGRAPHIC
TRAVELER

argentina

by Wayne Bernhardson
photography by Eliseo Miciu

National Geographic
Washington, D.C.

CONTENTS

Pages 2–3: Salta's Plaza 9 de Julio is the centerpiece of Argentina's most colonial city.
Opposite: Hikers contemplate the Moreno Glacier, in Parque Nacional Los Glaciares.

TRAVELING WITH EYES OPEN

Alert travelers go with a purpose and leave with a benefit. If you travel responsibly, you can help support wildlife conservation, historic preservation, and cultural enrichment in the places you visit. You can enrich your own travel experience as well.

To be a geo-savvy traveler:

- Recognize that your presence has an impact on the places you visit.

- Spend your time and money in ways that sustain local character. (Besides, it's more interesting that way.)

- Value the destination's natural and cultural heritage.

- Respect the local customs and traditions.

- Express appreciation to local people about things you find interesting and unique to the place: its nature and scenery, music and food, historic villages and buildings.

- Vote with your wallet: Support the people who support the place, patronizing businesses that make an effort to celebrate and protect what's special there. Seek out shops, local restaurants, inns, and tour operators who love their home—who love taking care of it and showing it off. Avoid businesses that detract from the character of the place.

- Enrich yourself, taking home memories and stories to tell, knowing that you have contributed to the preservation and enhancement of the destination.

That is the type of travel now called geotourism, defined as "tourism that sustains or enhances the geographical character of a place—its environment, culture, aesthetics, heritage, and the well-being of its residents." To learn more, visit National Geographic's Center for Sustainable Destinations at *www.nationalgeographic.com/travel/sustainable.*

NATIONAL
GEOGRAPHIC
T R A V E L E R

argentina

ABOUT THE AUTHOR & THE PHOTOGRAPHER

Wayne Bernhardson, author, first visited Argentina in 1979 and has returned repeatedly since then—with good reason, as he married an Argentine and owns an apartment in Buenos Aires. Spending four to five months every year in South America, he has visited every Argentine province and logged well over 100,000 miles on its highways, roads, and gravel tracks, from subtropical Jujuy to sub-Antarctic Tierra del Fuego. He holds a Ph.D. in geography from the University of California at Berkeley.

Eliseo Miciu, photographer, was born in Montevideo, Uruguay, but grew up in Córdoba and Patagonia, Argentina. His grandfather was an artist, as was his father, a well-known painter (Georg Miciu Nicolaevici). Miciu began his career as a photographer when he arrived in Patagonia at the age of 15; at 18, he started traveling and working for national magazines and agencies. He has since traveled through Europe and the United States learning the art of photography in museums and galleries, and continues to work as a freelance photographer in Argentina. Following his first published book about north Argentina, he is working on two others.

Charting Your Trip

From the world-class metropolis of Buenos Aires to the remote reaches of Patagonia, Argentina has everything. Within its boundaries lie some of the world's greatest river systems and biggest waterfalls, the world's highest mountain range, and one of its longest wildlife-rich shorelines. The world's eighth largest country also has subtropical forests, canyon-country deserts, countless alpine lakes, vast big-sky steppes, and growling glaciers.

Argentina has an epic history and thriving culture on its side as well. Buenos Aires is its urban flash point, but the surrounding Pampas are gaucho country. With its links to Peru and Bolivia, the northwest recalls the indigenous Andean past and Spanish colonial times, while the western Cuyo region has sophisticated wine country to match its mountains. Patagonia's grandeur evokes the age of exploration, and legendary Tierra del Fuego is the "uttermost part of the Earth."

Getting Around

Given that Argentina is such a large country, getting around is most efficient (albeit more expensive) by plane. The catch is that nearly all flights originate in Buenos Aires; meaning, if you want to fly from one province to a neighboring province, you'll typically have to go back through Buenos Aires in order to do so. Aerolíneas Argentinas (*www.aerolineas.com.ar*) offers the most flights, but LAN Argentina (*www.lan.com*) is considered more reliable.

Buses are another option, and overnight *coche cama* service is good value for trips, almost like business class on an airplane. At Buenos Aires's central bus terminal, you'll be confronted by a myriad of different bus companies; keep in mind you get what you pay for. You can also rent a car, though this option is better for shorter distances; you don't want to waste time arrowing through endless pampas or desert scrub.

NOT TO BE MISSED:

If You Have Only One Week

By consensus, Argentina has three major must-sees for the first-time visitor: the cosmopolitan capital city of Buenos Aires, the thundering torrents of subtropical Iguazú Falls in the northeast, and the grinding ice of Patagonia's Moreno Glacier in the

Visitor Information

The Argentine tourism ministry's official site *(www.turismo.gov.ar)* is comprehensive and serves the English speaker, but deals with destination information rather than specific services. Every Argentine province has an information office in Buenos Aires, and virtually every Argentine city and town has its own tourist information office, at least in summer. They keep long hours and, in the larger destinations,

there'll usually be an English speaker.

For a good English-language digest of Argentine news, see the *Buenos Aires Herald (www.buenosairesherald.com)*. The English-language newsgroup BA Expats *(www.baexpats.org)* contains plenty of information on coping with the day-to-day difficulties of life in Argentina, but also provides some good suggestions on what to do in and beyond the capital.

south. Seeing all three in a week is a challenge, though. It involves flying more than 700 miles (1,127 km) north from Buenos Aires to Iguazú, on the Brazilian border, then backtracking to the capital to make a connection to El Calafate, the gateway to the Moreno Glacier, nearly 1,300 miles (2,092 km) south. Thus any short trip will mean tight logistics, and would be best as a package tour (see Travelwise p. 288).

A less taxing one-week itinerary, flying less but living high, could combine Buenos Aires, its dining and nightlife, with the gaucho capital of San Antonio de Areco, 70 miles (113 km) west of Buenos Aires via RN 8 by bus or car. This arts and crafts center has a palpable gaucho presence that presents rural Argentina in an admittedly idealistic light.

Another option is to focus on the canyon country of the Andean northwest, centering around the lovely colonial city of Salta—about a 1.5-hour flight from Buenos Aires. This beautiful region, with its rainbow-hued canyons and Inca ruins, is underappreciated for its fine wines, produced at the highest elevations in the world. It's easy to drive around—the Salta-Cafayate-Cachi route is popular among drivers as well as bikers.

You could also focus solely on Patagonia, in the south. Its vastness makes flying imperative from Buenos Aires, but once there, with good planning, you can get around by rental car or long-distance buses. The top stops: Península Valdés, for its abundant wildlife, especially giant southern right whales that

A llama, a commonly seen resident in Argentina's Andean northwest

Currency

Argentina's currency is the peso ($), divided into 100 centavos. Banknotes, in denominations of $2, $5, $10, $20, $50, and $100, mostly depict figures from 19th-century history such as liberator Gen. José de San Martín. Coins come in denominations of 5, 10, 25, and 50 centavos and $1. As of press time, the U.S. dollar was worth about 7.8 pesos, but Argentine exchange rates are known for their volatility.

migrate April through December; El Calafate, along the shores of Lago Argentino; and the stunning Moreno Glacier.

Finally, you could also indulge in some of the world's finest wines in the region of Cuyo, where 70 percent of Argentina's wines are produced, including its signature Malbec. Base yourself in Mendoza, 1.5 hours by plane from Buenos Aires, and enjoy sipping, tasting, biking, and walking in the magnificent surrounding countryside, over-shadowed by the snowcapped Andes.

If You Have More Time

A country of Argentina's size and geographical diversity could fill a lifetime's itinerary, and more time lets travelers see more remote sights and indulge special interests. It's a particularly beguiling country for road trips. South of Trelew, the best sights to see along the Patagonian coast are Camarones, Puerto Deseado, and Puerto San Julián, all of which have wildlife reserves or national parks nearby. Penguins, elephant seals, and sea lions are common along the route, along with dolphins and many seabirds. Distances, however, are measured in the hundreds, even thousands, of kilometers. Turning inland to cover the legendary Ruta 40, at the foot of the Andes, can mean weeks of travel—plan at least two. Along the southernmost part of Ruta 40, you'll find few towns but plenty of guanaco and rhea.

Another possibility is to blend travel itineraries with specific activities, or to devote the entire trip to those activities. Many, for instance, travel to Buenos Aires just to dance tango—lots of schools offer day-, week-, and month-long classes. In Buenos Aires and at estancias in the surrounding countryside, horse lovers can indulge in gaucho-style galloping, formal English riding, even polo. While estancias generally offer hour-long rides, you can

Dodging the Roadblocks

In Argentina's dysfunctional politics, debate often takes place in the streets: Huge demonstrations, often vying to see who can pack more people into the Plaza de Mayo, are common in Buenos Aires.

In recent years, protest has spread to the highways. For more than a year, protestors at Gualeguaychú blocked an international bridge in opposition to a pulp plant across the Río Uruguay, and farmers

have barricaded highways with bulldozers to protest soy export taxes. Truckers have installed roadblocks to protest both the farmers (whose business they need) and government obstinacy.

Drivers encountering roadblocks, which can become contentious, should do nothing to agitate *piqueteros* (picketers). Serious confrontation is unlikely, but err on the side of solidarity.

When to Visit

Buenos Aires's attractions are rarely seasonal, but in summer (Jan.–Feb.) many museums close. Subtropical Mesopotamia, including Iguazú, is an all-year destination, but the northwestern desert canyons and even the altiplano (high steppe) are best in the winter dry season (July–Aug.). The Cuyo wine country is ideal at harvest time (March–April), but Patagonian travelers usually prefer January and February (though skiers and whale-watchers go in winter). Generally, the shoulder seasons (March–April and Nov.–Dec.) tend to be cheaper.

instead join a multiday pack trip in the northwest, the Mendozan Andes, and Patagonia.

Multiday trekking excursions are hugely popular in Argentina, especially in southern Patagonia's Fitz Roy range, near El Chaltén. The trails are less busy in November or March. In the Cuyo region near Mendoza, peak-baggers can spend three weeks or more training for and climbing towering Aconcagua. Others prefer to fish for days or weeks in the lakes and streams of Argentine Patagonia—particularly fly-fishing. You'll find trout and salmon in the rivers and lakes from Junín de los Andes to Esquel, as well as in Tierra del Fuego; the fishing season runs November through April.

Space prohibits more than a summary here but, as the above examples suggest, the options are almost infinite. Argentina should be more than just a one-time vacation. ∎

The vineyards of the Valles Calchaquíes, in the Andean northwest, produce high-altitude wines.

History &
Culture

In full gaucho gear, a young boy dances the *malambo* at the Feria de Mataderos, Buenos Aires.

Argentina Today

It takes the world's eighth-largest country to contain sights like the cosmopolitan capital Buenos Aires, thundering Iguazú Falls, and Patagonia's Moreno Glacier, but that's not all Argentina has to offer. There's world-class cuisine, including some of the world's most distinctive wines, and both high and popular culture: Argentina gave tango to the world.

The country can also boast one of the world's greatest rivers in the Paraná, some of its highest summits—including Aconcagua, tallest mountain in the Americas—and desert canyon country to match the U.S. Southwest. Add millions of penguins and thousands of whales on its Patagonian shores, Andean lakes, and herds of guanacos on the steppes, and there's more than enough for weeks or months of matchless sightseeing and recreation.

Statistically speaking, Argentines are city dwellers. In a territory nearly the size of India,

Buenos Aires's Obelisco was erected in 1936, on the 400th anniversary of Mendoza's landing.

Argentina has a population of only 40.1 million, a third of whom live in or around Buenos Aires. Nearly 90 percent of all Argentines live in urban areas, so much of the country is only thinly populated.

Ideologically, Argentines are a complex people. Despite their urbanity, they retain a romantic attachment to the gaucho, the legendary horseman of the Pampas. They particularly admire his idealized qualities of courtesy, generosity, and independence. This became part of the national narrative even among 20th-century immigrants who never moved beyond the port city of their arrival; in provincial festivals, a gaucho presence is almost imperative. It even became part of the language—a *gauchada* is a favor done without expectation of return, and even harried *porteños* (literally, "port dwellers," or natives of Buenos Aires) may exhibit remarkable courtesy toward Buenos Aires visitors.

> **Ideologically, Argentines are a complex people. Despite their urbanity, they retain a romantic attachment to the gaucho, the legendary horseman of the Pampas.**

National Identity

Conventional wisdom says that Argentina is the most European of South American countries. The preponderance of Spanish, Italian, Basque, and other European surnames would suggest so. Argentine intellectuals, especially writers and artists, have certainly looked to Europe for inspiration, but the gaucho heritage has spawned a fierce nationalism as well—in any other country, would Argentino (Argentine) be a man's given name, as it was with President Julio Argentino Roca (1843–1914)?

That said, these extremes are both misleading. With its ethnic heritage and large immigrant population—including Afro-Argentines, Anglo-Argentines, Irish, Welsh, French, Germans, Italians, Scandinavians, Jews, a multinational Middle Eastern community often erroneously referred to as *turcos* (Turks), and many others—Argentine society is a New World mosaic that resembles the United States. Just as the United States has many immigrants from Mexico and Central America, Argentina hosts numerous residents from neighboring countries, such as Bolivia and Paraguay, as well as an increasing number of Asian immigrants, mostly Hong Kong Chinese, Taiwanese, and Koreans.

Recent research has also suggested that contemporary Argentines may have to rethink who they are. DNA testing by investigators from the Universidad de Buenos Aires (UBA) has shown that 56 percent of Argentines carry genetic material from pre-Columbian peoples, though only 10 percent of today's population is purely indigenous. The remaining 44 percent—a minority, then—comes from exclusively European origins.

Indigenous Argentina

When the Spaniards first saw the Americas, they encountered great civilizations with large settled populations in Mexico, Central America, and the Andean highlands. They found far fewer people on the midlatitude periphery—North America and the Southern Cone—where most pre-Columbian peoples were agriculturalists or hunter-gatherers.

Argentina was part of the periphery, but its indigenous peoples have proved resilient. The Querandí of the Pampas were few, but northwestern Argentina was an outlier of the Andean civilizations, and, even today, according to official statistics, at least 70,500 Kolla raise potatoes on mountainside terraces and herd llamas

on the high plains of the puna. In the Mesopotamian provinces and the Gran Chaco, there are about 40,000 Guaraní, 48,000 Toba, and smaller numbers of Wichi, Mocoví, and others.

The most numerous of Argentine *indígenas* are the Mapuche (about 114,000), who made the Patagonian frontier a dangerous place for Spaniards and Argentines into the late 19th century. Like the Plains Indians of North America, the Mapuche quickly adapted to life on horseback, and horses became abundant as feral Spanish livestock proliferated. These horses and wild cattle made the gaucho lifestyle possible; many of today's Mapuche reflect the gaucho's origins.

Religion

Historically, Argentina is a Roman Catholic country, and the church here is often a conservative force. Cardinal Antonio Quarracino (1923–1998), for instance, was an apologist for the "Dirty War" dictatorship of 1976–1983 and a harsh opponent of homosexual rights. In 2005, military bishop Antonio Baseotto suggested that health minister Ginés González García should be "thrown into the sea headfirst with a large millstone around his neck"—similar to the fate of many Dirty War victims—for advocating free condom distribution and the decriminalization of abortion.

On the other hand, compassionate clergy such as the Jesuit Carlos Mugica (1930–1974) worked in the slums and made courageous human-rights stands—often at great personal risk. Mugica died in a terrorist assassination, probably by the extreme-right militia known as the Alianza Anticomunista Argentina (Argentine Anti-Communist Alliance, commonly known as the Triple A).

For all its lengthy history, the church has been losing influence. Since the constitutional reform of 1994, the president need no longer be a Roman Catholic, and former President Néstor Kirchner's government openly challenged the Vatican by firing Baseotto.

The official church has also failed to deal with the spread of irregular folk Catholicism. It disapproves of unofficial "saints" such as the gaucho Antonio Gil, of Corrientes Province, and the Difunta Correa (a 19th-century woman), of San Juan Province, but hundreds of thousands of pilgrims still visit their shrines regardless of the church's concerns.

While the church has been occupied with these minor heresies, it's lost even more ground to evangelical Protestantism, which has proliferated here as elsewhere in Latin America. In early 2013, the selection of Buenos Aires native Jorge Mario Bergoglio as Pope Francis, the first Latin American pontiff, did manage to inspire a wave of enthusiasm for official Roman Catholicism.

In addition to Christianity, Argentina has one of the world's largest Jewish communities outside Israel, and Jewish community landmarks are conspicuous in Buenos Aires—

so conspicuous, in fact, that two were destroyed by bombs in terrorist incidents in the early 1990s. Although half a million Argentines are of Middle Eastern descent, the capacity of the capital's Islamic Center far exceeds the number of observant Muslims. Of Syrian parentage and raised a Muslim in La Rioja Province, former President Carlos Menem formally converted to Roman Catholicism in the 1960s and was thus eligible, under the old constitution, for the country's top elected office.

A focus on Old World institutional religions often overlooks traditional indigenous beliefs such as those of the Andean peoples in northwestern Argentina, the Toba and Wichi in the Gran Chaco, and the Mapuche in Patagonia. In addition, there are cults such as Silo's Message, founded by the self-anointed "humanist" guru Mario Luis Rodríguez Cobos (1938–2010).

A Mapuche farmer leads his oxcart near San Martín de los Andes, Neuquén Province.

Standards of Living

Historically, Argentina has been one of Latin America's wealthiest countries, but an economic meltdown in 2001–2002 plunged the country into a bleak situation unmatched since the 1930s. Despite an impressive recovery, with sustained growth over a decade, private estimates suggest that at least 20 percent of Argentines live in poverty; more optimistic official statistics are unreliable.

Ideologically, Argentina is a middle-class country, but the gap between rich and poor has widened and the middle class has shrunk. Traditionally, wealth has been a function of land ownership, with the wealthy raising beef cattle on sprawling estancias and wheat farms, mirrored in a large, impoverished rural proletariat. There is also a large urban and suburban working class that suffered when the industrial sector went belly-up during the 2002 crisis. Unemployment reached at least 25 percent, and while it may now have

Soccer passions run high at River Plate Stadium, site of Argentina's 1978 World Cup triumph.

fallen into the 10 percent range, many Argentines are underemployed at menial jobs.

High growth rate statistics since the collapse may not be completely reliable, and many observers worry that Argentine authorities have not taken full advantage of favorable exchange rates and export markets to sustain the economy. At the same time, high inflation has eaten into everyday Argentines' purchasing power—official sources admit to 10 percent, but most private economists place the figure upward of twice that.

There are also major regional disparities. The capital city of Buenos Aires is prosperous, and its namesake province is the country's wealthiest and most populous, but northern and northwestern agricultural provinces such as Misiones, Santiago del Estero, Jujuy, and Tucumán have seemingly intractable poverty. Thanks to its flourishing wine and tourism sector, as well as energy resources that support local industry, westerly Mendoza Province is thriving, but the rest of Cuyo lags behind. With tourism and their energy-based economies, the Patagonian provinces are mainly prosperous but have poverty-stricken enclaves.

Government & Politics

Under the Constitution of 1853, Argentina has a federal system with a checks-and-balances national government that superficially resembles that of the United States. A popularly elected president, who may serve successive four-year terms, heads the executive branch. The legislative branch includes both a Senado (Senate) and Cámara de Diputados (Chamber of Deputies), and there's a nine-member Corte Suprema (Supreme Court). Twenty-three provinces and the Ciudad Autónoma de Buenos Aires (Autonomous City of Buenos Aires) have their own governments.

In reality, the systems are not so similar. The president enjoys great discretionary powers, often intervenes in provincial matters, and controls revenue-sharing purse strings. Legislators usually defer to presidential prerogative but, given any sign of executive weakness, many go quickly for the jugular. The Supreme Court usually acts independently, but it is subject to political pressure, as when former President Carlos Menem (1930–) added four select members in the 1990s (one of the new justices was his tennis coach). Its membership presently stands at seven, with two vacancies.

All the provinces are similarly organized, but few are well governed and some are near-hereditary fiefdoms dominated by caudillos (provincial strongmen). In the northwestern province of Santiago del Estero only military coups and federal intervention interrupted the reign of five-time governor Carlos Juárez (1916–2010) between 1948 and 2002, when his wife, Mercedes Aragonés de Juárez, succeeded him. She, in turn, appointed him provincial justice minister to give him immunity for covering up murders and other human-rights violations by his cronies; then she came under investigation herself.

Peronism's current leaders, though, have recently been the left-of-center President Cristina Fernández (1953–) and her husband/predecessor, former President Néstor Kirchner (1950–2010). Both of them, but especially Kirchner, gained reputations for intransigence toward their political opponents and willingness to exercise extraconstitutional power.

Nearly 30 different parties hold seats in the lower house, several of them with only a single representative.

Political Parties & Personalities: Given Argentina's fractured and impetuous politics, information about its parties and personalities can change suddenly. Nearly 30 different parties hold seats in the lower house, several of them with only a single representative. The heritage of the provincial caudillo has meant that personality often trumps party affiliation.

One constant, for more than six decades, is the Justicialist party—commonly known as "Peronist"—of former President Juan Perón (1895–1974) and his wife Eva Duarte (Evita, 1919–1952). Known for its corruption, the populist party has a range of factions from extreme left to extreme right. The leading faction is President Cristina Fernández's Frente para la Victoria (Victory Front), but she is facing a strong challenge from Tigre mayor Sergio Massa's Frente Renovador (Renovation Front).

Founded in 1891, the next most important party has been the Unión Cívica Radical (UCR). Since the presidency of their hapless Fernando de la Rúa (1937–) ended in political and economic meltdown in late 2001, the Radicals have fallen into disarray. Two ex-Radicals, the center-right Ricardo López Murphy (1951–) and center-left Elisa Carrió (1956–), have been presidential candidates and prominent opposition figures at the heads of the Propuesta Republicana (Republican Proposal, PRO) and the Coalición Cívica (Civic Coalition) parties. Buenos Aires city Mayor Mauricio Macri (1959–), a PRO member, is considered a future presidential candidate.

For much of Argentina's history, but especially after overthrowing President Hipólito Yrigoyen (1852–1933) in 1930, the military have played a major political role through extra-institutional pressure and repeated coup d'états. Since the notorious 1976–1983 Dirty War dictatorship and the 1982 Falklands War disaster, though, they appear to have subordinated themselves to civilian authority.

Celebrants at the Vendimia (Wine Harvest Festival), Teatro Griego Frank Romero Day, Mendoza

EXPERIENCE: Learning the Argentine Language

Argentina offers many opportunities to learn Spanish. Argentine Spanish, however, may surprise those who have learned the language elsewhere, and novices may acquire habits that are less useful in other countries. Thanks partly to its Italian intonation, the result of several centuries of immigration, the standard accent differs from that of other countries.

Similarly, Argentine speech is known for *yeísmo*, in which the *ll* and *y* sounds, both equivalent to English *y*, sound more like English *zh*.

Also characteristic is the *voseo*, in which the second-person familiar pronoun *vos* uses slightly different verb forms from the *tú* used in Spain.

Argentines, for instance, say *vos hablás* instead of *tú hablas* (you talk), and *vos decís* instead of *tú dices* (you say).

The Argentine vocabulary includes localisms and slang ranging from innocuous (*laburar* instead of *trabajar*, to work) to off-color (*quilombo*, a mess, but literally a "whorehouse"). It's also unselfconscious about borrowing words from other languages, including English—*pub*, for instance, or *delivery* and *sale*.

Among the many places in Buenos Aires to study the language are: **Centro Universitario de Idiomas** (*Junín 224, Balvanera, tel 011/5352-8000 ext. 24, www.cui.com.ar*) and **Coined** (*Suipacha 90, 2nd fl., tel 011/4331-2418, www.coined.com.ar*). There are many others and also private tutors.

Geography & Climate

With an area of almost 1.1 million square miles (almost 2.8 million sq km), Argentina is the world's eighth largest country. Latitudinally, it stretches about 2,300 miles (more than 3,700 km) from the subtropics to the sub-Antarctic. Longitudinally, it ranges from the Atlantic Coast to the Andean divide that separates the country from Chile.

Along with size, Argentina has diversity, starting with the almost endlessly level Pampas that stretch west from Buenos Aires, interrupted by only a few small mountain ranges. The great Río Paraná and its tributaries water the rolling riverine provinces of Mesopotamia and much of the Gran Chaco, which becomes a "green hell" desert in its western reaches. The canyon country of the northwestern provinces compares to the American Southwest, while the wine country of Cuyo sprawls at the base of the highest Andes. The southern vastness of Patagonia, with its lengthy shoreline, boundless steppe, and lakes and glaciers, gives way to the archipelago of Tierra del Fuego—shared with Chile—before the continent disappears beneath the South Atlantic Ocean.

In the Southern Hemisphere, seasons are reversed, but climate varies with latitude and altitude. Buenos Aires and the Pampas enjoy mild to warm, humid weather all year. The Mesopotamian provinces are hot in summer, mild in winter, and humid all year. Most of northwestern Argentina has hot, wet summers and mild, dry winters except at the highest altitudes, where nights are always cool and often freezing. East of the Andes, Argentine Patagonia can be arid, but sufficient storms sneak through mountain gaps to supply major lakes, rivers, and even a continental ice field. Summers are mild in the northern half, cool in the southern half, and the area is cold in winter; the climate's most trying feature is the nearly incessant wind, which abates somewhat in winter. ■

Food & Drink

Viewed from beyond Argentina's borders, the stereotypical diet seems to consist of beef and more beef. When Charles Darwin rode across the Pampas in the 1830s, he remarked that his gaucho guides ate "nothing but beef ... It is, perhaps, from their meat regimen that the Gauchos, like other carnivorous animals, can abstain long from food ... [S]ome troops voluntarily pursued a party of Indians for three days, without eating or drinking."

The reality, of course, is more complex. While few Argentines can pass up an *asado* (barbecue) of succulent beef, the country's fields and pastures produce a cornucopia of foodstuffs that, combined with a diversity of culinary traditions and recent innovations, offer something for everybody. Buenos Aires and other large cities have a wide range of ethnic and international food, but even some provincial towns have their enclaves—in the Andean Northwest, for instance, Middle Eastern food is common.

It's easy to be a vegetarian, theoretically at least— but the social pressure to share meat at the table forces some aspiring vegetarians back to the traditional diet. Committed vegetarians need to avoid misunderstandings about the word *carne,* which means "beef," not "meat," in Argentina—otherwise they may find chicken or ham in their plate of pasta, for instance.

> **Anyone who expects to dine before 9 p.m. may get an incredulous reception from waiters and restaurant staff.**

Argentine mealtimes deserve a mention here. Breakfast and lunch hours will be familiar enough to foreigners, though lunch may be more slowly paced than in North America. Dinner times, though, are as late as in Italy or Spain—anyone who expects to dine before 9 p.m. may get an incredulous reception from waiters and restaurant staff. Indeed, many Argentines eat even later.

Meat & Poultry

The signature Argentine meal is the *parrillada,* a mixed grill that ranges from *achuras* (offal) to chorizo sausages (far less spicy than their Mexican counterparts), *vacio* (flank steak), *costillas* (ribs), and other meats. It's often prepared with a mild, garlic-based *chimichurri* marinade—Argentines rarely abide spicy food—and may also include chicken or pork, and roast peppers. In Patagonia, though, the parrillada's centerpiece is succulent lamb, often grilled on a stake over an open fire; in some areas, it may even be goat. Most Argentines prefer their beef *bien cocido* (well done), but some take it *a punto* (medium) or *jugoso* (rare).

Several meat dishes qualify as Argentine comfort food. Often sold at mobile food carts, the *choripán* surrounds the grilled chorizo with a crusty roll, to be garnished with chimichurri or mustard. The *milanesa* is a breaded cutlet, usually fried (and thus greasy), but sometimes baked.

Game dishes, such as *venado* (venison), *jabalí* (wild boar), *ñandú* (rhea), and guanaco, mostly from Patagonia, are making their way onto Buenos Aires menus as well.

Fish & Seafood

Conventional opinion holds that Argentines are not great seafood consumers, but urban archaeologist Daniel Schávelzon has found evidence that early Buenos Aires residents consumed substantial quantities of fish. Spanish and Basque traditions are

Slicing the beef at an *asado*, La Rural, Palermo, Buenos Aires

A *mate* and *bombilla* await their *yerba*.

notable in dishes such as *abadejo al arriero* (pollack casserole), *gambas al ajillo* (garlic shrimp), and *rabas* (squid rings). *Merluza* (hake) may be the finest oceangoing fish available, while *centolla* (southern king crab) is the prime crustacean.

Patagonian *trucha* (trout) makes menus around the country, but the Mesopotamian rivers are renowned for game fish such as *boga, pacú* (a piranha relative), and *surubí* (Paraná catfish). Buenos Aires and some other cities support numerous sushi restaurants that vary in quality.

Comida Criolla

Argentina has many foods, including regional dishes, snacks, and desserts, that don't fall into any easy category but are distinctively Argentine. "Soul food" might be the closest equivalent for English-speaking audiences.

Puchero, for instance, is a stew of boiled beef, salted bacon, potatoes, and other vegetables. *Carbonada* has some of the same ingredients but also includes corn on the cob, raisins, and occasional regional touches. In a country where spicy food is uncommon, northwestern Argentina's *locro* is a hominy-based stew with a variety of meats, sausages, and vegetables seasoned with cumin, paprika, and hot peppers. Also from the northwest, *humitas* resemble Mexican tamales.

Pastel de papa is a sort of shepherd's pie. The Argentine empanada, a light phyllo-dough turnover with fillings that can include chopped beef, chicken, ham and cheese, or lamb, plus vegetables, eggs, olives, raisins, and seasonings, makes an extraordinary, savory appetizer or snack.

Pastas & Pizza

Almost every imaginable dish that ends with a vowel is available on Argentine menus, thanks largely to the prodigious Italian immigration that transformed the country in the 20th century. Quality Italo-Argentine food is available even at obscure truck stops in the Gran Chaco.

Standard dishes include lasagna, polenta, ravioli, and risotto. One specialty holds a unique niche in Argentine culture—by custom, the popular and inexpensive *ñoquis* (potato gnocchi) are eaten on the 29th of each month, when families are running short of cash. Ñoqui is also a *lunfardo* (slang) term for a public employee who does little or no work, but makes an end-of-the-month appearance to pick up his or her paycheck.

Argentine pizza is generally thin crusted *a la piedra*, topped with mozzarella and thinly sliced meats such as ham and pepperoni. Standards include the sauce-free, onions-only *fugazza* and its cousin, the onion-and-mozzarella *fugazzeta*. In recent years, some pizzerias have begun to produce more creative versions, with toppings such as grilled vegetables.

Fruits & Desserts

Argentina produces all the typical midlatitude fruits, such as apples, grapes, peaches, pears, plums, oranges, and the like. These are often ingredients of the *ensalada de frutas* (fruit salad, also known as *macedonia*), a standard on dessert menus throughout the country.

Flan (egg custard, often topped with caramel or whipped cream) is also an everyday dessert item. Argentines spread extraordinary quantities of *dulce de leche,* a caramelized condensed milk, onto almost everything, and even eat it straight out of the jar.

Rooted in the Italian tradition, Argentine *helado* (ice cream) is among the world's finest. Vanilla, chocolate, and strawberry are the standard flavors, but you may find dozens of often subtle variations on each—bittersweet chocolate or chocolate hazelnut, for instance—plus specialties such as lemon mousse and, of course, dulce de leche. The best *heladerías* are small-scale neighborhood shops that produce only limited quantities on a daily basis.

Wine, Beer, & Spirits

Argentina is the world's fifth largest wine producer, but only in the past couple of decades has it become a major exporter. Sophisticated wine bars are appearing in Buenos Aires and many provincial cities as well.

Mendoza Province is the dominant producer, with hundreds of wineries in and around its namesake capital, but there are also notable wine regions in San Juan and Salta Provinces and in the Patagonian provinces of Río Negro and Neuquén.. Growers raise all the usual varietals, but the country's distinctive vintages are the *tinto* (red) Malbec and the dry but fruity *blanco* (white) Torrontés.

Beer consumption is high, mostly of industrial beverages such as Quilmes, but regional producers make artisanal brews in towns such as El Bolsón in northern Patagonia. Most hard liquor is imported; *ginebra bol*s (distilled from barley, wheat, and rye) and *caña* (cane alcohol) are more typically Argentine. ∎

EXPERIENCE: Social Sipping in the *Mate* Ritual

Argentines can spend entire afternoons over coffee and croissants in city *confiterías,* but when they're with friends or family at home, the beverage of choice is *mate.* This infusion of the shredded dry leaf of *Ilex paraguayensis,* a relative of the common holly, is more than just a pick-me-up—"Paraguayan tea" is part of the social fabric of Argentina.

Grown in the subtropical northeast, *yerba mate,* the raw material, is available outside Argentina. Many tourists take home the necessary gear—a carved calabash (also known as a *mate,* sometimes truly elaborate) for brewing it and a *bombilla* (metallic tube) for sipping it.

It's much harder to export the ritual of its preparation. After the *cebador* (server) fills the gourd with dry yerba and adds hot but not boiling water, he or she usually dumps the first serving as too bitter or too hot, then refills it and passes it clockwise. In this egalitarian ceremony, everyone sips from the same bombilla until the last person says "*Gracias.*"

Because mate is more a household than a commercial custom, many visitors never have an opportunity to partake, but a conversation can bring an invitation to share. If so, don't refuse—the bitter brew may be an acquired taste, but the sociable ritual makes for sweet memories.

Land & Landscape

Argentina's extravagant geography contains some of the world's longest shorelines, widest rivers, greatest plains, broadest steppes, hottest deserts, and highest mountains. Its environments range from arid badlands to subtropical rain forests and continental and alpine glaciers. From the Bolivian border at La Quiaca to Tierra del Fuego's Beagle Channel, the latitudinal change is comparable to that from Guadalajara to Hudson Bay.

The Pampas

Sprawling west from midlatitude Buenos Aires, the Pampas are Argentina's heartland, the sediment-rich source of pastoral wealth. That wealth brought the phrase "rich as an Argentine" into English. Their verdant grasses fed the cattle that became a symbol of quality beef and, with ample rainfall and optimum temperatures, their rich loess soils yielded wheat exports that fed Europe in the early 20th century. Today, though, soybeans are a dominant crop.

> Sprawling west from midlatitude Buenos Aires, the Pampas are Argentina's heartland, the sediment-rich source of pastoral wealth.

Toward the drier south and west, rain-fed agriculture becomes difficult, and livestock estancias dominate the rural economy. Low igneous mountain ranges—the Sierra de Tandil, the Sierra de la Ventana, the Sierra de La Pampa—and the higher Sierras de Córdoba break the monotony. There are two national parks, La Pampa Province's Parque Nacional Lihué Calel, with its rounded granite inselbergs, and Córdoba's Parque Nacional Quebrada del Condorito, the Andean condor's easternmost habitat.

A sweeping coastline, with dramatic headlands, makes southern Buenos Aires Province a magnet for beachgoers. Some parts are highly urbanized in and around the resort of Mar del Plata.

Mesopotamia

From its Brazilian headwaters, the Río Paraná flows nearly 2,500 miles (4,000 km) to join the Río Uruguay and form the Río de la Plata (River of Silver) estuary. Between these navigable rivers, Entre Ríos, Corrientes, and Misiones Provinces form the region known as Argentine Mesopotamia, an area of rolling hills and gallery forests that becomes low mountains in its northeastern extremes. Rainfall is high and floods are frequent.

Corrientes's most notable feature is the Esteros del Iberá, an immense fauna-rich wetlands that's really a shallow, slow-flowing tributary of the Paraná. Stretching to the river bottom, long root systems anchor "floating islands" in this little-visited, vastly underrated provincial reserve.

In Misiones, on the Brazilian border, the region's highest-profile sight is the thunderously scenic Iguazú Falls, on their namesake Paraná tributary. They are part of Parque Nacional Iguazú, which preserves 260 square miles (670 sq km) of subtropical rain forest where wildlife is abundant. The climate is hot and humid in summer, mild and humid the rest of the year, except for occasional cold fronts from the south.

A peon gathers sheep at Estancia Sol de Mayo, Paso Roballos, Santa Cruz Province.

The Gran Chaco

Across the Paraná River from Corrientes, the Gran Chaco is an alluvial plain that comprises the entire provinces of Chaco and Formosa and includes parts of Santiago del Estero, Salta, and Jujuy. Hot, humid, and densely forested in its easternmost parts, the landscape rises almost imperceptibly toward the west, where it is drier and hotter yet in the sector known as El Impenetrable. Some of South America's highest temperatures ever have been recorded here, and it's one of few Argentine regions where tropical diseases such as malaria and dengue arouse concern. Winters can be dry.

Lago Cholila, Chubut Province

The Andean Northwest

Northwestern Argentina starts as a southerly extension of the high Andean landscape of Bolivia. While it lies within tropical and subtropical latitudes, altitude usually determines climate and weather.

At its westernmost edge, along the Chilean border, the altiplano or puna is an arid steppe, punctuated by salt flats and saline lakes, rising to 13,000 feet (4,000 m) above sea level. Isolated peaks may reach 19,000 feet (5,800 m) or even higher; Cerro Ojos del Salado, along the Chilean border in Catamarca Province, is the continent's second highest summit at 22,743 feet (6,932 m).

To the east, descending rivers dissect the landscape into a canyon country that resembles the U.S. Southwest—Jujuy Province's Quebrada de Humahuaca has terraced agriculture reminiscent of the central Andean civilizations. Summer rainfall can disrupt travel with floods and mud slides, so the dry winter months, with their warm days and cool nights, can be better times to travel.

Despite the general aridity, southern Salta Province and parts of La Rioja produce fine wines at elevations up to nearly 10,000 feet (3,000 m). On the eastern Andean slopes, a longitudinal band of well-watered cloud forest is home to several national parks, most notably Calilegua and El Rey; in Tucumán Province, the rainfall supports a major sugarcane industry.

Cuyo

Cuyo's geography is an extension of the northwest and, irrigated by runoff from the Andes, the vineyards of Mendoza Province are the heart of Argentina's wine industry. Mendoza is also a destination for those seeking to reach the 22,837-foot (6,961 m) summit of Cerro Aconcagua, the "roof of the Americas."

Brutally hot in summer, the northern and western deserts showcase badlands landscapes that are major paleontological sites. Dotted with hoodoos, San Juan's Parque Provincial Ischigualasto and La Rioja's Parque Nacional Talampaya are a collective World Heritage site where Argentine dinosaur hunters have found a wealth of Triassic fossils.

Patagonia

No Argentine region has a higher international profile than Patagonia, a Texas-size territory that's become a brand name. It lies in a rain shadow, and only a few of the Pacific storms that drench the Chilean coast make it through gaps in the Andes, which are lower here than farther north. Still, that's enough to maintain a lush lakes district in and around the city of San Carlos de Bariloche. Several national parks, including Parque Nacional Nahuel Huapi, hug the Chilean border for hundreds of miles, and ample snowfall makes the region a winter playground.

Farther south, Parque Nacional Los Glaciares includes the grinding Moreno Glacier and the exhilarating trekking country of pinnacled Monte Fitz Roy. To the east, though, lies a vast arid steppe of open skies, bunch grasses, and nearly incessant gales. Today, grazing Corriedale sheep make it the nucleus of Patagonia's wool industry.

Several major rivers cross the steppe to the Atlantic shoreline which, south from the Río Negro, alternates between scenic headlands and sandy beaches. Big tides cause problems for the scattered port cities, but they encourage the abundant marine mammals and seabirds that breed at reserves such as Península Valdés, a World Heritage site.

Despite Patagonia's reputation for inclemency, maritime influences on the tapering continent moderate extreme temperatures in both summer and winter. Visitors find summer's high winds the most trying aspect of the climate.

Tierra del Fuego

Tierra del Fuego's northern half is an extension of the Patagonian steppe and shoreline, but its southern half is a mountainous land of beech forests, glacial horns, and turbulent seas. The climate is wetter than in areas farther north. ∎

Argentina's Changed Landscapes

However impressive Argentina's sprawling grasslands and lush forests may be, it's worth remembering that very few parts of the country are pristine. Over millennia, and especially since the arrival of Europeans, the human presence has altered these natural landscapes.

To use the most obvious example, before the arrival of the Spaniards, the verdant Pampas grasslands were home to herds of wild guanacos hunted by Querandí Indians. Even after the first settlers of Buenos Aires abandoned the area—victims of starvation and Querandí warriors—European cattle and horses flourished in huge feral herds that displaced the guanaco and other game. Heavy grazing, in turn, impoverished the Pampas pastures, and the grain-farming boom of the 20th century brought even more dramatic changes, such as railroads and urbanization.

Institutions such as the cattle estancia also transformed the landscape. In the big-sky country of Patagonia, changes came in the form of vast open-range sheep ranches, oriented toward the export of wool and mutton. Even where settlements are few, no one should mistake these areas for unspoiled nature.

Flora & Fauna

On a mostly tropical continent that separated from the Gondwana supercontinent about 110 million years ago, Argentina's terrestrial flora and fauna have evolved largely in isolation. What you'll see often depends on latitude: Tropics often have high diversity with small individual numbers, while higher latitudes have less diversity with greater numbers.

Flora

Argentina is famous for its sprawling Pampas grasslands, which have fed the world with beef and grains since the early 20th century, but its flora is far more diverse than that. It ranges from subtropical wetlands, gallery forests, and cloud forests to desert scrub, dense coniferous and deciduous woodlands, vast steppes, and even a touch of tundra.

A hummingbird feeds on a blossom at Parque General San Martín, Mendoza city.

Grasslands: Argentina's easternmost Pampas are a well-watered plain where feral Spanish cattle and horses thrive on native grasses, but their drier southern and western sectors are a mix of grasses and scrub known as *monte*. In the subtropical Chaco, savanna grasslands mix with thorn forests.

Gallery Forests & Wetlands: Longer than the Mississippi, ending in a lush delta north of Buenos Aires, the Paraná and other northern rivers feature hundreds of miles of densely wooded banks. Key species include the *guayabo colorado*, a myrtle relative, and the *ceibo*, whose bloom is Argentina's national flower.

> **Since 1992, Argentina has designated a total of 17 Wetlands of International Importance under the Ramsar Convention.**

Since 1992, Argentina has designated a total of 17 Wetlands of International Importance under the Ramsar Convention. These total more than 15,000 square miles (40,000 sq km). The most spectacular wetland is the Esteros del Iberá, where floating islands of amphibious plants shelter a cornucopia of birds, mammals, and reptiles.

Subtropical Forests: Almost entirely below the Tropic of Capricorn, Argentina lacks tropical rain forest, but subtropical selva is the natural vegetation of most of Misiones Province. More than 90 tree species, including the ceibo and the *lapacho* (with bright pink flowers), grow in Parque Nacional Iguazú.

Across the country, the *yungas* of Jujuy, Salta, and Tucumán Provinces are a narrow longitudinal strip of cloud forest on the easternmost slopes of the Andes. Much of the Gran Chaco is covered with thorn forest distinguished by the quebracho (axe-breaker tree).

Puna: In the most northwesterly highlands, *tola* shrubs and *ichu* bunch grasses form a scanty cover on the rocky soils, while lichens and cushion plants colonize some of the stones. In a handful of well-watered places, there are thick grasses; in dry foothill canyons, the *cardón* cactus is a common sight.

Broadleaf & Coniferous Forest: In the Patagonian lakes region, along the Chilean border, several species of *Nothofagus* (false or southern beech) constitute most of the dense evergreen and deciduous forests. Conifers are rarer, but there are two narrow endemics. Known in English as the "monkey-puzzle tree," *Araucaria araucana* (*paraguas* in Spanish, for its umbrella shape) is *pehuen* to the Mapuche Indians, who collect its edible nuts in autumn. Resembling the California redwood, the *alerce* (false larch) takes its Linnaean name *(Fitzroya cupressoides)* from the captain of the H.M.S. *Beagle.*

Patagonian Steppe: Like the puna, the Patagonian steppe consists of patchy grasslands studded with thorny shrubs such as the *calafate,* an edible barberry. The river valleys, however, contain lusher pasture, often grazed by upland geese and domestic sheep.

Fauna

Amidst the grandeur of its landscapes, Argentina's fauna sometimes seems second fiddle, but almost everything will be new to visitors from the Northern Hemisphere. The birdlife is wildly diverse, especially in subtropical Mesopotamia, and profuse in Patagonia, where penguins cluster by the tens of thousands. Elsewhere, sharp-eyed observers will spot guanacos, rheas, and the emblematic Andean condor.

The American Camelids

Throughout the Pampas and much of Argentina, cattle-crossing signs are common. But in northwestern Argentina's Quebrada de Cafayate and the high puna, the icons on crossing signs have the long necks of the llama and the wild guanaco.

Most common in Salta and Jujuy Provinces, the llama is just one of four South American camelids found in Argentina— two domestic and two wild. The llama is traditionally a pack animal, though its meat now appears on Argentine menus. The domestic alpaca—far less common

because the marshy pastures it prefers are fewer in Argentina—produces fine wool that fetches high prices.

The vicuña, an endangered species with even finer wool, is rare in Argentina, though some are raised in semi-captivity in the northwest. The most widely distributed camelid, though, is the robust guanaco, found throughout the high Andes but also in Patagonia and more rarely in the Pampas. Leaping over fences that sheep can only nudge, its herds are one of Patagonia's signature sights.

Birds: Argentina is a paradise for birders. For bird-watchers from the Northern Hemisphere, almost everything will be new. The Iberá marshes are home to an astonishing 344 species, including cormorants, egrets, herons, storks, and horned screamers; tropical species, such as toucans, find their way south into Misiones Province. The pampas and gallery forests have many small birds, but the most conspicuous avians are the *tero* (southern lapwing) and *bandurria* (buff-necked ibis), with its curved beak.

Scattered wetlands in the puna, such as Laguna de los Pozuelos, host migratory birds such as coots, ducks, geese, and flamingoes. The condor is common in the Patagonian Andes, while distinct species of the flightless *choike* or *ñandú petiso* sprint like ostriches across the steppes of the northwest and Patagonia. Black-browed albatrosses, giant petrels, and black-necked cormorants frequent the shoreline. What really draws visitors, though, are the colonies of Magellanic penguins in Chubut and Santa Cruz Provinces.

Gato montés (wildcat) on the prowl, Esteros del Iberá, Corrientes Province

Mammals: Argentina has few conspicuous land mammals, but its marine mammals range from large to giant. The most emblematic land mammal is the widely distributed guanaco, a relative of the domestic llama common in the northwestern altiplano and throughout Patagonia. Other grazing mammals include the Andean *huemul*, a cervid with northern and southern subspecies, and the *pudú*, a spaniel-size deer.

Widely distributed, the puma is Argentina's largest carnivore, but the magnificent *yaguareté* (jaguar) occurs only in the forested subtropics. Related to the horse, the subtropical tapir is also a northern species. Other notable northern mammals include the tufted capuchin monkey, the howler monkey, and the riverine capybara.

Along the long Patagonian shoreline, southern sea lions, southern elephant seals, and southern fur seals breed on sandy beaches and rocky islands. In the southern winter, southern right whales breed in the shallow waters off Península Valdés, but there are also orcas, humpback, fin, and sei whales, and dolphins.

Reptiles & Amphibians: Two species of the crocodilian *yacaré* (caiman), which reaches 7 to 10 feet (2–3 m) in length, inhabit the northeastern wetlands. There are three species of the venomous *yarará*, a snake common in the subtropics but rare in northern Patagonia, the southern limit of its range.

Marine Life: Pelagic fish such as *merluza* (hake) and corvina (croaker) often appear on restaurant menus, as do shellfish and crustaceans such as *mejillones* (mussels), *calamares* (squid), and *centolla* (soutern king crab). The Paraná and other northern rivers are home to game fish such as *boga*, dorado, and *surubí* (Paraná catfish). Patagonia's rivers are popular for introduced trout and Atlantic salmon, plus native perch and *pejerrey*. ■

History of Argentina

Argentine history is an epic that, given the country's fractious politics, often becomes a polemic. Nevertheless, with larger-than-life figures such as José de San Martín and Juan Domingo Perón, the epic is always absorbing. And in recent years, democracy has happily survived and at times prospered.

Prehistory & Pre-Columbian Argentina

Humans first reached the Americas from Asia when low sea levels in a period of continental glaciation opened a land bridge across the Bering Strait. This happened no later than 12,500 years ago; by the time the land bridge closed, about 10,000 years ago, hunter-gatherer bands had occupied almost every environmental niche in North and South America.

Hunter-gatherers subsisted on game and other wild foods, but as their numbers increased some began to select and cultivate plants. In the present-day Peruvian highlands, this brought densely settled agriculture and the great civilizations that culminated in the Inca Empire. The main crops were beans, squash, and potatoes, with maize a later introduction from Mesoamerica. The llama and alpaca were the primary domestic animals.

Some of this agricultural complex reached northwestern Argentina, where the Diaguita practiced intensive terraced agriculture, but the Inca never quite managed to extend their power effectively in this area. Most indigenous societies remained nomadic hunter-gatherers or semisedentary shifting cultivators—along the southern Andes, for instance, the mobile Araucanian Indians were beyond Inca control, as were the Guaraní of Mesopotamia. In remote Patagonia, Inca rule had no impact on hunter-gatherers such as the Tehuelche.

> Magellan's supernumerary Antonio Pigafetta entertained the European imagination with tales of Tehuelche giants "so tall that the tallest among us reached only to their waists."

The European Invasion

South America's second wave of settlement began with Columbus and the age of exploration. The first to see the Río de la Plata estuary was Amerigo Vespucci's (1454–1512) expedition of 1501, sponsored by Portugal. In 1516 Juan Díaz de Solís (1470–1516) became the first European to set foot in what is now Argentina (Solís died in a confrontation with the Charrúa or Guaraní on the Uruguayan side).

Ferdinand Magellan (1480–1521) and Sebastian Cabot (1484–1557) also entered the estuary, in 1519 and 1527 respectively, and Magellan even wintered on the Patagonian coast, where his expedition had a peaceful encounter with the Tehuelche. Magellan's supernumerary Antonio Pigafetta entertained the European imagination with tales of Tehuelche giants "so tall that the tallest among us reached only to their waists."

Cabot, meanwhile, returned to Spain with bits of Peruvian silver that gave the River of Silver its name. Supplemented by rumors of the wealth of Cuzco, this drove Pedro de

Pre-Columbian handprint "stencils," Río Pinturas, Santa Cruz Province

Mendoza (1487–1537) to mount a large but poorly planned expedition that founded
Buenos Aires in 1536. In the same year, Diego de Almagro's almost equally poorly
organized expedition to Chile passed through northwestern Argentina, marking the first
Spanish presence there.

After many of Mendoza's men died from starvation, Querandí Indians drove most
of the rest out. Some headed north to found the city of Asunción (Paraguay), among
the more accommodating Guaraní. The Spanish abandoned European livestock—horses
and, later, cattle—that would proliferate to transform the Pampas from native grasslands,
grazed by troops of guanacos hunted by the Querandí, to a ranch without fences.

Colonial Argentina

In the ensuing years, the Spaniards subjugated the larger populations of the South
American highlands more easily than they did the scattered populations of the
Pampas, thanks to the highlands' more sophisti-
cated hierarchical political system.

In the process, they established forced labor
in a system known as the *repartimiento* and col-
lected tribute through the *encomienda*, but those
systems collapsed when European diseases
ravaged native populations. Infections such as
smallpox, measles, and typhus were new to
the Americas, whose peoples lacked immu-
nological resistance. In some areas, more
than 90 percent of the population died.

Moving into the vacuum, Spanish settlement moved south from the Viceroyalty
of Peru. The first city to be established in
Argentina was Santiago del Estero (1553),
followed by San Miguel de Tucumán
(1565) and Córdoba (1573); Mendoza
(1561) and San Juan (1562) were
settled from Chile. Not until 1580 did
Spaniards from Asunción refound
Buenos Aires, to be followed by
Salta (1582), La Rioja (1591), and
San Salvador de Jujuy (1593).
With political power concentrated
in the highlands, Buenos Aires
was a backwater that, despite its
Atlantic access, was forbidden
to trade with Europe except
through Peru. That would
not change for nearly two

**Gen. José de San Martín
astride his horse at Plaza San
Martín, Retiro, Buenos Aires**

centuries, and the local economy had to rely on meager resources such as beef and hides.

Hides were durable, but their low value-to-weight ratio could not justify shipping them overland to Lima, freighting them to Panama, transshipping them across the isthmus, and onward to Spain.

In response, Buenos Aires residents traded surreptitiously with Portuguese and British smugglers in the Paraná Delta's channels, where Spanish authorities exercised almost no control. Eventually, Spain ceded to reality by creating the Viceroyalty of the River Plate, encompassing most of what is now Argentina, in 1776. Exports and imports could now pass legally through the port of Buenos Aires.

By this time, the city's population had reached 24,000; it nearly doubled by century's end thanks to the establishment of *saladeros* (salting plants), where beef was salted for export to Spain. Well before then, though, the contraband economy had spawned a tradition of corruption that has plagued Argentina throughout its history. At the same time, criollos (Creoles, or American-born Spaniards), mestizos, *indígenas* (Indians), and caudillos grew dissatisfied with European rule and would soon challenge it.

The Ubiquitous San Martín

In the Argentine pantheon, José de San Martín (1778–1850) is the counterpart of George Washington. The Argentine liberator may not have slept in as many places, but his monuments are everywhere, and it's a rare town where neither the central square nor main avenue is named for him.

Equestrian statues, of course, are abundant—starting with Buenos Aires's Plaza San Martín—and he's always present on Argentine banknotes. The streets and plazas that bear his name often do so in an unwieldy manner. In the Patagonian resort of El Calafate, for instance, the main drag is Avenida del Libertador General José de San Martín.

Ironically enough, all this adulation goes to a man who, dismayed with postindependence events, moved to Europe in 1824 and spent the rest of his life in exile. He only returned 30 years after his death, when his remains were shipped to Buenos Aires.

The Independence Era & Caudillismo

By the early 19th century, Spain's American empire had become unwieldy, and its preoccupation with Napoleon in Europe meant that de facto autonomy devolved to the criollos. Independence movements began in peripheral places such as Buenos Aires, whose residents identified more closely with Argentina than with Spain.

The initial impetus toward independence began in 1806 and 1807, when British troops occupied Buenos Aires but soon encountered a popular resistance that drove them from the city. The Viceroy having already fled the British, city residents chose their own replacement in the French naval officer Santiago de Liniers (1753–1810).

Liniers, a committed royalist, was no independence campaigner, but the successful resistance raised local confidence and cemented an American identity. In 1810, criollos under the leadership of Corrientes-born José de San Martín (see sidebar above), who had attended military school in Europe, rebelled against Spanish rule. In July of 1816, delegates at Tucumán voted to declare the independence of the Provincias Unidas del Río de la Plata (United Provinces of the River Plate), soon to become Argentina. This shaky confederation of relatively cosmopolitan urbanites and violent provincial warlords managed to dislodge the Spaniards, but conflicts soon surfaced between the "Unitarists" of Buenos Aires and the "Federalists" of the provinces. Those conflicts have never gone away.

CHILI,
PLATA
ET
PATAGONIE.

Argentina in the 1870s was changing rapidly under aggressive military leaders.

Republican Argentina

Instead of a constitutional republic, the Provincias Unidas soon devolved into a mosaic of caudillo-run fiefdoms. The largest and most influential was Buenos Aires Province, whose caudillo, Juan Manuel de Rosas (1793–1877), was Argentina's greatest strongman until the emergence of Juan Perón.

From 1829 to 1852, except for a short period out of power, Rosas ruled by fear, but also enjoyed the loyalty of his gaucho followers. When Charles Darwin crossed the Pampas in 1833, he observed that "I never saw anything like the enthusiasm for Rosas," who kept the Indians from raiding frontier settlements. Rosas, though, was also responsible for unspeakable brutality through his violent political police, the *mazorca:* In the words of his rival, Domingo F. Sarmiento (1811–1888), Rosas "applied the knife of the Gaucho to the culture of Buenos Ayres." Sarmiento, who self-exiled several times in Chile to avoid Rosas's thugs, later became Argentina's seventh president.

In other provinces, the scenario resembled that in Buenos Aires. Sarmiento deplored figures such as La Rioja's Facundo Quiroga, a charismatic rancher and soldier who overthrew the government of Sarmiento's native San Juan Province because of its alliance with pre-Rosas Buenos Aires. A common salutation on Federalist documents of the era was "Death to the Unitarist savages!"

Rosas's federalism was opportunistic and, ironically, his concentration of power through political authoritarianism, military force, and export/import controls actually reinforced the dominance of the port city of Buenos Aires—which was not even the country's capital. Finally, in 1852, former ally Justo José de Urquiza (1801–1870) of Entre Ríos Province headed an army that defeated Rosas at the town of Caseros; after Rosas fled into British exile, Urquiza helped create the Constitution of 1853, which survives to this day.

Urquiza, though, did less well against the Unitarist army of Bartolomé Mitre (1821–1906), a talented soldier-politician whose concept of Argentina was more centralized and outward looking. It was so outward looking that, after defeating Urquiza and his allies to unite the country, Mitre joined Uruguay and Brazil to defeat Paraguayan dictator Francisco Solano López (1826–1870) in the War of the Triple Alliance (1865–1870).

In doing so, Mitre expanded Argentine territory to include the present-day provinces of Formosa and Misiones. Later politicians moved to establish control over the vast

Patagonian lands, initially through concessions to Welsh colonists in Chubut. Meanwhile, Gen. Julio Argentina Roca (1843–1914) fought to drive Araucanian raiders toward the Chilean border in his genocidal Conquista del Desierto ("conquest of the desert"). The government also invited British sheep farmers into the southern territories of Chubut, Santa Cruz, and Tierra del Fuego—in part to derail Chilean expansion.

Roca, who became president in 1880, made the city of Buenos Aires a federal district comparable to Washington, D.C.—nearly triggering a civil war and prompting angry provincial authorities to move their capital to the new city of La Plata. Doing so, though, consolidated the Argentine state and symbolized unity, despite lingering conflicts.

Immigration & Modernization

After Mitre and Roca, foreign trade, foreign investment, and immigration became the pillars of prosperity. Shipped to England's mills, wool from the Pampas was the first major commodity, but wheat and other grains soon superseded it. British capital built a web of railroads to carry goods to market, making fortunes for latifundios (large landholdings) but simultaneously squeezing out small farms, even as land speculation brought a near collapse toward the end of the 19th century.

What really changed the country, though, was the tsunami of immigration that engulfed Buenos Aires, the Pampas, and even interior provinces with millions of Spaniards, Italians, Britons, Russians, Ukrainians, Scandinavians, and other nationalities. A revived rural economy, based on beef and grain exports, brought increased revenues, but the gap between rich and poor grew. Corrupt clientelism (patron-client political machinery) ruled in tenement-filled city neighborhoods where immigrants barely got by, and political violence reappeared as anarchists provoked the police and military.

Twice elected to the presidency, the well-intentioned reformist Hipólito Yrigoyen (1852–1933) dealt ineffectually with working-class discontent and resorted to strike-breaking with army support. His second term ended in 1930 with Argentina's first—but not last—military coup. This conservative restoration started half a century of frequent

A Country of Caudillos

For nearly half a century after Argentine independence in 1810, political life was a struggle between the cosmopolitan Unitarists of Buenos Aires and the Federalist caudillos of the provinces, as well as among the caudillos themselves. Writing from exile, San Juan native Domingo F. Sarmiento stated that the bloody career of La Rioja's charismatic Facundo Quiroga (1788–1835) illustrated what Sarmiento called a struggle between "civilization and barbarism."

The real target of Sarmiento's polemic was Buenos Aires caudillo Juan Manuel de Rosas, "the Caligula of the River Plate," who was finally ousted by Justo José de Urquiza, another caudillo with reformist ideas, in 1852. Urquiza stabilized the Argentine Confederation but, even then, caudillismo did not go away.

The basis of caudillo power was personal loyalty and charisma, and that has never disappeared in the politics of a country whose leadership motto might well still be: "He who is not with me is against me." For example, Carlos Menem, who served a decade as Argentine president (1989–1999), got his start as a La Rioja governor in the 1970s—a time when he conspicuously sported thick mutton-chop sideburns of the style once favored by Quiroga.

The Perón Legacy

In a newspaper interview, Argentine historian Tulio Halperín once confessed that "I've grown accustomed to the idea that Argentina is a Peronist country, and I have to say that at this point I'm so beaten up by life that it doesn't bother me in the least."

Peronism, founded on the charisma of Gen. Juan Domingo Perón and his wife Eva Duarte (Evita), is a political ideology embodied by the Justicialist Party (combining the Spanish words for "justice" and "social," but more commonly identified as "Peronist"). The movement was a populist reaction to the long-standing alliance between the military-backed Argentine "oligarchy" of farmers and industrialists, which contrasted with a large marginalized working class.

With ideas derived from Mussolini, Peronism exploited class resentment in nationalizing or heavily regulating private enterprise and in making alliances with or taking over labor unions. Such measures, which many observers consider a cause of Argentina's repeated economic and political crises, have not ceased: In late 2008, the Peronist administration of President Cristina Fernández assumed control of private pension funds, ostensibly because of the global financial crisis. Many analysts saw this as a power grab that was unsurprising in a government where one minister was quoted as saying "I have a visceral hatred against the ... oligarchy."

military intrusion into politics, but it had unanticipated results. Its enduring legacy was the return of the caudillo in the person of Gen. Juan Domingo Perón, along with perpetually disorderly politics.

Perón & Peronism

Nobody has left a greater imprint on contemporary Argentina than the charismatic Juan Domingo Perón (1895–1974), who rose from provincial origins to the officer ranks and, eventually, the country's highest office. Parlaying a minor role in earthquake relief in the provincial capital of San Juan into a high public profile, he founded a political party, formally known as the Partido Justicialista but so closely identified with him that it's more commonly called "Peronista."

Peronism is full of contradictions. Ranging from extreme left to extreme right, its partisans have proclaimed fealty to their founder even as they've shot at each other. Their only apparent shared belief was that ruthlessness was the route to power, and that power was an end in itself. Perón himself was an ambiguous figure, in whom his followers could see what they wanted.

In the course of his military service, Perón had traveled widely within Argentina and overseas, and he saw the inequities of its social and economic order firsthand. His genius was to exploit class resentments against the prosperous landed elite and the foreign interests who exported commodities overseas, rather than reinvesting in Argentina.

Perón used a relatively minor post in the military regime's labor department to forge a contradictory coalition of union bosses and their membership, leftist intellectuals, and nationalist xenophobes. As president, he employed government revenues to support a large bureaucracy and an industrial infrastructure that, despite inefficiencies, provided jobs. His social safety net brought job security—firing workers became almost impossible—generous pensions, and better working conditions.

Perón could not have achieved what he did without his equally charismatic second wife, Eva Duarte, a soap opera actress better known as Evita. Her resentment of the oligarchy—she was a provincial landowner's illegitimate daughter—matched that of the impoverished *descamisados* (shirtless ones) who were Perón's natural constituents. She outraged residents of an exclusive Buenos Aires neighborhood by opening a center for homeless mothers from the provinces there. Her death from cancer, in 1952, brought millions of Argentines into the streets in grief.

Perón, meanwhile, misjudged the impact of his generous spending, which led to serious inflation, and he underestimated the opposition from other factions in the military, as well as from entrenched institutions such as the Catholic Church. In 1955, a coup known as the Revolución Libertadora drove him from power and into exile, setting the stage for Argentine history's darkest decades.

Disorder & "Dirty War"

In exile, Perón wandered the Western Hemisphere before finally settling in Spain, but he always expected to return to power in Argentina. In his absence, military dictatorships banned the Peronist Party, but political, economic, and social tensions continued to seethe just beneath the surface. In the late 1960s, a time of revolutionary turbulence worldwide, Argentina began to come undone, the result of political and economic instability, with roaring inflation, strikes, and urban and rural guerrilla warfare. Political kidnappings and assassinations became common occurrences.

In this context, the military lifted its ban on the Peronist Party and, after Héctor Cámpora's victory in the 1973 presidential election—Perón's own participation was still proscribed—the caudillo returned on a

Perón portraits in the Museo Evita, Buenos Aires

winter's night when millions gathered to greet him at Ezeiza, Buenos Aires's international airport. Fighting broke out between Peronist factions, with at least 13 killed and hundreds more injured, but new elections after Cámpora's resignation soon inaugurated Perón's third term.

Despite a brief euphoria in an increasingly polarized society, the aging Perón was no solution to Argentina's problems; he died in less than a year. His replacement was his vice-president and third wife, María Estela Martínez (1931–), 35 years his junior. Better known as Isabelita, she had been a nightclub dancer when he met her on his travels. The power behind the ineffectual Isabelita, though, was the sinister spiritualist José López Rega (1916–1989), who organized the right-wing Alianza Anticomunista Argentina (AAA) death squad and controlled enormous funds as social welfare minister.

Meanwhile, challenges mounted from urban guerrillas such as the Montoneros (a leftist Peronist faction that had kidnapped and executed former de facto president Gen. Pedro Aramburu) and Che Guevara–inspired revolutionaries like the Ejército Revolucionario del Pueblo (ERP, People's Revolutionary Army) in Tucumán Province. Such groups often used bank robberies and kidnappings to finance their activities.

In that setting, a junta led by army general Jorge Rafael Videla (1925–2013) deposed Isabelita on March 24, 1976. The coup was bloodless, but its aftermath was a seven-year reign of state terrorism unmatched in Argentine history except, perhaps, in Rosas's time. Tens of thousands of Argentines (many of them innocent bystanders) "disappeared" off the streets, to be tortured, and often killed, with no pretense of due process.

Pope Francis greets Gianluigi Buffon of Italy and Lionel Messi of Argentina during an audience with the two countries' soccer teams at the Vatican.

Soccer's 1978 World Cup was supposed to showcase a new Argentina, but it had to share top billing with the Madres de Plaza de Mayo, a courageous group of mothers who paraded around Buenos Aires's landmark plaza every Thursday to demand the return of their disappeared children. Some of those children had been thrown live, out of airplanes and helicopters, into the ocean.

Even as the Dirty War eliminated ostensible "subversives," the regime started to come undone with continued corruption and inflation, which led to massive public protests by 1982. In April of that year, the junta bought itself a little extra time by invading and occupying the British-governed Falkland Islands, which Argentina had long claimed as the Malvinas. An unexpectedly effective British response, combined with Argentine military ineptitude, ended both the occupation and the regime.

The following year, as Argentina returned to constitutional government, Videla and his fellow coupmongers were tried for human-rights violations. All went to prison for several years, but were later pardoned (though the pardons were overturned years later).

Democracy & Its Discontents

Raúl Alfonsín (1927–2009), the first post-junta president, was the UCR (Unión Cívica Radical) party's first president since the 1960s. Except for prosecutions of the military, his six-year term was so unsuccessful that he resigned months early. This allowed Peronist president-elect, Carlos Menem (1930–), to take office in July 1989.

Menem inherited inflation that sometimes reached 50 percent monthly, which his talented economy minister Domingo Cavallo (1946–) managed to tame by pegging the peso to the dollar at a one-to-one exchange rate, controlling the money supply, and privatizing inefficient state enterprises. Superfluous government employees, known as ñoquis (see p. 24), disappeared from the payrolls.

Cavallo's measures worked well enough to get Menem reelected, but in his second term the currency peg kept labor and production costs high, overvalued Argentine exports lost their markets, and unemployment skyrocketed. Menem's successor in 1999, Fernando de la Rúa (1937–), of the UCR, inherited a deteriorating economy. De la Rúa restricted bank withdrawals to stabilize currency reserves, resulting in rioting by a frustrated public.

Pope Francis

In 2013, the former Archbishop of Buenos Aires, Jorge Mario Bergoglio (1936–), was elected as the first Latin-American Pope. Bergoglio, a Jesuit, had previously used his pulpit to highlight the plight of Argentina's poor. He was highly critical of modern materialism, which, he claimed, had led to huge inequalities in Argentine society, a view that led him into ideological conflict with the Kirchners.

Bergoglio took the name of Francis in honor of Saint Francis of Assisi, and he has shunned the usual trappings of papal wealth—including the red shoes—in favor of a life of comparative frugality. As pope, he has reached out to a surprising mix of followers and nonbelievers, including Muslim prisoners (whose feet he washed), Italy's African refugees, divorcees, and atheists.

De la Rúa resigned in panic, and there followed a series of caretaker presidents who presided over Argentina's economic collapse: a default on the foreign debt, strikes, and massive unemployment. The new Peronist president Eduardo Duhalde (1941–), chosen by the congress, then devalued the peso, triggering its collapse. Duhalde advanced presidential elections to early 2003, when his designated successor, Néstor Kirchner (1950–2010), defeated former president Menem.

Kirchner, a left-of-center Peronist, oversaw the resurrection of the economy—which really had nowhere to go but up—but also endangered the recovery with populist measures such as price and export controls that resulted in food and fuel shortages. Deciding to focus on reorganizing the Peronist party, Kirchner declined to run for reelection in 2007, and his wife Cristina Fernández, a senator from Buenos Aires Province, succeeded him.

Most observers thought the confrontational Kirchner would remain the power behind the presidency and, when Fernández decreed an unpopular tax in 2008 on soybean exports, they saw their analysis validated. This ignited a crisis that went on for months, with roadblocks and mass demonstrations on the part of pro-government and pro-farmer factions, until Fernández finally relented and submitted her program to the congress. She lost that vote, which weakened her politically, but rallied to win reelection in 2011. ■

Arts & Literature

Politically and economically, Argentina has had its ups and downs, but its contributions to art, literature, music, dance, theater, and cinema have been impressive. As novelist, journalist, and cultural critic Tomás Eloy Martínez (1934–2010) wrote following the 2002 economic meltdown, "One of Argentina's riches ... is the quality, the leadership of our culture." In that, added Martínez, "[W]e can speak as equals to the U.S. or France."

Painting & Sculpture

For most of Argentina's history, the visual arts have been derivative, especially when compared with the indigenous syncretism of the Peruvian and Bolivian highlands, and public art has leaned toward the pompously nationalistic—Argentina's

In Buenos Aires, Eduardo Catalano's "Floralis Generica" closes at night, like a tulip.

density of military equestrian statues may be among the world's highest. More recent artists, though, have produced innovative work that's drawn attention around the world, and much of it makes strong political and social commentary.

One of Argentina's most important artists is Cándido López (1840–1902). When he took up painting in his teens, Argentine art often consisted of ecclesiastical imagery and solemn military portraits. In his youth, López himself painted a portrait of Gen. Bartolomé Mitre. Mitre changed López's life in unexpected ways. As president, Mitre went to war against Paraguayan despot Francisco Solano López in 1864; enlisting as a second lieutenant, Cándido López lost his right forearm to a grenade two years later. López might have despaired, but he turned injury into opportunity by learning to paint left-handed, producing an extraordinary series of watercolors on the war. Underappreciated in their time, his

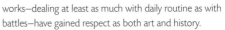

An antidote to the vulgar nationalism of most public art, Rogelio Yrurtia (1879–1950) sculpted larger-than-life tributes to the efforts of working-class Argentines.

works—dealing at least as much with daily routine as with battles—have gained respect as both art and history.

An antidote to the vulgar nationalism of most public art, Rogelio Yrurtia (1879–1950) sculpted larger-than-life tributes to the efforts of working-class Argentines. He achieved this in a country that most often honors military men atop their mounts. On a prominent plaza in the Buenos Aires neighborhood of San Telmo, his "Canto al Trabajo" ("Ode to Labor") honors the anonymous workers who were the foundation of Argentine prosperity.

Raised an orphan, Benito Quinquela Martín (1890–1977) put his Buenos Aires barrio of La Boca on the fine-arts map with his oils of everyday life in a working-class neighborhood of shipyards, stevedores, and factory laborers. While he had commercial and critical success and even gained praise from highly placed public officials, he never forsook his origins. His lasting legacy is his studio, donated to the city as a museum, along with many of his works.

A close friend of Jorge Luis Borges, watercolorist Alejandro Schulz Solari (1887–1963), better known as Xul Solar, also associated with spiritualists such as Aleister Crowley. His paintings—on surprisingly small, sometimes miniature canvases—reflect his obsession with astrology and other esoteric beliefs.

Wealthy collectors pay millions for the paintings of Antonio Berni (1905–1981), who created memorable characters in the person of prostitute Ramona Montiel and shantytown waif Juanito Laguna. Though he died nearly three decades ago, Berni's social realism series depicts urban poverty so powerfully that, for example, "Juanito Laguna Bañándose entre Latas" ("Juanito Laguna

Bathing at the Garbage Dump") might as well have been created for the 2002 crisis, when many poor Argentines resorted to scavenging for their livelihood.

Challenging conservative institutions, combative León Ferrari (1920–2013) pushed the envelope in the mid-1960s by depicting Christ crucified on a Vietnam-era fighter jet in "La Civilización Occidental y Cristiana" ("Western and Christian Civilization"). Age did not mellow him—his anti-clerical works at a 2005 Buenos Aires exhibition so enraged the church that it sought an injunction that, ironically, brought huge crowds to see what the fuss was about.

> The cornerstone of Argentine literature is José Hernández's (1834–1886) epic poem *Martín Fierro* (1872), which idealized the gaucho as the Argentine archetype even as the country rapidly urbanized.

Like Yrurtia, sculptor Alberto Heredia (1924–2000) resisted the paradigm of public monuments, but he went much further to produce scathing parodies and satire that attack middle-class conventions. Appearing just before the coup of 1976, "El Caballero de la Máscara" ("The Masked Horseman") sardonically depicts a headless rider who signifies Argentine militarism and authoritarianism; used sarcastically here, the word *caballero* also means "gentleman."

A Dirty War critic who had to go into exile, Juan Carlos Distéfano (1933–) shares Heredia's political sensibilities. Depicting the torture of a man with his hands tied behind his back as his head emerges from a toilet bowl, his sculpture "El Mudo" ("The Mute") is both topical and timeless.

Of a different generation, painter Guillermo Kuitca (1961–) produces collagelike abstracts that take their inspiration from architecture, cartography, theater, opera (he designed sets for the Teatro Colón, Buenos Aires's opera house), and even popular music. More recently, Kuitca has adopted Cubist techniques and made forays into surrealism; his work is more subtly political than that of some of his older counterparts.

Literature

Argentina is one of Latin America's most literate countries: Novelists and poets are celebrities and public intellectuals, and Buenos Aires hosts a massive international book fair every April. There are contradictions and conflict, though, between the literary traditions of the countryside and the cosmopolitan capital.

The cornerstone of Argentine literature is José Hernández's (1834–1886) epic poem *Martín Fierro* (1872), which idealized the gaucho as the Argentine archetype even as the country rapidly urbanized; it created a whole genre of writing known as *gauchesco* (gauchesque). Popular even with city dwellers, *Martín Fierro* has been widely translated.

Son of a wealthy landowner, Ricardo Güiraldes (1886–1927) was the literary heir of Hernández. His quasi-autobiographical novel *Don Segundo Sombra* (1926) romanticizes a rural society, as violent as it was picturesque, from the viewpoint of an oligarch's son. Like *Martín Fierro*, it has also been widely translated.

Despite provincial origins, author and seventh Argentine president Domingo F. Sarmiento (1811–1888) was the anti-Hernández, an urbane writer whose nonfiction *Life in the Argentine Republic in the Days of the Tyrants* (1845) depicted the gaucho as a tool of local warlords even as he acknowledged the gaucho's positive qualities.

It's *porteño* (natives of Buenos Aires) writers, though, who have given Argentine literature its highest profile. Many of them found their voices with encouragement from essayist Victoria Ocampo (1890–1979), publisher of the literary magazine *Sur* and organizer of a cultural circle resembling Britain's Bloomsbury Group.

The foremost of them was Jorge Luis Borges (1899–1986). From a prominent founding family that fought against the dictator Rosas, the multilingual Borges transcended the purely Argentine to become a cosmopolitan author and scholar who could write about Norse sagas as effortlessly as he could about petty urban scammers and gaucho knife fights. (Borges respected *Martín Fierro* even as he found its conventions limiting.) Best known for short-story collections such as *Labyrinths* (1962), he was also a prolific poet, but never wrote a novel.

If Borges failed to write a novel, his close friend Adolfo Bioy Casares (1914–1999) more than compensated for the shortage. His surrealistic novel *The Invention of Morel* (1940) was adapted for the screen as *Man Facing Southeast*, but his *Diary of the War of the Pig* (1969), set in the Buenos Aires barrio of Palermo, is a more accessible work on the generational tensions and political divisions that resulted in the Dirty War.

Spending much of his career in Parisian exile from Peronism, Julio Cortázar (1914–1984) is known for enigmatic fiction such as the novels *Hopscotch* (1963), with its experimental structure, and *62: A Model Kit* (1968), which picks up where *Hopscotch* leaves off. Cortázar also, notoriously, wrote the short story on which Michelangelo Antonioni based the award-winning film *Blow-Up*.

A physicist who quit science to devote himself to fiction, Ernesto Sábato (1911–2011) may be the most porteño of novelists. Set in Buenos Aires, using city landmarks to counter a sense of disorientation, his grim but engrossing psychological novel *On Heroes and Tombs* deals with the dark side of conflicts between the traditional and the contemporary, as symbolized by the landowning aristocracy and the cosmopolitan capital.

Compared with Sábato, Manuel Puig (1932–1990) seems almost frivolous for his absorption with popular culture in novels such as *Betrayed by Rita Hayworth* (1968) and

The Enigma of Borges

Argentina's single most famous literary figure, Jorge Luis Borges was a sophisticate who spent much of his life overseas and claimed that the "whole world is our country." With a multilingual command of world literature, he nevertheless identified with Buenos Aires—a city "I judge to be as eternal as water and air." Before going blind, he spent long nights walking its streets.

Descended from one of Argentina's founding families, distrustful of the masses (he detested Peronist populism), Borges could still write stories of urban lowlifes and temperamental gauchos. This was especially ironic for a writer who had been a weak and myopic young man, but Borges, with his interest in epics and fables from around the world, placed them in a universal context.

For that, some argued, Borges was divorced from Argentine reality; in fact, his universalism drew scorn from nationalist critics. Alarmed over the disorder of 1970s Argentina, Borges welcomed the 1976 coup that overthrew Perón's widow Isabelita. He even legitimated the dictatorship of Gen. Augusto Pinochet with an official visit to Chile that may have cost him a Nobel Prize in literature.

Still, at times, Borges could be candid about such matters. When Argentina and Great Britain went to war over the Falkland Islands in 1982, he sardonically commented that it was the equivalent of "two bald men fighting over a comb."

Kiss of the Spider Woman (1976), which became an award-winning English-language film. Puig wrote *Eternal Curse on the Reader of These Pages* (1980), about a Dirty War amnesiac in New York (where Puig himself lived for several years), in English.

Quoted in the introduction to this section, Tomás Eloy Martínez was a versatile writer whose journalism informed his fiction. Interviews with Juan Perón, for instance, led to *The Perón Novel* (1985), which the *New York Times* called "a brilliant image of a national psychosis." *Santa Evita* (1995) is an almost Gothic tale that traces Eva Perón's postmortem odyssey from Buenos Aires to an anonymous grave in Italy and back to her husband's Spanish home-in-exile.

Federico Andahazi (1963–), the bad boy of contemporary Argentine literature, is a former Freudian psychoanalyst who made his name with *The Anatomist* (1997), a sexually explicit story that won a literary prize whose scandalized sponsor made every effort to revoke it. That, of course, made the book a best seller in many languages.

Music & Dance

In various musical genres, Argentines have had a global impact. Classical, tango, folk, and rock performers have all made their mark within and beyond the country's borders, though some of them are little known in the English-speaking world. The tango's origins stem, at least in part, from the Afro-Argentine presence that, blended with massive European immigration, produced a hybrid music that bears a thematic resemblance to the North American blues (see pp. 68–69).

The word "tango" can mean song, orchestral music, or dance, though the three are not mutually exclusive.

Thanks to sustained public support for more than a century, the Teatro Colón has put Buenos Aires on the world opera map, and talented Argentine conductors, musicians, and dancers have become known well beyond the country's borders. Though he now lives in Berlin and also has Israeli and Palestinian citizenship, conductor Daniel Barenboim (1942–) has held opera and symphony posts in Europe and the United States and still makes appearances in his birth country. He has incorporated tango and Argentine folk themes into his work.

Brussels-based, Buenos Aires–born pianist Martha Argerich (1941–) avoids the limelight, but she has won two Grammys as a soloist with orchestra and one for best chamber music performance. Though he retired from performing in 2007, dancer Julio Bocca (1967–) has formed his own Ballet Argentino company to promote classical and contemporary dance. Boston-based composer Osvaldo Golijov (1960–) has won two Grammys and also written a score for Francis Ford Coppola's *Youth Without Youth* (2007).

Popular Music: The word "tango" can mean song, orchestral music, or dance, though the three are not mutually exclusive. The most universally beloved tango singer is Carlos Gardel (ca 1887–1935), who almost single-handedly took it onto the world stage. His own ambiguous origins—nobody knows his real birth date or birthplace (France, or possibly Uruguay, before he became Argentine)—contributed to the sense of nostalgic dislocation that has made tango the Argentine counterpart to the blues. His sudden death in a Colombian plane crash at the height of

Tango dancers take to the street in Buenos Aires's La Boca neighborhood.

A guitarist plays folkloric music at Salta's La Casona del Molino.

his fame left his charismatic smile as a symbol and his recordings as a sanctuary for fans, who still claim that "Gardel sings better every day."

As a singer, the Uruguayan-born Julio Sosa (1926–1964) is second to Gardel, but his approach was more traditional. Sosa's contemporary Roberto Goyeneche (1926–1994) played or recorded with legendary musicians such as Aníbal Troilo and Astor Piazzolla. Susana Rinaldi (1935–) was the first female singer to make a major impact on what had been a male-dominated genre.

Troilo (1914–1975) was a virtuoso with the accordionlike *bandoneón*, which gives the music much of its wistfulness; Piazzolla (1921–1992), who played with Troilo but also lived in New York City, was more innovative in incorporating jazz elements into his playing. A rock performer and producer, as well as Oscar-winning soundtrack composer for *Brokeback Mountain* (2005) and *Babel* (2006), Gustavo Santaolalla (1951–) has also introduced electronica into tango through his Bajofondo Tango Club.

Argentine folk music has its roots in the *payadores* of the Pampas, gauchos who conducted singing duels in rural *pulperías*; in the indigenous peoples of northwestern Andean provinces; and in the immigrant communities of northern Mesopotamia, where the accordion-based *chamamé* resembles Tex-Mex music. Its greatest figure is Pampas-born Atahualpa Yupanqui (1908–1992; real name Héctor Roberto Chavero Aramburo), a purist who blended gaucho and indigenous traditions in his singing and guitar playing.

In some ways a successor to Yupanqui, Mercedes Sosa (1935–2009) was more innovative in her willingness to collaborate with international figures such as Joan Báez, Sting, and Milton Nascimento, and even her erratic countryman Charly García, who is primarily a rock musician. Sosa's successor may be Soledad Pastorutti (1980–), who sometimes steers perilously close to gauchesco kitsch but has helped repopularize the genre, and the two performed together several times.

León Gieco (1951–) is a Dylanesque figure who bridges the divide between folk and rock; his album *De Ushuaia a La Quiaca* is a musicologist's delight that incorporates influences from Argentina's subtropics to its sub-Antarctic. He's performed with many international figures, including Pete Seeger and David Byrne.

The dominant figure in Argentine rock music, though, is the brilliant but erratic Charly García (1951–), who once nearly found himself in jail for an irreverent version of the national anthem. His frequently changing band has nurtured some of the best young talent in Argentine rock music.

In a category of their own, Les Luthiers are a musically sophisticated theater and comedy troupe whose closest analogue in the English-speaking countries might be Monty Python's Flying Circus. Then again, Monty Python's personnel never had to stand up in public and ridicule a military dictatorship. As the name implies, they make many of their own improvised instruments out of common household objects such as barrels and bicycles.

Buenos Aires supports a stable jazz scene, but the best known performers have gone abroad and made their names with movie soundtracks. New York–based saxophonist Gato Barbieri (1932–), for instance, wrote the score for *Last Tango in Paris*, while pianist Lalo Schifrin (1932–) has enjoyed a long Hollywood career with credits for *Bullitt*, *Cool Hand Luke*, and other movies.

Cinema

Throughout its history, Argentina has had one of Latin America's most vibrant cinema industries, and its films are a good way of getting to know the country. The country's cinema has also drawn recent attention from foreign producers and directors. Famous director Francis Ford Coppola, for instance, has located his new Zoetrope Argentina facilities in the Buenos Aires neighborhood of Palermo.

Argentine cinema more often stresses character over action, but for more than three decades it has had a presence in Hollywood, starting with Academy Award nominees for best picture in Sergio Renán's *The Truce* (1974) and María Luisa Bemberg's *Camila* (1984). In 1985, Luis Puenzo's *The Official Story* won the Oscar for its tale of the delicate theme of Dirty War adoptions by military families, but Puenzo took some heat in Argentina for the alleged implication that many Argentines were unaware that the military kidnapped babies of political prisoners they had tortured or killed. Eliseo Subiela's *Man Facing Southeast* (1986), Carlos Saura's *Tango* (1998), and Juan José Campanella's *Son of the Bride* (2001) also won nominations. In 2009, Campanella's *The Secret in Their Eyes* won the Oscar.

Argentina's most prolific director, Leopoldo Torre Nilsson (1924–1978), was the first to attract attention beyond its borders. Many of his subjects appealed to Argentine nationalism.

Argentina's most prolific director, Leopoldo Torre Nilsson (1924–1978), was the first to attract attention beyond its borders. Many of his subjects appealed to Argentine nationalism. These included the epic poem *Martín Fierro* and a biography of José de San Martín, but he also directed a screen version of Manuel Puig's unconventional novel *Boquitas Pintadas* (translated into English as *Heartbreak Tango*).

Taking It on the Road

Given Argentina's size and far-flung corners, taking to the highway has been a tradition since the days of the gaucho. Although Argentine directors don't get out of Buenos Aires often, a handful of films illuminate the Argentine experience through themes such as personal discovery and exile.

We might as well start in the Pampas, where director Héctor Olivera's *A Shadow You Soon Will Be* (1994) adapts Osvaldo Soriano's surrealistic novel about a Quixotic computer programmer who gets off a broken train and encounters other oddball characters. Marcelo Piñeyro's engaging *Wild Horses* (1995) is a caper film, with some similarities to *Dog Day Afternoon*, in

which a Robin Hood anarchist and a bank manager, having absconded with laundered money, flee to Patagonia. Piñeyro's *Kamchatka* (2002) is about a family on the run in Patagonia during the Dirty War dictatorship of 1976–1983.

Director Walter Salles might be Brazilian, but his award-winning biopic *The Motorcycle Diaries* (2004), about the youthful adventures of Ernesto "Che" Guevara, features young Ernesto's encounters with the winds and snows of Patagonia. Pablo Trapero's *Familia Rodante* (2004), by contrast, is a domestic comedy that follows a dysfunctional family in a motor home through the Mesopotamian provinces en route to a wedding.

In addition to *Camila*, a drama that blends politics with a fatal romance during Rosas's 19th-century dictatorship, Bemberg (1922–1995) filmed the English-language *Miss Mary* (1986), a tale of the rural oligarchy in the pre-Perón years through the eyes of an English governess (Julie Christie). *I Don't Want to Talk About It* (1993), Bemberg's highly metaphorical last film, features a love-struck Marcello Mastroianni in a conservative provincial town where the unconventional is taboo.

After winning the Oscar, Puenzo (1946–) got to direct Gregory Peck and Jane Fonda in *The Old Gringo* (1989), about the ostensible fate of American satirist Ambrose Bierce during the Mexican Revolution. He also filmed a version of Camus's *The Plague* (1992) in Buenos Aires with U.S. actors, including William Hurt and Robert Duvall.

One of the great tragedies of Argentine cinema was the early death of Fabián Bielinsky (1959–2006) after directing only two noirish films. Released on the eve of the recent economic and political meltdown, *Nine Queens* (2000) is a twist-filled story of trust and (mostly) betrayal that reveals Buenos Aires as a city of scammers. In *The Aura* (2005), an even more atmospheric descent into the genre, a hunting accident involves a timid taxidermist in a casino robbery through a serendipitously assumed identity.

Uruguayan-born Adrián Caetano (1969–) deals with the down-and-out in films such as *Pizza, Beer & Smokes* (1998), about a youthful group of disaffected squatters who collude with a Buenos Aires cabbie to rob his clients; it was codirected with Bruno Stagnaro (1973–). Caetano's *Bolivia* (2001) deals poignantly with the contemporary theme of undocumented immigrants and their fate, in this case a Bolivian restaurant worker confronting an ugly Argentine nationalism and random tragedy.

Theater

Like New York, Buenos Aires has a vibrant live-theater scene, but even small provincial towns often have their own companies. Much of the Buenos Aires theater consists of gaudy musicals, which move to the beach city of Mar del Plata in summer, but there is also a serious theater presence that ranges from committed amateurs to highly professional theaters and actors.

Buenos Aires, in fact, was such a major theater destination that France's Jean Cocteau and Spain's Federico García Lorca made between-the-wars pilgrimages to the city. The city government supports live drama through the Teatro San Martín, a complex of five theaters where classics by Shakespeare, Chekhov, and Molière are routinely on the program. The Buenos Aires Province capital of La Plata is also a hotbed of live theater.

That said, small independent theaters, sometimes seating no more than a few dozen patrons, often provide remarkable value with no-frills, often avant-garde, productions. At the other extreme is the *revista porteña*, a burlesque potpourri with vulgar comedians and scantily dressed dancers. In recent years, some of these have acquired a topical political edge, with titles such as *They Came, They Saw ... and They Stole*—dealing with the timeless theme of government and corporate corruption.

Filming a scene in Walter Salles's *The Motorcycle Diaries*, a biography of the youthful Che Guevara

In a category of its own is community theater, best exemplified by companies such as the Teatro Catalinas Sur (see sidebar p. 67), with a professional director but amateur performers in the working-class Buenos Aires neighborhood of La Boca. Their approach is unapologetically political and left-of-center. Children's theater is also a popular leisure activity.

Because Argentina's population is relatively small, many Argentine theater figures work in movies and television as well. Playwright Juan Carlos Gené (1929–2012), for instance, wrote five plays about García Lorca, but also created film and TV screenplays, and acted extensively on both the big and small screens. ■

World-class culture, dining, and tango—and getaways to the wildlife-rich Paraná Delta

Buenos Aires & the Delta

National polo championships in Palermo's Campo Argentino de Polo

Buenos Aires & the Delta

Buenos Aires is a metropolis of millions that's a world capital but, at the same time, a city of intimate neighborhoods. The cliché calls it the "Paris of the South," but it's really a New World immigrant city with a vigorous diversity and 24/7 energy that makes New York City a better comparison.

As Argentina's largest and most influential city, Buenos Aires is, like New York, sometimes a target of scorn and resentment by people from the provinces. Even so, its barrios (neighborhoods) conserve aspects of the 19th-century "great village" that existed until European immigrants inundated the city before World War I, and many provincial people seek their fortunes among the *porteños* (residents of the port city).

Back Then

In 1536, when Pedro de Mendoza founded Buenos Aires on the edge of the humid Pampas, it was only a scattering of indigenous encampments where the Querandí hunted guanaco and rhea and scavenged for wild foods. Reestablished by Juan de Garay in 1580, for nearly two centuries it was a colonial boondocks, but the creation of the Viceroyalty of the River Plate was a first step toward making it one of the world's great port cities.

Since independence in 1816, the city's colonial core has spread beyond the riverside and onto the Pampas, absorbing smaller towns to create a conurbation that now holds nearly a third of Argentina's population. Greater Buenos Aires has more than 13 million people, but the city proper—a federal district like Washington, D.C.—is a compact area with about three million inhabitants.

Grasping the Barrios

Buenos Aires has 47 barrios, but just a few easily accessible ones hold most sights and sounds a visitor needs to know. Political power finds a home in Monserrat's Plaza de

NOT TO BE MISSED:

Plaza de Mayo, where presidents address the public—and the public shouts back **58–60**

Feria de San Pedro Telmo—Plaza Dorrego's Sunday flea market **62**

Teatro Colón: refurbished opera house anticipating Argentina's bicentennial **72–73**

Historic Café Tortoni, tourist friendly but not a tourist trap **76**

Cementerio de la Recoleta— the Argentine elite's preferred boneyard **79–81**

Trendy Palermo's dining, nightlife, and shopping **83–88**

MALBA, Palermo's modern Latin American art museum **87**

The Delta boat trip to historic Isla Martín García **94–95**

Mayo, where the president and her bureaucracy reside; to the north, the "Microcentro" of San Nicolás is the city's commercial and financial axis. Immediately east, Puerto Madero is a revived, sophisticated counterpart to Baltimore's Inner Harbor.

South of Monserrat, San Telmo's cobbled colonial streets are steadily gentrifying, but their tangophile traditions and the Sunday flea market on Plaza Dorrego remain intact. Farther south, La Boca is still a working-class neighborhood with tourist appeal for its colorful Caminito pedestrian mall and the scrappy, popular Boca Juniors soccer club.

North of the Microcentro, Retiro's Plaza San Martín marks the spot where the Argentine oligarchy built massive mansions to give the city its Parisian pretensions. Immediately north, the trend spread to Recoleta and its residential "Barrio Norte" and even to the deceased in its celebrated Cementerio de la Recoleta. Once unsavory northern outskirts,

Palermo is now the nerve center of Argentine gastronomy, design, and entertainment, while Belgrano is a more sedate residential barrio with a cluster of fine museums.

Beyond the Avenida General Paz beltway, the riverside town of Tigre is an enticing getaway, especially for its access to the lush Paraná Delta and the historic island of Martín García. ■

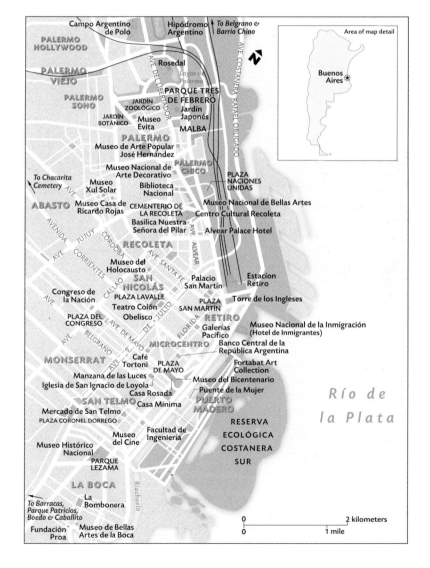

Buenos Aires

After two centuries as a cultural and political backwater, Buenos Aires began to flourish in the 19th century, and it has never looked back. Visitors to the city can take in a range of the urban Argentine experience, from the historic buildings around Plaza de Mayo to Recoleta's VIP cemetery, final resting place of Evita Perón.

Linking the Congreso with the presidential palace, Avenida de Mayo is Buenos Aires's civic axis.

Buenos Aires

Map p. 57

Visitor Information

☎ 011/4313-0187

Plaza de Mayo & Around

Monserrat, Buenos Aires's oldest barrio, is where Juan de Garay refounded the city nearly four decades after Pedro de Mendoza's starving settlers—some resorting to cannibalism—abandoned the city in 1541. Garay's more enduring settlement is now the center of Argentine public life, with all key institutions on or near the Plaza de Mayo. All roads to the provinces start nearby, at Plaza Mariano Moreno. Many visitors and even

porteños conflate Monserrat with San Telmo, which formally starts six blocks to the south.

Famously, the Plaza de Mayo is also the place where, in 1977, the Madres de Plaza de Mayo first confronted the junta that kidnapped and killed many of their children. The Madres have since divided into factions, but until recently they were still parading silently at 3:30 p.m. Thursdays around the plaza's obelisk.

The plaza's focal point is the pink-hued **Casa Rosada**

presidential palace, whose balcony was the site of Perón's often strident speeches to his followers. Supported by redbrick columns, the palace once held a colonial fortress and customhouse in the basement; alongside it is the **Museo del Bicentenario,** which provides an overview of the Argentine epic from pre-Columbian times to the present. A contemporary superstructure covers the remains of a colonial fortress and customhouse, which displays iconic artifacts of Argentine history, quirky items such as a Peronist sports car, and even a mural by Mexico's David Alfaro Siqueiros.

Opposite the museum, the chipped marble walls of the Ministerio de Economía y Finanzas Públicas are living testimony to the plaza's contentious history. These chips are bullet marks from the navy planes that strafed the Casa Rosada during a 1955 coup attempt.

On the plaza's north side, the neoclassical facade of the **Catedral Metropolitana** is a misleading face for a late-colonial church. Supported by massive columns, it has a line of cupolas from which dim lights stream onto the floor. The cathedral is to religion what the Casa Rosada is to politics, but not so long ago it was influential in both arenas—until a constitutional amendment in 1994, Roman Catholic membership was obligatory for the presidency. Draped with Argentine flags, the **Mausoleo del General José de San Martín,** the independence hero, occupies an exterior niche chapel with an eternal flame.

On the west side, the plaza's only surviving colonial building is the **Cabildo de Buenos Aires** (town council), entered via a shady portico. It's a truncated version of the original ever since 19th-century mayor Torcuato de Alvear knocked most of the building down to help create Avenida de Mayo. The building itself is more interesting than the **Museo Histórico Nacional del Cabildo y de la Revolución de Mayo,** with its scanty collections of maps, paintings, portraits, and photographs.

Alvear's controversial project razed narrow colonial streets to open a broad avenue that now leads west to the **Congreso de la Nación.** En route, it passes

INSIDER TIP:

For authentic dining, skip overpriced Palermo and try the *parrillas* and Spanish restaurants on Avenida de Mayo near Congreso, or in San Telmo.

—MICHAEL LUONGO
National Geographic writer

landmarks like **Café Tortoni** *(Avenida de Mayo 825, tel 011/4342-4328, www.cafetortoni.com.ar),* an institution since 1858; the elegant **Teatro Avenida** *(Avenida de Mayo 1222, tel 011/4812-6369, www .balirica.org.ar),* a substitute opera house for the Teatro Colón during the latter's recent restoration; and **Palacio Barolo** *(Avenida de Mayo 1370, tel 011/4383-1065,*

Microcentro
- ⊠ Florida & Diagonal Roque Sáenz Peña
- 🕐 Closed Sun.

Puerto Madero
- ⊠ Dique 4

Retiro
- ⊠ Terminal de Ómnibus, local 83
- 🕐 Closed Sun.

Recoleta
- ⊠ Avenida Quintana & Roberto M. Ortiz

www.bue.gov.ar

Museo del Bicentenario
- 🅰 Map p. 57
- ⊠ Paseo Colón 100
- ☎ 011/4344-3802
- 🕐 Closed Mon.– Tues., & holidays
- 🆂 Free
- 🚇 Subway: A, D, E

www.museo.gov.ar

Catedral Metropolitana
- ⊠ Avenida Rivadavia & San Martín
- ☎ 011/4331-2845

www.catedral buenosaires .org.ar

Museo Histórico Nacional del Cabildo y de la Revolución de Mayo
- ⊠ Bolívar 65
- ☎ 011/4342-6729
- 🕐 Closed Mon.– Tues.
- 🆂 $, Fri. free
- 🚇 Subway: A, D, E

www.cabildonacional .gob.ar

Manzana de las Luces

- 🅰 Map p. 57
- ✉ Perú 272
- ☎ 011/4342-3964
- 🕐 March–Jan.: guided tours daily. Feb.: tours Tues., Thurs.– Sun.
- 💲 From $
- Ⓜ Subway: A, D, E

www.manzanadelas luces.gov.ar

Iglesia de San Ignacio de Loyola

- 🅰 Map p. 57
- ✉ Bolívar 225
- ☎ 011/4331-2458

www.sanignacio deloyola.org.ar

Museo de la Ciudad

- ✉ Defensa 219
- ☎ 011/4343-2123
- 💲 $, Mon. & Wed. free
- Ⓜ Subway: A, D, E

www.museodela ciudad.buenosaires .gov.ar

www.pbarolo.com.ar), an ornately detailed office building themed after Dante's *Divine Comedy.* Facing the Congreso, **Plaza del Congreso** features a raised monument with statues representing past congresses, the Argentine Republic, and natural features of the country.

Taking a Taxi

Buenos Aires's black-and-yellow taxis are cheap and abundant, but taking them requires a little caution. For security, some people prefer ringing a radio taxi to flagging one in the street, but otherwise hail one that explicitly says "radio taxi." Or you can call meterless *remises* that charge per trip. In any cab, lock the doors to discourage robberies.

Before stepping in the taxi, clarify whether the price is in dollars or pesos. Tipping is unnecessary. Cabbies may even round down to avoid making change, but to avoid misunderstandings, mention the value of the banknote you pay with.

Monserrat

Two blocks south of Plaza de Mayo, Monserrat contains more landmarks from the colonial quarter, which extends into San Telmo. Many of these are ecclesiastical; the most prominent is the **Manzana de las Luces,** a full city block where the Jesuit Order built the foundations for the city's intellectual life until its expulsion from the Americas

in 1767. Fronting on Bolívar, the city's oldest church is the **Iglesia de San Ignacio de Loyola** (1722), based on Rome's 16th-century Il Gesú. Alongside it, the Colegio Nacional de Buenos Aires is an elite public school run by the Universidad de Buenos Aires.

The Jesuits valued the intellect, but their adjacent **Procuraduría de las Misiones** (storehouse), facing Alsina, suggests also they respected the peso. Combined with their commercial acumen, the produce from their mission farms made them the wealthiest and most powerful monastic order in the Spanish Empire. The building's restored defensive tunnels (later used for contraband) and the rest of the Jesuit facilities are open for guided tours.

One block east, embellished with burnished woodwork and tiled floors, the **Farmacia de la Estrella** (*Defensa 201, tel 011/4343-4040, www.farmaciadelaestrella.com*) feels like a 19th-century homeopathic apothecary—because that's exactly what it is. Its decorative details include the ceiling fresco "El Triunfo de la Farmacopea ante la Enfermedad" ("The Triumph of Pharmacopeia Over Illness"), by Italian painter Carlos Barberis, in a romantic style resembling his U.S. contemporary Maxfield Parrish.

Above the pharmacy, the **Museo de la Ciudad** avoids the chronology trap of city history with frequently changing, thematically organized exhibitions of everyday objects such as bathrooms, doors, floor tiles, and furniture. There's a special exhibit hall at street level, where the pharmacy's windows serve as display cases, so that even when the museum's closed there's something to see.

Across the street, a Jesuit designed the **Basílica de San Francisco** *(Defensa & Alsina, tel/011 4331-0625)* in 1726, but it belonged to the Franciscans. While the interior retains its colonial integrity, with decorative tile floors and a central cupola, it lost much of its ornamentation to Peronist arsonists after the 1955 coup attempt against Perón. Architect Ernesto Sackmann refashioned the facade in a Bavarian baroque style, with twin towers, in 1911.

One block south, the underrated **Museo Etnográfico Juan B. Ambrosetti** shows and tells more about indigenous Argentina—specifically the Kolla of the Andean northwest, the seminomadic Mapuche of Patagonia, and the hunter-gatherer bands of Tierra del Fuego—than any other museum in the city. Its pluralist orientation is an antidote to a widely held belief that Argentines are almost exclusively of European origins. In addition to its regular exhibits, the museum hosts frequent lectures by Argentine and foreign scholars.

Another block south, dating from the late 18th century, the **Basílica del Santísimo Rosario y Convento de Santo Domingo** played a major role in the British invasions of 1806 and 1807, but it lost almost all its colonial artifacts and documents when Peronist mobs set it ablaze in 1955. Its courtyard holds the **Mausoleo de Belgrano,** where an eternal flame illuminates the resting place of Gen. Manuel Belgrano, independence hero and designer of the Argentine flag.

San Telmo

Strictly speaking, San Telmo starts six blocks south of

Museo Etnográfico Juan B. Ambrosetti
- ⊠ Moreno 350
- ☎ 011/4345-8196
- ⏱ Closed Mon., holidays, & Jan.
- 💲 $
- 🚇 Subway: A, D, E

www.museoetno grafico.filo.uba.ar

Basilica del Santísimo Rosario y Convento de Santo Domingo
- ⊠ Belgrano & Defensa
- ☎ 011/4331-1668

Facing Plaza de Mayo, the Casa Rosada is Argentina's presidential palace.

Tango dancers perform in San Telmo.

**Centro Cultural
Torquato Tasso**
✉ Defensa 1575
☎ 011/4307-6506
🕐 Shows Tues.–
Sat.; *milonga*
(tango dance
party) Sun.
Closed mid-
Dec.–mid-Jan.

www.torquatotasso
.com.ar

**Museo Histórico
Nacional**
🅰 Map p. 57
✉ Defensa 1600
☎ 011/4307-1182
🕐 Closed Mon.–
Tues.,
Jan. 1,
& Dec. 25

www.aamhn.org.ar

Svenska Kyrkan
✉ Azopardo 1428
☎ 011/4361-7304

www.iglesia
suecaenbsas
.blogspot.com

Plaza de Mayo, but its bohemian spirit has spread north across Avenida Belgrano into the southern blocks of Monserrat—many of whose tourist-oriented businesses claim to be part of San Telmo. Occasionally ragged around the edges, San Telmo is where new money, old money, and little or no money coexist in a blend of traditional *PH*s (a *propiedad horizontal* is a single-story house on a deep lot), recycled lofts, boutique hotels, tango salons, chic restaurants and wine bars, and crumbling *conventillos*—aging mansions occupied by squatters. Its many hostels make it popular with backpackers.

Even though San Telmo's street plan is relatively regular, a handful of cobbled alleyways and dogleg streets bring out the barrio's palpable social informality. Its uncontested core is **Plaza Coronel Dorrego,** the cobbled plaza whose Sunday antiques flea market, the

Feria de San Pedro Telmo, is one of the city's top attractions for Argentines and foreigners alike. It's so popular that authorities have closed eight blocks of Defensa street to make more room for the vendors, dancers, mimes, musicians, and singers, who flood into the neighborhood every Sunday. The rest of the week, the shady plaza makes an ideal site for lunch or coffee from the surrounding cafés and restaurants that set up tables there.

It's been said, though it's uncertain, that Pedro de Mendoza's original encampment took place on the high ground of present-day **Parque Lezama,** four blocks south, where the river once lapped at the shore. Whether or not that's the case, an imposing bronze statue of Mendoza stands at the park's northwest corner on a marble monument with a bas-relief of a Querandí Indian. On Sundays, an artisans' market occupies the park's palm-studded pathways and even stretches north along Defensa toward Plaza Dorrego, stopped only by broad Avenida San Juan.

In mid-block across Defensa street from the monument, look for the *filete*-painted facade of the **Centro Cultural Torquato Tasso.** Despite its dim, no-frills interior, it's one of the city's top choices for live tango song and music—as opposed to the flashy floor shows that many porteños disparage as "for export."

Just south, on the park at Avenida Caseros, the **Museo Histórico Nacional** (National History Museum) underwent a long-overdue renovation in preparation for the bicentennial of the Revolution of 1810, both in its facilities and in its entire approach. Not so long ago, for instance, the handsome Italianate building's collections held almost nothing on pre-Columbian Argentina; the bulk of the exhibits focused on San Martín and other national icons, and the most recent presidential portrait was that of Hipólito Yrigoyen, overthrown by the military in 1930. Now the museum puts more emphasis on social history, including Argentina's

indigenous and immigrant origins and its mass movements (in that context, portraits of Juan and Evita Perón are an innovation here).

Argentina's immigrant religious diversity is on display nearby. Facing the park from Avenida Brasil, the **Catedral Ortodoxa Rusa de la Santísima Trinidad** *(Brasil 315),* a Russian Orthodox church, features bow windows and turquoise onion domes imported from St. Petersburg. Two blocks east, in a staid Nordic style, the **Svenska Kyrkan** (Swedish Lutheran Church) offers services in Spanish and Swedish—as well as tango lessons.

Three blocks north of the park, the **Museo de Arte Moderno de Buenos Aires** (Modern Art Museum) occupies a former tobacco factory; after undergoing a major renovation for Argentina's 2010 bicentennial, it showcases

Museo de Arte Moderno de Buenos Aires (MAMBA)
- ✉ Avenida San Juan 350
- ☎ 011/4342-3001
- 🕓 Closed Mon.

www.museode
artemoderno
.buenosaires.gov.ar

Filete & the Piropo

Piropos—witty, flirtatious remarks—often appear in the context of the traditional sign-painting art of *filete*. In Jorge Luis Borges's essay "Las Inscripciones de los Carros," he applauded the simple eloquence of the epigraphs that decorated the horse-drawn carriages of his 20th-century prime. These piropos, he pointed out, could range from arrogant (*¿Qué mira, envidioso?*: "What are you looking at, jealous one?") to enigmatic (*El perdido nunca llora*: "The lost one never weeps") and beyond.

Filete's flourishes decorated some city buses into the 1970s. The art was eventually banned from buses, but in recent years it has made a comeback through artists such as Martiniano Arce and Jorge Muscia—though not on public transportation.

The Dirty War & Its Monuments

The so-called Dirty War of 1976–1983, in which tens of thousands of Argentines perished or "disappeared" under one of the continent's most vicious military dictatorships ever, is something many citizens would like to forget. At the same time, they have sworn, "Never again"—to use the title of novelist Ernesto Sabato's summary report of the era.

For that reason, recent governments have created monuments at clandestine detention centers around the city. Under San Telmo's Autopista 25 de Mayo, the freeway to the international airport, both sides of Avenida Paseo Colón have pocket-park memorials to the euphemistically named Club Atlético, a warehouse that the military demolished to destroy evidence of the torture and murders that took place there.

Club Atlético, though, was not the most notorious of the bunch. That "honor" fell to the Escuela de Mecánica de la Armada (ESMA, the Naval Mechanics' School), on Avenida del Libertador in the northern barrio of Núñez. Former president Carlos Menem—himself a Dirty War detainee—helped make it even more controversial by proposing its demolition for a monument to national unity, but overwhelming public opposition forced him to retreat. It has now undergone conversion to make it the Espacio para la Memoria—the Space for Memory.

Museo de Arte Contemporáneo

✉ Avenida San Juan 328

☎ 011 / 5299-2010

💲 $

🕐 Closed Tues.

www.macba.com.ar

abstract rather than figurative art. Almost alongside it, the **Museo de Arte Contemporáneo** has rotating exhibitions of abstract Argentine art.

Even during the week, when Plaza Coronel Dorrego is quiet, antiques shops and galleries attract visitors along both sides of Defensa and Balcarce, one block east. One block north, under wrought-iron roofing that hasn't changed in a century, the **Mercado de San Telmo** remains a rough-around-the-edges fruit and vegetable market that's let in only a handful of crafts stands with tourist appeal. Two blocks east, the **Dansk Kirke** (Danish Lutheran Church) is another Scandinavian enclave—no tango lessons, but a Danish folkloric dance group meets most Fridays and Saturdays.

San Telmo is a traditional tango venue, where several supper clubs stretch north along twisting Balcarce street and into Monserrat. Nearly hidden behind a tree at the corner of Avenida Independencia, the inconspicuous **Plazoleta Leonel Rivera** contains a mural whose embracing dancers (he in hat, striped trousers, and spats, she in slit skirt and heels) are the quintessence of classic tango style.

Immediately east, the busy thoroughfare of Avenida Paseo Colón surrounds the ovoid **Plazoleta Coronel Manuel de Olazábal,** where sculptor Rogelio Yrurtia's massive bronze "Canto al Trabajo" is the antidote to all the capital's pretentious equestrian statues. In his statue, Yrurtia, whose Belgrano home is a museum (see p. 90) in its own right, honors the hard physical labor of the pioneers on the Pampas.

Across the avenue, the monumental **Facultad de Ingeniería** (Engineering School of the University of Buenos Aires) began its life as the Fundación Eva Perón, where Argentina's legendary first lady doled out patronage to the working-class clients that were her husband's natural constituency. It's no accident that the Confederación General del Trabajo, the Peronist trade union, built its nondescript headquarters immediately behind it, decorating the building with a corner portrait of Evita in her prime. After her death, it even harbored her mummified corpse for three years until military coupmongers overthrew Perón and spirited her body away to Italy in 1955.

At the northern end of the barrio, the block-long alleyways of **Pasaje Giuffra** and **Pasaje San Lorenzo** were once grassy arms

INSIDER TIP:

Soak up the atmosphere and essence of Buenos Aires at the Sunday morning flea market in the historic neighborhood of San Telmo.

—STEVE ST. JOHN
National Geographic contributor

of a flood-prone colonial arroyo that ran east to the river, but in the 1830s the city filled them with construction debris and cobbled them over. Today, they're a picturesque part of the Sunday street fair that's spread north from Plaza Dorrego. They are better seen, though, when the vendors' stalls don't clutter the sightlines. That's because of structures like Pasaje

San Lorenzo's so-called **Casa Mínima,** a balconied two-story house pinched between two later Italianate buildings. Barely 6 feet (2 m) wide, it's best appreciated from the other sidewalk and, even then, photographing it takes a good wide-angle lens.

Long closed to the public, once nearly crumbling, Casa Mínima is now under the administration of **El Zanjón de Granados,** an events center whose construction unearthed a series of colonial tunnels that the arroyo's debris had entombed. Urban archaeologist Daniel Schávelzon helped restore cisterns, wells, and even residences long lost to view, and salvaged centuries-old household artifacts for exhibit. Jorge Eckstein, the local businessman who paid for the restoration, also purchased the Casa Mínima, which is a chief component of local guided tours.

La Boca

Directly across from Parque Lezama on Avenida Paseo Colón, Omar Gasparini's flamboyantly inspired mural of three-dimensional caricatures is the gateway to La Boca, the colorful working-class neighborhood that, despite its palpable poverty, is also one of the city's artist colonies. Gasparini, a sculptor and a set designer for the equally flamboyant Catalinas Sur theater group, developed the **Mural Escenográfico** to represent the barrio's immigrant history. Salvaged materials from its tenements have been turned into a block-long facade that shows icons such as composer

Facultad de Ingeniería
🅜 Map p. 57
✉ Avenida Paseo Colón 850
☎ 011/4343-0891
www.fi.uba.ar

Casa Mínima
🅜 Map p. 57
✉ Pasaje San Lorenzo 380
☎ 011/4361-3002

El Zanjón de Granados
✉ Defensa 755
☎ 011/4361-3002
🕒 Closed Sat.
💲 $$$$–$$$$$. 60-min. tour Mon.–Fri.; 30-min. tour Sun. Ask in advance for tours on holidays.
www.elzanjon.com.ar

Museo de Bellas Artes de La Boca Benito Quinquela Martín

 Map p. 57

✉ Avenida Pedro de Mendoza 1835

☎ 011/4301-1080

🕐 Closed Mon.

💲 $ (suggested)

mnba.gob.ar

Fundación Proa

 Map p. 57

✉ Avenida Pedro de Mendoza 1929

☎ 011/4104-1000

🕐 Closed Mon., Jan. 1, May 1, & Dec. 1

💲 $$

www.proa.org

Juan de Dios Filiberto (1885–1964) and soccer legend Diego Maradona (1960–). Yet the art also acknowledges the firemen, stevedores, drunkards, gossips, prostitutes, and others who built the barrio's identity.

It was Filiberto who wrote the music to the wistful tango about **Caminito**, the curving rail spur that, today, is a cobbled walkway where tour buses leave Sunday strollers who come to photograph the brightly painted, metal-clad *conventillos* (tenements) that overlook clusters of busts, statuary, and painters at their easels. Barrio painter Benito Quinquela Martín helped to transform La Boca into an artists' colony with his evocative and sympathetic portrayals of fishermen, shipyards, stevedores, and grain elevators. It was also

Quinquela Martín, an orphan who adopted the barrio as much as his parents adopted him, who turned Caminito from a weed-strewn lot into the attraction it is today.

Caminito starts at the **Vuelta de Rocha,** the riverbend meander where, not so long ago, some of the same ships that Quinquela Martín had painted were rusting hulks on the heavily polluted Riachuelo. Most of those have since been cleared away, but the Puente Transbordador Nicolás Avellaneda, the steel girder bridge that crosses the river to Buenos Aires Province, remains a striking Boca symbol. Cleaning up the river may take another millennium.

Half a block east, Quinquela Martín's former studio—which he donated to the city—is now the **Museo de Bellas Artes de La Boca Benito Quinquela Martín.** In addition to his own works, it holds an assortment of vividly colored bowsprits and paintings by other eminent Argentine artists, including Antonio Berni, whose compassionate depiction of the underclass resembles Quinquela Martín's social realism.

Quinquela Martín's legacy is part of the reason that the **Fundación Proa,** a contemporary art museum, could locate its headquarters facing the Vuelta de Rocha immediately south of Caminito and expand it to include adjacent buildings. The expanded Proa has an auditorium for events, a specialized bookstore, and a renovated facade that integrates the interior with the surrounding barrio.

To the rest of the world, though, La Boca is not Caminito,

Vivid colors brighten La Boca's Caminito walkway.

EXPERIENCE:
Way off Corrientes at Teatro Catalinas Sur

Avenida Corrientes is Buenos Aires's traditional theater district. Recently, it has seen a revival as city authorities have widened the sidewalks to create a more inviting environment—the Broadway of Buenos Aires. Its standard, though, is the *revista porteña,* a musical revue with vulgar comics and scantily clad dancers. The topical Argentine jokes and slang escape most non-native speakers of Spanish.

That's not the case with at least one community theater, **Teatro Catalinas Sur** *(Benito Perez Galdós 93, tel 011/4300-5707, www.catalinasur.com.ar),* in a renovated warehouse in La Boca. It has a professional director, Adhemar Bianchi, but unlike mainstream theater

it uses nonprofessional actors, singers, and musicians from the barrio to present repertory works. *Venimos de Muy Lejos (We Came From Far Away),* for instance, deals with the Argentine immigrant experience, and *El Fulgor Argentino (The Brilliance of Argentina)* is an ironic take on the country's history from the perspective of a neighborhood social club.

Unlike conventional theater, Catalinas Sur is participatory from the moment that the ushers—who are also actors—pass out scripts in Spanish and English. It continues as they move through the audience during the play, and even after it ends—when they wait at the exits to say thank you.

nor Quinquela Martín. Rather, it's the legendary Boca Juniors soccer team and its equally legendary stadium colloquially known as **La Bombonera** ("The Chocolate Box," but formally **Estadio Alberto J. Armando**). Here, on game days, tens of thousands of rabid fans surge into the barrio to express their passion for a club whose former striker, Diego Armando Maradona, is considered one of the best players, if not the best, in the sport's history.

Along the Brandsen street side of the stadium, realist murals are worthy successors to the Quinquela Martín legacy, showing stevedores, streetside tango dancers, and a pickup soccer match. Its basement museum, though, is more than just a celebration of the franchise—the **Museo de la Pasión Boquense** puts everything

in perspective, including the sport's role in the community and beyond. It does not flinch from placing the 1978 World Cup, which Argentina hosted, in the context of a vicious military dictatorship that was desperate to prove its legitimacy.

Newly relocated to the barrio, the **Museo del Cine** is a showcase for Argentina's rich cinematic history, with displays of posters and artifacts, plus a micro-theater that provides repertory offerings from Argentina and around the world.

The Microcentro & Around

North of Plaza de Mayo, the "Microcentro" is a catchall phrase for the city's financial and commercial center in the barrio of San Nicolás, which

(continued on p. 70)

Museo de la Pasión Boquense

✉ Brandsen 805

☎ 011/4362-1100

⊕ Closed Jan. 1, Dec. 25, & during Boca Juniors games

💲 $$$

www.museo boquense.com

Museo del Cine

✉ Agustín Caffarena 51

☎ 011/4300-4820

💲 Free Wed.

www.museodelcine .buenosaires.gob.ar

The First Tango in Buenos Aires

For non-Argentines, tango evokes romantic images of lithe dancers in sophisticated surroundings. That's not entirely wrong, but it is a stereotype. Though they pay lip service to tango's lower-class origins, the floor shows of Monserrat, San Telmo, and Barracas are usually a sanitized version of a music and dance that began in the brothels and dance halls of the city's disreputable *arrabales* (outskirts).

Professional tango dancers at the Esquina Carlos Gardel, in the Abasto neighborhood

Tango's origins date from a time when those barrios had large Afro-Argentine populations, and the word itself may have come from sub-Saharan Africa's Niger-Congo family of languages. In a sense, that validates the comment of British musician Robert Fripp, a frequent visitor to Buenos Aires, that the nostalgic tango was the Argentine blues.

Buenos Aires's Afro-Argentine population, while it didn't completely disappear, lost its visibility in the flood of European immigration that started in the late 19th century. At first, the overwhelmingly male immigrants created a sexual imbalance in the population, at least in the poorer barrios where they tended to concentrate in *conventillos* (tenements). The men frequented brothels where, while waiting for the next prostitute, they often practiced

dancing among themselves in order to be able to impress the handful of women in their tenements. This would account at least in part for the wistfulness of tango lyrics.

Meanwhile, tango developed its own language, *lunfardo*—a dialect (according to some) or slang (according to others) that infused tango lyrics with their meaning. Today, lunfardo can be impenetrable to non-Argentines; in the early days even police were unable to decipher the conversations of *compadritos* and *malevos*, the small-time, knife-wielding hoods who dressed to impress.

It was only, according to British tango teacher and author Christine Denniston, when upper- and middle-class men slummed in the brothels that they came into contact with the tango, whose sensuality and class associations repelled *gente decente* (decent people). That, for the most part, kept tango out of the city's prestige venues until it gained legitimacy by crossing the Atlantic to Paris, where it became a sensation.

The Influential Carlos Gardel

Back in Buenos Aires, gente decente still had their doubts, but the charismatic Carlos Gardel made the *tango canción*, the tango song, into an international phenomenon. Gardel, whose immigrant origins were indisputable but ambiguous—the controversy whether he was born in France or Uruguay never seems to go away—became the Elvis of his era. In fact, though no one would suggest that Gardel still lives—he died in a plane crash in Medellín, Colombia, in 1935—his devotees maintain that "Gardel sings better every day."

Gardel grew up in the Abasto neighborhood west of downtown Buenos Aires, in the shadow of the wholesale market that has since been recycled as an upscale, art deco–style shopping center. In those times, the immigrant communities were starting to find their voice, and Gardel voiced their nostalgia, anxieties, and apprehension about the future. Songs such as "Mi Buenos Aires querido" ("My Dear Buenos Aires"), "Volver" ("To Return"), and "El día que me quieras" ("The Day That You Love Me") expressed nostalgia for times past, concerns about family and friends, and a longing for love that have proved to be durable themes.

Tango flourished during the Perón years as an expression of nationalism, but it faltered after Juan Perón's overthrow in 1955 unleashed nearly three decades of conservative authoritarianism and dictatorship. Since the return to democracy in 1983, though, its role in Argentine culture has solidified. Tango's increased popularity abroad and at home as a tourist attraction has helped to revive the form in recent years.

EXPERIENCE: Living the Tango

One of Buenos Aires's biggest annual events, the **Festival de Tango** *(www .tangobuenosaires.gob.ar)* is an elaborate program of dance and music performances—many of them free—that engages tango aficionados and newcomers alike. Traditionally held in March, following Brazilian Carnaval, it moved to August in 2008—immediately preceding the annual Campeonato Mundial de Baile de Tango (World Tango Championship).

Unlike Carnaval, a mass event, the tango festival is a potpourri of performances in more intimate settings—small theaters and parks—throughout the city. Spectators can see the performers up close. Many tourists get shuttled to expensive floor shows, but those in the know get their tango fixes at participatory *milongas* (tango dance parties) that take place every night, and some afternoons. There, more often than not, the music is recorded, but the dancers are passionate *porteños*, and they show how tango works beneath the glamorous facade. That said, some milongas feature live performances with professional musicians who are sometimes so close to the audience that you can touch their arms. Likewise, intimidatingly skilled dancers occasionally take the floor during breaks. You'll see them at a fraction of the cost of a floor show. The best source of information is the regularly updated English-language Hoy Milonga (www.hoy-milonga.com), which has daily schedules.

The tango festival was first held on December 11, the anniversary of tango legend Carlos Gardel's birthday. On that day, much of a major street near the Centro Cultural San Martín is still blocked off for the **Milonga de Calle Corrientes,** an open-air dance party that honors the singer's memory.

Banco de la Nación Argentina

✉ Avenida Rivadavia 205

☎ 011/4347-6000

www.bna.com.ar

Banco Central de la República Argentina

🗺 Map p. 57

✉ Reconquista 266, entrance at San Martín 275

☎ 011/4348-3500

www.bcra.gov.ar

Museo Histórico y Numismático Dr. Jose Evaristo Uriburu

✉ San Martín 216

☎ 011/4348-3882

🕐 Closed Sat.– Sun., & holidays

🚇 Subway: A, B, D, E

is rarely mentioned by its own name. Along with the rest of San Nicolás, it's also a traditional entertainment center, with its own share of museums and monuments.

The axis of the Microcentro is the Calle Florida pedestrian mall, which extends north for ten blocks into the barrio of Retiro; the other key streets are the east-west Avenida Corrientes, the traditional heart of the theater district, and the north-south Avenida 9 de Julio, multiple lanes of cars and buses that separate the Microcentro from the rest of San Nicolás.

Florida and the parallel streets that run north from Plaza de Mayo to Corrientes form the financial district known as **La City,** where Alejandro Bustillo's solidly neoclassical **Banco de la Nación Argentina,** the state-run bank, occupies an entire block facing the Casa Rosada. One of Argentina's most prolific architects, Bustillo

(1889–1982) is best known for his work in and around the Patagonian city of San Carlos de Bariloche.

It may be hard to picture now, but during the political and economic meltdown of 2002, most of the district's banks and exchange houses protected their facades with corrugated aluminum and plywood to thwart the wrath

INSIDER TIP:

For leather goods, hit Calle Murillo, rather than the more famous pedestrian mall called Calle Florida.

—MEI-LING HOPGOOD
National Geographic writer

of enraged depositors who had found their accounts frozen and their funds devalued—even though government action had forced the banks' hands. Vulgar graffiti even defaced such striking buildings as the Spanish Renaissance **Standard Bank** *(Florida 99),* and not all of it has disappeared.

No single building better embodies the Argentine paradox than the sturdy Italianate **Banco Central de la República Argentina,** designed by Englishman Henry Hunt, which has identical facades on San Martín and Reconquista. That's partly because the solid architecture of Argentina's central bank contrasts so starkly with the economy's boom-and-bust cycles, and partly because the bank's **Museo Histórico y Numismático Dr. Jose Evaristo**

EXPERIENCE:
Above the Pitch

Along with tango, soccer is an Argentine passion, and the national team is almost always in the top ten of FIFA rankings. On an everyday basis, Buenos Aires has half a dozen first-division teams with fan bases that are sometimes too energetic and enthusiastic—attending a match is quite an experience, but foreigners should wear neutral colors and avoid the cheap seats.

Boca Juniors *(Brandsen 805, tel 011/4309-4700, www.bocajuniors.com.ar)*

Club Atlético River Plate *(Avenida Presidente Figueroa Alcorta 7597, tel 011/4788-1200, www.cariverplate.com.ar)*

Uriburu, across the street, exhibits the country's chaotic monetary history so effectively. Its inconspicuous entrance monitored by federal police, this obscure second-story museum reminds us, for instance, how the face value of federal banknotes reached up to a million pesos in the hyperinflationary 1980s, and how the provinces have often printed their own currency to meet bloated government payrolls. The earliest 19th-century Buenos Aires banknotes, curiously enough, included portraits of the Venezuelan Simón Bolívar and, remarkably enough, George Washington.

Erratic monetary policy may have made investing in Argentina a challenge but, somehow, institutions like the **Bolsa de Comercio de Buenos Aires** (*Sarmiento 299*), the mansard-topped Francophile stock exchange, have managed to survive. Immediately to its east, toward Puerto Madero, the beaux arts **Correo Central** (central post office; *Sarmiento 151*) also sports a mansard roof, but architect Norbert Maillart took his inspiration from New York City's main post office.

Calle Florida itself is no longer the elite shopping area it once was—the Buenos Aires branch of Harrods, for instance, separated from its mother in the 1960s, and its storefront has stood vacant since closing in the 1990s—but there's one landmark exception to the rule. At the barrio's north end, occupying nearly an entire city block, the 1890s **Galerías Pacífico** went through multiple incarnations as an Italian-inspired shopping gallery and private and government railroad

The pedestrian mall of Calle Florida

offices before its resurrection as an elegant shopping mall in 1992.

It's not the shopping that makes the gallery worth visiting, but rather the 540 square yards (450 sq m) of frescos that adorn its central cupola. When the famous Mexican muralist David Alfaro Siqueiros visited Buenos Aires in 1933, he attracted a retinue that included Antonio Berni (1907–1981), Juan Carlos Castagnino (1908–1972), and Lino Spilimbergo (1896–1964). The artists later united with Demetrio Urruchúa (1902–1978) and the Galician Manuel Colmeiro (1901–1999) to create the Nuevo Realismo (New Realism) murals—differing dramatically from Berni's earlier surrealism—in 1945.

Galerías Pacífico
- 🅰 Map p. 57
- ✉ Florida 750
- ☎ 011/5555-5110
- **www.galerias pacifico.com.ar**

Centro Cultural Borges

✉ Viamonte & San Martín

☎ 011/5555-5359

🕐 Closed Jan. 1, May 1, & Dec. 25

💲 From $$

🚇 Subway: B, C

www.ccborges.org.ar

Teatro Ópera

✉ Avenida Corrientes 860

☎ 011/4326-1335

www.operaciti-teatro.com.ar

Teatro Gran Rex

✉ Avenida Corrientes 857

☎ 011/4322-8000

www.teatro-granrex.com.ar

Teatro General San Martín

✉ Avenida Corrientes 1530

☎ 011/4371-0111

Teatro Colón

🗺 Map p. 57

✉ Libertad 621

www.teatrocolon.org.ar

Integrating the murals on a concave surface was a challenge for the artists. They did a trial run on a model in Urruchúa's San Telmo studio before sketching them in charcoal in the cupola, dismantling the scaffolds for a better view, and then reerecting them for the painting. It took more than a year before Berni's "El Amor" ("Love"), Urruchúa's "La Fraternidad" ("Brotherhood"), and the others were ready. Berni oversaw a restoration in 1968 and a Mexican-Argentine team performed another in 1991, just before the mall opened.

Part of the Galerías Pacífico now serves as the **Centro Cultural Borges,** a performing arts center and exhibition hall dedicated to the memory of Argentina's most famous writer, whose permanent exhibit there is the closest thing to a Borges museum. The traditional entertainment district, though, is **Avenida Corrientes,** where the 220-foot (67 m) **Obelisco,** erected in 1936 for the 400th anniversary of Pedro de Mendoza's landing, rises at the intersection with Avenida 9

de Julio. Also visible from Plaza de Mayo, the white monolith is a point of orientation for the entire downtown area.

At the foot of Corrientes, **Luna Park** *(Avenida Corrientes & Leandro N. Alem)* is a covered stadium that hosts concerts, basketball games, boxing matches, and the like. Historically, it's a Peronist icon as the place where Evita met Perón. On both sides of Corrientes, venues like **Teatro Ópera, Teatro Gran Rex,** and **Teatro General San Martín** are all institutions with high-profile international performers, but there are countless other musical theater offerings and intimate halls that once made this the Broadway of Buenos Aires.

None of those, though, comes close to the high-culture tradition of **Teatro Colón,** the century-old opera house two blocks north of the Obelisco. After a centennial renovation, it once again has a full events schedule, even opening its stage to an orchestral presentation by the erratic rock star Charly García.

Facing the middle block of Plaza Lavalle, the seven-level

EXPERIENCE: Cycling the Costanera

Despite Buenos Aires's ferocious traffic, bike-friendly areas are abundant enough for a car-free afternoon. The best is a former landfill that, spontaneously colonized by plants and animals, is now Puerto Madero's **Reserva Ecológica Costanera Sur** *(Avenida Tristán Achával Rodríguez 1550, tel 011/4315-4129, closed Mon.).* Over an area of 860 acres (348 ha), crisscrossing trails take cyclists (and

runners and hikers—there are speed limits) from the Microcentro's bustle and onto the riverside.

In the process, sharp-eyed visitors may spot a wide variety of bird species native to the Pampas. At the northern entrance, at the extension of Avenida Córdoba, Bici Bus is a mobile bike rental that operates year-round. If it rains heavily, officials may close the trails to visitors.

Colón can seat nearly 2,500 spectators and accommodate another 500 in standing room. Designed by Francesco Tamburini, the Italian Renaissance-style theater employs its own 120-member orchestra, with first-rate acoustics and sets. Its forte, though, has been its

INSIDER TIP:

Head to Puerto Madero at sunset, when the water in the port reflects a fiery red and the city skyline is silhouetted behind. It's the riverfront at its most romantic.

—MICHAEL LUONGO
National Geographic writer

ability to attract globally prominent talent ranging from Igor Stravinsky to Leonard Bernstein, Enrico Caruso to Plácido Domingo, Maria Callas to Kiri Te Kanawa, and Rudolf Nureyev to Julio Bocca. Even in hard times, the Colón has managed to mount a credible schedule of performers.

Across the plaza, the third branch of Argentine government has its base at the eclectic **Palacio de los Tribunales** (formally called the Palacio de Justicia), the law courts building where the Corte Suprema de Justicia (Supreme Court) holds its deliberations. It is also, since 1994, the site where a moment of silence is observed every Monday at 9:53 a.m., the hour at which a terrorist bomb destroyed the city's Asociación

Mutual Israelita Argentina (AMIA), a Jewish community organization; judicial investigations have gone nowhere.

Immediately north of the Colón, the **Templo de la Congregación Israelita de la República Argentina** is a conservative synagogue that's the city's most impressive Jewish community landmark. It is also home to the **Museo Judío de Buenos Aires Dr. Salvador Kibrick,** which stresses the role of Jewish immigration and settlement in Argentina under the sponsorship of Baron Maurice Hirsch, who helped Russian Jews to flee from pogroms in tsarist Russia in the 1890s. The museum also contains Jewish and Jewish-Argentine art, along with documents and photographs (do not photograph the exterior, which has heavy security, without permission).

Puerto Madero

Along the riverfront, where penniless European immigrants first set foot on Argentine territory, the new barrio of Puerto Madero is fast becoming the city's most exclusive residential area, with luxury hotels and historical museums. Little more than an area of muddy riverbanks in colonial times, augmented by landfill in the late 19th century, it underwent a major port transformation as Argentine agriculture boomed. When the boom went bust after World War II, though, the handsome brick warehouses emptied and the cranes stood still and then rusted.

Museo Judío de Buenos Aires Dr. Salvador Kibrick
✉ Libertad 769
☎ 011/4123-0832
🕓 Open Tues. & Thurs.
www.museojudio .org.ar

Museo Nacional de la Inmigración

- Map p. 57
- Avenida Antártida 1355
- 011/4317-0285
- Closed until further notice

www.migraciones .gov.ar/accesible/? museo

Buque Museo A.R.A. Corbeta Uruguay

- Dique No. 4
- 011/4314-1090
- $
- Subway: B

www.ara.mil.ar/pag .asp?idItem=113

Buque Museo Fragata A.R.A. Presidente Sarmiento

- Dique No. 3
- 011/4334-9386
- $

www.ara.mil.ar/pag .asp?idItem=112

As the country stagnated, a military dictatorship further filled in the land with rubble as it planned for a satellite city, but an ill-conceived and ineptly executed war with Britain over the Falkland Islands brought the regime down. Ten years later, plants and animals had colonized much of the area, a civilian government had created a new barrio, and investors had recycled historic structures into stylish lofts, hotels, high-rise flats, and fancy restaurants. At the same time, the changes created vast public spaces for city residents.

From 1911 until 1953, at Puerto Madero's north end, the **Hotel de Inmigrantes** was where fresh-off-the-boat arrivals had five

INSIDER TIP:

Most restaurants don't open before 8 p.m. To survive, pop into a café for a *merienda*—an afternoon snack of coffee with *medialunas,* small sweet croissants.

—MEI-LING HOPGOOD
National Geographic writer

days, free of charge with meals included, to organize their departure into the city and beyond. Partially restored, it's now the **Museo Nacional de la Inmigración.** Here families come to track their genealogies from a computerized archive covering nearly four million immigrants who landed on Argentina's shores between 1882 and 1929. The museum is closed

at the time of publication, so please check the website (at left) for further details.

Immediately south of the museum, Dársena Norte is a *dique* (basin) where fast ferries now depart for the Uruguayan capital of Montevideo and that country's city of Colonia del Sacramento, a UNESCO World Heritage site. To the south, four rectangular basins were transshipment points for beef and grains from the dockside *depósitos* (warehouses) that now figure among the city's most prestigious addresses.

Today, those basins are home to a yacht harbor, two floating maritime museums, and **Puente de la Mujer,** a pedestrian suspension bridge designed by Spanish architect Santiago Calatrava. The graceful, harp-shape bridge swivels open to permit the passage of yachts between the middle basins.

At northernmost Dique No. 4, the British-built **Buque Museo A.R.A. Corbeta Uruguay** is a motorized corvette famous for having rescued Swedish explorer Otto Nordenskjöld's Antarctic expedition in 1903, jump-starting Argentina's presence on the frozen continent. One basin south, also British-built, the **Buque Museo Fragata A.R.A. Presidente Sarmiento** is a sailing vessel with a history: It owes its name to the Argentine president who created the Escuela Naval (Naval School), attended international diplomatic events including King Edward VII's coronation, and was even the subject of a feature film. Its bowsprit is the image of La Libertad Argentina (Argentine

Freedom), comparable to the Statue of Liberty.

Across the basins and beyond is a small grid of streets and avenues where modern luxury hotels and high-rise flats are fast dominating the skyline. In an out-of-the-way location here, the former Munich brewery is now the city's **Museo del Humor,** an exhibition hall focusing on the history of Argentine graphic humor, including caricatures.

Ironically, the barrio's current biggest attraction, **Reserva Ecológica Costanera Sur** (see sidebar p. 72), is the legacy of the Dirty War dictatorship that once blocked off the entire Puerto Madero waterfront and bankrupted the country with its political and economic ineptitude. When that regime ended and plants and animals had colonized the area, the new civilian government set it aside as one of the city's largest open spaces. With entrances opposite Dique No. 4 and Dique No. 1, the reserve is normally open during the day but there are also occasional full-moon tours.

Retiro

Immediately north of the Microcentro, surrounding **Plaza San Martín,** prosperous Retiro holds some of the most extravagant mansions from Argentina's golden age, when individuals like newspaper publisher José C. Paz could build his own Louvre-inspired **Palacio Paz** *(Avenida Santa Fe 750, tel 011/4311-1071, www.circulomilitar.org).* Paz, his wife, and three children then had 129,000 square feet

(12,000 sq m) of house to themselves—probably the largest private residence ever built in Buenos Aires—before selling the property to the military in 1938.

One of the capital's best-kept public parks, Plaza San Martín sits atop the barrancas (natural levees) of the Río de la Plata. Its centerpiece is French

Museo del Humor

✉ Avenida de los Italianos 851

☎ 011/4516-0944

$ $$, Mon.– Wed. free

www.museos.buenos aires.gob.ar/muhu/ index.html

Aboard a sailboat at redeveloped Puerto Madero

sculptor Louis-Joseph Daumas's monument to **General San Martín y a los Ejércitos de la Independencia** (1862), alleged to be Argentina's oldest equestrian statue. It's far from the river now, but several other open green spaces extend northeast across

(continued on p. 78)

Walk: Puerto Madero & Avenida de Mayo

Today, when most visitors arrive by air, it's hard to appreciate that in Argentina's golden years of the early 20th century, immigrants arrived by sea. This walk aims to follow the immigrant's steps, from his arrival through the center of town, and to point out some of the changes that have happened since.

The logical starting point is the **Hotel de Inmigrantes** ❶ *(Avenida Antártida Argentina 1355; see p. 74)*, where new arrivals could spend a few days while they tried to arrange housing and jobs; it's now the national immigration museum. Walking south, you pass **Dársena Norte,** currently the port for ferries to and from Uruguay, before arriving at **Puerto Madero** and the four oblong *diques* (basins) where freighters unloaded their cargo into brick warehouses. Two sailing ships docked here, the **Corbeta *Uruguay*** and the **Fragata *Presidente Sarmiento,*** are historical museums (see p. 74).

INSIDER TIP:

Visit the Fortabat Art Collection *(tel 011-4310-6600, www.coleccion fortabat.org.ar)* in Puerto Madero. The collection is the legacy of a cement heiress, and the building is itself quite artful, with a retractable roof and two exhibition halls.

—KENNY LING
National Geographic contributor

Today, Puerto Madero is one of the city's most fashionable neighborhoods. Those recycled warehouses hold lofts, restaurants, and offices; one of those basins is a yacht harbor; and Spanish architect Santiago Calatrava's avant-garde **Puente de la Mujer** ❷ bridges the water for pedestrians. It's positively cinematic—so much so that director Fabián Bielinsky shot part of his

NOT TO BE MISSED:

Puerto Madero • Plaza de Mayo
• Museo del Bicentenario
• Café Tortoni • Palacio Barolo

crime caper *Nine Queens* (2000) on the waterfront walkways and in the glistening **Hilton Buenos Aires,** one of several prestige hotels here.

From the Hilton, walk west along Macacha Güemes street and cross the railroad tracks to Perón. Then follow diagonal Avenida Rosales to **Plaza de Mayo** ❸ (see pp. 58–60), the flashpoint of modern Argentine history, home to the **Casa Rosada** presidential palace, the **Catedral Metropolitana,** the colonial **cabildo,** and **Museo del Bicentenario,** a contemporary museum that recycles colonial ruins into a narrative of the Argentine experience. Here, from the palace's balcony, Argentine politicians have risked everything to communicate with friendly crowds and angry throngs alike, while protestors have voiced their grievances at risk to themselves and others. The most effective protest ever, though, has been Thursday's weekly march by the Madres de Plaza de Mayo, whose dignified silence in support of their disappeared children said more than the screams and shouts of many others.

It's three blocks west along Avenida de Mayo to **Café Tortoni** ❹ *(Avenida de Mayo 825),* the city's iconic café since it opened in 1858; still, consider going underground at **Estación Perú** to take the continent's oldest subway to **Estación Piedras** at the café's front door. At any time of day, Tortoni's an ideal coffee break where locals and tourists mingle without distinction.

Barely a block west, most pedestrians need two changes of the light to cross the fast-paced traffic along **Avenida 9 de Julio.** The city government has widened the traffic islands but, in all circumstances, discretion is advisable—pedestrian right-of-way is only a theory here.

Dating from the early 20th century, the ornate **Teatro Avenida** ❺ *(Avenida de Mayo 1222)* served as Buenos Aires's opera house during renovation of the famous Teatro Colón. One block west, one of the city's most underappreciated marvels is the **Palacio Barolo** at No. 1370, an office building designed to reflect, thematically, Dante's *Divine Comedy.* Tours are

available, offering views that include **Plaza del Congreso** ❻, two blocks west, with its monumental sculptures and fountains that symbolize the historic assemblies and national rivers. They end with the neoclassical columns and copper dome of the **Congreso de la Nación** ❼—home of Argentina's notoriously dysfunctional legislature.

> 🅼 See also map p. 57
> ▶ Hotel de Inmigrantes
> ⏱ 2–3 hours
> ⟷ 3 miles (5 km)
> ▶ Avenida Rivadavia & Avenida Callao

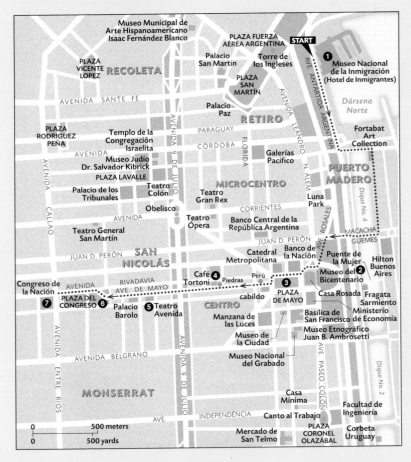

Palacio San Martín

- 🅰 Map p. 57
- ✉ Arenales 761
- ☎ 011/4819-8092
- 🕐 Open Mon. & Wed. for tours
- Ⓜ Subway: C

Museo de Arte Hispano-americano Isaac Fernández Blanco

- ✉ Suipacha 1422
- ☎ 011/4327-0272
- 🕐 Closed Mon., Jan. 1, May 1, & Dec. 25
- 💲 $, Thurs. free
- Ⓜ Subway: C

www.museo fernandezblanco .buenosaires.gov.ar

Avenida del Libertador toward Puerto Nuevo. Many traditional luxury hotels stand nearby, along with the Chicago-inspired **Edificio Kavanagh** *(Avenida Florida & San Martín),* an apartment building that was the city's earliest skyscraper in the 1930s.

On the slopes of the barrancas, facing Avenida del Libertador, the **Monumento a los Caídos en la Gesta de las Islas Malvinas y Atlántico Sur** commemorates the Argentine soldiers and sailors who died in the 1982 Falkland Islands War against Britain. Ironically, it faces the **Torre de los Ingleses** *(Avenida Del Libertador 49),* a clock tower donated by the Anglo-Argentine community during World War I. Since the 1982 war, though, the former Plaza Britania on which it stands is now **Plaza Fuerza Aérea Argentina,** honoring the only armed forces branch that performed creditably in the South Atlantic. Across Avenida Ramos Mejía, suburban commuters now arrive at Estación Retiro, but in its 20th-century heyday the British-built railway carried passengers to northern and western provinces.

The Palacio Paz may have been the biggest of Retiro's mansions, but the most elegant may be the **Palacio San Martín,** a complex of three beaux arts houses built for the influential Anchorena family. Sold to the foreign ministry in the 1930s, it's now used only for protocol events and guided tours. These include a look at an art collection with pre-Columbian pieces, as well as works by avant-garde artists including Berni, the Uruguayan Pedro Figari, and the Chilean Roberto Matta.

The arts remain a part of the barrio's legacy, with contemporary galleries dotting the streets on and around the plaza. The most notable institution is the **Museo de Arte Hispanoamericano Isaac Fernández Blanco,** but its focus is older: In a Spanish neocolonial residence dating from the 1920s, the museum holds collections of Spanish- and Portuguese-American colonial ecclesiastical art, both painting and statuary. Its adjacent administrative offices were the home of poet Oliverio Girondo (1891–1967), a romantic rival of Borges's.

Like other city neighborhoods, Retiro has its share of Jewish community landmarks. Even before

INSIDER TIP:

The Alvear Palace Hotel in Recoleta is a gilded confection. Even if you're not staying here, stop by for tea or drinks in the wooden lobby bar.

—MICHAEL LUONGO
National Geographic writer

the 1994 bombing of the AMIA building here, a 1992 car bomb destroyed the Israeli embassy in what is now the memorial **Plaza Embajada de Israel** *(Arroyo & Suipacha).* Poignantly, the embassy's outline survives on the adjacent building, and 22 lindens, freshly planted in two parallel rows, symbolize the diplomats and passersby who died in the attack—which has never been solved.

Tourists photograph the tomb of Eva Perón in the Cementerio de la Recoleta.

Recoleta & Around

Just inside the border of Recoleta, the city's wealthiest barrio, the **Museo del Holocausto** is a reminder that the Holocaust had repercussions all over the world. Its permanent collections relate events in Argentina to those in Europe—family ties were just as strong here as they were in the United States—and there are special thematic exhibits such as photographic portraits of Argentine Holocaust survivors and paintings of escape to Argentina via Palestine in the 1930s.

In life and death, Recoleta symbolizes power and privilege in Argentine society. In the city's wealthiest barrio, with seigneurial mansions, luxury lofts, and a glistening shopping district where Sotheby's seems downscale, residents expect deferential treatment—even after they've drawn their final breath and joined their forebears in an opulent necropolis

that's a global symbol of extravagance. In this neighborhood, crypts cost more than houses in other parts of the city.

In the capital's fashionable north, where the sidewalks are wider and cleaner than elsewhere, the elegant **Alvear Palace Hotel** is one of several classic buildings that help make this the city's most Eurocentric area. Seemingly untouched by economic distress elsewhere, the high-end shoppers who crowd its commercial arcade spill out onto **Avenida Alvear** for an even more extravagant shopping experience. Recoleta adjoins the area known as Barrio Norte, where the apartments are closer together and the open spaces are smaller, but where real estate values are still astronomical.

Cementerio de la Recoleta:

The sprawling green spaces along both sides of Avenida del Libertador help the city breathe,

Museo del Holocausto
- Map p. 57
- Montevideo 919
- 011/4811-3588
- Closed Sat.–Sun., & holidays
- $$
- Subway: D

www.museodel
holocausto.org.ar

Alvear Palace Hotel
- Map p. 57
- Avenida Alvear 1891
- 011/4808-2100

www.alvearpalace.com

Cementerio de la Recoleta

🅰 Map p. 57

✉ Junín 1790

☎ 011/4803-1594

www.recoleta
cemetery.com
(English-language)

www.cementerio
recoleta.com.ar
(Spanish only)

but Recoleta's centerpiece—if not exactly its heartbeat—is the Cementerio de la Recoleta, the famous cemetery where Evita Perón was eventually laid to rest. In the early independence years, Recoleta monks left only their name to the neighborhood graveyard, part of which was a vegetable patch. It lay alongside the colonial **Basilica Nuestra Señora del Pilar,** an 18th-century church with a remarkable silver baroque altarpiece.

But for a facade of Doric columns at the Junín street entrance, redbrick walls enclose the entire perimeter of the cemetery. Side by side within the walls, an orderly grid of lavish mausoleums faces onto a few broad tree-lined "avenues" and many more barren narrow "streets," occasionally divided by diagonals. Covering more than half a million square feet (46,000 sq m), this vast and prestigious city of the dead was a

pet project of modernizing mayor Torcuato de Alvear (1822–1890), who himself has his final resting place near the entrance portico.

Nearly all Recoleta decedents were wealthy, but just as importantly they had names that placed them in the upper echelon of Argentine society. Among them are presidents (Bartolomé Mitre, Domingo F. Sarmiento, Hipólito Yrigoyen); military men (Guillermo Brown, Julio Argentino Roca); and artists and literary figures (José Hernández, Cándido López, Adolfo Bioy Casares, Victoria Ocampo). The categories often overlap.

A few exceptions, though, stand out. Boxer Luis Ángel Firpo (1894–1960), the "wild bull of the Pampas" who nearly whipped Jack Dempsey at New York City's Polo Grounds in 1923, had an influential patron in oligarch Félix Bunge (himself buried at Recoleta). The most notorious case, though, is Eva Duarte—better known as

Chacarita: The People's Cemetery

For international connoisseurs of famous cemeteries, Recoleta ranks with Paris's Père Lachaise and London's Highgate, but Chacarita (Guzmán 680, tel 011/4553-9338) flies, so to speak, under the radar. Without great wealth and social standing, few Argentines can aspire to eternity in Recoleta, but just about anybody can share the hereafter with figures from the popular art and entertainment worlds in Chacarita's orderly necropolis—a grid of streets and diagonals, with monumental tombs and multilevel crypts that could take days to explore properly.

Many of Chacarita's residents are famous figures with whom Argentines

identify viscerally—most notably tango legend Carlos Gardel, who died in a plane crash in 1935. His tomb, that of the nearby faith healer Madre María Salomé, and comedian Luis Sandrini, are never without fresh flowers and, in Gardel's case, a lighted cigarette. Benito Quinquela Martín is the artist of the bunch.

Chacarita's most notorious figure, though, no longer resides here. The great caudillo Juan Domingo Perón—whose hands were amputated and stolen, postmortem, in a bizarre 1987 incident—was relocated to more exclusive surroundings in his former estate in the Buenos Aires Province town of San Vicente in 2006.

Evita—whose very presence here is a reproach to the rest. Evita, the resentfully illegitimate daughter of landowner Juan Duarte—whose crypt she now shares—made no effort to hide her hostility toward Argentina's upper classes. In fact, she boasted of it.

Marked by a simple plaque, Evita's latest resting place (her extraordinary postmortem travels

INSIDER TIP:

The silver altar at Basilica Nuestra Señora del Pilar is the work of Carlos Pallarol, Argentina's most famous silversmith.

—CAROL PASSERA
Director, Causana Viajes

have been the subject of a novel, Tomás Eloy Martínez's *Santa Evita*) draws more visitors than any other Recoleta celebrity. Truly diehard Peronists anticipate Evita's reunion with her late husband at his mausoleum in suburban San Vicente—a scenario that might allow her Recoleta neighbors to rest in greater serenity.

That said, the barrio has plenty for the quick as well as the dead. Immediately outside the cemetery, the adjacent **Plaza Intendente Alvear** hosts a popular weekend crafts fair; the plaza is the work of French landscape architect Carlos Thays (1849–1934), whose efforts are on display throughout the capital and in many other Argentine cities. Across the way, beneath the shade

of the sprawling *gomero,* neighbors and tourists sip espresso and nibble croissants at **La Biela,** one of the city's signature cafés.

Other Recoleta Sights: Like Retiro, Recoleta has plenty of upscale galleries and arts outlets. Alongside the Basilica, for instance, the **Centro Cultural Recoleta** promotes cutting-edge art exhibitions; it also keeps a full events calendar.

Across the avenue from Plaza Francia, the barrio's foremost arts institution is the **Museo Nacional de Bellas Artes.** The 19th-century building started life as a pumphouse for the city water system. In the 1930s, Bustillo tried to give the nondescript facade a makeover with a neoclassical portico. The results were mixed—its lack of streetside windows, for instance, makes the approach uninviting—but its transformed interior has proved suitably luminous for a permanent display of the national patrimony. It has since expanded some display areas and added a pavilion.

The "national" aspect of the museum is misleading, in that contemporary Argentine artists such as Berni, Ferrari, and Quinquela Martín are not the focus of its collections. They're present, but this is the most comprehensive of all Argentine art museums: Its permanent exhibits range from the pre-Columbian Andes to colonial religious art to French Impressionism and beyond. The upper floor features an open-air sculpture patio dedicated to Argentine artists.

The area's most imposing sculpture, though, stands in the nearby

Centro Cultural Recoleta

📍 Map p. 57
✉️ Junín 1930
☎️ 011/4803-1040
🕐 Closed Mon.

www.centrocultural recoleta.org

Museo Nacional de Bellas Artes

📍 Map p. 57
✉️ Avenida del Libertador 1473
☎️ 011/5288-9945
🕐 Closed Mon.

www.mnba.org.ar

Art & Design

For the longest time, the Buenos Aires art scene—both figurative and abstract—was so conservative that critic Jorge Glusberg suggested that the colonial period in Argentine art lasted until World War II severed connections with Europe. That was hyperbole, but Glusberg had a point that, fortunately, no longer applies.

Puerto Madero's Puente de la Mujer

In art, architecture, and contemporary design, Buenos Aires now has one of the planet's most flourishing scenes. Its flagship project may well be the Museo de Arte Latinoamericano de Buenos Aires (see p. 87), the Constantini Foundation's Palermo museum, designed by Córdoba architects Gastón Atelman, Martín Fourcade, and Alfredo Tapia. On an esplanade above a busy avenue, its facade comprises a series of angular prisms surfaced with a greige Spanish limestone, while the interior alternates between spacious public areas and exhibition halls housing some of Latin America's most avant-garde art.

Meanwhile, not so long ago, the docklands of Puerto Madero were one of the city's most rundown areas. Today, Spanish architect Santiago Calatrava's innovative pedestrian suspension bridge, the Puente de la Mujer, crosses an old shipping basin to link the recycled brick *depósitos* (warehouses)—now stylish restaurants, offices, and lofts—with developments on the other side.

One of those developments is the Faena Hotel & Universe (see p. 297), a former granary that French architect Philippe Starck transformed into a boutique hotel. Argentine owner Alan Faena sees the hotel as the anchor of a new Faena Art District, including the new Faena Arts Center exhibition space *(Aimé Paine 1169, tel 011/4010-9230, www.faena.com/artscenter-new, Sat.–Mon., $$$$)* in a recycled flour mill.

Like its hotels, Buenos Aires's restaurants have undergone a similar makeover. In the "Palermo Soho" and "Palermo Hollywood" districts, where the standard residence is a "sausage house" on a long deep lot, creative cuisine and night life have established a permanent presence. At Ølsen (see p. 296) owner/chef Germán Martitegui has recycled a storehouse into a showcase of clean Nordic design with a Scandinavian-Patagonian menu. The crowning touch, though, was turning half the lot into a birch, cypress, and pine woodland that merges into a grassy meadow.

Other buildings in those neighborhoods have been transformed into cutting-edge fashionista hangouts with casual styles. Artisan furniture makers may adapt the seats of sulkies—single-seat horse carts once common on the Pampas—into garden or patio benches, making the traditional stylishly urban.

Innovative urban designers are making an impact even in Francophile Recoleta. The Buenos Aires Design shopping center (see p. 323), for instance, holds a variety of contemporary furniture and household items, ranging from bathroom accessories to sleek living room combinations.

Palermo, though, remains the center of innovation, where Argentine creativity is on display seemingly wall-to-wall-to-wall. At the Tiendamalba (MALBA's museum store; see p. 87), products from jewelry and accessories to leather goods, toys, and textiles provide an ideal orientation.

Plaza Naciones Unidas, across Avenida Figueroa Alcorta from the museum. There, in the midst of a circular fountain, architect Eduardo Catalano's **"Floralis Generica"** is a stainless-steel flower whose "petals" open with the sunlight and close as the sun goes down. Nearly 75 feet (23 m) tall, it has become a symbol of the barrio.

Evita's mortal remains may repose in Recoleta but, according to legend, her spirit haunts the hallways of the nearby **Biblioteca Nacional,** the brutalist national library designed by architect Clorindo Testa (1923–) to replace the presidential palace after the military overthrew Perón in 1955. Some library employees even claim to have smelled her perfume, but the only confirmed presence has

INSIDER TIP:

Be sure to take a look at Recoleta's belle epoque Palais de Glace. It was originally an ice rink and ballroom (it's now an exhibition center).

—ROB LAFRANCO
National Geographic writer

been an exhibit devoted to her on the 50th anniversary of her death in 2002.

In a barrio that's so self-consciously derivative of European traditions, the **Museo Casa de Ricardo Rojas** is an exception to the stereotype that Argentines undervalue their American heritage. Born in the provincial capital

of Tucumán, Rojas (1882–1957) was a writer and educator who directed his architect to incorporate pre-Columbian elements into a colonial-style house that resembles the one in which Argentine independence was initially declared. In his Euro-Indian doctrine, Rojas proposed fusing "European technique with American emotion," and details such as the mixed Inca and Spanish colonial bas-reliefs reflect that ideological commitment.

Only a short walk away, the nonconformist **Museo Xul Solar** is utterly different from anything else in the area. Borges's close friend, the eccentric painter Alejandro Schulz Solari, who adopted the name Xul Solar, lived here most of his life. After his death, his widow turned it into a museum displaying his esoteric and often surrealistic paintings (Picasso was an obvious influence). Surprisingly for an artist to whom color was so important, the canvases are small and the accent lighting may make some viewers squint to see the details. Many of Xul's "paintings" are actually three-dimensional, even if they fall short of traditional sculpture—rather, they are something of a hybrid.

Palermo

North of Recoleta, Palermo is Buenos Aires's biggest, hippest, and most socially diverse barrio. In a borough with the city's largest parks and other open spaces, with some of its most cutting-edge cuisine and design, working-class families can still live behind auto body shops that

Biblioteca Nacional
🅰 Map p. 57
✉ Agüero 2502
☎ 011/4808-6000
🕐 Closed Jan. & holidays
www.bn.gov.ar

Palais de Glace
✉ Posadas 1725
☎ 011/4804-1163
www.palaisdeglace .gob.ar

Museo Casa de Ricardo Rojas
🅰 Map p. 57
✉ Charcas 2837
☎ 011/4824-4039
🕐 Closed Sat.–Sun.
🚇 Subway: D

Museo Xul Solar
🅰 Map p. 57
✉ Laprida 1212
☎ 011/4824-3302
🕐 Closed Sun.– Mon.
💲 $
🚇 Subway: D
www.xulsolar.org.ar

Jardín Japonés
- Map p. 57
- Avenida Casares & Adolfo Berro
- 011/4804-4922
- Closed Jan. 1, & Dec. 24, 25, & 31
- $

www.jardinjapones .org.ar

Hipódromo Argentino de Palermo
- Map p. 57
- Avenida del Libertador 4101
- 011/4778-2800
- Closed Tues.–Thurs.

www.palermo.com.ar

Club Alemán de Equitación
- Ave. Dorrego 4045
- 011/4772-6289
- Lessons Tues.– Sun.; reserve ahead Jan.–Feb.
- $$$$$

www.clubalemande equitacion.com

Campo Argentino de Polo
- Map p. 57
- Avs. del Libertador & Dorrego
- 011/4777-8005
- Main tournament Nov.–Dec.

www.aapolo.com

are themselves located between luxury lofts. The embassy row of Barrio Parque, also known as Palermo Chico, is affluent even by Recoleta standards, but modest middle-class apartments are only a few minutes' walk away.

Curiously, Palermo owes its open spaces to dictator Juan Manuel de Rosas, whose flight from Buenos Aires in 1852 put his private estate into the public trust. His ultimate humiliation was that the new Parque Tres de Febrero would take its name from the date of his defeat at the Battle of Caseros in that year. Despite its open spaces, Palermo is mostly residential but, except for Barrio Parque, it consists of high-density apartments and clusters of traditional propiedad horizontals. Along **Avenida del Libertador,** the most prestigious buildings are full-floor apartments and penthouses.

Palermo Viejo: In the Palermo Viejo neighborhood, where food, nightlife, and shopping are the most innovative, individual units are usually smaller, but there's plenty of new construction along the cobbled, tree-lined streets.

When Jorge Luis Borges lived here, Palermo Viejo was a marginal neighborhood of small-time hoods and knife-fighters. Today, by contrast, it's a fashionable zone that's colloquially subdivided into **Palermo SoHo,** the city's gourmet ghetto, and **Palermo Hollywood,** the home to movie, TV, and radio production complexes. On many streets, bending sycamores form a solid canopy

over mid-century cobbles where, in Walter Salles's 2004 film *The Motorcycle Diaries,* a youthful Ernesto "Che" Guevara and his friend Alberto Granado started the Patagonian adventure that would eventually lead to Cuba.

Palermo Viejo's nucleus is **Plaza Serrano,** where streets on all sides are lined with restaurants, bars, and fashion and design shops that show some of the most audacious styles on the continent. Nearby, picturesque alleyways like **Pasaje Russel,** barely wide enough for a compact car to pass, were once working-class clusters but have become too fashionable for those who work regular hours at proletarian wages.

INSIDER TIP:

Palermo's Argentine Polo Final every December features the world's best players (as well as the "beautiful people").

—KARIN SIMONCINI
National Geographic Channels International

Weekends start no later than Thursday and run into Monday, and the streets can be busier at 3 a.m. than at 3 p.m.

Parque Tres de Febrero:
Facing Avenida del Libertador, this park offers a diversity of attractions and activities, starting with the meticulously maintained **Jardín Japonés** (Japanese Garden), its lush **Rosedal** (Rose Garden), and cycling

trails (rental bikes are readily available) around the **Lagos de Palermo,** a cluster of artificial lakes. With some of its curving roads closed to automobiles, this is one of the city's most popular areas for jogging, pickup soccer, and outdoor workouts in general. Racing fans can bet on the ponies at the **Hipódromo Argentino de Palermo** or ride them at the **Club Alemán de Equitación.** Some of the world's best polo ponies and riders show their stuff at the **Campo Argentino de Polo,** across the avenue from the Hipódromo.

Also in the park is the **Jardín Zoológico** (also known as **Zoo de Buenos Aires**), wildly popular for family outings, its enclosures reflecting the animals' region of origin. The elephant house, for instance, displays an explicitly Hindu style. Lavishly planted with exotic species, the contiguous **Jardín Botánico** was the initiative of Carlos Thays, easily the most influential landscape architect in Argentine history.

Barrio Parque: In such an urbane barrio, the gaucho might seem the odd man out, but Barrio Parque's **Museo de Arte Popular José Hernández** (*Avenida del Libertador 2373, tel 011/4803-2384, museohernandez .buenosaires.gob.ar, closed Mon.– Tues., $*) brings the country to the city. It does so in an offbeat way, though—the museum takes its name from the gauchesque poet who wrote the epic *Martín Fierro,* but the French-Italianate building, with its marble staircases, was built by Félix Bunge (1894–1935), the oligarch who sponsored the rough-around-the-edges Luis Ángel Firpo in his fight with Jack Dempsey. (When Bunge lived here, it was also the site of the Boxing Club de Buenos Aires.) Now it promotes

Jardín Zoológico

- Map p. 57
- Aves. Las Heras & Sarmiento
- 011/4011-9900
- Closed Mon.
- $$
- Subway: D

www.zoobuenos aires.com.ar

Jardín Botánico Carlos Thays

- Avenida Santa Fe 3951
- 011/4831-4527
- Closed Jan. 1, Good Friday, May 1, Sept. 21, Dec. 25
- Subway: D

www.jardinbotanico .gov.ar

A jacaranda tree blooms in Palermo.

EXPERIENCE: Buenos Aires in the Saddle

Argentina is famous for the gaucho, the rugged rural horseman who tamed feral stallions, but even urban Argentines have an affinity for horses—and ponies—as spectators and participants. Among its high-rise office blocks and apartments, Buenos Aires has wide-open spaces where equine sports of all kinds are available.

Bettors can size up the ponies in person at the **Hipódromo Argentino** (*Avenida del Libertador 4101, tel 011/4778-2800, www.palermo.com.ar*) in the barrio of Palermo. Dating from 1908, but built in 17th-century Francophile style, the main building feels appropriate to the sport of kings, but the low admission prices and minimum bets make it a more democratic destination than it once was.

Likewise, you can see some of the world's finest polo players at the **Campo Argentino de Polo** (see p. 85). It seems far from the English countryside, but spectators still flock to events such as late spring's Campeonato Argentino Abierto de Polo, the national polo championships.

For those whose ambitions are more active, several clubs in Palermo and nearby Belgrano invite riders of all skill levels to ride and take lessons—invariably in the English style, with European saddles. For gaucho-style riding, it's better to head to estancias near San Antonio de Areco (see sidebar p. 109), in Buenos Aires Province, though even there English-style riding and polo ponies are possibilities.

No place in the city teaches polo, but several estancias in surrounding Buenos Aires Province do so—sometimes with attention by some of the world's finest players. This, of course, is a specialized and expensive option.

The gaucho makes his appearance in the capital, though, most notably in the barrio of Mataderos (see sidebar p. 91). At its weekend fair, the streets clear for speeding riders trying to grab the hanging ring known as the *sortija*—a thrill for spectators as well as players. The gaucho version of polo, though, is *pato*—once an unapologetically brutal sport in which riders tried to hurl a live duck, enclosed in a leather sack, into a goal. The annual pato championships take place at Palermo's genteel polo grounds, but times have changed—the "duck" is now a leather bag with handles.

For a taste of the sport, try (websites in Spanish only):
Club Alemán de Equitación (*Avenida Dorrego 4045, Palermo, tel 011/4772-6289, www.clubalemandeequitacion.com.*); **Club Hípico Argentino** (*Avenida Figueroa Alcorta 7285, Belgrano, tel 011/4787-1003, www.clubhipicoargentino.org.ar*); and **Federación Argentina de Pato y Horseball** (*Avenida de Mayo 749, 4th floor, Oficina 24, tel 011/4372-1080, www.pato.org.ar*). **La Martina Polo Ranch** (*Vicente Casares, Buenos Aires Province, tel 0222/643077*) is an estancia 50 minutes from the city, with polo lessons and accommodations.

A gaucho grabs for the ring at the Feria de Mataderos.

EXPERIENCE: Apartment for Rent

Buenos Aires has fine hotels but, to know the city as *porteños* live it, short-term apartment rentals are best. Ranging from studios to luxury penthouses, rentals offer options for everyone from singles to families and groups. All expenses included, they usually provide regular maid service, local telephone, cable TV, Internet access, and other amenities.

But their best amenity is the chance to live in neighborhoods such as San Telmo, Palermo, or Belgrano, where hotels are few and interaction with the neighbors is frequent. Many brokers can be found online. You can start a search at **Alojargentina** *(tel 011/4961-9385, www.alojargentina.com.ar)* and **B y T Argentina** *(tel 011/4876-5000, www.bytargentina.com).*

all things gaucho, most notably Hernández's classic poem, but also the material culture that was more typical of families like the Bunges—who had servants to prepare their *mate* in silver-plated gourds.

Bunge, in fact, would have felt most at home at places like the **Palacio Errázuriz,** a beaux arts single-family mansion that now holds the **Museo Nacional de Arte Decorativo.** He certainly would have felt at home with host Matías Errázuriz Ortúzar, a Chilean diplomat, and Errázuriz's Argentine wife Josefina de Alvear. When she died, both the house and their collections of Asian and European art passed into state control. Displayed in massive baroque salons with high ceilings, the statuary dates back to Roman times, and Flemish tapestries line many of the walls. Incongruously, Errázuriz's son's bedroom affects an art deco style. The museum now holds concerts, lectures, and special exhibits in addition to its permanent collections.

With his European tastes tempered by gauchesque pretensions, Bunge might have felt less comfortable in Palermo Chico's **Museo de Arte Latinoamericano de Buenos Aires** (MALBA), a cosmopolitan Latin American facility that places Argentina in the context of a regional avant-garde. Occupying a handsome structure of concrete, steel, and glass—designed by Córdoba architects—MALBA displays businessman Eduardo Constantini's private collection, which includes paintings, sculptures, sketches, engravings, collages, and photographs. Artists represented include Mexico's Frida Kahlo and Diego Rivera, Colombia's Fernando Botero, Chile's Roberto Matta, Uruguay's Joaquín Torres-García and Pedro Figari, and Argentina's Antonio Berni, Jorge de la Vega, León Ferrari, and Guillermo Kuitca.

MALBA, though, offers much more through its special exhibits, a full-size cinema with a repertory schedule from around the world and at least four shows daily, and literary lectures and classes. On balance, it has helped place Palermo on the international cultural map, even if Bunge might have felt awkward there.

Museo Nacional de Arte Decorativo

- Map. p. 57
- Avenida del Libertador 1902
- 011/4802-6606
- Closed Mon.
- $

www.mnad.org.ar

Museo de Arte Latinoamericano de Buenos Aires (MALBA)

- Map p. 57
- Avenida Figueroa Alcorta 3415
- 011/4808-6500
- Closed Tues.
- $$$, Wed. free

www.malba.org.ar

A carriage tour of Palermo Park

Museo Evita

🅜 Map p. 57

✉ Lafinur 2988

☎ 011/4807-0306

🕐 Closed Mon.,
Jan. 1, May 1,
& Dec. 24, 25,
& 31

💲 $$

www.museoevita.org

Bunge would have felt conspicuously unwelcome a few blocks away at today's **Museo Evita,** in a building that, in his day, was a private residence in a neighborhood of *palacetes* (mansions) just south of the zoo. Middle-class apartments now surround the Italian renaissance mansion, but in the late 1940s, the confrontational Evita enraged the upper-class neighbors by turning it into Hogar de Tránsito No. 2, a sanctuary for single mothers from the provinces.

Though it closed after the coup in 1955, the building reopened in 2002—the 50th anniversary of Evita's death—as a museum in her honor. It's not exactly interactive, but a surround-film chamber that puts the viewer in the midst of a rabid Peronist rally is effective in conveying the alarming enthusiasm, bordering on fanaticism, that the Peróns could inspire. Other than that, the museum follows a fairly chronological path dealing with Evita's youth and acting career, the Perón years, and her death and legacy. Astonishingly, there's little to suggest that Evita was ever a controversial figure in an increasingly polarized Argentine society. Today, most of its visitors are foreigners who probably know her mostly through musical theater and cinema.

Belgrano

Where the subway ends and the northern suburbs begin, Belgrano is a barrio with a history that includes a brief spell as capital of the republic in the late 19th century. At that time, it was a separate city, but as Buenos Aires grew the two eventually merged. Today the neighborhood is largely residential, but with a cluster of museums and other sights that make it worth a detour. Even the Juramento subway station is a mini-museum of art and history.

Belgrano is a large barrio, but its points of interest are clustered along Avenida Juramento between **Plaza Manuel Belgrano,** the main square, and the sloping city park known as **Barrancas de Belgrano,** on the levee where the river used to run. Across the railroad tracks, toward the river, is the capital's **Chinatown,** predominantly Taiwanese.

Opposite the plaza, which has a large weekend crafts fair, the **Iglesia de la Inmaculada Concepción** is known as La Redonda ("the circle") for its rounded shape. It's also known as the setting for Ernesto Sábato's

INSIDER TIP:

Head to Belgrano for Buenos Aires's little-known Chinatown district. If you're here during Chinese New Year, come catch the dragon parade.

—MICHAEL LUONGO
National Geographic writer

description of a "curious corner of Buenos Aires" where, in his psychological novel *On Heroes and Tombs*, his protagonist encounters a strange society of the blind.

Across the plaza, the **Museo Histórico Sarmiento** honors Argentina's 19th-century president. It was also the building that served as the seat of government during a near civil war in 1880. As a museum, it displays Sarmiento's personal effects and a reproduction of his San Juan Province birthplace.

On the north side of the plaza, bounded by walled Andalusian gardens with luxuriant trees and murmuring waters, the Spanish Renaissance **Museo de Arte Español Enrique Larreta** was

the residence of writer Enrique Larreta (1875–1961), who filled the building with Iberian art even as he was writing nostalgic novels, poems, and essays about Spain. That put Larreta well outside Argentina's literary mainstream, which could lurch between fierce nationalism and genteel cosmopolitanism, but it's what made him memorable. He left the house and its contents, much of which is religious imagery, to the city; oddly, it also includes the wardrobe of regional costumes that Evita acquired on her 1947 tour of Franco's Spain (most Argentines in Larreta's social circles detested the Peróns). In summer, the gardens also host music and theater events.

Belgrano's other art museums are less conventional. Overlooking the barrancas, the inconspicuous **Museo Líbero Badií** displays the work of an Italian-born artist whose *arte siniestro* approaches that of Xul Solar but is a little less esoteric. Badií (1916–2001) worked in ceramics, collage, engraving, and sculpture, the sculpture often a mix of colors, shapes, and moving parts.

Museo Histórico Sarmiento
- ✉ Avenida Juramento 2180
- ☎ 011/4782-2354
- 🕐 Closed Sat. April–Nov.; Sat.–Sun. Dec.–March; & holidays
- 💲 $, Thurs. free
- 🚇 Subway: D
- **www.museo sarmiento.gov.ar**

Museo de Arte Español Enrique Larreta
- ✉ Avenida Juramento 2291
- ☎ 011/4783-2640
- 💲 $, Thurs. free
- 🚇 Subway: D
- **www.museos .buenosaires.gov.ar/ larreta.htm**

Museo Líbero Badií
- ✉ 11 de Septiembre 1990
- ☎ 011/4783-3819
- 🕐 Closed Sat.–Sun., Jan.–Feb., & holidays
- **www.museoliberobadii .com.ar**

It's Chinatown

It's not big by international standards, but Belgrano's Barrio Chino, known as Chinatown even by Spanish speakers, has a presence beyond its small size. Dating from the 1980s, when Taiwanese immigrants established themselves around the Mitre railroad line just below the Barrancas de Belgrano, it has become a lively zone of restaurants, supermarkets, hairdressers, herbalists, souvenir vendors, video clubs, a Buddhist temple, and even feng shui consultants. On top of that, the Taiwanese Peronists have their headquarters here.

Its biggest annual event is Chinese New Year, when visitors from all over the city pack Arribeños street for the festivities. In August 2008, China's Ambassador Zeng Gang celebrated the opening of the Beijing Olympics in the neighborhood.

Museo Casa de Yrurtia

- ✉ O'Higgins 2390
- ☎ 011/4781-0385
- 🕐 Closed Mon. & Sat.
- 💲 $, Tues. free
- 🚇 Subway: D

Belgrano's most interesting museum, the **Museo Casa de Yrurtia,** manages to be accessible without being conventional. Yrurtia, uniquely, used his literally monumental talent to create sculptures like San Telmo's "Canto al Trabajo," putting the collective heroism of physical laborers on a

Mercado del Abasto's glitz and glamour

Museo Casa Carlos Gardel

- ✉ Jean Jaurés 735
- ☎ 011/4964-2015
- 🕐 Closed Tues.
- 💲 $, Wed. free
- 🚇 Subway: B

www.museos .buenosaires.gov.ar /gardel.htm

plane with the achievements of generals on horseback.

Yrurtia's house, designed as a museum to display his legacy, is worth seeing. Like Larreta's, its origins are Iberian—the Mudéjar style, with arched windows and decorative tiles, derived from southern Spain where Moorish and Christian influences mixed.

The museum does more than just display artwork—though it also holds a Picasso. Rather, it shows the process of creating a sculpture such as "Canto al Trabajo" through partial models of the original. The gardens are less elaborate than those of Larreta's house, but do include the larger-than-life-size work known as "The Boxers," first displayed at the 1904 World's Fair in St. Louis.

Around the *Arrabales*

Before the massive immigration of the late 19th century, when Buenos Aires was a *gran aldea* (great village), most of its outskirts were *arrabales* (outlying slums) where small-time hoods ruled. That's not so true today, and some of the city's less touristed barrios—closer than they once were, relatively speaking—have sights that are worth going out of the way to see.

One of those areas is the **Abasto,** in the barrio of Balvanera west of San Nicolás, where wholesale produce arrived at the vast interior of the **Mercado del Abasto** until the 1970s. During most of the 1980s, the landmark building stood empty, but in the 1990s U.S. investor George Soros turned it into a four-level shopping center that has helped revitalize the neighborhood.

The Abasto is notable partly because it was home to tango legend Carlos Gardel, and his modest house is now the **Museo Casa Carlos Gardel.** Loaded with Gardeliana, it stands on a block where some houses sport filete-painted facades and tango has been making a comeback at *milongas,* nightclubs, and a theme hotel—its suites named for his songs.

The western barrio of **Caballito** was once the *quinta* (rural getaway) of *La Nación* newspaper publisher Ambrosio Lezica, and today's **Parque Rivadavia** is what's left of that. As with Belgrano, the city and suburb have grown together. Even more notable is the ovoid **Parque Centenario,** whose **Museo Argentino de Ciencias Naturales Bernardino Rivadavia** (Argentine Museum of Natural Sciences) is especially strong on paleontology—a field in which Argentine researchers have, both literally and figuratively, made groundbreaking discoveries.

Because it's remote and because a comparable museum in La Plata is a national landmark, this one gets overlooked. The building itself has fitting details—the sculpted owls flanking the upper windows, for instance, are a symbol of wisdom. Numerous bas-reliefs—condors, flamingos, tapirs, sea lions, pumas, llamas, and vicuñas—represent Argentina's native fauna. The permanent exhibits include halls on geology (note the meteorites from Santiago del Estero Province), paleontology, plants, marine biology, amphibians and reptiles, contemporary mammals, quaternary mammals, and comparative osteology. Special exhibitions also take place—the Sala de Aves has hosted a display on flying dinosaurs in addition to its usual bird exhibits.

Southern barrios such as **Barracas** (with its historic factories, now mostly closed), **Boedo** (with its militant literary left), and **Parque Patricios** (with its model housing) can give visitors a sense of authentic, working-class Buenos Aires. Because the sights are so spread out here, they're best seen on a guided tour. Most of them are less conspicuous than **Pasaje Lanín** in Barracas, where painter Marino Santa María and his neighbors have turned three blocks' worth of houses into one nearly continuous abstract mural. ∎

Museo Argentino de Ciencias Naturales Bernardino Rivadavia

- ✉ Avenida Angel Gallardo 490
- ☎ 011/4982-4494;
- 🕐 Closed holidays
- 💲 $
- Ⓜ Subway: B

www.macn.secyt .gov.ar

Feria de Mataderos

Porteños—and most other Argentines, for that matter—may be urbanites, but they have a romantic affinity with the gaucho and the countryside. On the southwestern outskirts of a sophisticated city, the Feria de Mataderos *(tel 011/4342-9629, www.feriademataderos.com.ar)* keeps the capital in touch with its hinterland.

Here every Sunday from April to December, amid the sizzle of chorizos on the grill, Avenida de los Corrales and Lisandro de la Torre fill with fiesta-goers inching their way along street stalls. Rural crafts—including woven ponchos and the intimidating gaucho knife known as the *facón,* with its carved handle—alternate with fresh food for maximum snacking (cheeses, empanadas, and sweets). There is always live music, and visitors can join in workshops on guitar, weaving, and other skills.

When the streets clear, it's time for dancing to the traditional *chamamé* or *chacarera* or viewing rugged equestrian events such as the *sortija,* a race in which a galloping gaucho grabs a small hanging ring. Regular races and *doma* (broncobusting) are also on the docket.

The Delta

Like the bayous of the Mississippi under French and Spanish rule, the channels and islands of the Paraná Delta were home to smugglers and pirates in colonial times. At that time, the only legitimate commerce was charcoal from its gallery forests, shipped overland from the flood-prone port of Tigre, but the delta thrived with contraband. Today the port thrives as a charming day-trip destination, and visitors can safely tour the delta's waterways.

Aquatic buses run fixed routes from Tigre through the Paraná Delta.

Tigre

A Map on inside back cover C4

Visitor Information

✉ Mitre 305

☎ 011/4512-4497

🕐 Closed Jan. 1 & Dec. 25

www.vivitigre.gov.ar

Tigre & Around

After the railroad covered the 18 miles (28 km) from Retiro in 1865, Tigre became a weekend and summer getaway for well-to-do porteños, who built extravagant mansions and rowing clubs along the Río Luján and other riverine tributaries. Starting with the Great Depression of the 1930s, Tigre suffered setbacks that lasted until not so long ago. A recent revival—the

entire area houses almost 300,000 with progressive leadership and ample investment—has made it a desirable community for commuters to the capital via the Mitre railway, and an afternoon and weekend getaway for porteños at all economic levels. The rowing clubs survive, but visitors are just as likely to get around in kayaks or, more obtrusively, personal watercraft. Passenger launches operate like

EXPERIENCE: Paddling the Delta

For most visitors, getting around the Paraná Delta involves *lanchas colectivas*, the floating buses that carry dozens of passengers on the river's large and mid-size channels, stopping at restaurants, hotels, private clubs, and even the odd museum. Docking briefly to load and unload passengers, they're the equivalent of city buses, with regular routes on their broad "avenues" (where so-called personal watercraft often roar like motorcycles).

For those whose urban tastes tend toward picturesque alleyways, though, the Paraná has better options. In the maze of quiet, shallow channels, bordered by dense gallery forest, where the *isleños* (islanders) of the area have their hide-aways and homesteads, the fishing and wildlife are abundant, and flat-bottom launches and kayaks—available for rent in Tigre (see Travelwise p. 328)—are the best way to get around. The other option, for those who have the skills and contacts, are the rowing skulls that local clubs use for training. If venturing out onto the big channels like the Paraná de las Palmas, though, be aware of the big waves produced by the freighters and other large ships that cruise up and down the river.

city buses to deliver their clients to the docks of their weekend homes, hotels, and restaurants on the various watercourses.

On the Río Tigre, across from the train station and just above its confluence with the Río Luján, **Estación Fluvial** is the gateway to the delta and also the departure point for catamarans to Isla Martín García and the Uruguayan port of Carmelo. One of Tigre's most interesting sights is the **Puerto de Frutos**, where farm products from the delta arrive. There's a fine crafts market and above-average *parrillas* (grill restaurants) for day-trippers at lunchtime.

The streets along both sides of the Río Tigre make an ideal walking tour. On the right bank, the Tudor-style **Buenos Aires Rowing Club** building (1923) and the Venetian-style **Club Canot-tieri Italiani** (1921) are both remnants of Tigre's 20th-century heyday. On the left bank, Lavalle street leads to **Paseo Victorica**, a Río Luján promenade that faces the **Club de Regatas La Marina**, the stately boating club across the river.

Under the recent city administration, the Luján riverside has become a pedestrian-friendly zone of broad sidewalks that leads past several museums and other landmarks. The **Museo Naval de la Nación** started life as a 19th-century naval repair station—at that time, Argentine warships could still sail into these narrow channels. It has an interior full of model ships and their plans and an open-air sector (visible from the street) that includes antique weaponry, naval aircraft, and salvage from the 1982 Falklands War.

The newest attraction is the **Museo de Arte Tigre** (MAT), an early 20th-century masterpiece originally built as a casino alongside the since demolished Tigre Hotel. The two-story building

Museo Naval de la Nación

✉ Paseo Victorica 602

☎ 011/4749-0608

💲 $

www.ara.mil.ar/pag.asp?idItem=110

Museo de Arte Tigre (MAT)

✉ Paseo Victorica 972

☎ 011/4512-4528

🕐 Closed Mon.–Tues.

💲 $

www.mat.gov.ar

Museo Domingo Faustino Sarmiento

✉ Río Sarmiento & Arroyo Los Reyes

☎ 011/4728-0570

🕐 Open daily, 10 a.m.-6 p.m., including holidays

Isla Martín García

🗺 Map on inside back cover E5

features Doric columns, a mansard roof with a hexagonal central tower and semicircular towers on each side, an upper-level walkway that leads to a river overlook, and an array of details that include a spiderweb chandelier and marouflage ceiling murals. Its current collections contain landscapes, portraits, and still lifes connected to Tigre, but it also holds figurative works by famous Argentine artists such as Benito Quinquela Martín and Juan Carlos Castagnino.

Not all of Tigre's sights are right in town. Now protected under glass, the **Museo Domingo Faustino Sarmiento** was the island getaway of former president Domingo F. Sarmiento, who built it of fruit boxes. Local launches drop off and pick up passengers here.

Isla Martín García

North of Tigre, the Paraná Delta is a maze of sedimentary islands with placid backwater channels, where houses stand on stilts above broad lawns to escape frequent flooding. Unlike the Mississippi, the Paraná gets no hurricanes, but upstream storms can raise the river level; in some places, the main channel of the Paraná de las Palmas has so eaten away at flood defenses that some dilapidated buildings might slide into the river at any moment.

In the quieter backwaters, gallery forests still line both sides of the waterway and birds abound, but mosquitoes can be the most abundant fauna. Fishermen troll for game species such as *surubí*

(Paraná catfish). In some areas woodcutters are clearing the islands for timber and charcoal and grazing livestock on them, but in many places forests are still well preserved.

Beyond the delta, the main channel of the Río de la Plata is open water except for Isla Martín García, a Precambrian bedrock enclave of Argentine territory barely 2 miles (3 km) off the Uruguayan coast. Reached by fast catamaran from Tigre, it's both

INSIDER TIP:

Don't miss the Puerto de Frutos in Tigre, a nice little market with local products.

–KARIN SIMONCINI
National Geographic Channels International

a natural and a historic site, with luxuriant vegetation and a rich heritage that started with Juan Díaz de Solís's sighting in 1516. In colonial times, Spain and Portugal disputed its possession. Since 1814, when Irish admiral Guillermo Brown claimed it for the Argentine confederation, it's been a naval base, a quarantine center, a common lockup, a political prison, and even a detention camp for German POWs (at the beginning of World War II, after the battleship *Graf Spee* sank in Montevideo harbor). Four Argentine presidents have been confined here: Hipólito Yrigoyen (1930), Marcelo T. de Alvear (1932, after his presidency), Juan Domingo Perón (1945, before his presidency), and Arturo Frondizi (1962). What might be called the "Alcatraz of Argentina" is still a halfway house for non-violent prisoners from Buenos Aires Province.

Up to 4,500 residents once lived here, but only about 150 remain. Most of the island is now a nature reserve with forests of *ceibo* (cockspur coral), acacia, and other species. Its 250 bird species include hummingbirds, parakeets, cormorants, storks, and owls. The occasional capybara and even *yacaré* (caiman) can come ashore.

The point of entry is the lovingly landscaped **Plaza Guillermo Brown,** uphill from the passenger jetty. Among the rusting gun emplacements and crumbling barracks is the outlandish **Cine-Teatro General Urquiza,** with a twin-circle facade (each with its own double doors), set among three fluted columns, with gold-tinted rococo details. The nearby **Museo de la Isla** contains shipwreck relics and items linked to its illustrious detainees, such as an English toilet that accompanied Alvear. An abandoned lighthouse still stands at the island's highest point, and a small cemetery holds the remains of conscripts who died in an epidemic a century ago.

One of the island's constructions is a landmark: The Panadería Rocío, dating from 1913, is still known for its fruitcakes. Beyond the settlement, to the northwest, most residents lived in now-rotting wooden buildings at the **Barrio Chino** (Chinatown) near the **Puerto Viejo,** the island's abandoned port. This is the best area for wildlife-watching, at least for those who remember their mosquito repellent. ■

Tigre's Puerto de Frutos is a popular handicrafts market.

Famed for their sweeping grasslands, home of the gaucho, with majestic mountains and vacation-friendly beaches

The Pampas

Córdoba Province's Altas Cumbres highway yields impressive views of Villa Carlos Paz.

The Pampas

Nearly surrounding Buenos Aires, stretching from the Atlantic shoreline to a distant horizon where the Andes are only a mirage, the Pampas are the Argentine heartland. Where the Spaniards' feral cattle and horses multiplied on the lush level grasslands, the gaucho created an open-range lifestyle that remains part of Argentine mythology long after the great cattle estancias fenced the pastures.

Many Argentines were ambivalent about what they called the *pampa gringa* (in Argentine Spanish, "gringo" means a light-skinned European), lands transformed by European immigrants into an export-led economic juggernaut that overran the gaucho and turned him into a dependent laborer. The exact extent of the pampas is open to debate, but for most purposes the area includes the provinces of Buenos Aires, La Pampa, Santa Fe, and Córdoba. All of them, except for thinly populated La Pampa, were major contributors to the boom, and Buenos Aires (exclusive of the federal capital) holds almost 40 percent of the country's population. Vying to be the republic's "second city," the riverside port of Rosario (Santa Fe Province, birthplace of the Argentine flag) and Córdoba (capital of its namesake province) both have vigorous economies and active cultural calendars.

The city of La Plata, capital of Buenos Aires Province, is a cultural force with major universities, performing arts venues, and the country's top natural history museum, the Museo de La Plata. The Pampas' sentimental capital, though, is San Antonio de Areco, where the gaucho is an icon; the pace is leisurely, both in town and on the historic estancias that are now popular guest ranches. A bit closer to Buenos Aires, the city of Luján is Argentina's major devotional center and home to a cluster of important historical museums.

For most Argentines, though, the Pampas' biggest attraction is the long Atlantic shoreline and, in particular, the beach resort of Mar del Plata. Many *porteños* spend their summer

vacations here, greeting the same neighbors they see all year on the streets of the capital. Even much of the entertainment calendar moves to the coast in summer. Since the elite started summering at Uruguay's Punta del Este decades ago, Mar del Plata is no longer exclusive, but it has its own impressive galleries, museums, and theaters.

Most of the Pampas is, of course, unrelentingly flat, but in a few select areas resistant rocks have withstood weathering to form isolated mountain ranges that fall short of Andean grandeur but still have their appeal. In Buenos Aires Province, the Sierras de Tandil are a rolling granitic range, while the jagged folded sediments of the Sierra de la Ventana rise sharply above the plains. La Pampa's Lihué

Calel is a unique igneous archipelago in the western desert, while the Sierras de Córdoba are the Andean condor's easternmost habitat. The foothills town of Alta Gracia was the boyhood habitat of famed revolutionary Ernesto "Che" Guevara. ■

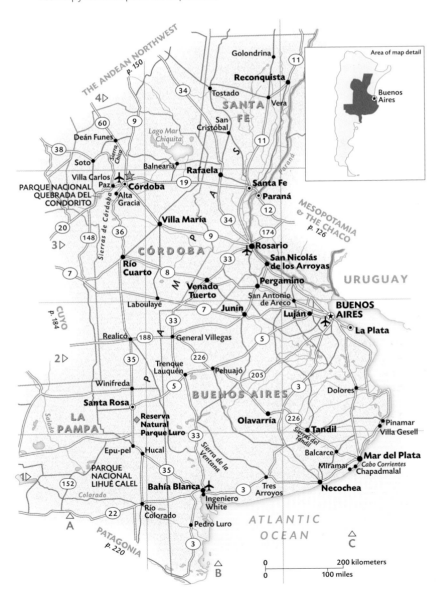

La Plata

Less than an hour from Buenos Aires, the Buenos Aires provincial capital of La Plata affects the airs of a national center. Its monumental architecture and design—the city grid, with its connecting diagonals, resembles that of Washington, D.C.—imply a rivalry with the federal capital. In fact, it owes its existence to such a rivalry. After a near civil war in 1880, the province formed its new capital some 37 miles (60 km) to the southeast of Buenos Aires.

Saber-toothed tigers guard the entrance to the Museo de La Plata.

In the interim, it has become a city of more than half a million people, and its cultural institutions—theaters, concert halls, universities, research libraries, and museums—are among the country's best. The architecture is self-consciously continental, with Flemish, French, and German elements, but a handful of contemporary buildings struggle to fit in. City planner Pedro Benoit (1836–1897) ensured an abundance of well-distributed plazas and parks to guarantee easy access to open spaces. On Evita Perón's death in 1952, the city was renamed Ciudad Eva Perón in her memory, but it reverted to its original name after the military overthrew Juan Perón in 1955.

Plaza Mariano Moreno & Around

La Plata's center point is Plaza Mariano Moreno, which occupies four full but surprisingly barren blocks covered mostly with grass and paving tiles, with only a scattering of trees. Its major landmark is the **Catedral de la Inmaculada Concepción** (also known as Catedral Metropolitana de La Plata), whose basement **Museo Catedral** holds the tomb of founding father Dardo Rocha (1838–1921), a provincial governor who faced down strong opposition in order to locate this rival power center outside the city of Buenos Aires—which soon became a separate federal district.

Designed by Benoit and two other architects, begun in 1885, the neo-Gothic cathedral took more than a century to complete. So slow was its construction that

INSIDER TIP:

In La Plata's Vieja Estación, be amused by jugglers and acrobats, a tango or jazz show, and have a coffee amid the atmosphere of the early 20th century.

—SERGIO F. VIZCAINO
National Geographic field scientist

its first restoration ended two years before the completion of its triple towers in 1999, but an elevator to the 207-foot (63 m) level now offers access to a panoramic view of Plaza Moreno, an ideal way to appreciate the city's layout.

Across the plaza, the **Palacio Municipal** (City Hall; *Calle 12 bet. 51 & 53*) is a German Renaissance structure with a central clock tower, marble staircases, and an eclectic mix of Greek, Roman, French, and German details. The 24-member city council meets in a semicircular hall easily identified from the back of the building.

With a new art gallery, it's open for guided tours on weekdays.

Two blocks northeast, the original **Teatro Argentino de La Plata** was La Plata's answer to the Teatro Colón in Buenos Aires—many of the same performers played at both—but it burned to the ground in 1977. Its replacement, decreed under the Dirty War dictatorship of 1976–1983 but not completed until 2000, is a concrete monolith with all the personality of a parking garage. The interior, though, is a worthy successor to the original, with a main theater seating 2,000 spectators, a smaller hall seating about 300, and a subterranean gallery with rotating exhibits of painting and sculpture. The theater has its own orchestra, chorus, and ballet, and is open for guided tours.

Two blocks farther northeast, the **Palacio de la Legislatura** *(Plaza San Martín)* is another German Renaissance building that houses the provincial Senate and Chamber of Deputies; the entrance to each chamber has a neoclassical facade. Across wooded **Plaza San Martín,** the Flemish Renaissance **Casa de Gobierno,** housing the governor's offices, trumps the federal government's mishmash Casa Rosada.

On the plaza's west side, the **Pasaje Dardo Rocha** was the city's first train station, but today it's a cultural center with two worthwhile museums: the **Museo de Arte Contemporáneo Latinoamericano** (Museum of Contemporary Latin American Art) and the **Museo Municipal de Bellas Artes,** with local artists.

La Plata

🅰 99 C2

Visitor Information

✉ Centro Cultural Pasaje Dardo Rocha, Calle 50 bet. 6 & 7

☎ 0221/427-1535

🕐 Closed Jan. 1, May 1, & Dec. 25

www.laplata.gov.ar

Museo Catedral

✉ Calle 14 bet. 51 & 53

☎ 0221/427-3504

🕐 Closed Jan. 1 & Dec. 25

💲 $

www.catedral delaplata.com

Teatro Argentino de La Plata

✉ Avenida 51 bet. 9 & 10

☎ 0221/429-1700

🕐 Tours Tues.–Sat.; book at least a week in advance. No tours Jan.–Feb. & holidays

www.teatroargentino .gba.gov.ar

Museo de Arte Contemporáneo Latinoamericano

✉ Centro Cultural Pasaje Dardo Rocha, Calle 50 bet. 6 & 7

☎ 0221/427-1843

🕐 Closed Mon., Jan. 1, May 1, & Dec. 25

www.macla.com.ar

Museo Municipal de Bellas Artes

✉ Centro Cultural Pasaje Dardo Rocha, Calle 50 bet. 6 & 7

☎ 0221/427-1198

🕐 Closed Mon., Jan. 1, May 1, & Dec. 25

Four blocks northeast, the **Casa Curutchet** (1954) is a pilgrimage site for architectural students in search of South America's only Le Corbusier building. Its modernism may not match La Plata's original style, but the combination residence and dental offices can stand on its own. Le Corbusier never visited the site, nor even met the client, but a poplar tree that he added softens the starkness of the building.

the Iraola family, who planted most of the trees that now shade it; after its expropriation, the *casco* (big house) successively housed the governor, a police station, law courts, and a telegraph office. Around 1917 it was, for no apparent reason, demolished.

Founded in 1907, the **Jardín Zoológico** shared the post-Victorian sensibilities of its time, both in its construction and in the collections of exotic animals

EXPERIENCE:
Political Disneyland? República de los Niños

It might not seem that a children's amusement park, with scale-model versions of European castles, Asian palaces, and public institutions, would have an explicit political purpose. Still, it's more than symbolic that Eva Perón herself helped create La Plata's República de los Niños *(Camino General Belgrano & 501 Manuel Gonnet, tel 0221/4841409, www.republica.laplata.gov.ar)* on the site of an expropriated, previously British-owned golf course.

To appreciate República de los Niños, it's necessary to imagine yourself in the minds of two people: The first is that of Evita Perón, whose resentment of the

Argentine oligarchy and its institutions was almost limitless. The second is that of an underprivileged child, who could at least dream of influencing those institutions under Peronist patronage.

Evita died less than a year after the 131-acre (53 ha) park opened in late 1951, but the enterprise fit her modus operandi of challenging the oligarchy for the presumptive benefit of the underprivileged. According to legend, Walt Disney visited the park shortly after it opened and incorporated some of its concepts into Disneyland, but Disney archivist Dave Smith says Walt's only Argentine visit took place in 1941.

Casa Curutchet

✉ Avenida 53 No. 320

☎ 0221/482-2631

🕐 Closed Sat.–Sun., Jan., & holidays

💲 $$$$$

www.capba.org.ar

Paseo del Bosque

La Plata's real pride, though, is the sprawling Paseo del Bosque, a public park that's the city's counterpart to Buenos Aires's Parques de Palermo. It covers more than 150 acres (60 ha) with gardens, an artificial lake with paddleboats, a zoo, an amphitheater, sausage stands, and one of the country's top museums. Before La Plata's founding, it was the estancia of

that it sheltered. It has since given a greater emphasis to housing native Argentine fauna, but it is still primarily an outing for the kids. The Universidad Nacional de La Plata operates the **Observatorio Astronómico de La Plata,** which offers evening tours on Fridays and Saturdays.

Museo de La Plata: The park's gem, though, is the

Museo de La Plata (also known as Museo de Ciencias Naturales de La Plata), the legacy of Patagonian explorer Francisco Pascasio Moreno—better known as "Perito" ("Expert") Moreno, for his experience and knowledge of Argentina's southernmost frontier. Moreno's work was critical in clarifying the borders between Argentina and Chile. The museum's first director, he donated his entire paleontological, archaeological, and anthropological collections to the museum, which opened only six years after the city's founding in 1882. Like the observatory, the museum is now part of the Universidad Nacional de La Plata.

The museum has a commanding exterior that matches those of La Plata's other public buildings. At the entrance, flanked by carved saber-toothed tigers, six fluted neoclassical columns support a portico whose pediment features a winged allegorical sculpture representing science, standing atop a three-dimensional globe. The inference is that this is a serious endeavor; rising to a stained-glass skylight, the circular vestibule reinforces the solemn mood with a central bust of the founder and paintings of the Argentine countryside on the surrounding walls.

However impressive the structure, the museum rises and falls on the collections that fill 21 exhibition halls on two floors. Some of this means a stuff-in-glass-cases approach, but the university's efforts have improved its thematic approach to the earth sciences, life sciences, and anthropology. Dinosaur fans will find much to like.

The permanent exhibits follow a logical progression from the origins of the Earth through the mechanisms of evolution, paleontology (including Argentina's impressive Triassic and Jurassic dinosaur discoveries), zoology, entomology, and botany. Nearly

INSIDER TIP:

Don't miss the Museo de La Plata, with its dinosaurs and other ancient animals.

—NICOLAS KUGLER
National Geographic contributor

reaching the ceiling of the evolution exhibit, the full-size *Diplodocus* reproduction (sent here by Andrew Carnegie) is native to the western United States; the smaller *Herrerasaurus* is authentically Argentine, from the canyon country of San Juan Province. (Argentina has other, equally massive dinosaurs, but no other complete skeleton is on display here.)

On the human side, there are displays devoted to physical anthropology, the ethnography of Argentina's native peoples from the subtropical high Andes to the sub-Antarctic Tierra del Fuego, the Jesuit mission experiment of northeastern Argentina, and Andean archaeology north into Bolivia and Peru. An exhibit on early Egypt (Ramses II) feels out of place except in the context of the museum's Victorian origins. ∎

Jardín Zoológico

✉ Paseo del Bosque, Avenida Iraola bet. Avenida Centenario & Avenida 52

☎ 0221/427-3925

🕐 Closed Mon., Jan. 1, May 1, & Dec. 25

💲 $

www.jardinzoologico
.laplata.gov.ar

Observatorio Astronómico de La Plata

✉ Paseo del Bosque, Avenida Centenario & Avenida Iraola

☎ 0221/423-6593

🕐 Tours Fri. & Sat. No tours Jan.–Feb. & holidays

💲 $

www.fcaglp.unlp
.edu.ar

Museo de La Plata

✉ Paseo del Bosque; access from Avenida Iraola

☎ 0221/425-7744

🕐 Closed Mon. (except holidays), Jan. 1, May 1, & Dec. 24, 25,& 31

💲 $

www.museo.fcnym
.unlp.edu.ar

The Pampa Gaucha & the Pampa Gringa

West of Buenos Aires, the interior of Buenos Aires Province is the gaucho's symbolic homeland, even if fenced cattle estancias and wheat and soybean fields nearly monopolize the lush open range of earlier times. Some historic estancias are now guest ranches, partly because economic circumstances forced them to change over in the aftermath of various financial crises.

A gaucho surveys the landscape, Sierras de Córdoba.

Luján

⚑ 99 C2

Visitor Information

✉ Edificio La Cúpula, Parque Ameghino, San Martín 1

☎ 02323/427-082 or 0800/333-1061

🕐 Closed Jan. 1, May 1, & Dec. 25

www.lujan.tur.ar

Luján & Around

Barely an hour from Buenos Aires, Luján draws millions of pilgrims to Argentina's holiest site. Here, according to legend, a 17th-century oxcart stalled in the mud until its owner removed a statuette of the Virgin Mary—a sign that the image should remain on the spot. On weekends and holidays, thousands of pilgrims may line up to view the statuette, painted in the Argentine colors of celeste and white, in a tiny chamber behind the **Basílica**

Nacional Nuestra Señora de Luján.

Recently restored to its original luster, Lujan's cobbled plaza holds tens of thousands of people for outdoor masses. Even secular events, including an annual folklore festival, take place here, and pilgrims find time to barbecue in the open air until the early hours.

Almost immediately west, the **Complejo Museográfico Provincial Enrique Udaondo** is a cluster of historical museums that presents Luján's secular side in the 18th-century **cabildo** (town council building) and the so-called **Casa del Virrey** (no viceroy ever lived here). Besides the usual homages to historic figures such as Manuel Belgrano and Gen. Bartolomé Mitre, its **Museo Colonial e Histórico** samples the darker side of Argentine history—for example, the assassination of caudillo Facundo Quiroga and Rosas's trial of Córdoba's Reinafé brothers for the murder. Meanwhile, the **Museo del Transporte** shows the quirkier side of Argentine history through the stuffed specimens of Gato and Mancha, the rugged criollo horses that Swiss adventurer A. F. Tschiffely rode from Buenos Aires to Washington, D.C., in the 1920s.

On Luján's outskirts, **Estancia Los Talas** (RP 47 Km 1, tel 02323/494-995, www.estancias argentinas.com) is one of Argentina's most historic, least pretentious guest ranches, with an important research library.

San Antonio de Areco & Around

Only an hour northwest of Luján, San Antonio moves at a gaucho pace—except on the slow-moving highway bypass that connects Buenos Aires with Mendoza. Thanks largely to the legacy of novelist Ricardo Güiraldes (1886–1927), who wrote the Argentine horse opera *Don Segundo Sombra*, November's annual **Fiesta de la Tradición** is an homage to all things gauchesque.

San Antonio also supports a remarkable concentration of silversmiths and other craftsmen who produce gaucho gear and other traditional artifacts. Many of the brick buildings on its narrow colonial streets have been, and are being, recycled as boutique hotels, B&Bs, and bar/restaurants, but San Antonio (continued on p. 108)

Basílica Nacional Nuestra Señora de Luján
- San Martín 51
- 02323/420-058
- www.basilicadelujan.org.ar

Complejo Museográfico Provincial Enrique Udaondo
- Lezica & Torrezuri bet. San Martín & 25 de Mayo
- 02323/420-245
- Closed Mon.– Tues., Nov.– March
- $

San Antonio de Areco
- 99 C2/C3
Visitor Information
- Zerboni & Ruiz de Arellano
- 02326/453-165
- www.sanantonio deareco.tur.ar

EXPERIENCE: Walking to Luján in the Peregrinación de la Juventud

For Argentina's conventionally faithful, there's no more profound an experience than early October's "youth pilgrimage" to Luján but, given the city's devotional importance, it's a surprisingly recent tradition, dating from 1975. Anyone can join the 37-mile (59 km) walk from Buenos Aires.

According to anthropologist María Laura Massolo, under the 1976–1983 dictatorship's state of siege, the pilgrimage became one of the few forms of mass expression where young people felt safe. When she walked the route in 1977, she says, "I followed the crowd."

Along with 300,000 others—she and her friends could outspokenly "jump for life and hope" without fear or apprehension on an all-night walk ending with an early morning mass.

Anyone who wants to participate in the pilgrimage to Luján can join in at any of various stations along the route. The procession now begins in the Buenos Aires city barrio of Liniers, at the city's western edge, at Avenida Rivadavia and Avenida General Paz.

For more information, contact the **Peregrinación Juvenil a Pie a Luján** (www.peregrinacionlujan.org.ar).

The Silverwork of San Antonio

According to the late San Antonio de Areco silversmith Juan José Draghi, "Being a silversmith and being an Argentine is to share the same etymological root." In a Pampas town in a country that gave its name, in a slightly different form, to the Río de la Plata—"river of silver"—San Antonio de Areco is the center of the universe for Argentine *plateros* (silversmiths).

A silversmith peers at his work at the Primer Museo y Taller Abierto de Platería Criolla.

Draghi was perhaps San Antonio's most prominent, but far from its only, silversmith. No other town of its size has had so many, and many of Draghi's protégés and competitors have spread their craft throughout the country. Draghi's work, appropriately, was the subject of an elaborate retrospective at Palermo's Museo de Arte Popular José Hernández, and was later shown at the Argentine embassy in Paris.

Most silversmiths are also *orfebreros*—*orfebrería* is the art of making precious metals, including gold, into objects of everyday use—but Draghi and other San Antonio silversmiths excelled at making items of the highest craftsmanship without abandoning their gaucho traditions. Thus they produce dress versions of the gaucho *rastra* (a leather belt embellished with silver coins or equivalents), *facón* (dagger, with varying ornamentation depending on its region of origin), *estribos* (stirrups), and *espuelas* (spurs). *Boleadoras*, the balls on leather cords originally used to bring down wild game such as guanacos and rheas, date from pre-Columbian times, but gauchos used them to capture feral cattle on the Pampas. Like their boleadoras, gaucho *rebenques* (short rawhide riding whips) contain silver details—in this case, a knob—and a wrist strap.

EXPERIENCE:
Watching the Artisans

Many silversmiths sell their wares in San Antonio, but the best place to watch them at work is at the late Juan José Draghi's **Primer Museo y Taller Abierto de Platería Criolla** (*Lavalle 387, tel 02326/454-219, www.draghi plateros orfebres.com*). Still run by Draghi's heirs, the "museum" is an outlet for high-end *gauchesco* silverwork—even during the 2002 economic crisis, Draghi had plenty of hard-currency commissions from overseas. For all its wealth of artifacts, though, the museum and its open workshop are a low-key locale where visitors can observe the artisans closely, photograph them, and question them about their craft (there is a bilingual guide, and some of the Draghi family handle English well).

As the gaucho morphed from an open-range horseman who lived off the wild herds to a dependent laborer on the cattle estancia, the silversmith's task came to include luxury items for the wealthy *estancieros* whose herds roamed the newly fenced pastures. Some of the owners' horses, for instance, came to sport parade bridles on which the crownpiece, cheekpieces, band, and bits consisted almost entirely of gold and silver, and the reins ended in braids or laces. When polo became a pastime of the rural elite, silversmiths made the trophies for their competitions.

Household Silver

The silver extravagances extended into household goods. Gauchos made their own mate and sipped it from carved calabashes, but the oligarchy—who sometimes employed a servant for the sole purpose of preparing Argentina's favorite infusion—insisted on encasing their gourds in finely crafted silver or sometimes ceramics, often with a

pedestal to match. They would, of course, need a comparable *bombilla* (straw) for sipping it from the gourd, and a matching set for their house in Buenos Aires.

Meanwhile, the silversmiths made other household accessories and personal items for the fortunate of the country: candlesticks, chalices, cuff links and jewelry, tankards, and wine cups. As the Argentine economy suffered a meltdown in 2002, Draghi and his colleagues were to some degree crisis-proof as they found export markets for their goods—a set of custom cutlery, for instance, might be commissioned by a rancher in Texas. Even as unemployed workers scavenged cardboard and plastic bottles in the streets of Buenos Aires, San Antonio maintained an air of quiet prosperity thanks to its silversmiths.

The socially prominent of Buenos Aires have a saying that, until your obituary appears in the Buenos Aires daily *La Nación*, you're not really dead. By that standard, Juan José Draghi (1943–2008) is unquestionably dead, but he helped revive a rural tradition that some said was on the point of disappearing. His family, protégés, and their apprentices are carrying on the work in San Antonio and elsewhere.

Ceremonial mate gourds

Centro Cultural Usina Vieja

✉ Alsina 66

☎ 02326 /454-722

🕐 Closed Mon.

💲 $

Parque Criollo y Museo Gauchesco Ricardo Güiraldes

✉ Camino Ricardo Güiraldes

☎ 02326/455-839

🕐 Closed Tues.–Wed.

💲 $

www.blogmuseo guiraldes.com.ar.

Museo Atelier del Pintor Osvaldo Gasparini

✉ Alvear 521

☎ 02326/453-930

💲 $ (suggested)

Rosario

🄰 99 B3

Visitor Information

✉ Avenida Belgrano & Buenos Aires

☎ 0341/480-2230

🕐 Closed Jan. 1, May 1, & Dec. 25

www.rosarioturismo .com

remains truer to tradition than to stereotype.

Bordered by historic buildings, wooded **Plaza Ruiz de Arellano** is the traditional town center and, unlike many provincial towns, it's not cluttered with gaudy retailers and video parlors. Most of its buildings, such as the **Iglesia Parroquial San Antonio de Padua,** date from the mid-19th century.

Half a block north of the plaza, once the town's power plant, the **Centro Cultural Usina Vieja** is a museum and events center that focuses less on personalities and more on neighborhood institutions such as the *boliche* (general store).

Two blocks north of the plaza, both sides of the Río Areco are grassy parkland, studded with

INSIDER TIP:

To see the country's best traditional celebrations, be in San Antonio de Areco between November 1 and 10.

—ELISEO MICIU
National Geographic photographer

occasional trees and flooded when it rains heavily. Open to pedestrians, bicycles, and horses, the mid-19th-century **Puente Viejo** bridges the river and leads to **Parque Criollo y Museo Gauchesco Ricardo Güiraldes,** honoring the novelist (who lived at nearby Estancia La Porteña) and his protagonist. What the

museum has done best is its restoration of the **Pulpería La Blanqueada,** a typical roadhouse where gauchos played cards, raced horses, cheered cockfights, and drank themselves under the table. It was also where they stocked up on supplies. The main **Casa del Museo** replicates an 18th-century *casco* (big house) with several rooms devoted to Güiraldes and his family. Other rooms cover gauchesque literature, large landowners (the prize exhibit is Rosas' bed), and horse gear and gauchesque art. The museum, though, lacks information about the contentious relations between landowners and the gauchos who became their virtual chattels. After flood damage, only parts of the museum are open to the public.

Six blocks south of the plaza, opposite Plaza Gómez, visitors can still hitch their horses at the **Museo Atelier del Pintor Osvaldo Gasparini** (many of Areco's artists and craftsmen have Italian surnames), where painter Luis Gasparini gives guided tours *(Spanish only)* through his father's atelier and continues the tradition of providing each visitor with a small souvenir—usually a pencil sketch on a gauchesque theme. Most of the exhibits at this cozy family museum address such themes, but there are also works by urban artists such as Benito Quinquela Martín.

Rosario

Upriver from Buenos Aires, on the right bank of the Paraná, Rosario is the port for the grains that grow on the *pampa gringa,*

EXPERIENCE: Guest Ranches of the Pampas

A century ago, as their servants brought the silver-plated mate cups to the salons of their Francophile castles, the patricians of the Pampas could never have imagined opening their estancias to a paying public—much less one beneath their social class. Hiring out their polo ponies would have been unthinkable.

A luxury guesthouse at Estancia El Rocio

That was then, and this is now. Just as North American ranchers opened their doors to dudes from the East Coast, so the Argentine landowners, after decades of economic chaos, decided to diversify into tourism.

San Antonio de Areco is one of the centers of rural tourism—**Estancia La Cinacina** (*Lavalle 1, San Antonio de Areco, tel 02326/452-045, www.lacinacina.com.ar*), in fact, is only a few blocks west of Plaza Ruiz de Arellano, and is a favorite for day visitors with its *fiesta gaucha*. Don't expect intimacy for its barbecues, with their folkloric dances and horse races—its cavernous *quincho* (barbeque area) seats up to 400 lunch-going spectators.

For polo players, or aspiring players, **Estancia El Rosario de Areco** (*RP 41 Km 6, San Antonio de Areco, tel 02326/451-000, www.rosariodeareco.com.ar*) has converted stables into fashionable accommodations with its own quincho for barbecues and "day in the country" visits. Non-polo guests are welcome.

Of all Areco's estancias, **El Ombú de Areco** (*Ruta 31, Cuartel VI, Villa Lía, San Antonio de Areco, tel 02326/492-080, www.estanciaelombu.com*) is the most opulent, its Italianate casco surrounded by 9 acres (more than 3 ha) of formal gardens on a larger property raising cattle. Founded in 1880 by Gen. Pablo Ricchieri, its rooms feature period decoration but also urban amenities such as satellite TV. Like others in the area, it offers riding, cycling, and other outdoor activities.

If **Estancia La Bamba** (*Ruta 31, San Antonio de Areco, tel 02326/454-895, www.la-bamba.com.ar*) looks like a movie set, that's partly because it was—part of the Oscar-nominated 19th-century drama *Camila* was filmed here. It has a casual feel, and its buildings add to the charm—one of the guest rooms occupies an Italianate tower, for instance. Typical activities include riding, birding, swimming, and Saturday night folklore programs.

Showcasing warm colors, handpicked decor from the owners' world travels, and crackling fires, the colonial-style buildings at **Estancia El Rocio** (*Ruta 3 Km 102.5, San Miguel del Monte, tel 54-9-11-6293/7887 [from U.S.], www.estanciaelrocio.com*) sit on a secluded 325-acre (131 ha) ranch 60 miles (100 km) south of Buenos Aires. Polo aficionados (and beginners) will appreciate the two polo fields and the 60 ponies, while anyone seeking solitude will revel in the outdoor swimming pool and the earthy walking trails, not to mention the delectable asado feasts.

**Museo del
Paraná y las Islas**
✉ Avenida de los
  Inmigrantes 410
☎ 0341/440-0751
🕐 Closed Mon.–
  Fri.
💲 $

**Museo Municipal
de Bellas
Artes Juan B.
Castagnino**
✉ Avenida
  Pellegrini 2202,
  Rosario
☎ 0341/480-2542
🕐 Closed Wed.
💲 $

www.museocastag
nino.org.ar

but historically it's the "Cuna de la Bandera," where Gen. Manuel Belgrano first raised the Argentine flag that he had designed here. It's also an arts and entertainment center, with museums, theaters, and galleries.

Rosario's cornerstone is the **Monumento Nacional a la Bandera** *(Santa Fe 581, tel 0341/480-2239, www.monumentoalabandera .gov.ar, $)*, which overlooks the harbor from high ground between Avenida Córdoba and Santa Fe street. There's a certain hubris, though, in architects Alejandro Bustillo and Angel Guido's massive boat-shaped monument to the flag, whose symbolic mast is a 230-foot (70 m) tower that offers panoramas of the city and the river.

Stretching along the waterfront, the **Parque Nacional a la**

Bandera contains the Estación Fluvial, a passenger terminal that's a starting point for excursions into the upper delta. More notably, it contains the **Museo del Paraná y las Islas,** where local muralist Raúl Domínguez (1918–1999) vividly depicted life on the river.

Rosario's top arts museum is the **Museo Municipal de Bellas Artes Juan B. Castagnino,** which specializes in modern Argentine art from the likes of Berni (a local) and Quinquela Martín, but also displays some European masters and landscapes from the 19th and 20th centuries. The museum also operates in additional premises focused on contemporary Argentine art, the **Museo de Arte Contemporáneo de Rosario (MACRO),** located in renovated old granaries, known as Silos Davis, by the river.

On Maundy Thursday, the faithful take part in a pilgrimage to Cerro Calvario, Tandil.

Across from the Castagnino, **Parque Independencia** is a 311-acre (126 ha) park with pedestrian and bicycle trails, fountains, rose gardens, a soccer stadium, a race-course, and the **Museo de la Ciudad de Rosario,** covering Rosario's urban history.

INSIDER TIP:

Santa Fe is known for its unique old recipe for *alfajores.* Try them at Confitería Las Delicias (1924), at San Martín 2898.

—NICOLAS KUGLER
National Geographic contributor

Santa Fe

Capital of its namesake province, Santa Fe can't match Rosario's commercial and cultural vigor, and its riverside location is vulnerable to floods. Nevertheless, it can boast a colonial core that Rosario (a 19th-century city) and other towns along the Paraná can't match, even if some of that heritage disappeared in the prosperous 19th century and the early 20th.

Four blocks west of the river, studded with palms and conifers, the colonial **Plaza 25 de Mayo** is the civic and ecclesiastical center. Though the colonial cabildo was demolished in favor of the French Renaissance government house, the lack of commerce here has kept the surroundings relatively intact. The Jesuit-built **Iglesia de la Compañía** (also called **Santuario**

de Nuestra Señora de los Milagros**), for instance, dates from the late 17th century, and the **Catedral Metropolitana** from the mid-18th century.

Only a block south, the flood-prone open spaces of **Parque General Belgrano** are also home to several colonial monuments and museums, though the contents and presentation aren't up to standards elsewhere. The most notable is the 17th-century **Iglesia y Convento de San Francisco,** with its solid adobe walls, red-tile roof, and ceiling beams held in place by dowels and leather straps in lieu of nails. It has survived repeated floods even if there have been casualties—the oddest of them Padre Magallanes, interred here after being killed by a jaguar that entered the cloisters in 1825. Within the cloisters, the **Museo del Convento de San Francisco** covers both religious and secular history.

Also within the park, the **Museo Histórico Provincial de Santa Fe Brigadier General Estanislao López** occupies a 17th-century structure with collections on colonial and postcolonial art and history. The nearby **Museo Etnográfico y Colonial Juan de Garay** stresses the province's native peoples, both historically and today, and the city's original site at Cayastá (50 miles/80 km northeast and even more flood prone).

Tandil

In a few areas, resistant bedrock breaks the monotony of the Pampas to form low mountain ranges. In the case of Tandil, the highest peak reaches only about

Museo de Arte Contemporáneo de Rosario (MACRO)
- ✉ Bulevar Oroño & el Río Paraná, Rosario
- ☎ 0341/4804-9812
- 🕐 Closed Wed.

www.macromuseo.org.ar

Museo de la Ciudad de Rosario
- ✉ Bulevar Oroño 2300, Rosario
- ☎ 0341/480-8665
- 🕐 Closed Mon. & holidays

www.museodelaciudad.org.ar

Santa Fe
- 🅰 99 B3
- **Visitor Information**
- ✉ Terminal de Ómnibus, Belgrano 2910
- ☎ 0342/457-4124

www.santafeturismo.gov.ar

Museo del Convento de San Francisco
- ✉ San Martín & Amenábar, Santa Fe
- ☎ 0342/459-3303
- 💲 $ (suggested)

Museo Histórico Provincial de Santa Fe Brigadier General Estanislao López
- ✉ San Martín 1490, Santa Fe
- ☎ 0342/457-3529
- 🕐 Closed Mon.
- 💲 $ (suggested)

www.museohistorico-sfe.gov.ar

Museo Etnográfico y Colonial Juan de Garay

✉ 25 de Mayo 1470, Santa Fe

☎ 0342/457-3550

🕐 Closed Mon. & Jan. 1, May 1, first Friday of Sept., & Dec. 25.

$ $ (suggested)

www.santafe -conicet.gov.ar/ etnografico

Tandil

🗺 99 C2

Visitor Information

✉ Avenida Espora 1120

☎ 0249/443-2073

🕐 Closed May 1

www.turismo.tandil .gov.ar

1,720 feet (524 m), but that's been enough to make it the recreation mecca of southern Buenos Aires Province. Barely blocks from the central Plaza Independencia you'll find hiking, cycling, and horseback trails. For technical climbers, the challenges of steep granite faces compensate for modest altitudes.

For Argentines, Tandil is also a devotional destination, especially for outdoor Easter masses at Monte Calvario. Surrounded by dairy farms, it's also known for its cheeses and cured meats (both sold throughout the country), and traditional gaucho crafts.

Surrounded by cobbled streets that have disappeared in most of the rest of the city, **Plaza Independencia** is the city center. In the 19th century, it was a frontier fortress in a war zone. The city's most entertaining sight is the

sprawling **Museo Histórico Fuerte Independencia,** an everything-to-everyone museum with 16 vast rooms—one of which accommodates a fighter aircraft.

Even as the indigenous attacks on the town ceased in the 1870s, Tandil experienced one of the most peculiar assaults in Argentine history, from a healer known as Tata Dios, whose gaucho followers murdered 35 European settlers in 1872. Tata Dios and his devotees met at one of Tandil's strangest natural features, a wobbling 300-ton (272 metric ton) boulder known as **La Piedra Movediza,** which took another four decades to tumble off its precarious perch. At the site, about 2 miles (3 km) from the plaza, authorities erected a reproduction of the stone in 2007. What's genuine is the one-pitched bolted face that brings climbers here.

EXPERIENCE: Peaking the Pampas

To hear Charles Darwin tell it, no foreigner had climbed this part of the Sierra de la Ventana before him, and it was a struggle: "The climbing up such rough rocks was very fatiguing; the sides were so indented, that what was gained in five minutes was often lost in the next." It might surprise him, then, that **Cerro de la Ventana,** a peak famous for its natural arch, is now an easy two-hour (one way) hike. In all likelihood, it is Argentina's most frequently reached summit. You'll find the trailhead at the ranger station (tel 0291/491-0039) on RP 76 Km 225, west of the village of Sierra de la Ventana.

From Darwin's perspective, the mountains were "steep, extremely rugged, and broken, and so entirely destitute of

trees and even bushes" that he and his gaucho guides could barely build a fire. Nearly two centuries later, though, exotic conifers dot the lower slopes of Cerro de la Ventana's well-marked trail. Countless city dwellers make the climb every year, enjoying expansive panoramas of the Pampas in all directions.

There is one obstacle Darwin did not encounter and could never have anticipated. Wandering solo, he worried about Indian raiders, but he didn't have to deal with park rangers: As a rule, you are not permitted to begin the hike after midday, even in midsummer, on the rationale that descending in the dark is dangerous. Insistent hikers may get permission—but only by signing a waiver.

Sierra de la Ventana & Around

The Sierra de la Ventana is the sedimentary-metamorphic mountain range that runs southeast-northwest in southwestern Buenos Aires Province, and it's also the name of the village that's the main base for exploring it. Most visitors are day-trippers and weekenders from the port of Bahía Blanca and surrounding Pampas towns, who enjoy camping, hiking, cycling, and other activities in Ventania, as the range is also known.

One of Argentina's few remaining passenger rail lines passes through town, via a handsome girder bridge over the Río Sauce Grande, but otherwise there's little to see in town. Most services, including bicycle rentals and restaurants, are in the **Villa Tivoli** sector west of the river, but the easterly **Villa Arcadia** sector has better and quieter accommodations.

The range takes its name from the rugged 3,720-foot (1,134 m) peak known as **Cerro de la Ventana,** which in turn takes its name ("the window") from a natural opening, measuring more than 39 feet (12 m) deep, in the intensely folded strata. The peak lies within **Parque Provincial Ernesto Tornquist,** donated by a wealthy German-Argentine family to the province. Cerro de la Ventana makes a suitable day hike, but the area's highest summit, 4,065-foot (1,239 m) **Cerro Tres Picos,** is a longer trek over private property, requiring permission and a small fee. As the area is almost treeless, the route is easy to follow.

About 11 miles (18 km) northwest of Sierra de la Ventana, the smaller village of **Villa Ventana** is a picturesque alternative with unpaved but tree-lined streets and slightly better access to the park.

INSIDER TIP:

Pay a visit to rural Tornquist, 15 miles (25 km) west of the provincial park.

–NICOLAS KUGLER
National Geographic contributor

Santa Rosa & Around

As the Pampas stretch west, they're still flat, but far drier, in the thinly populated province of La Pampa. That said, the area has extensive forests of *caldén* (a relative of the common mesquite), patches of pasture that support dairy cattle, and vast shallow saline lakes filled with migratory birds. The provincial capital of Santa Rosa de Toay is the only substantial city in an area that, almost into the 20th century, was an insecure frontier subject to Indian raids and bandits.

Today, though, Santa Rosa is a tidy modern town that supplies the agricultural sector and serves as a back door into the legendary region of Patagonia, which it resembles in some ways. Its **Museo Provincial de Historia Natural** (*Quintana 116, tel 02954/422-693, closed Sat.*) focuses on local paleontology, with specimens of the herbivorous hadrosaur (duck-billed dinosaur) and the massive Titanosaurus, plus more recent fossils and exhibits on local flora

Museo Histórico Fuerte Independencia

- 4 de Abril 845, Tandil
- ☎ 0249/443-5573
- 🕐 Closed Mon., May 1, & Dec. 15–Jan. 15
- 💲 $

www.museodelfuerte .org.ar

Sierra de la Ventana
- 🅰 99 B1

Visitor Information
- Avenida del Golf
- ☎ 0291/491-5303

www.sierradela ventana.org.ar

Parque Provincial Ernesto Tornquist
- RP 76 Km 222
- ☎ 0291/491-0039
- 🕐 Closed Jan. 1 & Dec. 25
- 💲 $$

La Pampa Province
- 🅰 99 A2

Visitor Information
- Avenida Pedro Luro & San Martín, Santa Rosa
- ☎ 02954/424-404

www.turismolapampa .gov.ar

Santa Rosa
- 🅰 99 A2

Visitor Information
- Pellegrini 180, Santa Rosa
- ☎ 02954/422-693

Museo Provincial de Artes

✉ 9 de Julio & Villegas, Santa Rosa

☎ 02954/427-332

Reserva Natural Parque Luro

🗺 99 A2

✉ RN 35 Km 292

☎ 02954/499-000

💲 $

www.parqueluro .gov.ar

Parque Nacional Lihué Calel

🗺 99 A1

✉ RN 152, 229 km SW of Santa Rosa

☎ 02952/436-595

and fauna. The **Museo Provincial de Artes** exhibits works by artists from around the country, including Berni and Castagnino.

La Pampa may be below the radar for most international tourists, but not for hunters—whose activity the province still actively promotes. However, provincial leaders do not sponsor hunting at the nearby **Reserva Natural Parque Luro,** now a preserve that had its origins as a private hunting grounds for politician-businessman Pedro Luro (1860–1927), who stocked his 58,600-acre (23,700 ha) ranch with Carpathian deer, European boar, and pheasants. Luro also built a lavish lodge, now known as **Castillo Luro,** but repeated

INSIDER TIP:

In Reserva Natural Parque Luro, you'll see many Pampas creatures: deer, flamingos, and lots of other birds.

—ELISEO MICIU
National Geographic photographer

financial setbacks eventually left it in provincial hands. Less than half its original size, the reserve still has hiking and cycling trails, Castillo Luro is open for guided tours, and the **Museo San Huberto** displays carriages from Luro's brief heyday.

Parque Nacional Lihué Calel

Many people claim to seek solitude in nature, but isolated Lihué

Calel is the place to find it. In La Pampa's arid southwest, it's a chain of low granite summits that rise above the desert surface to create a diversity of micro-environments including grasslands, dense scrub forests, and *caldén* woodlands. Together, these support an abundance of Patagonia wildlife that includes guanacos, foxes, hares, rheas, and other species.

Lihué Calel has a history as a refuge for Araucanian Indians during guerrilla wars with Spaniards and Argentines. It also has a prehistory, as pre-Columbian hunter-gatherers left a record of their presence in several rock-art sites. In more recent times, it was an estancia expropriated by the province and transferred to Argentina's national park service in the 1970s.

Lihué Calel's finest hike reaches its highest summit on the awkwardly named **Cerro de la Sociedad Científica Argentina.** Though it's not even 2,000 feet (600 m) above sea level, it yields panoramas in all directions, particularly toward the marshes and salt lakes to the southwest. The **Sendero Valle Namuncurá** is a marked trail from the park campground, but when it emerges from the scrub there are numerous routes to the top. (The granite is slippery when it rains.)

A shorter nature trail, the **Sendero El Huitru,** leads through park flora near the caldén-studded campground, which thrums with birdlife at sunset. Reached by a 13-mile (21 km) loop road that also passes the old casco of the estancia, the **Sendero Valle de las Pinturas** is a short trail that leads to a large rock-art site. ∎

Córdoba & Around

Where the Pampas merge with the highlands, the provincial capital of Córdoba and its nearby Sierras are popular with Argentine tourists but get few foreign visitors. In colonial times, the area's importance dwarfed that of Buenos Aires. Now, some of the country's biggest music festivals take place in the region's small provincial towns.

The boyhood home of Ernesto "Che" Guevara is now a museum in Alta Gracia, Córdoba Province.

Córdoba

Córdoba was colonial Argentina's link to the Viceroyalty of Perú and, thanks to the Jesuits and other monastic orders, it was also the colony's high-culture capital.

Córdoba's sprawling outskirts mark it as an industrial city, but part of its central core retains a colonial integrity in several key landmarks; some of them are Jesuit monuments that, along with other provincial sites, comprise a UNESCO World Heritage site. To this day, Córdoba's nickname is La Docta, the learned city, and *cordobeses* consider themselves rivals to the porteños of Buenos Aires.

Most of Córdoba's colonial heritage is found on or around the central **Plaza San Martín.** The late colonial **Cabildo de la Ciudad,** with its handsome arched portico, replaced an earlier council building, but the adjacent **Iglesia Catedral de Nuestra Señora de la Asunción** dates from the 17th century, though it took nearly a century to complete.

A joint effort of Franciscan and Jesuit architects, the cathedral has towers flanking its neoclassical facade, while a decorative cupola rises from its center. The lavish interior contains many features, such as the altars and pulpits, plated in gold; the detailed ceiling

Córdoba
A 99 A3
Visitor Information
✉ Cabildo de la Ciudad, Independencia 50, Córdoba
☎ 0351/434-1200
www.cordoba turismo.gov.ar

Museo Histórico Provincial Marqués de Sobremonte

✉ Rosario de Santa Fe 218, Córdoba

☎ 0351/433-1661

🕐 Closed Sat.–Sun., & holidays

💲 $, Wed. free

Museo Municipal de Bellas Artes Dr. Genaro Pérez

✉ Avenida General Paz 33, Córdoba

☎ 0351/434-1646

🕐 Closed Mon.

www.museogenaro perez.wordpress.com

Manzana Jesuítica & Museo Histórico de la Universidad Nacional de Córdoba

✉ Obispo Trejo 242, Córdoba

☎ 0351/433-2075

🕐 Closed Sun.

💲 $$ for tour

www.unc.edu.ar

Cripta Jesuítica del Antiguo Noviciado

✉ Rivera Indarte & Colón, Córdoba

☎ 0351/434-1228

🕐 Closed Sat.–Sun.

💲 $

Alta Gracia

🅰 99 A3

Visitor Information

✉ Calle del Molino & Avenida Padre Domingo Viera

☎ 03547/428-128

www.altagracia .gov.ar

frescos are the work of painter Emilio Caraffa (1863–1939). The cathedral is also notable for its celebrity crypts, including local independence figures Gregorio Funes (1749–1829) and José María Paz (1791–1854).

Barely a block east of the plaza, the **Museo Histórico Provincial Marqués de Sobremonte** occupies an 18th-century building, the best conserved residence of its period. Its ample collections are strongest on religious statuary, but its 26 exhibition rooms also display paintings, weapons, and furniture.

Córdoba's traditional art museum is the **Museo Municipal de Bellas Artes Dr. Genaro Pérez,** also decorated by Caraffa. Occupying a Francophile residence from the early 20th century, its collections focus on contemporary Argentine artists such as Berni, Castagnino, and Quinquela Martín.

Internationally, though, Córdoba is notable for its **Manzana Jesuítica,** the colonial center of learning that's survived along the pedestrian mall two blocks south of the plaza. Córdoba's counterpart to Buenos Aires's Manzana de las Luces (see p. 60), it includes the **Rectorado de la Universidad Nacional de Córdoba** (South America's second oldest university) and the **Colegio Nacional de Monserrat.** The former's central courtyard was once a botanical garden, surrounded by colonnades with marble floors, but only a few raised beds suggest its history.

It's four blocks north of the block proper, but the **Cripta**

Che Guevara continues to influence Latin American politics.

Jesuítica del Antiguo Noviciado offers an underground view of colonial Córdoba. Recently restored, the subterranean Jesuit chapel was part of an aborted construction project.

Alta Gracia

Only half an hour from the capital, the colonial estancia of Alta Gracia is now a tidy foothills town with two claims to fame: its colonial Jesuit monuments, which form part of the province's UNESCO World Heritage site, and the boyhood home (but not the birthplace) of Ernesto "Che" Guevara. In Che's time, the town was a fashionable getaway for the Argentine elite, but today it's a more middle-class destination.

Alta Gracia's two main Jesuit monuments sit side by side on a slight rise above the central **Plaza Manuel Solares.** Originally built by the Jesuits, the domed **Iglesia**

Parroquial Nuestra Señora de la Merced went to the Mercedarian Order after the Jesuit expulsion of 1767. Its elaborate baroque facade is its outstanding feature; across the street, to the left, the inconspicuous 17th-century workshops known as the **Obraje** are now a public school.

Most of the building and grounds above the plaza, though, are now the **Museo Nacional Estancia Jesuítica de Alta Gracia y Casa del Virrey Liniers,** a brick-and-stone building separated from the church by a large interior patio. Most of its 17 salons are decorated

in the style of colonial and early republican Argentina, and the exhibits are diverse and far from stereotypical—guided tours, for instance, deal with such mundane matters as disposal of human waste with the basement latrines.

When Che Guevara lived in town, his family rented a series of houses in a middle-class neighborhood. One of those residences, **Villa Nydia,** is now the **Museo Casa de Ernesto Che Guevara,** which provides an idyllic view of his boyhood with no real insight into what he eventually became. The Norton motorcycle, like "La Poderosa," the one he rode through Patagonia and Chile, is a nice touch though.

When the Guevaras lived here, the center of their social life was the **Sierras Hotel,** which has undergone a tasteful renovation and added a casino. Alta Gracia's other notable museum is the **Museo Manuel de Falla,** where the Spanish composer spent four years while in exile from the Franco dictatorship.

Villa Carlos Paz

In the Sierra Chica immediately west of the city of Córdoba, Villa Carlos Paz is the Mar del Plata of the mountains. Here hordes of beachgoers swarm the shores of **Lago San Roque,** a freshwater reservoir big enough for sailboating and windsurfing. In summer, the crowds come from Buenos Aires, but the rest of the year it's a weekend or even an afternoon destination from the provincial capital. The resort has

(continued on p. 120)

The Guevara Paradox

Before becoming a revolutionary icon in Cuba, Ernesto Guevara de la Serna was an asthmatic adolescent in Alta Gracia. He was born to an elite pedigree—the Guevaras and the de la Sernas were both prominent Argentine families—but young Ernesto's branch of the family could no longer sustain an elite lifestyle.

Because of his economic circumstances, Ernesto was as likely to socialize with working-class kids as he was with his parents' peers' children. Still, he cultivated upper-crust hobbies, such as poetry and photography. He was also an avid golfer—a sport he pursued even after the Cuban revolution's triumph.

Museo Nacional Estancia Jesuítica de Alta Gracia y Casa del Virrey Liniers

- ✉ Avenida Padre Domingo Viera 41, Alta Gracia
- ☎ 03547/421-303
- 🕐 Closed Mon., Jan. 1, May 1, & Dec. 25
- 💲 $, Wed. free

www.museoliniers .org.ar

Museo Casa de Ernesto Che Guevara

- ✉ Avellaneda 501, Alta Gracia
- ☎ 03547/428-579
- 🕐 Closed Jan. 1, Good Friday, May 1, Nov. 8, & Dec. 25
- 💲 $$$$$, Wed. free

www.altagracia.gov .ar/cultura/museo -casa-del-che.html

Sierras Hotel

- ✉ 198 Avenida Vélez Sarsfield, Alta Gracia
- ☎ 3547/431-200

www2.hojoar.com /hoteles/hotel .php?idhotel=18

Museo Manuel de Falla

- ✉ Avenida Pellegrini 1011, Alta Gracia
- ☎ 03547/429-292
- 🕐 Closed Jan. 1, Good Friday, May 1, Nov. 8, & Dec. 25
- 💲 $

www.altagracia.gov .ar/cultura/museo -manuel-de-falla .html

Drive: Sierras de Córdoba

West of the provincial capital, the Sierras have a road network that's ideal for auto touring, on both paved highways and unpaved back roads. A countryside drive takes one long day or two shorter ones, with a possible overnight at Cosquín or La Falda.

A visitor views the condors at Parque Nacional Quebrada del Condorito, Córdoba Province.

Beginning in the provincial capital city of **Córdoba ❶** (see pp. 115–116), make your way to the piedmont town of **Alta Gracia ❷** (see pp. 116–117), 22 miles (36 km) southwest by smoothly paved RP 5. Alta Gracia, of course, is Che Guevara central—his boyhood house is a museum there and the Sierras Hotel where his family hung out has even surpassed its early glory—but it's most notable for its colonial Jesuit heritage.

From Alta Gracia, another paved road leads straight north before zigzaging west for 12 miles (19 km) to the **Estación Astrofísica de Bosque Alegre ❸**, where the Universidad Nacional de Córdoba's astronomy department operates a classic 1942 telescope, recently adapted to digital technology. At 4,100 feet (1,250 m) above sea level, it's open for tours daily in summer, less often at other seasons.

NOT TO BE MISSED:

Alta Gracia • Parque Nacional Quebrada del Condorito • Cosquín • Jesús María

From the observatory, it's another 5.5 winding miles (9 km) to the junction with RN 20, which climbs 19 miles (31 km) west onto the high steppe of **Parque Nacional Quebrada del Condorito ❹** (see p. 120), the Andean condor's easternmost nesting site. After backtracking to the junction, it's another 15 miles (24 km) northeast via RN 38 to **Villa Carlos Paz ❺** (see pp. 117, 120), which draws big summer crowds to its **Lago San Roque** beaches.

North of Carlos Paz, RN 38 climbs slowly and steadily for 15.5 miles (25 km) up the Valle de Punilla to **Cosquín,** the Sierras' summer events center for January's Festival Nacional del Folklore (National Folklore Festival) and February's Cosquín Rock. At this time of the year, accommodations here and nearby fill up fast, and traffic slows to a near standstill. Immediately east of town, via a gravel road, the views from the 4,130-foot (1,260 m) **Cerro Pan de Azúcar** make a nice detour; reaching the summit requires half an hour's hike or a short chairlift ride.

Only 12 miles (19 km) north of Cosquín on RN 38, the woodsy hillside town of **La Falda** ❻ was once an elite hangout thanks to the **Hotel Edén** (*Avenida Eden 1400, tel 03548/421-080, www.edenhotellafalda.com*), which, in the first half of the 20th century, lodged both the Prince of Wales and Albert Einstein. La Falda still makes an ideal overnight stop but not at the Edén—after World War II, it fell into ruins when the Argentine government expropriated it from its second owners, who were Nazi sympathizers. Today, the hotel is partially restored and offers guided tours and some recently refurbished accommodations.

From La Falda, unpaved RP E57 switchbacks up the western slope of the Sierra Chica before dropping into the village of **Salsipuedes,** 23 miles (37 km) west, where it intersects paved RP E53. About 3.5 miles (6 km) north at the crossroads of **El Manzano,** another gravel road leads 6 miles (10 km) west to the former Jesuit estancia of **Candonga** ❼, whose simple baroque chapel sports a distinctive semicircular archway; in the words of architect Mario Buschiazzo, "It's beautiful, without trying to be."

North of El Manzano, the road leads 11 miles (17 km) to the town of **Ascochinga** to intersect eastbound RP E66 to **Jesús María** ❽, 12.5 miles (20 km) farther. Like Candonga, Jesús María was Jesuit property and is home to the **Museo Jesuítico Nacional de Jesús María**—and part of the province's World Heritage site. From here, it's a quick 31 miles (50 km) back to Córdoba city via RN 9.

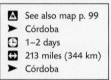

⚑ See also map p. 99
➤ Córdoba
🕐 1–2 days
↔ 213 miles (344 km)
➤ Córdoba

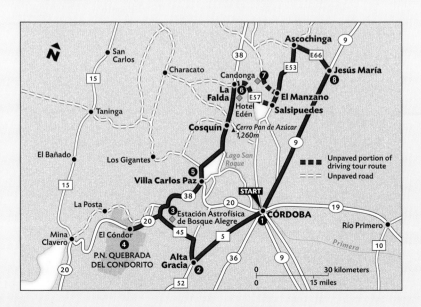

■ ■ ■ Unpaved portion of driving tour route
= = = Unpaved road

Villa Carlos Paz

 99 A3

Visitor Information

✉ Avenida San Martín 1000

☎ 03541/421-624 or 0810/888 2729

🕓 Closed May 1

www.villacarlospaz .gov.ar

Parque Nacional Quebrada del Condorito

 99 A3

✉ RN 20, Paraje La Pampilla, 34 miles (55 km) SW of Villa Carlos Paz

☎ 03541/433-371

www.condoritoapn .com.ar

an enormous hotel capacity, but much of it shuts down in winter.

There's no skiing in Carlos Paz, where the summit of **Cerro de la Cruz** reaches only about 3,100 feet (950 m) above sea level, but for more than half a century an *aerosilla* chairlift *(Florencio Sanchez s/n, $$$)* has carried Argentine families to the top for views of the city and the Altas Cumbres ("high peaks") to the west. There's also a footpath to the top but, if using it, beware the kamikaze mountain bikers who take the chairlift to the top and ride down the trail at breakneck speed. Alternatively, it's possible to rent a bike at the base station and ride down with them.

At the summit, there's a *confitería* that sells short orders and beverages, an open-air monorail snakes around the hillside, and hikers can enjoy a short nature trail with native flora and birds.

Condor Flight School

From the north side of Quebrada del Condorito, at trail's end, several *balcones* (scenic viewpoints) overlook the canyon to the Escuela de Vuelo ("flight school"), where condor chicks spend up to two years with their parents, though they can fly after six months. The view across the canyon is direct but, given the distance, binoculars are essential except when the birds soar on the thermals in search of carrion. After taking off, they rarely flap their wings.

In most areas, condors nest above 10,000 feet (3,000 m), but here and in southernmost Patagonia the nests are lower. The female lays one or two eggs every other year but, with their long adolescence, birds are frequently hurling themselves into the skies.

Parque Nacional Quebrada del Condorito

Beyond the Sierra Chica front range, the Altas Cumbres are a higher chain in an area with scattered farmsteads. On the road to San Luis Province, covering 140 square miles (364 sq km), the Parque Nacional Quebrada del Condorito marks the easternmost limit for nesting populations of the Andean condor. It enjoys easy trailhead access from the highway, which passes the highest parts of the park.

At this altitude, in a landscape of rolling hills more than 7,000 feet (2,100 m) above sea level, the predominant vegetation is bunchgrass. Toward the east, streams flow through deep ravines whose rocky sides provide ideal condor nesting sites. The park's most appealing activity is the 6-mile (10 km) hike from the highway to the V-shaped **Quebrada del Condorito,** about 2,500 feet (750 m) deep, where the birds breed on stony "balconies." Even in foggy weather, the well-signed fire road—closed to all traffic but official vehicles—is usually easy to follow. If doing this as a day trip, budget your time, as the hike starts high and drops into the canyon, which means the walk back takes longer than on the way in. There is no water beyond the new visitor center, which is barely a mile (1.6 km) in.

In addition to its signature species, the park is home to many other birds as well as guanacos, pumas, foxes, and the deadly pit viper *yarará ñata;* when wandering off trail, watch your step. ∎

Check Out Receipt

Linda Vista Library
858-573-1399
https://www.sandiego.gov/public-
library/locations/linda-vista-li

Friday, November 26, 2021 12:17:57 PM
92126

Item: 31336095880127
Title: Argentina
Call no.: 918.204/BERNHARDSON
Due: 12/27/2021

Total items: 1

Renew at www.sandiegolibrary.org or by
calling your local branch library. Your library
card number is needed to renew borrowed
items.

Mar del Plata

The interior of Buenos Aires Province may be gaucho country, but its southern coastline is Argentina's Jersey shore. In the city of Mar del Plata, beachgoers from all over the country rent shade tents for their two-week summer stays. In January and February, sunseekers are stepping over each other to find an open patch of sand. After sunset, they're lining up outside grill restaurants and, after midnight, they head to dance clubs until dawn.

A rainbow shines over Playa Bristol, Mar del Plata.

At the same time, "Mardel" (as it is known locally) is one of Argentina's cultural capitals, with a literary history that made it a "Bloomsbury of the South" thanks to publisher Victoria Ocampo and an active events calendar that includes music, theater, and film.

However, Mar del Plata is no longer an elite destination, especially since Peronist trade unions built hotels in the city center in the late 1940s. This development gives the seaside city a democratic diversity uncommon in the resorts to the north (which are more exclusive) and the south (which are more proletarian). Still, non-Argentines often prefer the spring and fall shoulder seasons, when Mardel is less frenetic and prices are more affordable.

Mar del Plata

🅜 99 C1

Visitor Information

✉ Rambla Edificio Casino local 51, Bulevar Marítimo P. Peralta Ramos 2270

☎ 0223/495-1777

www.turismomar delplata.gov.ar

Museo Municipal de Ciencias Naturales Lorenzo Scaglia

✉ Avenida Libertad 3099

☎ 0223/473-8791

🕐 Closed Tues. & holidays

💲 $, Wed. free

Water sports are the default option at **Playa Popular** (People's Beach), where a fishing pier juts into the South Atlantic and swimmers immerse themselves in the warm summer waters. (Remember though, that summer in Argentina falls in the months of January and February). A waterfront walk takes visitors along the restored **Rambla Bristol,** whose **Casino Central** is a striking brick building designed by renowned architect Alejandro Bustillo. On the plaza between the casino and its twin, the former **Hotel Provincial** (now occupied by government offices), nearly every Argentine snaps family photos at the massive statues of sea lions that symbolize the city. Slightly farther south, the beaches along the **Cabo Corrientes** headlands attract a more affluent following that indulges in the more

upmarket outdoor activities such as paragliding.

Facing Playa La Perla, just north of Playa Popular, the **Museo Municipal de Ciencias Naturales Lorenzo Scaglia** has bright display spaces with uncluttered exhibits stressing paleontology and zoology, with fossil glyptodonts and megatheriums. Contemporary species, such as the rhea, appear in environmental dioramas. Both freshwater and maritime fauna from in and around Mar del Plata inhabit its aquarium.

South of the Rambla, **Barrio Stella Maris** is a neighborhood of stuccoed chalets with red-tile roofs that's still one of the city's prime residential areas. Its most conspicuous landmark is the **Torre Tanque,** the municipal waterworks tower that rises 157 feet (48 m) from its base. Climbing the spiral staircase or taking its

Small fishing boats motor out of Mar del Plata.

elevator to the top yields the finest possible vistas of the cityscape and the South Atlantic.

Stella Maris has two key museums. On a dramatic elevated site, with Norman-style battlements and art nouveau furnishings, the century-old **Villa Ortiz Basualdo** was built as a summer home for a patrician family in

INSIDER TIP:

The most beautiful town in the whole of Argentina is the seaside Mar del Plata, preserving the finest architecture of the 19th and early 20th centuries.

—FERNANDO NOVAS
National Geographic field scientist

Mardel's golden age. It now houses the **Museo Municipal de Arte Juan Carlos Castagnino,** honoring the famous local painter. Comprising various paintings, sketches, engravings, sculpture, and photography, the collections concentrate on Argentine art, about a third of it Castagnino's.

To the south of Stella Maris, **Barrio Los Troncos** was the neighborhood where the porteño literati and high-culture icons from around the world gathered at the home of Victoria Ocampo, which is now the **Centro Cultural Victoria Ocampo.**

Founder of the literary magazine *Sur,* whose contributors were a who's who of Latin American literature, Ocampo inherited the Anglophile kit house, surrounded by 2 acres (1 ha) of gardens, from her great-aunt. After her death, it became a cultural center that's now a reminder of her achievements— and privileged lifestyle.

Less than a block away, the **Archivo Museo Histórico Municipal Don Roberto T. Barili** occupies the **Villa Mitre,** built by descendants of General and President Bartolomé Mitre. Its exhibits chronicle Mardel's urban development from the 1850s, when the city was still a somewhat provincial nondescript port for salted meat exports. Its photographs and other exhibits also show the city's transformation as it began to welcome middle- and working-class beachgoers with the rise of Peronism (and the elite began to move to the Uruguayan resort of Punta del Este).

In the city center it's easy to forget that Mardel is still a major fishing port because the **Banquina de Pescadores,** with its brightly painted boats and scavenging sea lions, is several miles to the south. Named for a local painter, the central city's **Museo del Hombre del Puerto Cleto Ciocchini** takes an interesting anthropological and historical approach to the fishing industry, and the surrounding complex is the place to order fresh fish right off the boat. ∎

Museo Municipal de Arte Juan Carlos Castagnino
- ✉ Avenida Colón 1189
- ☎ 0223/486-1636
- 🕐 Closed Tues. & holidays
- 💲 $, Wed. free

Centro Cultural Victoria Ocampo
- ✉ Matheu 1851
- ☎ 0223/492-2193
- 🕐 Closed Mon.– Tues., holidays
- 💲 $

Archivo Museo Histórico Municipal Don Roberto T. Barili
- ✉ Lamadrid 3870
- ☎ 0223/495-1200
- 🕐 Closed holidays
- 💲 $

Museo del Hombre del Puerto Cleto Ciocchini
- ✉ Centro Comercial Puerto
- ☎ 0223/489-7901
- 🕐 Closed Sun., Mon., & Wed.
- 💲 $

Around Mar del Plata

Smaller beach resorts, some of them exclusive and others less so, dot the coast north and south of Mar del Plata, but not all the attractions are along the seashore.

Excursion at Pinamar, north of Mar del Plata

Centro Cultural y Tecnológico Museo del Automovilismo Juan Manuel Fangio

✉ Dardo Rocha & Mitre, 44 miles (70 km) NW of Mar del Plata via RN 226

☎ 02266/425-540

💲 Closed Jan. 1 & Dec. 25

💲 $$$

www.museofangio.com

Balcarce

About an hour northwest of Mar del Plata, the otherwise nondescript Pampas town of Balcarce is notable as the birthplace of Formula One legend Juan Manuel Fangio (1911–1995), and home to the **Centro Cultural y Tecnológico Museo del Automovilismo Juan Manuel Fangio,** created in his memory. More than just an homage, though, it's a trip through transportation history that places Fangio into a broad context of world events. That said, the display of classic cars, on eight levels in a magnificently recycled building, is enough to sustain the interest of both generalists and specialists.

Villa Gesell

Planting a barren dunescape northeast of Mar del Plata with exotic acacias and conifers, Carlos Idaho Gesell (1891–1979) helped create a beach resort that has also become a summer center for art and music. Gesell designed a pedestrian-friendly street plan that, even today, has only one paved street. That makes it popular with cyclists, equestrians, fishermen, and windsurfers, in addition to beachgoers.

Gesell's history is accessible in the **Parque Cultural Pinar del Norte,** his own beachfront property whose original 1931 residence is now the **Museo y Archivo Histórico Municipal**

(Alameda 201 & Calle 303, tel 02255/468-624, closed Mon.–Tues. in off-season). His **Chalet de Don Carlos,** a more elaborate villa, hosts special events. The entire park is now city property.

Pinamar

Up the road from Villa Gesell, Pinamar resembles its predecessor in its irregular city plan, wooded dunes, long sandy beaches, and outdoor activities, but it's best known for its hyperactive nightlife. Architect Jorge Bunge devised a fan-shaped city plan that bewilders the unfamiliar, and its very name—a combination meaning a pine forest by the sea—suggests that Bunge followed the example of Villa Gesell. Pinamar is more exclusive and pricier than Gesell, and its greatest fame is that it's the coast's biggest party town.

INSIDER TIP:

A dammed stream 18 miles (30 km) southwest of Balcarce, in Parque Idoyaga Molina, makes a perfect summer escape.

—NICOLAS KUGLER
National Geographic contributor

Necochea

Southwest of Mar del Plata, the landscape changes from sandy dune-lined beaches to dramatic headlands with occasional gaps that offer access to the seashore. The first notable resort is **Chapadmalal,** where Juan and Eva Perón promoted "social tourism" for their trade union supporters, partly through expropriations. Passing the middle-class beach town of **Miramar,** with its casino and high-rise hotels, you arrive at the city of Necochea.

Like Villa Gesell and Pinamar, Necochea has its own greenbelt beachfront in the **Parque Miguel Lillo,** but it's a more diverse city with a Danish colony—cars with "DK" decals are a common sight.

Bahía Blanca

The last large city in Buenos Aires Province, Bahía Blanca is no beach resort, but a home port for the Argentine Navy and the coastal gateway to Patagonia. The best reason for stopping, though, is the unconventional **Museo del Puerto** *(Carrega & Guillermo Torres, tel 0291/457-3006, closed Sat.–Sun. Jan.–Feb.),* which tells Argentina's 19th-century history through the microcosm of immigrant communities and their institutions in the suburb of **Ingeniero White.**

It does so in a light-hearted manner, portraying its fishermen, stevedores, and railroad employees and their families through their bars, barbershops, clubs, kitchens, and the material culture of everyday life. When the museum is open, its café prepares plates and snacks that come not just from the main Spanish and Italian communities, but also from the Arabs, Croats, Greeks, Lithuanians, and other immigrants who populated the polyglot port. ■

Villa Gesell
🅜 99 C2
Visitor Information
✉ Camino de los Pioneros 1921
☎ 02255/458-596
www.gesell.gov.ar

Pinamar
🅜 99 C2
Visitor Information
✉ Avenida Shaw 18
☎ 02254/491-680
www.pinamar.gov.ar

Parque Idoyaga Molina
✉ RP 55, 15 miles (25 km) from Balcarce, San Agustin
☎ 0223/491-075

Necochea
🅜 99 C1
Visitor Information
✉ Avenida 2 & Avenida 79
☎ 02262/425983

Bahía Blanca
🅜 99 B1
Visitor Information
✉ Avenida Colón & Drago
☎ 0291/481-8944
🕐 Closed Sun.
www.bahiablanca .gov.ar

Jesuit missions and expansive wetlands, and the world-famous attractions of the falls of Iguazú

Mesopotamia & the Chaco

The thunderous Garganta del Diablo waterfall is the backdrop for the smaller Salto Bossetti at Parque Nacional Iguazú.

Mesopotamia & the Chaco

Between the Paraná and Uruguay Rivers, Argentine Mesopotamia encompasses the wildlife-rich provinces of Entre Ríos, Corrientes, and Misiones, where the earliest Spaniards found a welcome after the Pampas Indians drove them from Buenos Aires. The dense indigenous populations soon drew Jesuit evangelists, who named one province and explored the Chaco lowlands west of the Paraná.

Except for the world-famous Iguazú Falls—one of the continent's greatest sights—Mesopotamia and the Chaco have a low international profile, but the region deserves more attention. Throughout the area, Carnaval has undergone a revival in riverside cities like Corrientes and, especially, Gualeguaychú. The Entre Ríos littoral also has lush gallery forests, fine fishing, birds, and other wildlife, and it offers hikes through soothing palm savannas at Parque Nacional El Palmar.

Mesopotamia's most underrated sight, one that matches or even surpasses Iguazú for those who have been there and seen it, is the vast slow-moving river of floating islands known as the Esteros del Iberá. Its birds, mammals, and reptiles, easily seen and almost as easily photographed, make the Everglades of Corrientes an unforgettable experience. All it lacks is the crowds—with no international or domestic airport nearby, only dedicated wildlife-watchers make it over the rugged, but far from impassable road from the town of Mercedes.

In the rolling mountains of Misiones, where Guaraní Indians grew tubers and shifted their

NOT TO BE MISSED:

settlements from year to year, Jesuit missionaries created a state-within-a-state that also thrived in adjacent parts of Brazil and Paraguay. When their power, and the numbers they governed, threatened Spanish hegemony, they were expelled from the Americas, but they left a visible legacy. Not only were their red sandstone missions architectural masterpieces, but they trained the Guaraní to embellish them with remarkable baroque details at sites like San Ignacio Miní, the best-preserved example on Argentine soil.

Parque Nacional Iguazú & Beyond

With its spectacular waterfalls, Parque Nacional Iguazú is a UNESCO World Heritage site, and rightfully so. Its popularity, though, has made it almost impossible to enjoy the solitude of nature when the crowds descend on the paved, manicured footpaths and catwalks that provide access to the falls. In the surrounding subtropical rain forest, birds are abundant, but other wildlife is harder to observe or photograph in the dense canopy and forest floor.

Across the Paraná, in the Gran Chaco, two other distinctive wetlands get only a handful of visitors but brim with wildlife. At Parque Nacional Chaco, some 340 bird species inhabit the marshes along the slow-moving Río Negro and the scrub and hardwood forests that surround it. In Formosa Province, by contrast, the remote Parque Nacional Río Pilcomayo is an area of shallow subtropical lagoons where caimans float like logs on the placid surface, and marshes are home to countless birds and other fauna. Both bear similarities to Iberá, but the animals cannot be so easily seen and identified. ■

Entre Ríos & Corrientes

In Entre Ríos and Corrientes Provinces, low rolling hills fill the land between the Paraná and the Uruguay Rivers, while gallery forests line their shores. The Iberá wetlands, though, are the area's top natural attraction.

The sun sets over Parque Nacional El Palmar, Entre Ríos Province.

Gualeguaychú

  129 D1

Visitor Information

  Paseo del Puerto, Tiscornia & Goldaracena

  03446/422-900

www.gualeguaychu turismo.com

Gualeguaychú

With its riverside beaches, Gualeguaychú has been a popular *porteño* getaway for years, but it's famous for its Carnaval del País. At the midsummer event, the country's liveliest Carnaval celebration, accommodations are at a premium, and visiting requires plenty of advance planning. The celebration is every bit as colorful, not quite so racy, and rather more orderly than Brazilian Carnaval. Spontaneous participation is not so simple in Gualeguaychú's enclosed stadium—but the fun-loving atmosphere is infectious.

Gualeguaychú has also become famous, though, for vigorous and often ill-tempered environmental protests against the Finnish pulp mill on the Uruguayan side of the border, and for the picketers who have used the dispute to block access to the international bridge after 2006. For a time, cross-border traffic nearly ceased and, even if the occasional bus or private car got through, most public transportation and private cars were forced to use more northerly border crossings.

Despite a handful of colonial buildings, Gualeguaychú has no really notable museums, but its riverfront greenbelt makes an attractive walk. The big sight is the seasonally important **Corsódromo,** the open-air stadium along Avenida Parque where Carnaval takes place, on the site of the former railroad station. For trainspotters, the station does feature **Museo Ferroviario,** with steam locomotives and other antique stock.

Parque Nacional El Palmar

Fronting on the Río Uruguay, midway between the cities of Colón and Concordia, the park of El Palmar has no dramatic landscapes but does feature a subtly appealing savanna, cut by arroyos, where the native

park also has abundant wildlife, and not just birds—the capybara, the world's largest rodent, thrives here, along with introduced mammals such as axis deer and European boar. The latter two compete with native species, hamper the yatay's recovery by consuming its seeds, and, in the boar's case, damage bird habitat. Boar populations are being reduced, but it's a slow process.

A gravel road from the highway leads east to the riverside campground, but at roughly the midway point a southbound footpath leads through the savanna to **Mirador La Glorieta,** an overlook on the Arroyo El Palmar that has some of the park's most mature, picturesquely distributed palms (which

Museo Ferroviario
- ✉ Calle El Tala & Ayacucho, Plaza de la Estacion
- ☎ 03446/437-034
- **www.estacion gualeguaychu .blogspot.com**

Parque Nacional El Palmar
- 🄰 129 D1
- ✉ RN 14 Km 198, Ubajay
- ☎ 03447/493-053
- 🅢 $$$$
- **www.elpalmarapn .com.ar**

EXPERIENCE: Carnaval at Gualeguaychú

Every February or March, Brazilian Carnaval draws millions of tourists but, at one time, Argentina had similarly vigorous celebrations that have only recently made a comeback. Unlike those in Brazil, they're relatively small—if colorful—neighborhood affairs. The spectacle survives best in the Mesopotamian provinces, and the Entre Ríos city of Gualeguaychú is its epicenter.

In fact, Gualeguaychú's annual event goes by the name of Carnaval del País, or Carnival of the Nation (www.carnaval delpais.com.ar). Unlike those in Brazil, it takes place in the enclosed Corsódromo, seating 35,000 people, so go early for the best vantage points. Also unlike Brazilian Carnaval, it takes place weekends only—Argentina doesn't shut down for the duration.

---

yatay palm has survived grazing, farming, and wood-cutting. Along the river, forests crowd the shore, but there are sandy beaches where campers can enjoy a swim, paddle canoes and kayaks, and fish for game species like dorado and *surubí.*

Despite its proximity to one of Argentina's busiest highways, the

reach nearly 60 feet/18 m and can live upward of 200 years). This is also the place to see the flightless rhea and, possibly, the large and poisonous pit viper *yarará,* related to the fer-de-lance.

The commonest grounddweller, though, is the 8-inch (20 cm) toad that frequents the campground. Nearby, the **Paseo**

Paraná
⚑ 129 C1

Visitor Information

✉ Buenos Aires 132

☎ 0343/423-0183

🕐 Closed Jan. 1, Nov. 8, & Dec. 25

www.turismo enparana.com

Parque Nacional Pre-Delta
⚑ 129 C1

✉ 4 miles (6 km) S of Diamante; offices at 25 de Mayo 389, Diamante

☎ 0343/498-3535

www.parquenacional predelta.wordpress .com

Yapeyú
⚑ 129 C2

Visitor Information

✉ Gregoria Mattora & Sargento Cabral

☎ 03772/493-198

Arroyo Los Loros is a vehicle trail better explored on foot or bicycle to spot the abundant birds along the river: caracaras, cormorants, herons, kingfishers, and the parakeets that give the trail its name. Related to the wild chinchilla, the vizcacha burrows in and around the campground as well.

Paraná & Around

On a bluff above the east bank of its namesake river, the provincial capital of Entre Ríos is a newer twin city of Santa Fe, capital of its namesake province on the west bank. Its **Parque Urquiza,** which runs nearly a mile (1.6 km) along the flood-prone riverside, is part of a tidy, tree-shaded city with a political history. After local caudillo Justo José de Urquiza overthrew

---

Argentina's Softbol Capital

In soccer-mad Argentina, baseball is below the radar. But since 1970, when accountant Víctor Centurión and a group of friends sought a youth activity to promote, *softbol* has become a Paraná tradition. Both fast- and slow-pitch versions are popular. The midsize city has eight fields—three of them lighted—and many adults continue to play. In 1995, Paraná hosted the Pan American Games tournament, and local teams have traveled as far as New York for top competition.

General Rosas in 1852, the city was briefly Argentina's capital, and even the Túnel Subfluvial Raúl Uranga-Carlos Sylvestre Begnis, which links the city to Santa Fe beneath the main channel of the Paraná, was a challenge to Buenos Aires. After the federal government vetoed a bridge, the two provinces defiantly united to build the 1.5-mile (2.4 km) tunnel.

Paraná's heart, though, is palm-studded **Plaza 1° de Mayo,** where nearly the entire population seems to enjoy a Saturday morning walk down the nearby pedestrian mall of San Martín street. There are no colonial monuments, but the plaza's 19th-century buildings, including the **Catedral Metropolitana,** with its neoclassical facade and twin bell towers, form an appealing urban backdrop.

About an hour south of town, near the city of Diamante, **Parque Nacional Pre-Delta** is a wetlands-and-gallery-forest park, with numerous sedimentary islands, on the braided upper Paraná Delta. At the park entrance, a ranger station called **Paraje La Jaula,** you may rent launches to explore its marshes, channels, and native forests of *ceibo* (coral cockspur) and *timbó* (black ear). In the process, visitors may well come across paddling capybaras and otters, silent lurking caimans, waterfowl, and the emblematic kingfisher.

Yapeyú

Traditional Argentine history often keeps national heroes like José de San Martín under glass. That's almost literally true in the languid Corrientes village of Yapeyú, where a modern **Templete Sanmartiniano** (Gregoria Mattora & Sargento Cabral) with high ceilings and cathedral windows shelters the walls and foundations of the liberator's simple stone birthplace from rain, wind, sun, and graffiti artists.

The only truly worthwhile stop along the Río Uruguay north of El Palmar until the Misiones border,

saint. His shrine, **Santuario del Gauchito Gil**, on the outskirts of town draws hundreds of thousands of pilgrims every year, and huge crowds gather on the January 8 anniversary of his death. Roadside shrines, their red flags flying, are also a common sight.

Contemporary Corrientes gauchos, with their tilted black felt sombreros, seem to stand

Museo de la Cultura Jesuítica R. P. Guillermo Furlong

- ✉ Sargento Cabral & Obispo Romero, Yapeyú
- ☎ 03772/493-320
- 🕐 Closed Mon., Jan. 1–8, Good Friday, May 1, & Dec. 25

The River by Numbers

Sharing a continent with the mighty Amazon, the Paraná seemingly gets no respect, but it's one of the world's great unsung river systems. Statistics vary, depending on which tributary is deemed to be its source, but its length may be anywhere from 2,452 miles (3,945 km) to 3,015 miles (4,851 km).

According to the World Resources Institute, the Paraná drains a watershed of 997,248 square miles (2,582,672 sq km) in four countries—Bolivia, Brazil, Paraguay, and Argentina. At its southern end, it meets the Río Uruguay to form the

Río de la Plata, the great River Plate estuary. Within that watershed are 54 cities of more than 100,000 inhabitants—some of them, such as São Paulo, Brazil, with many more. It has 29 large dams—including Brazil's huge Itaipú on the Paraguay border—with four more planned.

Only 3 percent of the Paraná watershed is protected, but the area includes 14 wetlands that are recognized by the international Ramsar convention—including Argentina's stunning, wildlife-rich Esteros del Iberá and Parque Nacional Río Pilcomayo.

Yapeyú was a colonial Jesuit mission. Just the foundations and a few other features remain, but its open-air **Museo de la Cultura Jesuítica R. P. Guillermo Furlong** provides a photographic summary of its history. The Argentine Army's Granaderos regiment also keeps the **Museo Sanmartiniano** in town.

Mercedes

At the virtual geographic center of Corrientes Province, Mercedes is famous for the gaucho Antonio Gil, a 19th-century Robin Hood figure who has become a popular

on almost every street corner. Mercedes is also the main access point to the Esteros del Iberá, the magnificent wildlife-rich wetlands about 75 miles (120 km) to the northeast. Because of inconvenient early morning bus schedules to the Iberá village of Colonia Carlos Pellegrini, visitors without their own cars often have to sleep here.

Esteros del Iberá

In the sprawling roadless center of Corrientes Province, the fauna-rich subtropical wetlands

(continued on p. 136)

Museo Sanmartiniano

- ✉ Avenida del Libertador & Aguado, Yapeyú
- ☎ 03772/493-011

Santuario del Gauchito Gil

- ✉ RN 123, 5 miles (8 km) W of Mercedes

Saving Iberá: The Mission of Doug Tompkins

Since 1990, when he cashed out of the Esprit clothing company that he helped found in the 1970s, U.S. entrepreneur Doug Tompkins has become the most famous—infamous to some—environmental philanthropist in Latin America. A dedicated sportsman, Tompkins began his second career by buying up large tracts of native forest in northern Chilean Patagonia and consolidating them into a de facto national park.

U.S. conservationist Doug Tompkins

Protection of the coniferous *alerce*, false larch, also present on the Argentine side of the border, was one of the key reasons for creating Parque Pumalín. Despite official and extra-official opposition—both left and right expressed suspicion of a foreigner acquiring so much land in a border area, and the Catholic Church objected to his "deep ecology" beliefs that humans are just one of many species in the natural environment—Tompkins managed to turn his lands into a legal nature sanctuary. At the same time, he opened the area to the public

for hiking, camping, and other low-impact activities. Meanwhile, he turned his attention toward Argentina.

One acquisition was Estancia Monte León, a 153,000-acre (62,000 ha) ranch in the Patagonian province of Santa Cruz, where 70,000 pairs of Magellanic penguins nest every year along more than 25 miles (40 km) of shoreline. Guanacos and rheas sprint across the steppe. Through his Conservation Land Trust, with cooperation from the Fundación Vida Silvestre Argentina (Argentine Wildlife Foundation), Tompkins donated all but 740 acres (300 ha) to Argentina's federal government, creating the country's second coastal national park—with the support of the late President Néstor Kirchner, despite his skepticism of foreigners and their investments. (The remaining acreage belongs to Hostería Monte León, owned by Conservación Patagónica—Patagonia Land Trust.)

Esteros del Iberá

The real gem of Tompkins's acquisitions, though, was the endangered wetlands around the Esteros del Iberá, part of which was already a provincial reserve. Tompkins now spends the mild southern winter at his Estancia Rincón del Socorro here, and summers in Chile, at Pumalín, and at Valle Chacabuco in more southerly Patagonia.

Less well known than Brazil's huge freshwater Pantanal, which these wetlands resemble in many ways, Iberá is threatened by overgrazing, massive hydroelectric projects, deforestation, the construction of drainage embankments for rice cultivation and plantations of exotic trees, and other environmental problems.

Despite Tompkins's successes in Chile and Argentine Patagonia, Iberá has been a tougher nut to crack. Certain projects have met with success: The preliminary reintroduction of the giant anteater could, if the species recovers sufficiently, help reduce the alarming explosion of anthills in areas overgrazed by domestic livestock. Tompkins has also cleared non-native eucalyptus woods in hopes of restoring the area's natural vegetation.

Opposition

Meanwhile, Tompkins has run up against political opposition from both ends of the spectrum. On the one hand, the influential Forestal Andina timber company is responsible for allegedly illegal earthworks that have desiccated parts of the marshes, and the provincial government of Corrientes has been slow to move against them despite protests taken to Buenos Aires. At the other extreme, the xenophobic agitator Luis D'Elía, while a Néstor Kirchner administration minister, once encouraged local peasants to cut down Tompkins's fences and argued for expropriation of his land.

While other Corrientes landowners may have distrusted Tompkins's environmental evangelism, they closed ranks behind him when faced with a takeover that could have spread to their own properties. At the same time Kirchner, who appreciated the establishment of Monte León as a national park in his home province, quickly distanced himself from D'Elía's questionable tactics, and in short order D'Elía lost his post. The irony, of course, is that Tompkins's plans, including a national park on the Monte León model, would return much of the land to the Argentine state.

Caiman, Esteros del Iberá, Corrientes Province

Reserva Natural Iberá

✉ RP 40, access to Colonia Carlos Pellegrini

☎ 03773/154-59110

www.coloniapellegrini.gov.ar

Parque Nacional Mburucuyá

Ⓜ 129 C2

✉ RP 86, 7 miles (12 km) E of Mburucuyá

☎ 03782/498-907

www.parques nacionales.gov.ar

Corrientes

Ⓜ 129 C2

Visitor Information

✉ 25 de Mayo 1330

☎ 0379/442-7200

🕔 Closed Sat.–Sun. & holidays

Museo Histórico de la Provincia de Corrientes

✉ 9 de Julio 1044

☎ 0379/447-5946

🕔 Closed Sun.–Mon. & holidays

of **Reserva Natural Iberá** are a dazzling natural treasure that, covering more than 5,000 square miles (13,000 sq km), is one of Argentina's largest protected areas. Long before Europeans saw this slow-moving river, with its shallow lagoons and "floating islands" tenuously anchored to the river bottom, the Guaraní appreciated how dazzling it was. The Spanish word *iberá*, a compound adapted from their native idiom, means "bright water."

INSIDER TIP:

To see capybaras, boas, yacarés, and hundreds of birds, take the boat at Reserva Natural Iberá in Corrientes Province. In the evening stroll along the monkey's path.

—SERGIO VIZCAINO
National Geographic field scientist

About 75 miles (120 km) northeast of Mercedes by a rocky, sometimes muddy road, the village of **Colonia Pellegrini** is the main access point to **Laguna Iberá**, a broad stretch of calm open water crossed, at an isthmus, by an army-style Bailey bridge. Covering an area of more than 13,000 acres (5,200 ha), the lake is the starting point for outboard-driven skiff excursions into the *embalsados*, the floating islands that harbor most of the park's wildlife. When the guides reach the embalsados, they have to cut the motor and pole

through them at a turtle's pace.

The quantities and diversity of Iberá's wildlife are overwhelming. Outside the visitor center, on the west side of the bridge, packs of placid capybaras munch on lush grasses and, on occasion, flightless rheas may even sprint past. Opposite the visitor center, the **Sendero de los Monos** is a self-guided nature trail loop where, in all likelihood, hikers will see howler monkeys in the dense gallery forest.

Easily seen from the skiffs, the semiaquatic capybaras also swim between the islands, where marsh deer sink almost to their shoulders in the muddy soils before pulling themselves free with a loud sucking sound. In a few relatively dry spots, passengers can even go ashore, but they need to watch their steps to avoid sinking into knee-deep mud. Caimans can float like rotting logs on the water's surface, but they also sun themselves on the embalsados. Only about 6 feet (1.8 m) long, they're not a menace to humans, but provoking them is still unwise.

Despite the thin peaty soils on these islands, fairly large trees like the ceibo still manage to flourish. They also give habitat and shelter to upward of 300 different bird species, including the turkey-size crested screamer, cocoi heron and other herons, storks, cormorants, kingfishers, owls, and smaller birds such as hummingbirds and swallows.

Most of the excursions take place in early morning or around sunset, when the wildlife is most active, but some of the wildlife is nocturnal. With luck, for instance, moonlight tours might spot the rare maned wolf.

On the south side of the marshes, Colonia Pellegrini makes an ideal starting point because of exceptional accommodations in all price ranges. There are limited options for eating outside hotels and guesthouses, but it is possible for nonguests to eat at most of them with advance notice.

While Colonia Pellegrini is the main access point to the reserve, the north side of the marshes can boast of **Parque Nacional Mburucuyá**, a smaller protected area with lesser infrastructure. Much of the same wildlife is present here as at Pellegrini.

Corrientes & Around

Near the confluence of the Paraná and Paraguay Rivers, the provincial capital of Corrientes takes its name from the river's swirling currents. Settled by Spaniards who moved south from Asunción, it's a slightly ragged subtropical city with just enough Guaraní heritage and colonial character to offer some insight into Mesopotamian life. Its Carnaval Correntino, second only to Gualeguaychú's in Argentina (see sidebar p. 131), approaches the euphoria of Brazilian-style Carnaval celebrations.

The city's most appealing feature, ideal for a long sunset walk, is the **Costanera General San Martín**, with its broad riverside promenade, massive shade trees, and small zoo with regional species. At the west end, the **Puente General Belgrano** is a suspension bridge over the river that leads to the Chaco provincial capital of Resistencia. Near its east end, at

San Juan street, **Paseo Italia** honors Italian immigrants, but its more interesting sight is the **Gran Mural**, with a colorful representation of the province's Guaraní heritage.

The most notable colonial remnant is the 17th-century **Convento de San Francisco**, with an ecclesiastical art museum in the early stages of restoration. The **Museo Histórico de la Provincia de Corrientes**, in a colonial-style 20th-century building, has a well-arranged collection of colonial religious art and current materials.

The Paraná is renowned for its game fish, and the nearby town of **Paso de la Patria** is a mecca for fishermen seeking the legendary dorado (see sidebar below). Paso de la Patria, in fact, hosts mid-August's **Fiesta Nacional del Dorado** to promote sportfishing of the "tiger of the Paraná." ■

Paso de la Patria

✉ Avenida Santa Coloma & Dorado

☎ 0379/449-4556

www.posadapaso patria.com.ar

FISHING LICENSES & GUIDES: Licenses are available through **Provincial Direccíon de Recursos Naturales** (*Av. Costanera Gen. San Martín 99, Corrientes, tel 0379/423-1245*). There are other offices in smaller towns, including Paso de la Patria, where you'll also find fishing guides at **Posada Paso de la Patria**.

EXPERIENCE: Fighting the Dorado

A big river breeds big fish, and the dorado—so called for its golden color—is the meanest and toughest of the bunch. More than 3 feet (1 m) long and weighing upward of 40 pounds (18 kg), with powerful jaws, this aggressive predator hunts the omnivorous *boga* in fast currents around dusk. A powerful jumper with sharp teeth, *Salminus maxillosus* is the river's prime game fish. The season runs mid-January to mid-October, but the fishing is best in the summer months, January to March.

By consensus, the best place to fish for dorado is the town of **Paso de la Patria**, near the provincial capital of Corrientes. All types of techniques, from fly-fishing to trolling, are possible. Licenses are obligatory, but they are easy to obtain.

Misiones

Misiones, with its rolling mountains, Jesuit ruins, powerful rivers, and the incomparable Iguazú Falls, has the highest international profile of any Mesopotamian province. Although its Guaraní heritage is apparent, it's also known for its European immigrant communities, including Italians, Germans, Poles, and Ukrainians.

Misión San Ignacio is the best preserved of Argentina's colonial Jesuit missions.

Province of Misiones

🗺 129 C3/D3

Visitor Information

✉ Colón 1985, Posadas

☎ 0376/444-7539

www.turismo
.misiones.gov.ar

Museo Ferrobarco Ezequiel Ramos Mexía

✉ Puerto de Posadas

Posadas & Around

On a bluff above the Paraná, the Misiones provincial capital is a sweltering subtropical city with an increasingly attractive redeveloped riverfront, a border crossing to Paraguay via an international bridge, and a gateway to the Jesuit missions on both sides of the river. In the central city, a nearly unbroken canopy of street trees compensates for the mostly unremarkable architecture.

As late as 1990, before the suspension bridge crossed the Paraná, travel to Paraguay involved ferrying across the river by train, on a boat that could carry four passenger carriages to link up with a locomotive that would continue to Asunción. Trains as well as motor vehicles cross the new bridge, and the former ferry terminal is now the **Museo Ferrobarco Ezequiel Ramos Mexía,** showcasing the Scottish-built vessel that started service in 1913. The museum also serves as a cultural center, with special events.

Along the redeveloped riverfront, part of Parque República del Paraguay, the **Museo Regional Aníbal Cambas** holds ethnographic materials on the Guaraní, Jesuit carvings and other relics, and exhibits on Misiones's immigrant communities.

About an hour west of Posadas, near the town of Ituzaingó, the **Central Hidroeléctrica Yacyretá** is a colossal Paraná dam project that provides about 15 percent of Argentine electricity. A joint undertaking with Paraguay, it has driven about 40,000 people, mostly Paraguayans, out of their riverside homes, and it has raised water levels in the Esteros del Iberá. Its visitor center museum, though, has an impressive assortment of pre-Columbian artifacts unearthed during the dam's construction.

San Ignacio Miní & Around

In the 17th century, the Jesuit Order founded a series of more than 30 missions in present-day Argentina, Brazil, and Paraguay.

In the process, the Jesuits taught their charges to be highly skilled carvers, bookbinders, and even luthiers, as well as farmers and herders. Throughout the upper Paraná, their red sandstone structures created an architectural style known as Guaraní baroque, with elaborate sculptured details that, in some cases, have withstood nearly 400 years of weathering and invasive plants.

Unfortunately for the Jesuits, their success brought their downfall. In both Portuguese and Spanish America, other colonists—especially Brazilian *bandeirantes* (slavers)—resented the Jesuits' near monopoly of indigenous labor. After the Spanish crown started to view the Jesuits as a state-within-a-state, it expelled them from

Museo Regional Aníbal Cambas

- ⊠ Parque República del Paraguay, Alberdi 600
- ☎ 0376/442-2860
- 🕐 Closed Sun. & holidays
- 💲 $, Wed. free

www.museocambas .blogspot.com

Central Hidroeléctrica Yacyretá

- 🅰 129 C3

Visitor Information

- ⊠ Avenida Ing. Roque Carranza & Entre Ríos, Barrio General Belgrano, Ituzaingó
- ☎ 03786/421-543
- 🕐 No tours Jan. 1 & Dec. 24, 25, & 31. Passport needed.

www.eby.org.ar

The Paraguayan Missions

San Ignacio Miní is the best preserved of Argentina's Jesuit missions, but anyone impressed with Roland Joffé's 1986 movie *The Mission* should consider crossing the Paraná from Posadas to view the Paraguayan missions of Trinidad and Jesús. Late additions to the Jesuit empire—Trinidad was finished in 1760 and Jesús was unfinished when Carlos III expelled the order from the Americas—they both occupy scenic hilltop sites that were also defensible against Brazilian slave raiders. Hiring a taxi in the Paraguayan city of Encarnación is the easiest way to see them—but not before getting a visa at Posadas's Paraguayan consulate (*San Lorenzo 179, tel 0376/442-3858, weekday mornings only*).

In the process of evangelizing the Guaraní Indians in what the Spaniards euphemistically called *reducciones*—a word whose English equivalent, "reductions," doesn't quite communicate the exploitation it sometimes implies in Spanish—the Jesuits created outposts of high culture on the South American frontier.

the Americas in 1767. When they left, the Guaraní abandoned the missions, and the fast-growing subtropical forests reclaimed them.

Of the remaining Argentine missions, the UNESCO World Heritage site of San Ignacio Miní is the gem. Nearly demolished by Paraguayan dictator Gaspar Rodríguez de Francia in 1817, it

Ruinas de San Ignacio Miní, Centro de Interpretación

🗺 129 C3

✉ Alberdi bet. Rivadavia & Bolívar

☎ 0376/447-0186

💲 $$$$

was rediscovered 80 years later and restored in the 1940s. Before entering the grounds, everybody passes through the **Centro de Interpretación,** a museum that tries to place the Jesuit efforts in context. In a neocolonial building, with a red-tile roof, its collections show artifacts such as stringed instruments crafted by the Guaraní and an explanatory model of the original mission.

The Argentine Hemingway

Horacio Quiroga (1878–1937) may not have fought in World War I or reported on the Spanish Civil War, but the Argentine writer of supernatural short stories had a Hemingwayesque taste for the wild—and for firearms. Quiroga went first to Paris but later moved to the province of Misiones and helped uncover the mission of San Ignacio Miní. Quiroga remained in San Ignacio—his house is now a museum—but his first wife committed suicide, as did Quiroga himself and two of his children— another sad parallel with Ernest Hemingway.

On leaving the museum, visitors emerge onto the grassy **Plaza de Armas,** surrounded on three sides by the foundations of the Guaraní quarters—which once housed 4,000 of them. The most impressive landmark, though, is the **Iglesia de San Ignacio Miní,** the red sandstone church with an 80-foot-wide (24 m) facade so detailed that its survival, despite almost two centuries of neglect, is a tribute to the skills of the Guaraní craftsmen who executed Italian architect Juan Brasanelli's design.

Flanked by the cemetery and cloisters, the decorations on its graceful arches and columns include figures of angels, doves, and local flora. The floors are a jigsaw puzzle of handsome flagstones but, unavoidably, wooden scaffolding supports the precarious walls. Other structures include the original workshops and even the jail.

San Ignacio may be the best preserved of the Argentine Jesuit missions, but it's not the only one in the vicinity. At **Misión de Nuestra Señora de Loreto,** about 6 miles (10 km) west of San Ignacio and 2 miles (3 km) east of the highway, visitors can get an idea of what San Ignacio might have looked like long before its restoration. Still covered by secondary forest, much of the site is only understandable through explanatory plaques.

About 10 miles (16 km) south of San Ignacio and only half a mile (almost a kilometer) south of the highway, two-by-four scaffolding supports the crumbling brick walls at **Misión Santa Ana.** It's possible to discern the church, the Guaraní residences, the workshops, and the cemetery—which, reused and then abandoned in the 20th century, looks more like a set for a 1930s Hollywood horror movie. Both Loreto and Santa Ana have been slated for restoration, but progress on the work has been slow.

Puerto Iguazú & Around

Where the Paraná and Iguazú Rivers converge, and the borders of Argentina, Brazil, and Paraguay are within sight of each other, Puerto Iguazú is the downstream portal to **Parque Nacional Iguazú** and its celebrated cataracts. Smaller and friendlier than the fast-paced Brazilian city of Foz do Iguaçu, it's the most convenient service center for visiting both sides of the falls.

Placid Puerto Iguazú has no knockout sights in its own right, but within those limits its lush subtropical townscape and asymmetrical plan give it a genuine appeal. Its symbolic center is the triangular **Plaza San Martín,** whose adobe **Casa del Pionero** *(Santa Maria 890)* is a small-town museum with such limited resources that it tells local history through family photos donated by townspeople. Across the avenue, a series of bas-relief murals on a recently created plaza deal with themes of environment, ethnohistory, and the European invasion.

At the west end of Avenida Tres Fronteras, overlooking the confluence of the two rivers, **Hito Argentino** is one of three markers indicating the Argentine, Brazilian, and Paraguayan borders. The catamaran *Victoria Austral* occasionally cruises the river to the point where the borders actually intersect. (It's worth adding that the so-called Triple Border is infamous for smuggling and corruption of all sorts; the Argentine side is generally considered the safest place to stay.)

The nearby national park is known for its diverse birdlife but, in its lushly landscaped grounds right in town, the **Jardín de los Picaflores** purports to have all 17 of the hummingbird species found in the province—just sitting here suffices to see them. On the eastern

Puerto Iguazú
🅰 129 C3
Visitor Information
✉ Avenida Victoria Aguirre 311
☎ 03757/423-951
www.iguazuturismo .gov.ar

Jardín de los Picaflores
✉ Fray Luis Beltrán 150
☎ 03757/424-081
🕐 Closed Sun.
$ $$

From the air or from the ground, Iguazú Falls are among Argentina's greatest sights.

La Aripuca

✉ RN 12 Km 4.5

☎ 03757/423-488

💲 $$$$$

www.aripuca.com.ar

Parque Nacional do Iguaçu

✉ Rodovia BR 469 KM 18 Foz do Iguaçu, Paraná Brazil

☎ 55 (45) 3521-4400

💲 $$$$$

www.cataratas doiguacu.com.br

outskirts of town, **La Aripuca** is an ethnological museum and forest conservation project whose name derives from the game traps used by the Guaraní.

Iguazú Falls are a binational attraction, and Puerto Iguazú is the place to arrange a day trip to Brazil's **Parque Nacional do Iguaçu.** The falls are the same, of course, but the perspective is different—most people think the views are better on the Brazilian side, but there are far fewer activities other than the trail from the hotel to the overlook. The

The catwalk to Garganta del Diablo, Parque Nacional Iguazú

Usina Hidrelétrica Itaipú

✉ 7 miles (12 km) from Foz do Iguaçu

☎ 0800/645-4645 (from Brazil)

www.itaipu.gov.br

other drawback is that several nationalities, including U.S. citizens, need advance visas to cross the bridge over the Río Iguazú. Puerto Iguazú's Brazilian consulate can provide same-day service, but it's better (and cheaper) to do this in your home country.

Also on the Brazilian side, the **Usina Hidrelétrica Itaipú,** a massive hydroelectric project that

submerged the even more voluminous Sete Quedas falls in 1982, is open for public tours. For those seeking yet another passport stamp, it's possible to continue through Brazil to the Paraguayan city of **Ciudad del Este,** a grubby commercial town with a vigorous street life, and return to Argentina before nightfall. Paraguay also requires visas for U.S. citizens and some others, however.

While it's a little more distant than the national park, **Yacutinga Lodge** *(www.yacutinga.com)* on the upper Río Iguazú is a private wildlife reserve of about 1,400 acres (570 ha) with a biological research station. Only a tiny fraction of the property constitutes the lodge's accommodations, while the rest consists of several nature trails through dense subtropical forest, including an elevated walkway through the forest canopy. Yacutinga picks up its clients in Puerto Iguazú and shuttles them to the lodge via a little-visited provincial park.

Parque Nacional Iguazú

Along with Buenos Aires and the Moreno Glacier, the Iguazú Falls are one of Argentina's big three attractions, but the national park that surrounds some of the world's most magnificent cascades also encompasses more than 260 square miles (670 sq km) of subtropical rain forest. With 2,000 species of vascular plants, it teems with birds and other wildlife—anteaters, jaguars, tapirs, and ocelots—that most visitors never see. For its awesome landscapes and its biodiversity, the park has been a UNESCO World Heritage site since 1984.

EXPERIENCE: Iguazú, Without the Crowds

No one can deny that the powerful cascades of Iguazú are one of South America's most dramatic sights. It's also undeniable that their accessibility makes the most popular sights claustrophobically overcrowded at times. Getting to the platform railing to see the falls can be like fighting your way out of a crowded subway car.

Going early in the morning is certainly one option, saving the later hours for exploring areas like the Sendero Macuco, the little-used subtropical rain forest trail. Another option—not mutually exclusive—is contracting to take a moonlight tour

(tel 03757/491-469, www.iguazuargentina .com). This requires timing, as they take place only on the five nights surrounding the full moon, but the smaller groups—only about 50 people—are more leisurely. You'll amble at a relaxed pace, with the guide pointing out such natural phenomena as fragrant, night-blooming flowers. Guides are park rangers, as opposed to the concessionaire's contract personnel, used during the day.

Probably the best part: When you reach the Garganta del Diablo, there's plenty of room to gape over the railing at Iguazú's most impressive cascade.

INSIDER TIP:

Look for tiny elements to photograph amid the chaos and magnitude of Iguazú Falls, such as mist dripping from leaves.

—JASON EDWARDS
National Geographic photographer

Still, there's no denying that the falls, especially the torrents that plunge over the basalt amphitheater known as the **Garganta del Diablo**—"devil's throat"—are the center of attention. About 100 million years ago, a series of Cretaceous lava flows cooled to create a step formation that, its weaknesses exploited by rushing water, became a series of perhaps 275 falls that stretches more than a mile and a half (2.7 km) from Argentina into Brazil. Other statistics tell more of the story: Iguazú is more than twice the width, and at 269 feet (82 m)

nearly twice the height, of Niagara. At roughly 60,000 cubic feet (1,700 cubic m) per second, its average volume is lower than Niagara's, but its maximum volume of 450,000 cubic feet (12,740 cubic m) per second is at least 50 percent greater than Niagara's.

Numbers, of course, tell almost nothing about Iguazú's stunning visual impact. Suffice it to say that, for better or worse, films as diverse as the historical epic *The Mission* and the action potboiler *Indiana Jones and the Kingdom of the Crystal Skull* all exploited the falls' stunning scenery. Only *The Mission* did so in context, as the falls helped director Roland Joffé's tale of the colonial Jesuits and their Guaraní converts win an Oscar for cinematography.

In reality, the park's entrance may be a disappointment to anyone expecting forested wilderness, as it more closely resembles a commercial cluster with restaurants, souvenir shops, tour operators,

Parque Nacional Iguazú

🗺 129 C3/D3

Visitor Information

✉ 11 miles (17 km) SE of Puerto Iguazú via RN 12 & RN 101

☎ 03757/491-444

💲 $$$$$

www.parques nacionales.gov.ar

www.iguazu argentina.com

and, after the mid-morning tour buses arrive, crowds to rival those at Niagara. The Argentine park service's **Centro de Visitantes Yvyrá Retá** has organized a systematic introduction *(Spanish only)* to the park's ecology, ethnology, and history that few visitors bother to appreciate before heading lockstep to the falls.

Chamamé: The Argentine Polka

The Tex-Mex borderlands have conjunto, and Argentine Mesopotamia has *chamamé.* Just as Germans settled in Texas, adapting to Mexican traditions, a polyglot population of immigrants came to Misiones to blend their accordion-based music with indigenous subtropical rhythms to create a new sound that's gaining prominence in the world music era.

Contemporary chamamé's highest-profile figure is Chango Spasiuk (1968–), the grandson of Ukrainian immigrants, who has made the accordion hip enough to headline Buenos Aires rock clubs such as La Trastienda. He has also toured Europe and the United States.

It's possible to walk to the falls, but most visitors take the **Tren Ecológico de la Selva,** a short-line, narrow-gauge, open-sided tourist train. From the commercial area, it carries passengers to **Estación Cataratas** for overviews of the falls and **Estación Garganta del Diablo** for close-ups of the park's most famous cascades.

From Estación Cataratas

Near Estación Cataratas, the **Circuito Superior** is an easy half-hour walk on a partial loop through dense forest on paved paths and catwalks, some of which cross watercourses. With no climbing whatsoever, it's even wheelchair-friendly as it passes the falls of Salto Bossetti, Salto Guardaparque Bernabé Méndez, and Salto Mbiguá. Around this area, the only conspicuous wildlife is the common coatimundi, a raccoon relative that's too tame for its own good.

That circuit is a good introduction to the park, but the longer **Circuito Inferior** descends to river level; en route, it gets up close and personal with several falls, such as Álvar Núñez and Lanusse, that range from 130 to nearly 200 feet (40–60 m) in height. At river level, a free launch shuttles hikers across the river to **Isla San Martín** for the only straight-on view of the Garganta del Diablo. The Circuito Inferior is a loop that returns to Estación Cataratas and, in the hot humid weather so typical of this climate, the steep walk back up can be tiring even though it's shady.

From Estación Garganta del Diablo

As the Río Iguazú flows deceptively slowly before plunging over the Garganta del Diablo's horseshoe falls, it's hard to envision its strength at flood. In the 16th century, Alvar Núñez Cabeza de Vaca (the first European to see the falls) wrote that "the current of the Yguazú was so strong that the canoes were carried furiously down the river." Judiciously, his party decided on a difficult portage to avoid plummeting to their deaths.

Built of metal grates with handrails on both sides, the new, sturdy catwalks—also wheelchair-accessible—take hikers from Estación Garganta del Diablo to a larger overlook that often fills with tourists. The spray from the falls is so great that it sometimes blocks the view entirely, and sightseers get a soaking that can leave them shivering. When the mist clears, though, the close-up views make it all worthwhile, even if humans can only imagine the perspective of the ashy-tailed swifts that nest behind these inexorable sheets of falling water.

Beyond the Falls

If the Garganta del Diablo and other falls are overrun with tourists, the trails through the forest are a different matter. Even the short **Sendero Verde,** a paving-stone path that passes a bird-rich marsh en route from the commercial sector to Estación Cataratas, is far less peopled than any of the busy waterfalls trails.

For solitary hikers, the **Sendero Macuco** is an easy 4.5-mile (7 km) round-trip from the commercial sector through the rain forest to the **Salto Arrechea,** a 70-foot (23 m) waterfall that's a miniature by Iguazú standards. This is the most easily accessible fauna-rich forest area, but its drawback is that, because of the dense multilevel forest, wildlife such as capuchin monkeys and toucans can be more audible than visible. Still, the forest, with its flowering *lapachos* (trumpet trees), *guapoys* (strangler figs), and orchids, has its own appeal.

Visiting more remote parts of the park or undertaking specialist activities, such as early morning bird-watching via 4WD vehicle, requires hiring an operator at the park entrance. The most sedentary of these activities is the private boat excursion from the Circuito Inferior that goes to the base of the Garganta del Diablo. **The Sendero Yacaratiá** is a 5-mile (8 km) vehicle safari road, open only to park concessionaires, that focuses on wildlife viewing, including the rarely seen jaguar and monkeys.

More active alternatives include 2.5 miles (4 km) of Class III white-water rafting below the falls, rappelling into the canyon of the Iguazú, and mountain biking on trails through the selva. ■

TOURING THE FALLS:
For eco- and adventure tours of Iguazú Falls, outfitters include **Iguazú Jungle** *(tel 03757/421-696, www.iguazujungl explorer.com)* and **Explorador Expediciones** *(Perito Moreno 217, tel 03757/491-469, www.rainforest evt.com.ar).*

A toucan in Parque Nacional Iguazú

The Chaco

West of the Paraná River, the Gran Chaco is a vast subtropical lowland that rises slightly, and gets drier and hotter, toward the west. A paved road leads across the country to the northwestern Andean provinces, but the Chaco also extends north into Paraguay and Bolivia.

Marshes in the humid Chaco

Resistencia

While it dates from the founding of a Jesuit mission in 1750, Resistencia is a more contemporary twin city of Corrientes that, surprisingly, has a remarkable fine arts tradition. Originally a port for woodcutters, who extracted tannin from surrounding thorn forests, it became a jumping-off point for agricultural colonization of a region where soy and sunflowers are royalty. It's also known as the Ciudad de las Esculturas (City of Sculptures) or the Museo de Aire Libre (Open Air Museum) for the stone and wooden statuary that seems to stand on almost every corner.

The greatest abundance of these outdoor sculptures, which number about 500, is at the **Museo de las Esculturas Urbanas del Mundo (MUSEUM),** where they are displayed in a public park and in a small building dedicated to temporary exhibitions. In July of even-numbered years, the park fills with chain saw sculptors in the competitive Bienal Internacional de Escultura, where the artists have a week to fashion a finished product from marble or hardwood.

But for more than half a century, the heart of the city's arts community has been the downtown bar/restaurant/cultural center known as **El Fogón de los**

Arrieros. In a country of pompous equestrian statues, what other place would erect a sidewalk monument, covered in tiles, to a street mongrel known as Fernando, who, "wandering the streets of the city, aroused beautiful sentiments in an infinity of hearts"? The center's facade, covered with whimsical sculptures, murals, and random objets d'art, literally invites any traveler to enter with the motto "walk right in, don't bother knocking." The informality continues with tango or accordion-based *chamamé* (see sidebar p. 144) or just a drink at the bar. The art includes works by some of Argentina's best known artists, including Libero Badíí, Carlos Páez Vilaró, Raúl Soldi, and others.

INSIDER TIP:

For a good taste of a northern estancia, visit Las Curiosas *(tel 03732/417-932)*, 120 miles (200 km) from Resistencia, which offers not only ranch activities but exotic animals.

—ELISEO MICIU
National Geographic photographer

The Chaco was, and still is, home to substantial indigenous Mocoví, Toba, and Wichí populations. The **Museo Provincial del Hombre Chaqueño Profesor Ertivio Acosta** tells their story through well-organized maps and artifacts including pottery and weavings in its Sector Indígena. Sector Criollo and Inmigración Europea cover the contributions of European immigrants, with exhibits such as early agricultural implements that helped turn a territory of hunter-gatherers into farmland. What the museum doesn't really cover is the conflict between those first peoples and the immigrants.

Parque Nacional Chaco

In the humid lowlands, only an hour-plus drive northwest of Resistencia, Parque Nacional Chaco is a small but diverse reserve where reed-lined wetlands alternate with forests of subtropical hardwoods. In this low-relief landscape, gallery forests line the slow-moving Río Negro, but where the river has changed course it has left soggy marshes—some so soggy that the only way to travel through them is on horseback. In summer, it's a steam bath with clouds of mosquitoes, but at other seasons it's an ideal day trip from the provincial capital or a detour for trans-Chaco travelers.

Only the northeastern quadrant of the park's 58 square miles (150 sq km) is easily accessible, but it's enough to see plenty of the 300-plus bird species plus reptiles such as the caiman and, with luck, mammals such as the collared peccary and the howler monkey. Daybreak and sunset are the best times for wildlife viewing.

At the campground, a mile-long (1.6 km) loop trail provides an introduction to the forest, but the best site for seeing wildlife is at the end of a road so narrow

Chaco
128–129 B2
Visitor Information
Avenida Sarmiento 1675
0362/443-8880
Closed Sat.–Sun.
www.chaco.travel

Museo de las Esculturas Urbanas del Mundo (MUSEUM)
Parque 2 de Febrero, Avenida de los Inmigrantes 1001, Resistencia
0362/441-5020

El Fogón de los Arrieros
Brown 350, Resistencia
0362/442-6418
Closed Sun. & holidays
$

Museo Provincial del Hombre Chaqueño Profesor Ertivio Acosta
Juan B. Justo 280, Resistencia
0362/445-3005
Closed Sun.–Mon. & holidays
www.museodel hombrechaco.com.ar

Parque Nacional Chaco
129 B2
69 miles (110 km) W of Resistencia via RN 16 & RP 9 to Capitán Solari
03725/499-161
www.parques nacionales.gov.ar

Presidencia Roque Sáenz Peña

▲ 129 B2

Visitor Information

✉ San Martín & Brown

☎ 0364/443-0030

💲 $ for access to Complejo Termal

Complejo Termal

✉ Almirante Brown 545

☎ 0364/442-9590

Complejo Ecológico Municipal

✉ RN 95 Km 1111

☎ 0364/442-9660

💲 $

and densely wooded that there's almost nowhere to turn around if a vehicle appears from the other direction (which, however, is rare). The road takes you to a short trail leading to the elevated platform at **Laguna Carpincho,** a good place to spot birds and capybaras foraging at water's edge. A little farther by car on the same route, **Laguna Yacaré** has a similar overlook; truly alert visitors might spot the Chaco side-necked turtle.

In the park's more open areas, where *caranday* and *pindó* palms predominate, it's possible to sight sprinting rheas. Open in dry weather only, a 7.5-mile (12 km) southbound road from the campground passes through quebracho (axe-breaker) forest to the **Laguna Panza de Cabra,** another prime wetland.

Presidencia Roque Sáenz Peña & Around

The "cotton capital" of Sáenz Peña is not quite on the road to nowhere, but it's a stop

---

World's Largest Fish?

Easily identifiable as the world's largest rodents, capybaras measure 4 feet long (1.2 m), 1.5 feet tall (0.5 m), and weigh 100 pounds (45 kg). In the 16th century the Vatican officially classified the water-browsing mammals as fish. Since then the capybaras have been a pious, non-meat option for parts of South America.

INSIDER TIP:

Don't miss a visit to Campo del Cielo, a crater field caused by the impact of at least 22 meteorites thousands of years ago.

—ROGELIO DANIEL ACEVEDO
National Geographic field scientist

along the long, arrow-straight Trans-Chaco Highway, possibly Argentina's loneliest paved road, to the northwestern Andean provinces. It does have two notable attractions: a municipal hot springs complex and a surprisingly good zoo that specializes in native regional fauna.

At the north end of town, the resurrected **Complejo Termal** offers not only saunas and soaks in its hot mineral baths, but also inexpensive massages and physical therapy by qualified professionals. By international standards, it's pretty plain, but an outstanding value for what you get.

South of the highway, the **Complejo Ecológico Municipal** is the place to see rare mammals such as giant anteaters, maned wolves, and tapirs, in enclosures that approximate their natural environments—the capybaras, for instance, can immerse themselves in artificial ponds that attract migratory birds for wintering over. Its 50-acre (20 ha) botanical garden mimics the native Chaco forests and harbors small reptiles, birds, and mammals.

Northwest of Sáenz Peña, it's a long drive on the Trans-Chaco to the province of Salta, gateway to the Andean northwest. En route, the most unpropitious place-name in all of Argentina must belong to the town of **Pampa del Infierno,** (Hell's Flats), but the truck stop of **Taco Pozo** has one of Argentina's best roadside restaurants for a lunch break.

namesake national park resembles Parque Nacional Chaco but is three times its size. Its premier sight is **Laguna Blanca,** nearly 2,000 acres (800 ha) of still, shallow waters where capybaras feed, caimans lurk on the surface, and boas slink through the water.

Sendero a la Laguna Blanca is a short nature trail that traverses

Parque Nacional Río Pilcomayo

 129 B3

✉ 28 miles (45 km) NW of Clorinda via RN 86

☎ 03718/470-045 in Laguna Blanca

www.parques nacionales.gov.ar

Among Parque Nacional Chaco's flora hide woodpeckers, *ñandúes,* foxes, viscachas, and capybaras.

Two hours southwest of Sáenz Peña, the **Campo del Cielo** (field of the sky) is one of the world's biggest meteorite fields, dating from some 4,000 years ago.

Parque Nacional Río Pilcomayo

Perhaps the least visited of all Argentina's provinces, Formosa shares a long border with Paraguay along the Río Paraguay and the Río Pilcomayo, whose

a marsh via catwalks to arrive at the lagoon, where a series of piers extend into the water for easy wildlife viewing beneath a thatched open-sided shelter. In addition to the common capybaras, the marshland is home to ground-nesting birds. Extensive palm savannas and gallery forests are present in other parts of the park, most notably along the road that goes to the interior via the **Estero Poí** marshes. ∎

Campo del Cielo

🅰 129 B2

✉ Gran Chaco Gualamba

www.meteorite market.com/CCinfo .htm

Desert canyons, indigenous culture, and wine to quench your thirst at the end of the day

The Andean Northwest

Desert landscapes around Seclantás in the Río Calchaquí Valley

The Andean Northwest

For travelers who see Argentina as Buenos Aires, Iguazú, and the glaciers of Patagonia, the Andean northwest is a real eye-opener. With its polychrome desert canyons, pre-Columbian ruins, indigenous Andean peoples, and conspicuous colonial heritage, this region delivers on all fronts. With the bonus of one of the world's most underrated wine regions, the northwest alone is worth an extended trip to Argentina.

NOT TO BE MISSED:

In the lush Lerma Valley, surrounded by mountains, Salta is a destination in itself for its colonial churches, museums, and a nightlife district that's smaller but just as lively as parts of Palermo Viejo. Its centrality also makes it an ideal base for day trips and longer tours into the altiplano, the wine country of Cafayate, and the Andean history route of the Quebrada de Humahuaca.

On the easternmost Andean foothills beyond Salta, the *yungas* are a discontinuous longitudinal strip of cloud forest that's best visited in winter, when the roads are drier, at Parque Nacional El Rey. To the west, the Andes rise steeply to the arid altiplano, where the Kolla herd llamas and the famous Tren a las Nubes hauls passengers on one of the world's highest rail routes.

To the north, designated a UNESCO World Heritage site in 2003, the Quebrada de Humahuaca has an increasingly high international profile. The gateway city of San Salvador de Jujuy is nondescript, but it's not far up the steep-sided canyon to the sandy colonial streets of Purmamarca, beneath the vivid red chevrons of the surrounding hills. Farther up, the picturesque village of Tilcara is an artists' colony with four fine museums and a pre-Columbian fortress whose panoramic views are no longer the realm of Tilcara defenders. In the northern heights, where the nights are colder, the town of Humahuaca is still Kolla country, but the area's real revelation is a detour to the end-of-the-road hamlet of Iruya—with its cobbled streets and stone terraces, it might well have been airlifted intact from highland Peru.

South of Salta, the road to Cafayate is the starting point for one of Argentina's finest drives or cycling circuits, north through the Calchaquíes valleys and down the vertiginous zigzags of the Quebrada de Escoipe. When the road is too much, there's often a winery for a sample of the fruity white Torrontés, the signature grape grown at altitudes that, in some parts of the world, would have snow half the year.

Tucumán Province

Argentina's smallest province, Tucumán, is the cradle of Argentine independence, site of a scenic hill station in Tafí del Valle, and home to a sprawling art museum that takes indigenous themes into the 21st century.

Only a short distance away, the mountain-side ruins of Quilmes are a reminder that the indigenous past, displaced by more recent Spanish influence, is still a presence in this part of the country.

Travelers should note that north-western Argentina has a wet summer climate that can bring flash floods, making some areas, such as narrow desert canyons, impassable. ■

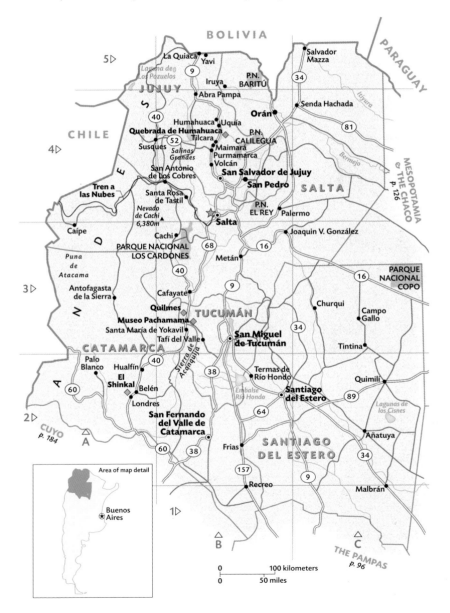

Salta

In a subtropical valley encircled by verdant mountains, Salta la Linda ("Salta the Beautiful") is a city to match its setting. In colonial times, it supplied food to the bonanza silver mine at Potosí, in present-day Bolivia, and forage for the mules that hauled the produce there. After independence, it began to look toward the south, especially after the railroad arrived from Buenos Aires, but even today Salta seems a city where the past is still a presence.

The brightly painted Iglesia San Francisco is one of Salta's most eye-catching landmarks.

Salta
🅰 153 B4
Visitor Information
✉ Caseros 711
☎ 0387/437-3340
or
0800/777-0300
**www.saltalalinda
.gov.ar**

**Catedral Basílica
de Salta**
✉ España 558
☎ 0387/431-8206
www.catedralsalta.org

Plaza 9 de Julio & Around

Salta's center is the colonial Plaza 9 de Julio, a subtropical palm garden with a circular band shell and central monument—the standard equestrian statue—to Juan Antonio Álvarez de Arenales. On the north side, its rococo facade flanked by twin clock towers, the 19th-century **Catedral Basílica de Salta** holds the tomb of provincial caudillo Martín Miguel de Güemes (1785–1821), whose gaucho followers waged

an effective guerrilla campaign against the Spaniards during the wars of independence. In the postindependence aftermath of intrigues and rivalries, Güemes lost his own life.

Several nearby buildings are late colonial structures, such as the **Cabildo Histórico de Salta** (Caseros 549), a two-story building whose double porticos extend the length of the south side of the plaza to provide shade and shelter. Part of it is now the

Museo Histórico del Norte, which traces provincial history from pre-Columbian times until the early 20th century. Arranged in chronological order, in well-lighted cases, its indigenous artifacts include the usual pottery but also finely carved and polished stone sculptures. The second story, dedicated to colonial history, is strong on religious art, with items like an elaborately carved Jesuit pulpit and 18th-century Peruvian paintings, plus a fine coin collection. Another exhibition room details the city's architectural evolution, including features salvaged from buildings since demolished, while yet another deals with historical figures from postindependence times. An interior patio contains an assortment of carriages and other transportation technology.

At the east end of the plaza, the **Museo de Arte Contemporáneo (MAC)** is a modern art museum that occupies a 19th-century Italianate building. It has permanent collections by lesser known Argentine painters and sculptors and frequently changing exhibitions of paintings, photographs, sculptures, and engravings.

The plaza's most cutting-edge museum, though, is the **Museo de Arqueología de Alta Montaña (MAAM),** where crampons, ice axes, and down-filled sleeping bags are among the tools of high Andean archaeology. With their help, in 1999, anthropologists recovered the mummies of three children (an adolescent girl, a seven-year-old boy, and a six-year-old girl) ceremonially sacrificed by the Inca on Llullaillaco, a 22,111-foot (6,739 m) summit along the Chilean border (see sidebar below). (A similar mummy, found on a peak near Cafayate in the 1920s, is also on exhibition here in a badly deteriorated state.) The museum has been utterly renovated to permit rotating exhibition of the recently recovered mummies, under tightly controlled temperatures, humidity, and atmospheric pressure.

Museo Histórico del Norte
- Cabildo Histórico de Salta, Caseros 541
- 0387/421-5340
- Closed Mon.
- $
- www.museonor.gov.ar

Museo de Arte Contemporáneo (MAC)
- Zuviría 90
- 0387/437-0498
- Closed Mon. & last working day each month
- $
- www.macsaltamuseo.org

Museo de Arqueología de Alta Montaña (MAAM)
- Mitre 77
- 0387/437-0592
- Closed Mon. & Dec. 31–Jan. 2
- $$$$, Wed. free
- www.maam.gob.ar

The Llullaillaco Sacrifices

The discovery of youthful mummies on high Andean peaks has always been an indicator of the religious significance of high places. Recent research on Salta's Llullaillaco mummies, though, suggests that the political imperatives of the lords of Cuzco had at least as much to do with the sacrifice of young children and adolescents in northern Argentina as did religion.

The Inca ruled an empire, and a relatively recent one—dating from the mid-15th century—when they expanded into the high Andes of what is now Argentina and Chile. According to archaeologist Timothy Taylor, of the University of Bradford, the three mummies found atop Llullaillaco in 1999 were not Inca royalty, but rather were chosen from among conquered peoples.

Having lived on peasant food for most of their lives, the sacrificial youths were placed on a year's special diet of maize and dried jerky to fatten them up, then drugged with maize beer and coca before being abandoned to die from exposure on the 22,111-foot (6,739 m) summit. This act, the research suggests, helped intimidate local peoples into collaborating with the invading Inca.

Museo Provincial de Bellas Artes–Casa de Arias Rengel

✉ Florida 20
☎ 0387/421-4714
🕒 Closed Sun. & holidays

Museo de la Ciudad–Casa de Hernández

✉ Florida 97
☎ 0387/437-3352
🕒 Closed Sun. & holidays

www.museociudad salta.gov.ar

Museo Presidente José Evaristo Uriburu

✉ Caseros 417
☎ 0387/421-8174
🕒 Closed Sun.–Mon. & holidays
💲 $

www.museonor .gov.ar

The museum places the discovery of the mummies in the context of pre-Columbian cosmology, which venerated high summits as holy places. Stylized interior murals communicate the structure of Inca society, and display cases exhibit its material culture (ceramics, gold figurines of humans and llamas, and especially textiles). Projected onto the walls, video footage of the expedition gives the sensation of being there. In special exhibits, curators have even re-created the journey that took the children to their mountaintop crypt.

Beyond the Plaza

One block west, the **Museo Provincial de Bellas Artes** fills one room of the upper floor of the 18th-century **Casa de Arias Rengel** with colonial religious art, most notably from the time when European and indigenous traditions began to blend in the so-called "Cuzco school." The 19th-century collections are a more secular version of the colonial styles, but the three rooms dedicated to contemporary *salteño* art break that mold. The downstairs salons, some of whose walls are more than 7 feet (2 m) thick in this earthquake-prone city, host temporary exhibits of local, Argentine, and foreign artists.

Half a block south, the **Museo de la Ciudad** occupies the 18th-century **Casa de Hernández,** an adobe with a corner balcony and spacious interior patio; elaborate grillwork adorns its staircases and second story. Its most memorable exhibit is painter Lorenzo Gigli's

oil of a heroic Güemes leading his gaucho troops into battle. Separate rooms deal with more commonplace matters, such as the city's architectural evolution, furniture, and photography.

INSIDER TIP:

Traditional *salteños* young and old head to *peñas,* or folk music clubs, where waiters serve mounds of beef on wooden platters and locals break into song and guitar-playing.

—MICHAEL LUONGO
National Geographic writer

Only a block east of the plaza, under the administration of the Museo Histórico del Norte, the **Museo Presidente José Evaristo Uriburu** is an 18th-century adobe with multiple patios, a tiled roof, and a wrought-iron streetside balcony. It takes its name from a later owner, José Evaristo Uriburu (1831–1914), who served as Argentina's president from 1895 to 1898. Its collections deal more with traditions of the 18th and 19th centuries, and it includes portraits painted by Frenchman Amadeo Gras in the 1840s.

Just across the street, the late colonial **Iglesia de San Francisco** is one of Salta's signature buildings for its flashy baroque facade, four-story bell tower (a 19th-century addition), and, not least, its attention-grabbing burnt red and gold paint job. Probably Salta's most photographed building, the church has an equally extravagant interior with marble columns, ceiling frescoes surrounding a central dome, and intricately painted walls. Three blocks east, the 16th-century **Convento de San Bernardo** presents a more sober image in its simple cobblestone plaza and whitewashed adobe walls: Its finely carved *algarrobo* (carob tree) doors are not open to the public.

Two blocks south of the convent, wooded **Parque San Martín** is central Salta's biggest open space, with lush landscaping surrounding an artificial lake and fountains. Leaving from its eastern edge, the **Complejo Teleférico Salta** hosts a cable gondola that climbs to the summit of San Bernardo, more than 800 feet (250 m) above its base station, for panoramic views of the bowl in which the city lies. From the summit, a trail switchbacks downslope to the **Monumento al General Martín Miguel de Güemes,** a boulder-strewn shrine symbolizing the Andes, at whose base the caudillo's gaucho guerrillas await their leader's order.

Some ten blocks north of Plaza 9 de Julio, the crumbling sheds and rusting railcars of the former **Estación del Ferrocarril General Belgrano** are a haven for trainspotters. In winter, it's the departure point for the **Tren a las Nubes** (see sidebar p. 166), the tourist train that climbs the Andean foothills to the high, dramatic La Polvorilla viaduct before returning to town in the evening.

Immediately south of the station, **Balcarce** street is the

heartbeat of Salta's nightlife, a miniature Palermo Viejo, with restaurants, bars, and live music locales side by side by side for several blocks. On weekends the sidewalks fill with revelers almost until daybreak.

In this neighborhood, an ethnographic museum might seem out of place but, one block west, the private **Museo de Arte Étnico Americano–Pajcha** complements the MAAM with its extensive collections of Andean ceramics, textiles, and other artifacts. Its cultural café displays traveling exhibits beyond its own collections, and it also hosts a regular calendar of lectures and workshops. ∎

Complejo Teleférico Salta

✉ Avenida San Martín & Hipólito Yrigoyen

☎ 0387/431-0641

$ $$$$

Museo de Arte Étnico Americano–Pajcha

✉ 20 de Febrero 831

☎ 0387/422-9417

🕐 Closed Sun. & Dec. 22–Jan. 5

$ $$

www.museopajcha salta.com.ar

Complejo Teleférico Salta

Wines of the Northwest

For its Andean altitudes and subtropical latitudes, northwestern Argentina is one of the world's most distinctive wine regions. Salta and La Rioja Provinces are the primary producers, famous particularly for their dry white varietals.

Laborers haul the harvest from the vineyard to the vats at Bodega Lavaque, Cafayate.

In a high desert, with warm days, cool nights, and sandy, sometimes rocky soils, the signature varietal is the dry but fruity white Torrontés. Argentina is, in fact, the only country that produces Torrontés in commercial quantities; the closest analogues would be Albariño and Viognier, grown in Spain and France, respectively, which are similarly dry and aromatic.

In fact, there are three varieties of Argentine Torrontés: the Mendocino, the Sanjuanino, and the Riojano, each associated with its respective province. The grapes of the first may be a rather different varietal; the latter two are closely related, but Salta Province produces most of the best. Origins of the Torrontés grape are unclear; recent DNA research suggests that it's a hybrid between the Mission wine grapes of Galicia and the Muscat of Alexandria, and missionaries may have brought it to Argentina. Historically, though, there appear to be links to the Malvasia group from Greece via the Portuguese island of Madeira.

Thanks to the combination of dry climate, with 300 sunny days per annum and low latitude, the northwest enjoys a long

INSIDER TIP:

For a unique experience, visit the small vineyard of Bodega José L. Mounier–Finca Las Nubes *(tel 03868/422-129, www.bodegamounier.com),* near Cafayate, in late March. You can participate in the harvest celebration; call ahead for the date.

—SUSAN RIGGS
National Geographic contributor

growing season. With only about 4 to 7 inches (100–200 mm) of rain per annum, snowmelt from the area's streams and groundwater from its aquifers are essential for successful cultivation. In the northwest the grapes grow at high altitudes, often upward of 5,280 feet (1,600 m). Mendoza vineyards are at lower altitudes; some Mendoza wineries, though, acquire their grapes from vineyards in the northwest.

Flood irrigation still exists, especially using the traditional *parral* system with widely spaced vines and dense leaf coverage. High evaporation, though, means that drip systems are increasingly important for efficient water usage. The climate can be an advantage: Since pests do not proliferate as they might in, say, France, growers can limit their use of pesticides and fungicides. Many northwestern vineyards are tacitly, if not officially, organic.

Northwest Varietals

After the grape known as Pedro Giménez or Ximénez, Torrontés is Argentina's second-most widely planted white-wine grape, though only a small percentage of that is found in the northwest (even if it's the best). While Torrontés is the northwest's signature grape, Malbec also occupies a major niche, and there are smaller acreages of reds including Cabernet Sauvignon, Syrah, and Tannat.

Even though the northwest produces only about 4 percent of Argentine wines in total—compared with Mendoza's 80 percent—it occupies an important niche.

Along with Salta, La Rioja produces fine Torrontés near the town of Chilecito, and ex-president Carlos Menem has his own winery at his Anillaco birthplace. Producers in Tucumán's Amaicha del Valle—a pebble's toss from Cafayate—and in Jujuy's Quebrada de Humahuaca have recently brought their wines into the marketplace.

With its aromas and citric taste, Torrontés matches well with seafood and Asian specialties. In Chile and Peru, where small quantities are grown as "Torrontel," the grape is used to produce the potent brandy, *pisco.* The most creative use of Argentine wine, though, is in the Salta town of Cafayate, where one shop makes ice cream—sorbet, really—from Torrontés and Cabernet Sauvignon.

Torrontés: aromatic, smooth, and moderately acidic

Around Salta

Salta the city has plenty to see and do, but its hinterland offers a diversity of lush cloud forests, red desert canyons, high wine country, and an even higher scenic steppe as you travel toward the border with Chile.

The red-rock canyons of the Quebrada de las Conchas, in Salta Province

Parque Nacional El Rey

🅼 153 B4

✉ 121 miles (195 km) from Salta via RN 9 E, RN 34 S, RP 5 E, & RP 20 N

✉ Offices: España 366 3rd floor, Salta

☎ 0387/431-2683

www.parques nacionales.gov.ar

Parque Nacional El Rey

On the eastern edge of the Andes, bordering the Gran Chaco, the yungas are a narrow, interrupted belt of cloud forest that extends through Jujuy, Salta, and Tucumán Provinces. Once an estancia, but declared a national park in 1948, the park's woodlands have recovered from the days when the ranch produced beef and timber for regional and national markets.

East of Salta, 121 miles (195 km) away as you drive but probably half that far as the crow flies, El Rey has only a basic campground, but it provides a variety of nature trails in an area that's ideal for bird-watchers in particular. The longest of them is the 15-mile (24 km) round-trip on the **Senda Pozo Verde**, the first 2 miles (3 km) of which are drivable, but then it's footpath-only to a circular lake with forest so dense that it's hard to walk the shoreline. The toucan is its symbol, but this dense woodland also hides rare mammals such as peccaries and tapirs.

In the wet summer, the main road into the park is impassable without a four-wheel-drive vehicle and can be tricky with it. Contracting a tour in Salta is advisable to anyone unsure of his or her driving skills.

INSIDER TIP:

Stop for goat cheese between Salta and Cafayate. There are several good places, including La Posta de las Cabras, between Talapampa and Alemania.

—KATHY BELL
National Geographic contributor

Parque Nacional Calilegua

Larger and higher than El Rey, and only about 105 miles (169 km) northeast of Salta by good paved roads, the Serranía de Calilegua is lush canyon country. It's filled with short hiking trails along its shallow watercourses and atop the **Mesada de las Colmenas,** a high plateau where the forest gives way to open grassland. Its highest point, **Cerro Amarillo,** reaches 11,963 feet (3,646 m) above sea level, but most of the park is far lower. Even so, it's rugged terrain where the dense forest

holds pumas and even the endangered jaguar.

Like Parque Nacional El Rey, Calilegua has limited infrastructure—camping only within the park boundaries—but there are accommodations near the park headquarters at the town of Calilegua. The road through the park, controversially used by logging trucks, is more transitworthy than the road into El Rey.

Cafayate

In southernmost Salta Province, near the Tucumán line, the town of Cafayate is the best base for sampling Argentina's number two—but by no means inferior—wine region. It's also convenient to the red-rock landforms of the nearby **Quebrada de las Conchas** and the desert canyons of the **Valles Calchaquíes** and the pre-Columbian ruins of **Quilmes** (see pp. 180–181), just across the provincial border.

On the south bank of the Río Chuscha, nearly 5,280 feet (1,600 m) above sea level, Cafayate is a low-rise town with an orderly grid centered on **Plaza 20 de Febrero,** which is surrounded by restaurants and handicrafts outlets, with most accommodations on nearby blocks. On weekends, when the town can fill with visitors from Salta, accommodations can be at a premium.

In addition to its wineries (see pp. 162–163), Cafayate has the notable **Museo Arqueológico Rodolfo Bravo,** containing a good collection

La Posta de las Cabras

✉ RN 68, Km 88 Camino a Cafayate, Valles Calchaquíes, Salta

☎ 387/499-1093

www.lapostade lascabras.com.ar

Parque Nacional Calilegua

🅰 153 B4

✉ 105 miles (169 km) from Salta via RN 9 E, RN 34 N, & RP 83 W

✉ Offices: San Lorenzo, Calilegua

☎ 03886/422-046

www.parques nacionales.gov.ar

Cafayate

🅰 153 B3

Visitor Information

✉ Plaza 20 de Febrero, Avenida General Güemes Sur & San Martín

☎ 03868/422-442

Museo Arqueológico Rodolfo Bravo

✉ Colón 191, Cafayate

☎ 03868/421-054

🕒 Closed Sun. & holidays

Bodega Domingo Hermanos

✉ Nuestra Señora del Rosario & 25 de Mayo

☎ 03868/421-225

🕐 Closed Sun. & holidays

www.domingo
hermanos.com

of artifacts from pre-Columbian hunter-gatherers and agricultural-ists. The legacy of scholar Rodolfo Bravo, it also covers colonial and postcolonial weapons and is par-ticularly strong on gaucho horse gear, but its antiquated presenta-tion detracts from the quality of its materials.

Cafayate's Wineries: With its warm days and cool nights,

Cafayate is home to several win-eries that specialize in the fruity white Torrontés—in fact, local ice creameries even make sorbet flavored with Torrontés and Cabernet Sauvignon. Nearly all of those wineries are within easy walking distance of the main plaza, and most of the rest are a short bike or taxi ride away. The town even has a winery museum, the **Museo de la Vid y el Vino** (Museum of Vine and Wine; *Avenida General Güemes Sur & Chacabuco*).

You could start the day at **Bodega Domingo Hermanos,** a modern midsize winery only three blocks south of the plaza, though its vineyards are scattered around the region. Portions of its own goat cheese complement samples of Malbec, Torrontés, and Cabernet Sauvignon, its only varietals, though it blends Merlot and Tannat with its Malbec.

A short hike south of town, **Bodegas Etchart** is Cafayate's big-name industrial winery, and its Torrontés Etchart Cafayate is one of Argentina's great wine bargains—a full bottle costs less than a glass of average white wine at most restaurants. Having undergone a modernization in the 1990s, with stainless-steel tanks in lieu of wooden barrels, it produces a wider range of varietals—Pinot Noir is a novelty here—than the area's smaller wineries.

At **Bodega José L. Mounier–Finca Las Nubes,** a boutique winery 3 miles (5 km) southwest of town, the entire harvest takes barely a day—but with good timing, travelers can participate

A weaver at the loom in the Valles Calchaquíes

El Poncho Salteño

Traveling around Salta Province, you're sure to spot the traditional *poncho salteño*—a blanket-like cloak of vibrant red, trimmed with black bands and bows. Woven with wool from sheep, vicuña, llama, guanaco, or alpaca, they've been worn for generations. There is, however, more to them than meets the eye. The black trimmings—modifications to the original red poncho—pay tribute to two *salteños*. The bands, added in the early 16th century, memorialize Inca Emperor Atahualpa, killed by invading Spaniards. And the black bows honor Gen. Martín Miguel de Güemes, who died fighting the Spaniards in the 19th-century War of Independence.

You may also note the strong resemblance between the poncho and Salta's official flag—indeed, Güemes's troops were gaucho soldiers who often wore the emblematic poncho. Today's flag represents those who died protecting the region.

INSIDER TIP:

If you are a *Star Wars* fan, then you must see the landscape between Cafayate and Angastaco. Some scenes of the desert planet Tatooine were filmed here. It definitely looks like another planet.

—SUSAN RIGGS
National Geographic contributor

in the picking and enjoy lunch, dinner, and a party. Unusually for this area, it makes a rosé in addition to the usual varietals.

Only four blocks north of the plaza, **Vasija Secreta–Antigua Bodega La Banda** is a historic winery—its adobe cellars are also a museum—whose production more closely resembles Etchart than it does small wineries like Las Nubes. About 5 miles (8 km) northwest of town, nearly 6,800 feet (2,070 m) above sea level, the French-Argentine **Bodega**

San Pedro de Yacochuya is another small winery, with fewer than 40 acres (16 ha) of vines. Malbec/Cabernet blends and Torrontés are the featured varietals.

Cachi

Along with Cafayate, the village of Cachi makes the best break on the long loop from Salta through the Valles Calchaquíes and back, but the real reason for stopping here is the colonial charm of the town's cobbled streets and squat houses. At the foot of the **Nevado de Cachi,** a 20,933-foot (6,380 m) behemoth of a mountain, its oblong **Plaza 9 de Julio** is the center of local life, with most institutions and services on or around it.

Where the ornamented churches of Salta may overawe worshippers, Cachi's 18th-century **Iglesia de San José** soothes them with the simplicity of its austere adobe facade and the native *cardón* cactus timber so prominently used in its interior. The village also has a surprisingly

(continued on p. 166)

Bodegas Etchart
- ✉ RN 40
- ☎ 03868/421-310
- 🕐 Closed Sun. & holidays

www.bodegasetchart.com

Bodega José L. Mounier–Finca Las Nubes
- ✉ El Divisadero
- ☎ 03868/422-129
- 🕐 Closed Sun. except Holy Week & July
- 💲 $$

www.bodegamounier.com

Vasija Secreta– Antigua Bodega La Banda
- ✉ RN 40 & RP 68
- ☎ 03868/421-850

www.vasijasecreta.com

Bodega San Pedro de Yacochuya
- ✉ 5 miles (8 km) NW of Cafayate
- ☎ 03868/15-570-6798
- 🕐 Closed Sun. & holidays

www.sanpedrode yacochuya.com.ar

The Salta-Cafayate-Cachi Loop

Red-rock canyons, shifting dunes, verdant vineyards, colonial churches, and *cardón* cactuses are highlights of this multiday loop that starts and ends in Salta. It needs at least three days, preferably more, and is also suitable for mountain bikers in good condition—with at least two or three more days.

From the city of **Salta ❶** (see pp. 154–157), southbound RN 68 skirts **Embalse Cabra Corral ❷,** a reservoir whose eastward-flowing Río Juramento outlet is a year-round detour for adventurous white-water rafters and kayakers.

About 60 miles (100 km) south of Salta, the smooth paved road begins to climb through the **Quebrada de las Conchas ❸** (also known as the Quebrada de Cafay-ate), where the Río de las Conchas and its ephemeral tributaries have created a

NOT TO BE MISSED:

Quebrada de las Conchas
• Cafayate • Molinos • Cachi

canyon-country landscape that recalls Utah's Bryce Canyon in its variety of hoodoo landforms such as **El Sapo** ("the toad") and **Los Castillos** ("the castles"). With no services along the route, though, it's a good idea to bring empanadas, snacks, and water from Salta and enjoy a picnic while exploring sites like **Garganta del Diablo** ("devil's throat") and **El Anfiteatro** ("the amphitheater").

Just before arriving at the town of Cafayate, the highway passes through the dunefields of **Los Médanos.** About 118 miles (189 km) south of Salta, **Cafayate ❹** (see pp. 161–163) is wine country. With its warm and welcoming colonial ambience, outstanding accommodations, and choice of restaurants, the town is the ideal place to break the journey overnight before continuing north up the Río Calchaquí Valley toward Cachi.

Before heading to Cachi, it's well worth considering a detour to the pre-Columbian fortress of **Quilmes** *(RN 40 just N of RP 357; see pp. 180–181),* 34 miles (54 km) south across the Tucumán line. The morning hours, when sun hits the hillside, are ideal for photog-raphy and cool enough for hiking through the cactus-studded ruins.

From Cafayate, northbound RN 40—the country's longest highway (see sidebar p. 270), from the Bolivian border to southernmost Patagonia—is paved only to the village of **San Carlos ❺,** 14 miles (23 km) away.

El Anfiteatro, Quebrada de las Conchas

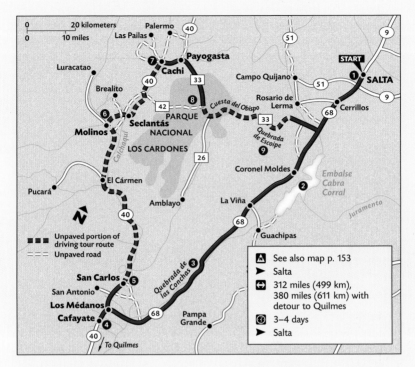

See also map p. 153

From there, it becomes a narrow, dusty road that weaves through and over dramatically folded sedimentary strata, occasionally emerging onto alluvial flats whose greenery contrasts dramatically with the monochrome hills.

Another 55 miles (88 km) north, the village of **Molinos** ⑥ is home to the 18th-century **Iglesia de San Pedro Nolasco de los Molinos**, a colonial residence that has been turned into a hotel, and the excellent **Casa de Entre Ríos** crafts market on its outskirts, a great place to puchase authentic Argentine gifts.

Cachi & Beyond

Continuing north, RN 40 passes the picturesque hamlet of **Seclantás** before arriving at **Cachi** ⑦ (see pp. 163 & 166), 29 miles (46 km) from Molinos; for those not staying at Molinos, Cachi has the best overnight services before Salta. Dominated by the summits of the snow-topped **Nevado de Cachi,**

its low-slung adobes sometimes dwarfed by cardón cactuses, the town's attractions include the 18th-century **Iglesia de San José** and the **Museo Arqueológico Pío Pablo Díaz.**

Paved for 7 miles (11 km) north to the village of Payogasta, RN 40 intercepts paved RP 33, an arrow-straight road that climbs to **Parque Nacional Los Cardones** ⑧, home to the saguaro-like cactus that dots the landscape at altitudes upwards of 11,000 feet (3,400 m). The pavement ends about 5.5 miles (9 km) into the park and the road peaks at 10,985 feet (3,348 m) at the **Cuesta del Obispo** before descending an awesomely steep, zigzag route where, in summer, low clouds and drizzle can obscure the view for days on end. When the weather clears, though, the **Quebrada de Escoipe** ⑨, dropping from high desert into subtropical woodlands, is one of the most spectacular descents in the country—and the best argument for cyclists to do the route clockwise.

Cachi

A 153 B3

Visitor Information

✉ Avenida General Güemes, Cachi

☎ 03868/491-902

www.cachi.todo websalta.com.ar

Museo Arqueológico Pío Pablo Díaz

✉ Pasaje Juan Calchaquí, Cachi

☎ 03868/422-1343

$ Donation

San Antonio de Los Cobres

A 153 B4

good archaeological museum in its **Museo Arqueológico Pío Pablo Díaz.** While it lacks the diversity of Cafayate's museum, it compensates with superior organization and better commentary *(Spanish only)* about the upper Calchaquí Valley's cultural evolution from hunter-gatherer times to the colonial period.

San Antonio de Los Cobres & Around

In colonial times and well into the 20th century, cattle drovers from Salta ascended the steep, deep canyon of the **Quebrada del Toro** en route to Chile's Atacama Desert, a rich mining area so arid that it could never produce enough food to support its hard-working labor force. When U.S. geographer Isaiah Bowman explored the high borderlands in the early

20th century, San Antonio de Los Cobres was the only town above 10,000 feet (3,000 m) whose population exceeded 500. It was the last breather before tackling bitterly cold, oxygen-thin trans-Andean passes that had claimed human and animal lives ever since the first Spanish expedition in the 16th century.

Today the town, which takes its name from the copper mined nearby, is a lunch stop for bus tours that climb the canyon past pre-Inca ruins at **Santa Rosa de Tastil** and sometimes loop to the **Salinas Grandes** salt flats before returning to Salta via the Quebrada de Humahuaca. The big attraction, though, is the rail line (see sidebar below) that parallels the road and still reaches the border, though tourists can only go as far as **La Polvorilla** viaduct. ∎

EXPERIENCE: Train to the Clouds

When the Transandino del Norte first pulled out of Salta's Estación del Ferrocarril General Belgrano in 1948, passengers were an afterthought on a line intended to carry food and freight to Chile's Atacama Desert mines. The journey averaged barely 9 miles (14 km) per hour on the 360-mile (901 km) route to the Chilean Pacific port of Antofagasta, with a change of trains at the frigid border post of Socompa—12,684 feet (3,866 m) above sea level.

Today, train enthusiasts can once again climb the Quebrada del Toro in comfort on the tourist-oriented Tren a las Nubes, the Train to the Clouds *(Ameghino & Balcarce, Salta, tel 0387/422-3033, www.trenalasnubes.com.ar, closed Dec.–March, $$$$).*

En route from **Salta,** the train zigzags and spirals twice, through terrain too rugged to tackle head-on, to reach **San Antonio de los Cobres.** Finally, before reversing direction, the train rolls onto the dramatic **Viaducto La Polvorilla,** which spans a 735-foot (224 m) gap, 207 feet (63 m) above the barren puna.

It's arguably misnamed—the altiplano's big skies are usually cloudless—but the trip can still take your breath away. If that's literally the case at nearly 14,000 feet (more than 4,200 m), the train carries oxygen for anyone who falters in the thin air. Fortunately, freed from the need to carry freight, the new train averages 22 miles (35 km) per hour on a trip that still lasts from daybreak to midnight.

Quebrada de Humahuaca & Around

Well before it became a UNESCO World Heritage site in 2003, the Quebrada de Humahuaca ("Humahuaca gorge") was one of the sights most worth seeing in the Andean northwest. A journey up this canyon of the Río Grande and its tributaries is a trip through geological time, from pre-Columbian cultures to their modern-day counterparts.

Sedimentary chevrons cover the hillsides at Maimará, in the Quebrada de Humahuaca.

San Salvador de Jujuy

The capital of the province of Jujuy, San Salvador de Jujuy is the gateway to the Quebrada de Humahuaca, but only traces of its colonial past remain on and around its central **Plaza General Manuel Belgrano.** The most notable building there is the 18th-century **Iglesia Catedral** *(Belgrano 556),* famous for its burnished baroque gilt pulpit and for the Cuzco school paintings in the nave and sacristy.

Two blocks west, the **Museo Histórico Provincial Juan Galo Lavalle** is a true historical site. During the struggle between Rosas' federalists and Lavalle's unitarists, Lavalle died here when a Montonero bullet penetrated the original wooden door—a copy is displayed separately—in the 1841 equivalent of a drive-by shooting. As a museum, it covers revolutionary Gen. Manuel Belgrano's dramatic evacuation of the city to avoid its falling under royalist

Province of Jujuy

🅰 153 A5/B5

Visitor Information

✉ Gorriti 295

☎ 0388/422-1326

🕐 Closed Jan. 1, May 1, & Dec. 25

www.turismo.jujuy .gov.ar

A restaurant made largely of salt at Salinas Grandes.

Museo Histórico Provincial Juan Galo Lavalle

- ✉ Lavalle 256, San Salvador de Jujuy
- ☎ 0388/422-1355
- ☎ Closed Jan. 1, May 1, & Dec. 25
- 💲 $

Museo Arqueológico Provincial

- ✉ Lavalle 434, San Salvador de Jujuy
- ☎ 0388/422-1315
- ☎ Closed Jan. 1, May 1, & Dec. 25
- 💲 $

control, colonial and sacred art, and, of course Lavalle's death and its curious aftermath. (Lavalle's forces carried his remains with them for fear the opposition would mutilate the corpse.)

Two blocks north of the history museum, the **Museo Arqueológico Provincial** places the Inca influence where it belongs in provincial historical perspective—dead last, as that culture's late arrival in what is now Argentina meant its authority was just a veneer on top of previous pre-Columbian cultures. Instead, the museum stresses the earliest peoples with exhibits on the hunter-gatherers, rock art, and ceramics that preceded the Inca. Today's indigenous *jujeños* (natives of Jujuy) are a notable presence at the **Mercado de Abasto** (*Dorrego & Leandro N. Alem*), a Kolla market located south of the Río Xibi Xibi.

Purmamarca & Around

The *quebrada* really starts at the hamlet of Volcán, 25 miles (40 km) north of San Salvador, where the roadside **Centro de Visitantes de la Quebrada de Humahuaca** (Visitor Center; *closed Jan. 1, May 1, & Dec. 25*) occupies the former railroad station (repeated floods long ago knocked out the precarious line to the town of Humahuaca). The first real destination, though, is the slow-paced village of **Purmamarca,** 14 miles (23 km) farther north off RN 9.

Beneath the polychrome **Cerro de los Siete Colores,** the "hill of seven colors," Purmamarca's oblong plaza, dusty streets, squat adobes, and 18th-century **Iglesia de Santa Rosa de Lima** (*Plaza Principal*) render it a picture-postcard colonial village. Its proximity to the provincial capital and Salta has made it a favorite with weekenders and newcomers who, so far, have not changed its character—visibly, at least. Tour buses, increasingly common, have to park on the outskirts so that their clients must walk the narrow streets to the plaza's popular **Mercado Artesanal** (crafts market).

Beginning at the plaza, the **Paseo de los Colorados** is a 2-mile (3 km) vehicle trail, also suitable for hikers and cyclists, that snakes through the hills behind town before returning to the plaza. Sunscreen is essential—the sun's nearly direct rays are powerful in this shadeless environment, just below the Tropic of Capricorn.

Purmamarca is also the starting point for a spectacular drive up and over the Andes to the Chilean town of San Pedro de Atacama via smoothly paved RN 52. Switchbacking up the precipitious **Cuesta de Lipán,** the highway emerges onto the puna at the Salinas Grandes salt flats, where it's possible to loop back to Salta via the Quebrada del Toro (see p. 166). Highway RN 52, though, continues west to **Susques,** a village of Kolla llama herders known for its 16th-century **Iglesia Nuestra Señora de Belén** and the simple, saintly murals that adorn its adobe interior. The frontier is 75 miles (121 km) west, at the 14,518-foot (4,425 m) **Paso de Jama.**

Andean Cuisine

In the Quebrada de Humahuaca region, the cuisine is influenced by its Inca heritage. Potatoes, corn, beans, pumpkin, and *cayote* (a local fruit) abound. You'll also find quinoa and *kiwicha,* extremely nutritious grains that were staple foods of the Inca. Your dishes may be seasoned with red chili pepper. Be sure also to try *locro,* a hearty stew of corn, squash, and beef; steamed maize parcels; and tamales.

La Comarca
✉ RN 52 Km 3.8, Purmamarca
☎ 0388/490-8001
www.lacomarca hotel.com.ar

Maimará
🔼 153 B4

Tilcara
🔼 153 B4

INSIDER TIP:

A good place to stay in Purmamarca is La Comarca, an upscale resort. After driving for days on the northwest's winding dirt roads, it's a great place to relax.

—SUSAN RIGGS
National Geographic contributor

Maimará & Around

About 9 miles (14 km) north of Purmamarca, the highway skirts **La Posta de Hornillos,** a colonial roadhouse on the route between Lima and Buenos Aires that's now an archaeological and historical museum. Only a few miles farther north, above the village of Maimará, the series of

chevron-shaped foothills known as **La Paleta del Pintor—**"the painter's palette"—aren't quite so colorful as Purmamarca's Siete Colores, but the contrast with the verdant valley is almost equally striking.

That verdant valley is now the site of the quebrada's first commercial winery, **Bodega Fernando Dupont** (*RN 9 Km 1770, tel 0388/15-473-1918, www.bodegafer nandodupont.com),* producing Cabernet Sauvignon, Malbec, Syrah, and Tannat. From the highway, the hillside cemetery seems positively pre-Columbian even if its individual cement tombs, decorated with artificial flowers, look better from a distance than up close.

Tilcara

Only a few miles north of Maimará, two artistic traditions—the indigenous and the

Museo Arqueológico Doctor Eduardo Casanova

✉ Belgrano 445, Tilcara

☎ 0388/495-5006

🕐 Closed Jan. 1, May 1, & Dec. 25

💲 $$ (includes access to Pucará de Tilcara)

metropolitan—meet in the village of Tilcara. With its archaeological monuments and Kolla population—not to mention its scenery and benevolent climate—Tilcara has also attracted painters and sculptors from around the country who have produced a hybrid art that pays tribute, not always successfully, to regional tradition.

West of the highway, **Plaza Coronel Manuel Álvarez Prado** is Tilcara's geographical center,

where Kolla vendors sell crafts of varying quality, and all the town's museums are conveniently on or near it. On the south side of the plaza, the **Museo Arqueológico Doctor Eduardo Casanova** sets the stage with its exhibits on pre-Inca Tiwanaku, from present-day Bolivia, and on the Diaguita culture that straddled the Andes of Chile and Argentina. Likewise, an entire room displays ceramics from the coastal Peruvian Nazca, Mochica, and Chimú

Humahuaca's narrow streets are barely wide enough for bicyclists.

that preceded the Inca, who only arrived in northwestern Argentina a few decades before the Spaniards. Most of the remaining five exhibition halls, though, focus on the diversity of local cultures in northwestern Argentina, including a tomb that was uncovered in the very street, Belgrano, on which the museum stands.

It's a 15-minute walk south to the museum's restored **Pucará de Tilcara,** a pre-Columbian fortress that's under the administration of the archaeological museum. Climbing to the top, it's easy to appreciate how the unobstructed views of the valley were a boon to defenders; appropriately, it has an overlay of Inca

INSIDER TIP:

Every August in Humahuaca, locals venerate the cult of Pachamama, Mother Earth, with a festival that showcases Andean culture. It's a traveler's must-see.

—FERNANDO NOVAS
National Geographic field scientist

features atop a structure at least 500 years older.

Immediately east of the museum, the **Museo de Escultura Ernesto Soto Avendaño** has showcased the Olavarría-born sculptor (1886–1969), whose heroic sculptures made an effort to blend indigenous valor with

Argentine nationalism. Unfortunately, in early 2008, an unauthorized construction project nearby collapsed the building's ceiling and destroyed many of Avendaño's plaster of Paris works, including a 1:10 scale model of his monument to Argentine independence in Humahuaca.

Half a block west of the plaza, the **Museo de Bellas Artes Fundación Hugo Irureta,** founded by La Boca sculptor Hugo Irureta (1929–), focuses on modern Argentine artists whose works adapt patterns from indigenous crafts, such as ponchos, into abstractions of form and color.

On the east side of the plaza, the **Museo Regional de Pintura José Antonio Terry** is the legacy of its namesake painter (1878–1954), whose landscapes and portraits, such as "El Tuerto del Pucará" ("The One-Eyed Man of the Fortress"), communicated his commitment to the region and its people without unduly romanticizing them.

Humahuaca & Around

Beyond Tilcara, the highway rises gradually and then steeply to the conspicuously Kolla town of Humahuaca. Higher and more exposed than Tilcara, its narrow cobbled streets and low adobe houses haven't seen the incursion of lowlanders that Purmamarca and Tilcara have experienced, but it still welcomes visitors to explore its sights and monuments.

Opposite Plaza Sargento Gómez, the main square, the

(continued on p. 174)

Museo de Escultura Ernesto Soto Avendaño
- Belgrano s/n, Tilcara
- 0388/495-5354
- Closed Tues. & holidays
- $

Museo de Bellas Artes Fundación Hugo Irureta
- Belgrano & Bolívar, Tilcara
- 0388/495-5124
- Closed Mon. & holidays

Museo Regional de Pintura José Antonio Terry
- Rivadavia 459, Tilcara
- 0388/495-5005
- Closed Mon., & Jan. 1, May 1, & Dec. 25
- $

Humahuaca
- 153 B4
Visitor Information
- Cabildo de Humahuaca. Tucumán & Buenos Aires
- 0388/742-1375
- Closed Sat.–Sun. & holidays

Art & Architecture From the Andes to Argentina

In colonial times, when Buenos Aires was still a struggling backwater, Argentina's Andean northwest was, if not thriving, then certainly more central to the Spanish empire. Spain's empire depended on the viceroyalty of Peru, from which both political and ecclesiastical authority emanated.

In reality, the Spaniards had replaced the Inca at the apex of the Andean political pyramid, and the twin influences of Spanish Lima and Inca Cuzco—not always easily separated—are apparent throughout the Quebrada de Humahuaca and beyond. This gorge was a royal highway in pre-Columbian times and, after the Spaniards took Peru, the gateway to the Southern Cone.

To be sure, the Inca and their predecessors left a lasting impact on Argentina's cultural landscape through their *pucarás* (fortresses), which commanded strategic high points; *pircas* (dry stone walls); and terraces where native peoples cultivated high-altitude tubers. In a

Humahuaca's Iglesia Catedral de Nuestra Señora de la Candelaria y San Antonia

landscape that often resembles New Mexico, thick-walled adobe houses were the rule both before and after the Spanish invasion.

Cuzco School

One of the Spaniards' goals was the conversion of the Americas to Roman Catholicism, and, to that end, Cuzco was the base for a new school of painting that quickly spread throughout the central Andes. Dealing with biblical themes, the so-called Escuela Cuzqueña (Cuzco school) quickly filled newly built adobe churches and chapels, often in extremely remote areas, with didactic, earth-toned oils, intended to complement sermons by the clergy. Over time, even a utilitarian church such as that of San Francisco de Yavi, east of today's border town of La Quiaca, came to feature imposing wooden doors embellished with forged ironwork and, most notably, a gilt altar and pulpit.

Many, if not most, of the native and mestizo artists worked anonymously, and few of their canvases bear any signature or other identifying mark. Derived initially from European Renaissance paintings, their work soon began to incorporate regional landscapes and themes, often in a subversively elegant manner. In the Chilean altiplano church of Parinacota, for instance, elaborate murals depict the soldiers marching Christ to the cross as Spaniards. In fact, native Andean artists took the idea of Christian soldiers literally—in the 17th-century chapel at Uquía, for instance, oils by Cuzco school painters depict angels flourishing 15th-century matchlock rifles.

Well after Argentine independence, this heritage attracted artists from elsewhere in the

The Cuzco school painting "Saint Joseph and the Christ Child" now hangs at Brooklyn's Museum of Art.

country. The village of Tilcara (see pp. 169–171), for instance, became home to painter José Antonio Terry and sculptors Ernesto Soto Avendaño and Hugo Irureta—all of them from Buenos Aires or Buenos Aires Province—who incorporated regional artistic traditions into their own work.

Meanwhile, the original heritage is under threat, because thieves have begun to take advantage of poorly guarded churches to abscond with original artworks and artifacts such as chalices and cruets to sell them on the black market. Ecclesiastical authorities have floated the idea of relocating some of these treasures to a museum to be built at Humahuaca—which would wrench them from their original context, but at least save them for posterity.

Iruya
153 B5
Visitor Information
Calle San Martín s/n
Open irregular hours
www.iruyaonline.com

17th-century **Iglesia Catedral de Nuestra Señora de la Candelaria y San Antonio**'s interior, with its rococo altar and Cuzco-school murals, is more authentic than its frequently renovated exterior. Across the plaza, the **Cabildo de Humahuaca** replaced an earlier, simpler municipal office building demolished in the 1930s. A life-size replica of San Francisco Solano appears out of its clock tower at noon every day.

Tilcara sculptor Ernesto Soto Avendaño created the overwhelming **Monumento a la Independencia,** a series of bronzes topped by a pre-Columbian warrior, at the summit of a broad stone staircase just north of the church. While Soto Avendaño's monument is imposing, it's also wrongheaded in implying that indigenous people were the vanguard of independence—in reality, it was criollos—American-born Spaniards—who spearheaded the movement.

A few miles south of Humahuaca, the highway passes the hamlet of **Uquía,** known for the

Cuzco school paintings (see pp. 172–173) of musket-toting angels in its **Iglesia de San Francisco de Paula.** About 6 miles (10 km) northeast of Humahuaca, the ruins of **Coctaca,** their piedmont bench terraces now studded with cactuses, are the province's largest pre-Columbian agricultural complex. When the Inca moved here in the 15th century, they left their mark on a site where farmers grew potatoes, other tubers, and possibly corn.

Iruya
Roughly 20 miles (33 km) north of Humahuaca, graveled RP 13 fords the Río Grande and climbs northeast to the 12,800-foot

EXPERIENCE: Exploring Iruya's Backcountry

Iruya's backcountry, an intriguing stark, high desert landscape of mountains, canyons, and meandering streams, is popular among hikers and horseback riders alike.

One well-trodden trek is to the nearby hamlet of **San Isidro,** taking in great gorge and river views, and more often than not accompanied by condors soaring high above. A local guide should be hired, since signposts are not reliable

and the rainy season *(Dec.–March)* often makes passage difficult. Iruya's **Hosteria de Iruya** *(tel 0387/ 15-407-0909)* arranges horseback-riding trips; schedule at least a day in advance.

Salta's tourism office *(Caseros 711, tel 0387/437-3340 or 0800/777-0300, www.saltalinda.gov.ar)* can provide additional information on outfitters and assorted adventure trips.

(3,890 m) pass known as the **Abra del Cóndor** before dropping into a breathtaking canyon of steep-sided crop terraces clinging to precipitous slopes. At road's end in Iruya, the most isolated settlement in Salta Province, the cobbled streets make up an indigenous enclave that seems to belong in Peru. Its colonial **Iglesia de Nuestra Señora del Rosario y San Roque** *(off Plaza Principal)* is worth a look, but the high open country that surrounds it is the real highlight for hikers or, to get around as locals do, for those on burros.

Monumento Natural Laguna de Los Pozuelos

About 53 miles (85 km) north-west of Humahuaca, just beyond the barren altiplano outpost of **Abra Pampa,** graveled RP 7 leads 30 miles (50 km) northwest to **Laguna de los Pozuelos** *(tel 0388/749-1349).* This high-altitude wetland is home to more than 40 species of breeding birds, notably some 25,000 flamingos of three different species. In the wet summer, roads can be impassable.

La Quiaca & Around

The highway ends at La Quiaca and the Bolivian border. In an exposed puna environment, with freezing night temperatures at nearly 11,300 feet (3,442 m) above sea level and nothing to stop the wind, the town of La Quiaca is nondescript, but the nearby village of **Yavi** deserves more than just a brief visit.

Canyon walls surround the remote Kolla village of Iruya.

Set in a sheltered valley, Yavi's outstanding landmark is its 17th-century **Iglesia de Nuestra Señora del Rosario y San Francisco** *(Plaza Mayor),* with its forged iron doors, Cuzco school statuary, and spectacularly rendered gold altarpiece. Almost next door, and of comparable vintage, the **Casa del Marqués Campero** *(Plaza Mayor)* was the colonial *encomendero's* (holder of a royal grant) residence and is now a museum. ∎

La Quiaca
153 B5

Tucumán

Argentina's smallest province, about the size of Israel, Tucumán looms large as the cradle of the country's independence, declared here in 1816. In colonial times, it was a stop on the royal road to present-day Bolivia, but after independence the sugar industry kept the province on the map. The historic provincial capital, San Miguel de Tucumán, is surrounded by scenic mountain villages with impressive pre-Columbian ruins.

The cathedral of San Miguel de Tucumán

The province has a troubled history. In the revolutionary ferment of the 1960s and 1970s, the dense forests of the sierras harbored leftist guerrillas whose presence provoked a ferocious military response and left a legacy of polarization. In late 2008, former army commander Antonio Domingo Bussi—at different times provincial governor and mayor of the capital city— was found guilty of numerous murders and "disappearances" in the 1976 coup that initiated the Dirty War (see sidebar p. 64). Because of his age, the unrepentant Bussi was able to avoid physical incarceration in favor of house arrest.

In the aftermath of the 2001 economic collapse, Tucumán was one of the country's hardest-hit provinces, leaving some businesses unable even to change small banknotes. Rural poverty and infant mortality reached unprecedented levels, but devaluation revived the sugar industry and sparked an uneven economic recovery.

San Miguel de Tucumán

At the foot of the steeply rising Sierra de Aconquija, the provincial capital is one of Argentina's most historic cities, even if contemporary construction has left only a scattering of colonial buildings in its central core. After independence, it turned its attention away from the highlands of the Andes to the lowlands of the Pampas, a trend that accelerated with construction of the railroad from Buenos Aires and Córdoba.

Tucumán's traditional center is **Plaza Independencia,** planted with jacaranda, laurels, palms, and trumpet trees. The

street, the 19th-century **Templo y Convento de San Francisco** *(Calles San Martin & 25 de Mayo)* sits on colonial Jesuit ruins.

At the plaza's southeast corner, the 19th-century **Iglesia Catedral** sports a neoclassical construction with twin bell towers, a pediment whose bas-reliefs depict the flight of Moses, and a tiled central cupola that recalls Eastern Orthodox churches. Its interior, with perfectly preserved ceiling frescos and a golden altar,

Tucumán

153 B3

Visitor Information

24 de Septiembre 484

0381/422-2199

www.tucuman turismo.gov.ar

Casa de Gobierno

25 de Mayo 90

0381/430-7894

The Argentine Barbecue

As a restaurant, the Argentine *parrilla* is an institution, and the mixed-grill of *parrillada* is the default option on the menu. In terms of its components, the barbecue known as *asado* is virtually identical, with prime beef cuts supplemented by chorizo (sausage) and *achuras*, a diversity of offal that most commonly includes *chinchulines* (small intestines) and *morcilla* (blood sausage). Chicken, lamb (especially in Patagonia), and pork can also be part of the mix.

The difference between the two, though, is their social context. The

more formal parrillada is most commonly served by professional waiters in a commercial context. The asado, by contrast, normally means a gathering of family or friends, where the host usually occupies the position of *asador*, monitoring the coals, determining when the meat is ready, and distributing it among the guests. The meal also includes a variety of salads and traditional desserts such as flan or fruit salad—not to mention plenty of red wine, sometimes diluted with soda water, to wash it all down.

unconventional sculptor Lola Mora (1866–1936), a daughter of the province, created the central statue of **La Libertad,** Argentina's counterpart of New York's Statue of Liberty. Occupying nearly the entire block facing the plaza from the west side, the French baroque **Casa de Gobierno** (Government House) replaced the colonial cabildo in the early 20th century, symbolizing the prosperity brought by development of the sugar industry. Immediately north, across the

is immaculate. Around the corner, the **Museo Histórico Presidente Nicolás Avellaneda** was Tucumán's first two-story house and the birthplace of President Nicolás Avellaneda (1837–1880); its seven exhibit halls display numismatic artifacts, maps, paintings, and most notably an entire section dedicated to the 19th-century civil wars, with perfectly preserved clothing, weapons, and imagery of the era.

Immediately south of Government House, the Italianate

Museo Histórico Presidente Nicolás Avellaneda

Congreso 56

0381/431-1039

Closed Mon.

$

Museo Casa Padilla

✉ 25 de Mayo 36
🕐 Closed Mon. &
   holidays

Museo Folclórico Manuel Belgrano

✉ 24 de Septiembre 565
☎ 0381/421-8250
🕐 Closed Mon.

Museo Provincial de Bellas Artes Timoteo E. Navarro

✉ 9 de Julio 44
☎ 0381/422-7300
🕐 Closed Mon., some holidays, & summer weeks
💲 $, Sun. free

Museo Casa Histórica de la Independencia

✉ Congreso 141
☎ 0381/431-0826
🕐 Closed Jan. 1, May 1, July 8, July 9 (a.m. only), & Dec. 24-25, 31
💲 $
www.museocasa historica.org.ar

Museo de la Industria Azucarera–Casa del Obispo Colombres

✉ Parque 9 de Julio
☎ 0381/452-2332

Museo Casa Padilla was the residence of an influential local family that donated its collection of decorative Eurocentric art, along with their traditional furnishings plus a handful of colonial and Asian pieces, to the province. Around the corner, the **Museo Folclórico Manuel Belgrano** was once the residence of bishop, independence figure, and sugar pioneer José Eusebio Colombres (1778–1859). It now houses an archaeological folklore museum that's also a crafts market.

Within a Francophile building half a block south of the plaza, the luminous **Museo Provincial de Bellas Artes Timoteo E. Navarro** holds works by famous Argentine artists including Berni, Quinquela Martín, and Lino Spilimbergo, but it devotes two full rooms to the locally born painter (1909–1965) from whom it takes its name.

For Argentine patriots, Tucumán's iconic sight is the **Museo Casa Histórica de la Independencia,** a block-plus south of the plaza. Here, on July 9, 1816, delegates from around the country confirmed the independence of the Provincias Unidas del Río de la Plata. Nearly demolished at one point, then rebuilt in the 1940s on the basis of documentary evidence, the building suffered decades of heavy automobile traffic that damaged its facade. With the street newly cobbled and closed to motor vehicles, the colonial building is more appealing than ever.

On the other hand, only the salon in which the signatories met, and where their portraits now hang, is truly original. Information about them is scant and, in English, nonexistent. The shady patios and gardens, with their brick pathways, lead to Lola Mora's outdoor bas-reliefs—commissioned by President Julio Argentino Roca (1843–1914)—that depict the independence movement not just through its elite signatories but also through humble gauchos. In fact, the artwork says more without narration than the other exhibits say with text.

INSIDER TIP:

At the Museo Casa Histórica de la Independencia, don't miss the show of light and shadows as the sun goes down over Lola Mora's relief sculptures.

—CARLA SORANI HLUCHAN
Organization of American States

Tucumán's largest open space, barely six blocks east of Plaza Independencia, **Parque 9 de Julio** was once Bishop Colombres's sugar plantation; its looping roads slow the pace of traffic and make it ideal for an easy getaway, except when heavy storms flood the low-lying ground. It is still the site of the **Museo de la Industria Azucarera–Casa del Obispo Colombres,** the bishop's residence and home to a functional ox-powered *trapiche*—once used to mill the harvested cane; it's now there for show. ∎

Around Tucumán

Tucumán is a central location for exploring the surrounding provinces of Santiago del Estero and Catamarca, but its own highlands are the best destination for first-time visitors.

Fuchsias on the road to Tafí del Valle

Tafí del Valle & Around

San Miguel de Tucumán may be a subtropical hothouse but, in any season, the mountain town of Tafí del Valle can be an escape from the crowded provincial capital. Just getting there is a highlight, as the paved highway—subject to washouts in wet weather—zigzags up the Río de los Sosas Valley through lush cloud forest before emerging into an enormous valley ringed by the summits of the Sierra del Aconquija, the Cumbres Cal-chaquíes, and the Cumbres de Mala-Mala. Tafí's microclimate is often wet and foggy, but at lower elevations—the town itself sits nearly 6,500 feet (almost 2,000 m) above sea level—the area's farmers can grow pota-toes and orchard fruits like apples and pears.

Though Tafí has only a few thousand permanent residents, it had a densely populated coun-tryside even in pre-Columbian times. The initial Spanish presence greatly reduced the indigenous Calchaquí population, who suc-cumbed to European diseases and forced labor. The Jesuit Order's intervention, however, revived the

Tafí del Valle
🅰 153 B3
Visitor Information
✉ Peatonal Los Faroles
☎ 03867/421-880

Museo Jesuítico de La Banda

✉ Avenida Gobernador Silva, Tafí del Valle

☎ 03867/421-685

💲 $

Ruins of Quilmes

🔺 153 B3

✉ RN 40, 14 miles (23 km) NW of Amaicha del Valle

💲 $

Santa María de Yokavil

🔺 153 B3

Belén

🔺 153 A2

community until the Jesuit expulsion in 1767. The only remaining evidence of the Jesuit presence is the **Capilla de La Banda,** a colonial chapel that now holds Tafí's **Museo Jesuítico de La Banda;** its highlights include Cuzco school paintings and carvings and pottery from Tafí's early peoples.

At the nearby village of **El Mollar,** the **Parque de los Menhires** is an assortment of pre-Columbian standing stones displaced, unfortunately, from their original locations around the valley. The highway from Tucumán switchbacks up the foggy mountainside to the 10,000-foot (3,050 m) pass known as the **Abra del Infiernillo** before dropping into the arid **Valles Calchaquíes,** site of the Quilmes ruins. On the Tafí side of the pass, there is access to guided hikes and horseback trails, arranged at the local tourist office.

Quilmes

West of the village of **Amaicha del Valle,** home to the remarkable **Museo Pachamama** (see sidebar opposite), the highway from Tafí del Valle intersects RN 40 which, only a short distance north, leads to the pre-Columbian ruins of Quilmes. Dating from about A.D. 1000, the former Diaguita fortress climbs the mountainside in a series of terraces that provided both observation points and strong defensive positions against invaders. Briefly under Inca control, the Quilmes Indians held out against the Spaniards until their final defeat, and forced march to Buenos Aires, in 1667.

Roaming through the restored, cactus-studded ruins of Quilmes—Argentina's single most impressive Andean archaeological site by a long shot—is one of the region's

A young man guards traditional sulky carriages in Simoca, Tucumán Province.

highlights. The views up and down the Valles Calchaquíes in the clear desert air are stunning.

Recently, though, Quilmes has become the scene of renewed struggle that, fortunately, has avoided the violence of the 16th century. In March 2008, the Colalao-based Comunidad India Quilmes occupied the ruins. With the adjacent hotel, restaurant, and museum closed, the

Nuestra Señora del Rosario, a simple colonial chapel, is a national historical monument in a scenic desert valley whose irrigated fields stand out from a distance.

Another 37 miles (60 km) south, the town of **Belén** has the small **Museo Arqueológico Cóndor Huasi,** which focuses on regional topics rather than the big picture. About 9 miles (14

Museo Arqueológico Provincial Eric Boman

✉ Centro Cultural Yokavil, Belgrano & Sarmiento, Santa María de Yokavil

---

Museo Pachamama

If pre-Columbian Argentina was a mosaic of cultures, Amaicha del Valle's Museo Pachamama *(RP 307 Km 118, tel 03892/ 421-004, www.museopachamama.com, $$)*— also known as the Casa de Piedra (House of Stone)—expresses the fact literally. On sprawling grounds with cactus gardens, scattered trees, and occasional pools, the traditional Andean figures of Pachamama (Mother Earth) and Inti (Sun) stand among artful paths and walls of colored stones. Depicting toads, serpents,rheas, pumas, and other wildlife, the mosaics

reflect the indigenous cosmology.

Created by local artist Héctor Cruz, even Pachamama's indoor spaces encourage visitors to experience the local environment. The geology exhibit, for instance, is arranged as a walk through a mine shaft, acknowledging the origins of the raw materials that created what is, in effect, an outdoor sculpture. Pachamama also exhibits regional textiles and paintings on indigenous themes to provide as complete a symbolic exploration of the Valles Calchaquíes as can be found.

---

indigenous community—which calls Quilmes its "sacred city"—has been conducting guided tours of the ruins at no charge, with tips accepted.

Belén & Around

South of Quilmes, RN 40 enters Catamarca Province and the town of **Santa María de Yokavil,** whose **Museo Arqueológico Provincial Eric Boman** is rich in materials but poor in presentation and organization. Another 70 miles (113 km) southwest, the road passes the village of **Hualfín,** where the **Capilla de**

km) south of town, though, the walnut-growing village of **Londres** is the gateway to substantial Inca ruins at nearby **El Shinkal,** where dozens of paths, platforms, and warehouses fill an area of some 45 acres (21 ha). It's not one of the most spectacular Inca ruins but, for anyone touring the vicinity, it's well worth a detour.

Termas de Río Hondo

There's nothing really scenic or absorbing about the Santiago del Estero town of Termas de Río Hondo, but it makes an ideal place to break a journey

Museo Arqueológico Cóndor Huasi

✉ San Martín & Belgrano, Belén
🕐 Closed Sun.
💲 $

El Shinkal

✉ 4 miles (6 km) W of Londres
🕐 Closed Sat.–Sun. & holidays
💲 $

www.shinkalde quimivil.com.ar

The Heartless Padre Esquiú

In an era of nearly endless civil war, Catamarca native Fray Mamerto de la Ascensión Esquiú (1826–1883) was a peacemaker who pled for constitutional government and national unity. In the course of a long and distinguished career, in which he traveled extensively and promoted education among provincial children, he became a priest at age 23 and, as the culmination of his career, the bishop of Córdoba only three years before his death.

Esquiú's body lies in Córdoba's cathedral (see pp. 115–116) but, in a manner of speaking, he left his heart in Catamarca. After an autopsy found no damage to the "incorruptible" organ, it resided in San Fernando's Franciscan church except for a brief 1990 incident when it briefly disappeared, only to be found on the adjacent monastery's roof. After that, it went on public display in a glass case until January 2008, when a vandal smashed the glass and absconded with it.

Detained by police, the young homeless man claimed to have discarded the relic in a streetside trash can, despite their suspicions that he had hidden it somewhere. If he was telling the truth, unless there's some genuine miracle, what's left of Padre Esquiú's heart is likely buried under tons of trash.

Termas de Río Hondo

📖 153 B2

Visitor Information

✉ Caseros 132

☎ 0385/842-2143

Santiago del Estero

📖 153 B2

Visitor Information

✉ Avenida Libertad 417

☎ 0385/421-4243

Museo de Ciencias Antropológicas y Naturales Emilio y Duncan Wagner

✉ Avenida Libertad 439

☎ 0385/422-4858

🕓 Closed Sat.–Sun. & holidays Jan.– March

www.ccbsantiago.gov.ar

for one reason: It has abundant spa accommodations and, befitting its name, in-room tubs for long hot soaks. Some spas also have more elaborate services that include massages, physical therapy, and personal trainers.

Termas is most popular for midwinter holidays; the summer climate is so stiflingly hot and humid that most hotels close but, even then, there's always a good option at bargain prices. On the outskirts of town, the 127-square-mile (330 sq km) **Embalse Río Hondo** is a reservoir for swimming, sailing, and fishing; otherwise, activities consist of Vegas-style gambling and entertainment at the downtown casino.

Santiago del Estero

Capital of its namesake province, dating from 1553, Santiago del Estero is Argentina's oldest city, but history—aided by a notoriously corrupt provincial elite—has mostly passed it by. It has only a scattering of colonial remains, but does hold two exceptional museums.

Shady **Plaza Libertad,** with its fountains and band shell, is the center of Santiago's slightly irregular grid. On its west side, the 19th-century **Catedral Basílica Nuestra Señora del Carmen** has a neoclassical facade and a soaring, richly decorated interior.

In new quarters facing the plaza, Santiago's top museum is the **Museo de Ciencias Antropológicas y Naturales Emilio y Duncan Wagner,** an anthropology and natural history institution begun by French anthropologist brothers in the early 20th century. Worth a special stop, its six impressively organized exhibition halls specialize in pre-Columbian ceramics associated with early farmers and fishermen from the third century A.D. Most come from the hot Chaco lowlands to the north rather than the Andes to the east. Prior to the arrival of the Spaniards, ceramics—most notably funerary urns—were much more complex and decorative. The natural history materials include fossil mastodons, glyptodonts, and smaller animals present into the Holocene.

Two blocks farther east, the 18th-century **Convento de San Francisco** stands on the site of a 16th-century namesake where Spanish missionary San Francisco Solano once resided. In the adjacent church, dating from the late 19th century, the **Museo de Arte Sacro San Francisco Solano** contains beautifully presented colonial religious artwork, paintings, and especially statuary, including a carving of the saint himself, which was done in Peru.

San Fernando del Valle de Catamarca

In all of Argentina, probably only the Buenos Aires devotional center of Luján can equal the significance of Catamarca's provincial capital among the Catholic faithful. Every December 8, hundreds of thousands of pilgrims converge on the city to pay homage to the image of the Virgen del Valle (Virgin of the Valley) who, as it happens, is also the "national patron saint of tourism." Many arrive on foot, having walked hundreds of miles in withering summer heat.

Like other Argentine cities, Catamarca's civic focus is a central plaza which, in this case, is French landscape architect Carlos Thays's **Plaza 25 de Mayo.** Thays

(1849–1934) created countless public parks and private gardens in Buenos Aires, Córdoba, Mendoza, and Tucumán that made him a legend in the country.

Thays's sunken gardens form the approach to the 19th-century **Catedral Basílica y Santuario de Nuestra Señora del Valle** (*Plaza 25 de Mayo*), whose neoclassical facade, with twin bell towers, is easy to appreciate since the street it faces is closed to traffic. Both the dome above its altar and the central nave contain Orlando Orlandi's ceiling frescoes depicting miracles attributed to the Virgen del Valle. Pilgrims stand in line to see her 17th-century image, which sports its diamond-studded crown only on December 8.

INSIDER TIP:

The thing to do in Tucumán is paraglide (*www.argentina.travel/ en/xp/paragliding-in- tucuman/4311*)—it's truly unforgettable to soar high over deep mountainous jungle.

—ELISEO MICIU
National Geographic photographer

Catamarca's other landmark church is the **Iglesia y Convento de San Francisco** (*Fray Mamerto Esquiú y Rivadavia*), a 19th-century building that preserves some original colonial features. It was the refuge of Fray Mamerto Esquiú (1826–1883; see sidebar opposite), a prominent priest and civic figure. ∎

Museo de Arte Sacro San Francisco Solano

✉ Avenida Roca Sur 716
☎ 0385/421-1548
🕐 Closed Sun.
💲 $

San Fernando del Valle de Catamarca

🅰 153 B2
Visitor Information
✉ República 524
☎ 0383/345-5385
🕐 Closed Sat.–Sun. & holidays

Centered on the capital city of Mendoza, a region famous
for wines, fossils, and South America's highest peak

Cuyo

In the echo chamber of the Chimenea del Eco, Parque Nacional Talampaya

Cuyo

Where the Andes reach their peak—literally so, on the soaring summit of Cerro Aconcagua—so do Argentine wines. Mendoza wineries irrigate their vineyards with water from the spring snowmelt, even as trekkers make their way up the Río Horcones Valley to the Roof of the Americas. Across the Río Mendoza, visitors can view the Cristo Redentor monument to peace.

Comprising the provinces of Mendoza, San Juan, San Luis, and, by some accounts, La Rioja, the Cuyo region has more than just high peaks and fine wines. Though the capital of Mendoza is the best base for visiting hundreds of nearby wineries, it's a liveable city by any standard, with fine services, cultural resources, and a wooded townscape that cools its hot summers.

In southern Mendoza Province, the city of San Rafael is a lesser known wine district whose rivers are also white-water magnets. Farther south, near the city of Malargüe, Las Leñas has become one of South America's premier ski

resorts, but in summer it has opened its lands to hikers, climbers, mountain bikers, and other outdoor enthusiasts. South of Malargüe, the volcanic caverns, scablands, and wetlands of Payunia are ideal for anyone seeking solitude in nature.

North of Mendoza, the provincial capital of San Juan has its own small but excellent wine district, but the province's most absorbing sight is the offbeat shrine to the Difunta Correa, a folk saint whose dedicated following obliged the Catholic Church to acknowledge—reluctantly—their sincerity and legitimacy. More conventionally, the province is also home to Parque Provincial Ischigualasto, a UNESCO World Heritage site where Triassic dinosaurs once roamed. Today the area boasts a noteworthy paleontological museum and a circuit of wildly eroded landforms that has developed since the dinosaurs died off.

To the north, part of the same UNESCO designation, La Rioja's Parque Nacional Talampaya is so close that many travelers visit both in the same day. Beneath the nearly vertical walls of its sandstone canyons, paleo-Indians left evidence of their time here in petroglyphs scattered among native thorn forests; in more open country, the dry Talampaya River has left equally intriguing but more colorful landforms than those at Ischigualasto. The colonial capital of La Rioja has a smattering of museums, but the province's most interesting city is Chilecito, an ex-mining town named for its Chilean immigrants that's also home to a small wine-growing district.

East of Mendoza, San Luis might be Cuyo's forgotten province but for the scenic

---

hill country bordering Córdoba Province and, especially, the red sandstone canyons of Parque Nacional Sierra de las Quijadas. Like Ischigualasto and Talampaya, the national park is keeping Argentine paleontologists, particularly

dinosaur specialists, provided with raw materials. It's also keeping hikers and campers happy with its views and trails, though descending too deeply into its badlands without a guide is inadvisable. ■

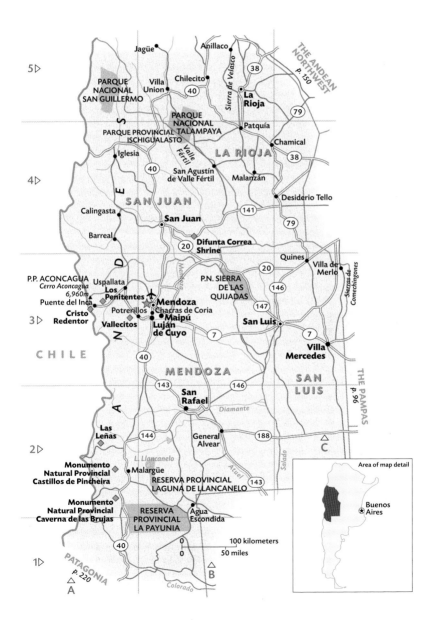

Mendoza City & Around

Mendoza is the heart of Argentina's wine industry, an industrial powerhouse with abundant energy resources, and the eastern terminus of the country's most important Andean crossing to Chile. The city dates from 1561, but its colonial remains are few because it stands in one of the country's most earthquake-prone areas. Today, its universities and cultural institutions help make it an arts and entertainment center.

Candidates for queen of the wine harvest festival parade through the streets of Mendoza city.

Mendoza City

🗺 187 B3

Visitor Information

✉ Avenida San
Martín &
Garibaldi

☎ 0261/420-1333

**www.ciudadde
mendoza.gov.ar**

In colonial times, the entire Cuyo region was under Chilean administration. Even today it's friendlier to Chile than almost any other Argentine city—after Argentina's political and economic collapse of 2002, provincial authorities openly encouraged Chileans to spend their own mid-September independence days here. That was a wise idea, as steady growth in the regional tourism industry continues to complement the

growth of a wine-tasting international clientele, spurring the construction of new hotels and the renovation of others. Tourism has also created a demand for fine food to match the wines and for excursions into the provincial backcountry.

Mendoza played a key role in the South American wars of independence as Gen. José de San Martín organized his forces for the liberation of Chile here—crossing the Andes in midsummer—but reoriented itself to Buenos Aires after the railroad arrived in the 1880s. Because of earthquakes, much of its architecture is nondescript and utilitarian, but a solid canopy of street trees above its broad sidewalks, plus a wealth of public parks and plazas, help make it one of Argentina's most livable cities.

Mendoza proper, the provincial capital, is a relatively small city surrounded by the sprawling suburbs of Gran Mendoza (Greater Mendoza): Guaymallén, Godoy Cruz, Las Heras, Maipú, and Luján de Cuyo. Most visitors will be hard-pressed to note where one ends and the other begins, which can sometimes lead you astray.

Sights

The city center is **Plaza Independencia,** the axis around which nearly everything revolves. Its fountains, trees, and footpaths support a weekend crafts fair *(Thurs.–Sun. eves.)* and surround a subterranean theater and the **Museo Municipal de Arte Moderno,** which hosts frequently changing exhibitions of contemporary painting, photography, sculpture, and mixed media. Despite the museum's underground location, its exhibition halls are strikingly luminous.

East of the plaza, the pedestrian mall of **Paseo Sarmiento** is home to the surprisingly inconspicuous **Legislatura Provincial** (Provincial Legislature), but for most Mendocinos it's a broad walk of shady sidewalk cafés and public benches in the midst of the central business district. West of the plaza, beyond the landmark facade of the Park Hyatt Hotel (now hiding a casino), the same street and parallel blocks shelter a cluster of hotels, hostels,

Museo Municipal de Arte Moderno
- ✉ Plaza Independencia
- ☎ 0261/425-7279
- 🕐 Closed Mon.
- 💲 $, Wed. free

EXPERIENCE: Plazas of Mendoza

Much of quake-prone Mendoza's architecture is utilitarian, but its verdant plazas help make it a city with, in the words of novelist Carlos Fuentes, "a roof of leaves woven together like the fingers of a huge circle of inseparable lovers."

To experience the city as Mendocinos do, spend at least part of a day strolling Mendoza's plazas. The city's axis is **Plaza Independencia,** four full blocks nearly encircled by a tiled walkway where, on warm nights, souvenir hunters stroll past crafts stalls and lovers gaze at its central fountains. If the spray doesn't cool you off, the subterranean modern art museum offers a refuge.

Four satellite plazas—occupying a full block each—lie two blocks from each of Plaza Independencia's corners, and each tells a story. To the northeast, at **Plaza San Martín,** an equestrian statue of the country's founding father expresses the heroic strain in Argentine nationalism. At **Plaza Chile,** two blocks northwest, San Martín embraces his Chilean colleague Bernardo O'Higgins in a friendship that waxed and waned over the years.

To the southwest, **Plaza Italia's** statuary honors Rome's myths and the immigrants who helped found the local wine industry. The most striking of all Mendoza's plazas is **Plaza España**—with its Moorish fountains, tilework, murals, and statuary, it could fit easily into Seville.

Terraza Jardín Mirador Arq. Gerardo Américo Andía
- ✉ Palacio Municipal, 9 de Julio 500
- ☎ 0261/429-6500
- 🕐 Closed holidays

Museo del Área Fundacional
- ✉ Beltrán & Videla Castillo
- ☎ 0261/425-6927
- 🕐 Closed Mon.
- 💲 $, Wed. free

Acuario Municipal
- ✉ Parque Bernardo O'Higgins, Ituzaingó & Buenos Aires
- ☎ 0261/425-3824
- 🕐 Closed holidays
- 💲 $

restaurants, and wine bars. Most of the restaurant and entertainment district, though, is a few blocks southwest, along **Arístides Villanueva** street to its terminus at **Parque General San Martín.**

Three blocks north of the plaza, the **Mercado Central** is the place to purchase wine, cheese, and other fixings for a picnic. A few blocks west, the **Museo Popular Callejero** (*Avenida Las Heras, bet. 25 de Mayo & Perú*) is an innovative museum that brings its exhibits out of the buildings and onto the street—its historical dioramas, in sturdy cases, chronicle the evolution of Avenida Las Heras ever since it was an intermittent stream in colonial times.

Some blocks south of the plaza, the **Barrio Cívico** is the site of city offices that offer one major amenity. Within the Palacio Municipal, reached by elevator, its 11th-floor **Terraza Jardín**

Mirador Arq. Gerardo Américo Andía offers a rooftop overlook of the city center to the north and, when conditions are clear, the Andean foothills to the west. Filled with flower beds, it even provides telescopes for more distant views.

The city's historical center, though, lies about a mile (1.6 km) northeast of Plaza Independencia, where the **Museo del Área Fundacional** has unearthed quake-demolished foundations of the colonial cabildo (which later served as a slaughterhouse).

The museum, in addition to its archaeological resources, focuses on Mendoza itself through accounts of its Huarpe Indian heritage, historical dioramas, and photographs. Its real strength, though, is its detailed examination of the role of water in Mendoza, a city whose downtown streets are lined with *acequias* (canals) that now irrigate street trees but, in times past, made life in this desert city possible. Among the exhibits is the aqueduct-fed fountain where residents came to collect water for their daily needs.

Immediately north of the adjacent Plaza Pedro del Castillo, their brick arches fenced for safety, the **Ruinas de San Francisco** are the remains of a building that belonged to the Jesuits until their expulsion from the Americas in 1767. The Franciscans who replaced them had to abandon the site after the 1861 earthquake.

Just south of the museum, **Parque Bernardo O'Higgins** is a strip of green space that extends several blocks south to the improbable **Acuario Municipal**

Bodega Escorihuela

Most of Mendoza's wineries are in the distant suburbs, but it's less than a 2-mile (3 km) walk to Bodega Escorihuela (*Belgrano 1188, Godoy Cruz, tel 0261/424-2744, www.escorihuela.com.ar*). **Just across the Godoy Cruz line, dating from 1884, Escorihuela is a historic winery that produces a classic red Carcassone label for everyday consumption, but it has also plunged into finer versions of Malbec, Syrah, Viognier, and others. Its vineyards are now in the countryside and, in December 2008, a fire destroyed much of the complex, which had to be rebuilt. Celebrity chef Francis Mallman's 1884 restaurant, which had turned part of the building and a patio into an intimate dining experience, survived.**

(Municipal Aquarium). In waters culled from Mendoza's withering desert, most of the aquarium's fish species come from the flood-prone Paraná River.

Wine mania peaks at the close of the grape harvest in March, during the Vendimia festival, a city-wide street party with parades, bands, and brimming glasses of *tinto* (red wine).

—MEI-LING HOPGOOD
National Geographic writer

Parque General San Martín

At the west end of Avenida Emilio Civit, crowned by an Andean condor atop the provincial coat of arms, iron-filigree gates imported from Glasgow mark the entrance to one of landscape architect Carlos Thays's most impressive achievements. Covering more than 750 acres (307 ha) with 10.5 miles (17 km) of looping roads, extensive footpaths, and an artificial lake, the park began as a wasteland, but it is now a major public asset that also includes museums, a plant nursery, a rose garden, and more than 30 outdoor sculptures.

Since Thays's day, the park has added a soccer stadium (for the 1978 World Cup), and its **Teatro Griego Frank Romero Day,** an outdoor amphitheater on the southwest corner, is the main venue for March's **Fiesta Nacional de la Vendimia,** the national wine harvest festival. The four-day event tests the capacity of city hotels, restaurants, and wineries.

The park's literal high point, reached by a spiral road, is the

The high Andes are the backdrop for the city of Mendoza.

Meltwater from the Andes irrigates the vineyards of Luján de Cuyo, Mendoza Province.

Museo de Ciencias Naturales y Antropológicas Juan Cornelio Moyano

✉ Parque General San Martín, Avenida de Las Tipas & Prado Español

☎ 0261/482-7666

🕐 Closed Mon., Jan. 1, Good Friday, May 1, & Dec. 25

💲 $

promontory known as **Cerro de la Gloria,** a panoramic overlook where Uruguayan sculptor Juan Manuel Ferrari (1874–1916) created the **Monumento La Patria al Ejército de los Andes** as a tribute to San Martín and his army. Open-air *bateas* (buses) take passengers from the gates to the peak *(summer & main tourist season only),* but it's also a popular ride for cyclists.

Topped by a squad of bronze horsemen including San Martín, beneath a winged figure of La Libertad Argentina, the monument's lower level includes a conspicuously African-Argentine rider—a segment of the country's population that historian George Reid Andrews once described as "forgotten, but not gone."

At the south end of the lake, the **Museo de Ciencias Naturales y Antropológicas Juan Cornelio Moyano** has reopened after a lengthy closure. It features

thematically arranged exhibits blending landscapes and cultures of the region, including not just visuals, but also sound recordings of wildlife such as the parakeets that inhabit native algarrobo trees, and the scent of the *jarilla* shrub. In addition, it covers phenomena, such as the volcanic Payunia scablands near Malargüe, which get little publicity

Wineries of Maipú

Stretching east through industrial suburbs into the countryside, the department of Maipú is home to numerous wineries with national and international reputations, several of which have museums and/or restaurants and host events for the public. Because of their scattered locations, organized tours or rented cars are the most efficient means of visiting them. Most of them have their vineyards elsewhere.

In the General Gutiérrez neighborhood, **Bodegas López** is a family-run industrial winery that dates from 1898, but its production facilities include modern stainless-steel tanks and the latest technology. Tours in either Spanish or English, with limited free tastings, take place in a new visitor center integrated with the original building; more extensive tastings cost extra and require reservations. López also offers half-day tours that include its vineyards and lunch at its restaurant.

Seven blocks south of López, **Antigua Bodega Giol** is more of a historical relic that hosts rock concerts and other performing arts events. A cooperative with precarious production, it's most notable for its elliptical 19,800-gallon (75,000 L) French oak barrel, embellished with a bronze sculpture created for the centennial of the Revolution of 1810. Immediately south, the **Museo Nacional del Vino y la Vendimia** (National Wine & Wine Harvest Museum) was once the founding Gargantini-Giol family's mansion, and its art nouveau architecture alone is worth a visit.

In the Coquimbito neighborhood, by contrast, **Cavas del Conde** dates from 1919 but has transformed itself into a boutique winery with gracious guides and an intimate underground tasting facility. It pales in comparison, though, with its Coquimbito neighbor **Bodega La Rural,** now owned by the Catena Zapata conglomerate but still operating autonomously. One of the province's oldest (1885) and largest

(2.8 million gallon/10.7 million L capacity) wineries, it also cultivates a fraction of its grapes—Cabernet Sauvignon only—on 25 acres (10 ha) here; it's best known for its premium Rutini line.

The technology is sophisticated—pneumatic presses, stainless-steel tanks, and French oak casks—but La Rural is a family favorite for its **Museo del Vino San Felipe,** with artifacts salvaged from over a century in the industry. Ceramic vessels, manual bottling and corking machines, plus

INSIDER TIP:

For a complete gourmet experience, don't miss La Casa del Visitante in Bodega Familia Zuccardi (see p. 194).

—CLAUDIA A. MARSICANO
National Geographic field scientist

antique carriages, tractors, and trucks make it a comprehensive history lesson in local winemaking. If possible, though, try to arrange an English-language tour and tasting—La Rural's Spanish-language tours draw large crowds. Alternatively, go early in the morning.

Also in Coquimbito is the smaller **Bodega Viña El Cerno,** a family-run effort with on-site vineyards and intimate cellars where the owners conduct tastings of their Cabernet, Malbec, Merlot, Syrah, Chardonnay, and blends. Annual production is fewer than 10,000 bottles of each varietal.

Bodegas López
- Ozamis 375, General Gutiérrez, Maipú, 8 miles (13.5 km) SE of Mendoza
- 0261/497-2406
- Tours Mon.–Sat. Advance arrangements needed for English tours Sun. & holidays
www.bodegaslopez.com.ar

Antigua Bodega Giol
- Ozamis 1040, General Gutiérrez, Maipú
- 0261/1560-12093

Museo Nacional del Vino y la Vendimia
- Ozamis 914, General Gutiérrez, Maipú
- 0261/497-7763
- Closed Jan. 1, May 1, & Dec. 25

Cavas del Conde
- Dorrego s/n, Coquimbito, Maipú
- 0261/497-2624
- Closed Sat.–Sun.
www.cavas.tawert.com

Bodega La Rural/Museo del Vino San Felipe
- Montecaseros 2625, Coquimbito, Maipú
- 0261/497-2013
- Closed Sun.
www.bodegalarural.com.ar

Bodega Viña El Cerno

✉ Moreno 631, Coquimbito, Maipú

☎ 0261/481-1567

🕐 Closed Sun.

www.elcerno.com.ar

Bodega Familia Zuccardi

✉ RP 33 Km 7.5, Fray Luis Beltrán, Maipú

☎ 0261/441-0000

🕐 Closed Jan. 1 & Dec. 25

www.familiazuccardi.com

In the countryside of Fray Luis Beltrán, half an hour from downtown Mendoza, **Bodega Familia Zuccardi** is on another scale entirely—surrounded by its own vineyards, Zuccardi produces prodigious amounts of domestic table wines and substantial amounts of fine wines for both urban consumption and export. Cultivating more than 30 varieties, it lets visitors (English-speaking guides are always available) sample its experiments as well as typical Mendoza vintages such as Malbec. Its mid-November **Degustación Anual** (*$$$$*) lets participants sample almost anything on the list and it provides entertainment on top of that. At other times, its restaurant is open to the public.

EXPERIENCE:
All Wine, All Day at Cavas Wine Lodge

On Mendoza's outskirts, facing the Andes whose spring snowmelt irrigates the grapes of Luján de Cuyo, Cavas Wine Lodge (*Costaflores s/n, tel. 0261/410-6927, www.cavaswinelodge.com*) is the place to surround yourself with wine—the 14 scattered adobes sit among 35 acres (14 ha) of vineyards. Its subterranean cava provides some of Argentina's finest vintages, its restaurant is the place to pair them with some of the area's finest dining, and it also arranges winery visits and tastings.

Cavas doesn't disdain Mendoza's other recreational pursuits—it will arrange activities such as hiking or white-water rafting in the nearby cordillera. At day's end you can literally immerse yourself in wine appreciation, as the Moorish-style spa offers vinotherapy baths of honey and wine.

Chacras de Coria & Around

South of Mendoza proper, **Luján de Cuyo** is a sprawling department that covers more than 1,871 square miles (4,847 sq km) from the alluvial piedmont to the highest Andes on the Chilean border. Only 20 minutes south of the city, the woodsy suburb of Chacras de Coria is an outlying "gourmet ghetto" that has become a fashionable residential area. Once covered with orchards and vineyards—the noun *chacra* derives from a Quechua term meaning "a small field"—it's also popular with tourists for its easy access to wineries (some within walking distance, many within cycling distance), easygoing pace, arts community, and quality accommodations.

Chacras's vital center is **Plaza Gerónimo Espejo,** whose Sunday crafts and antiques fair is one of the area's best. The plaza's mini-amphitheater is also the site for outdoor entertainment, sometimes including tango song and dance, on weekends. Nearby streets offer outstanding dining and entertainment as well—the erratic Argentine rock legend Charly García has played at the plaza's Cacano Bar—but it's generally more sedate than big-city nightlife.

Even on days when it's otherwise quiet, Chacras can offer an arts and entertainment space at the **Museo de Chacras de Coria** (*MUCHA; Pueyrredón 2124, tel 0261/496-5871, closed Mon., $*), a luminous new gallery and cultural center that showcases Mendocino artists, hosts lectures and book signings, has a small cinema, and sponsors live music and dance.

MUCHA complements Luján's traditional fine-arts museum, the **Museo Provincial de Bellas Artes Emiliano Guiñazú–Casa de Fader** *(Avenida San Martín 3651, tel 0261/496-0224, www.casafader .com.ar, closed Mon., $)* in the Mayor Drummond area southeast of Chacras. Named for local painter Fernando Fader (1882–1935), whose oils and watercolors deal with rural people and landscapes, the museum's collections specialize in regional artists. Fader also painted the murals in its hallways and pools for Emiliano Guiñazú, whose residence it was. Reflected in the exterior pools, with neoclassical statuary in its gardens, the somber brick building is forbidding on approach—the windows are few and tiny—but its interior is more luminous than might be expected. Like MUCHA, it also hosts special events.

Wineries of Luján de Cuyo:

The meltwater rivers that descend from the Andes into Luján de Cuyo irrigate the vineyards of some of Argentina's most prestigious wineries, many of them with their own accommodations and restaurants that make ideal lunch breaks.

The poplar-lined streets of Chacras de Coria are the home of **Bodega y Cavas de Weinert,** locally founded in the 1890s but acquired by the German-Brazilian Bernardo Weinert in the mid-1970s. The descent into its brick cellars, with their arched niches and decorative French oak casks, suggests tradition, but this was one of the earliest Mendoza wineries to adopt contemporary winemaking technology and to foresee a future for fine Argentine wines, especially Malbec, in the international market.

Bodega y Cavas de Weinert
- ✉ Avenida San Martín 5923, Chacras de Coria
- ☎ 0261/496-4382
- 🕐 Closed Sun., Jan. 1, May 1, & Dec. 24–25
- www.bodegaweinert .com

Malbec casks at Bodega y Cavas de Weinert, Luján de Cuyo

Just a few blocks south of the Fader museum, in the Mayor Drummond area, **Bodega Lagarde** is another classic winery that has been modernized with pneumatic presses and supplemented its epoxy-lined cement tanks with state-of-the-art stainless steel. Here, by contrast with Weinert, tours include a vineyard walk.

Like Lagarde, **Bodega Luigi Bosca** includes the vineyards in

Bodega Lagarde
- ✉ Avenida San Martín 1745, Mayor Drummond, Luján de Cuyo
- ☎ 0261/498-0011
- 💲 $$$
- www.lagarde.com.ar

Bodega Luigi Bosca

✉ Avenida San Martín 2044, Mayor Drummond, Luján de Cuyo
☎ 0261/498-1974
$ $$$
www.luigibosca
.com.ar

Bodega Ruca Malén

✉ RN 7 Km 1059, Agrelo, Luján de Cuyo
☎ 0261/413-8909
🕒 Closed Sun. & holidays
$ $$$$$
www.bodega
rucamalen.com

Bodega Séptima

✉ RN 7 Km 6.5, Agrelo, Luján de Cuyo
☎ 0261/498-9550
🕒 Closed Sun.
$ $$$$
www.bodega
septima.com.ar

its tours of its Mayor Drummond facilities. Its highlight, though, is winemaker Hugo Leytes's bas-relief cement murals chronicling the local wine industry, from the arrival of early immigrants through everyday activities such as planting, harvesting, bottling, and tasting. Leytes also depicts hazards, such as the hailstorms to which Cuyo vineyards are vulnerable; the tours end in a handsome tasting room.

Where the suburbs become the countryside and the highway to Chile starts westward, the Agrelo area is home to several important Luján wineries and their vineyards in contemporary facilities. **Bodega Ruca Malén,** for instance, is a boutique winery where everything is pneumatic presses, stainless steel, and new French and American oak barrels. Its post-tour tasting includes some of its best wines, along with snacks. Its restaurant, meanwhile, takes advantage of unobstructed Andean views while pairing wines with the day's lunch menu *(reservation only)*.

Immediately east, **Bodega Séptima,** a modern winery in the style of a pre-Columbian *pirca* (fortress), sits among more than 740 acres (300 ha) of relatively young vines. Its rooftop terraces offer vast Andean panoramas atop a building whose interior holds the latest in winemaking technology on a larger scale than at Ruca Malén.

A few miles south, **Bodega Catena Zapata** *(Cobos, Agrelo, Luján de Cuyo, tel 0261/413-1100, www.catenawines.com)* has built an attention-grabbing winery, in the style of a Maya pyramid, in the midst of its 260-acre (105 ha)

La Pirámide vineyards. The sole contemporary note is a glassed-in cupola that leads to a terrace with panoramas of the snow-topped Cordón del Plata. Unlike many Argentine wineries, it takes its inspiration not from Europe, but from California, where owner Nicolás Catena lived in the early 1980s. Its multilingual guides start the tours with a glass of Chardonnay and end them with a glass of

INSIDER TIP:

For the most stunning photographs you can take in Luján de Cuyo, go to its vineyards at sunrise and look toward the snowy Andes.

—ELISEO MICIU
National Geographic photographer

Malbec in well-lighted quarters decorated with modern paintings. For more comprehensive tastings, with premium vintages, there's an extra charge.

If Catena Zapata rises above the landscape, nearby **Bodega Dolium** *(RP 15 Km 30, Agrelo, Luján de Cuyo, tel 0261/490-0190, closed Mon. & holidays, $$$$$, www.dolium.com)* snuggles beneath it, taking advantage of ramped earth to place all its production underground—maintaining steady temperatures year-round in a torrid desert that sometimes gets snow in winter. The tasting facilities are aboveground in a small winery whose owner, Ricardo Giadorou, often shares a sip with visitors. ∎

Mendoza Province

The backcountry of Mendoza is one of Argentina's great recreational resources, with hiking and rafting in summer and skiing in winter, in a landscape that resembles the Himalaya. So closely does it recall the Himalaya, in fact, that it served as a stand-in for Central Asia in French director Jean-Jacques Annaud's *Seven Years in Tibet* (1997). Not many ranges could do that. Its mountains include South America's highest peak, Cerro Aconcagua.

The gateway to Aconcagua, Uspallata is an oasis in the arid Andes.

Potrerillos & Around

At Agrelo, RN 7 climbs slowly and then sharply up the Río Mendoza Valley to Potrerillos, a settlement whose model houses owe their existence to the **Embalse de Potrerillos,** a reservoir that submerged an earlier, much smaller hydroelectric project. Today it's a place to organize hiking and horseback riding, but most often visitors come for the white-water rafting and kayaking on the Río

Mendoza. Operators have their offices in Potrerillos and shuttle their clients up the valley to the put-in. Windsurfing is another option.

About 17 miles (27 km) west of Potrerillos, **Vallecitos** is a small ski area in the Cordón del Plata, about 9,500 feet (2,900 m) above sea level. The ski season runs from July to October, but on this dry side of the Andes, the snow cover can vary dramatically from year to year, so check before you go.

Vallecitos

- 187 A3
- ✉ 59 miles (95 km) W of Mendoza, access via RP 89

Visitor Information

- ☎ 0261/429-7338 in Mendoza

Uspallata

A 187 A3

Visitor Information

✉ RN 7 & RP 52, Uspallata

☎ 02624/420-410

www.turismo .lasheras.gov.ar

Bóvedas de Uspallata

✉ RN 149, 2 miles (3.5 km) N of RN 7

Los Penitentes

A 187 A3

✉ RN 7, 114 miles (183 km) W of Mendoza

☎ 0261/429-9953

www.lospenitentes .com

Uspallata & Around

Above Potrerillos, the winding two-lane highway passes through a series of short tunnels and, with so many trucks headed to Chile, traffic slows down dramatically before the landscape opens onto the scenic crossroads town of Uspallata, with the best services along the entire route. Lined with poplars, the main road continues toward the Chilean border, but the most interesting sights are to the north and east.

From the downtown crossroads, RP 52 is a scenic secondary road that loops northeast back to Mendoza via the **Caracoles de Villavicencio,** a series of switchbacks. The road passes a former hot-springs hotel site where a museum is planned on what is now a private nature reserve. Only 4.5 miles (7 km) outside Uspallata, **Cerro Tunduqueral** is a faded roadside rock-art site. This route,

which San Martín's army took in the successful campaign to liberate Chile, reaches 9,840 feet (3,000 m) but is more scenic than the main highway. It is also safer for cyclists, who can avoid tunnels and truck traffic en route to Mendoza.

From the same Uspallata crossroads, you can also try RP 149, which continues north toward the high country of San Juan Province. Only 2 miles (3.5 km) north of the junction, the **Bóvedas de Uspallata** is an archaeological and historical site where the Spaniards built three conical kilns, now restored, atop a pre-Columbian metallurgical site. In the campaign to liberate Chile, Gen. Gregorio de Las Heras used this as a base, and the on-site museum covers that and earlier usages.

Los Penitentes & Around

Los Penitentes, 39 miles (63 km) west of Uspallata, is a winter ski

Abandoned thermal baths and mineral deposits at Puente del Inca, Parque Provincial Aconcagua

resort that, in summertime, is the main base camp for exploring Aconcagua and vicinity. At roughly 8,500 feet (2,580 m) above sea level, it has better infrastructure and a more reliable snowpack than Vallecitos, as it's more exposed to Pacific storms, but the year-to-year variability can be significant.

Some 4.5 miles (7 km) west, the natural arch over the Río de las Cuevas at the roadside hamlet of **Puente del Inca** consists of stratified shingle cemented by chemicals secreted by nearby hot springs. Darwin, though, was unimpressed: "The Bridge of the Incas is by no means worthy of the great monarchs whose name it bears." Formerly visitors could cross the bridge to enjoy the baths but, due to recent weaknesses, it's off-limits except for photography from a distance.

Just before you reach Puente del Inca, you'll reach the climber's cemetery known as **Cementerio de los Andinistas**—Aconcagua has claimed more than a hundred lives—on a rugged outcrop on the south side of the highway. It's traditional for summit-bound expeditions to stop here before beginning the ascent, but not everyone who died on the mountain is buried here. Nor did everyone buried here die on the mountain; some successful summiteers have chosen to spend eternity at Puente del Inca.

Puente del Inca is also home to a large binational customs and immigration complex for travelers arriving from Chile; Chile-bound travelers do their paperwork at

---

EXPERIENCE: Descending the Mendoza

In general, Argentina's white-water rafting and kayaking take a distant second to Chile's, but when the spring runoff rushes down some of the Andes' highest summits, the Río Mendoza is a worthy challenge. While the rapids are few, big waves make for an exciting descent from a put-in above the foothills town of Potrerillos.

Two reliable operators have base camps in Potrerillos and on the highway: **Argentina Rafting Expediciones** *(Ruta Perilago, tel 02624/482-037, www.argentinarafting .com)* and **Ríos Andinos** *(RN 7 Km 55, tel 0261/517-4184, www.riosandinos.com).*

Portillo on the Chilean side of the border. Those remaining on the Argentine side can bypass the complex here.

Parque Provincial Aconcagua

A member of the famous "seven summits," the highest peaks on each continent, 22,837-foot (6,960 m) **Cerro Aconcagua** is one of the easiest to climb, but that's also the reason the Roof of the Americas is one of the most dangerous mountains in the world. The usual route to the peak of the "Stone Sentinel" is a walk-up, but its high altitude and changeable weather make it a challenge even for vigorous, well-conditioned individuals in the prime of life.

The Western Hemisphere's highest peak was always destined to be a magnet for mountaineers, and Swiss climber Matthias Zurbriggen (1856–1917) made

---

Parque Provincial Aconcagua

🅰 187 A3

Visitor Information

✉ Park Visitor Center, Valle de Horcones. Access from RN 7, 2 mi (3 km) W of Puente del Inca

🕐 Closed March 16– Nov. 14 except Holy Week

💲 $$$$$

www.aconcagua .mendoza.gov.ar

PERMITS: Ascent permits are required beyond Plaza de Mulas. You can obtain them at the **Permit Office** in Mendoza *(Avenida San Martín 1143, 1st floor, tel 0261/425-8751, closed Sat.–Sun. & holidays April–Nov. 15; passport required).*

the pioneer modern ascent—solo—in 1897. Many since have followed his route across the scree and snow but, in 1985, the discovery of an Inca mummy at almost 17,400 feet (5,300 m)—a precursor of Salta's Llullaillaco mummies—suggested that pre-Columbian peoples might have gotten there first.

Even if it's a climber's mecca, Aconcagua has something for everyone. The mountain is barely visible from the highway, but almost anyone can hike from the visitor center (a mile/1.5 km north via a

INSIDER TIP:

If you hire mules for Aconcagua, spend time with the gauchos; try their *mate*, and don't forget to return their generosity.

—PETER MCBRIDE
National Geographic photographer

gravel road) to **Laguna Horcones** (elevation 9,679 feet/2,950 m) for better views in half an hour or so. A lack of natural cover means that there is little shelter for wildlife, and the only large mammals are guanacos, foxes, and the rarely sighted puma. The Andean condor, though, is a common sight.

For a longer excursion, hikers can continue to **Confluencia,** about 5.5 miles (9 km) north of the ranger station, and return in the afternoon. It's also possible to camp there with permission. (All hikes in the park, except for Laguna Horcones, require written permits and a fee; overnight permits must be obtained and paid for at the Secretaría de Turismo in Mendoza city.)

At Confluencia, the trail bifurcates. The northeastern fork climbs 8 miles (13 km) to **Plaza Francia.** At 13,780 feet (4,200 m) it's the base camp for the **Pared Sur** (South Face) to the summit, which is a difficult technical climb from here, but overnighters will find the best views of Aconcagua.

Meanwhile, the northwestern fork climbs for 11 miles (18 km) to the **Plaza de Mulas,** 13,888 feet (4,230 m) above sea level,

Argentine Finger Food

Fastidious Argentines may eat them with knife and fork, but the light-crusted turnovers known as empanadas may be the continent's finest finger food. Many Latin American countries, of course, claim the empanada, but the Argentine version differs in its flaky phyllo covering and in the variety of filling. Ground beef is the default option, but ham and cheese, chicken, and mozzarella-tomato-basil are also popular.

Northwestern Argentina's *salteñas* are spicier than the norm and, in Cuyo and the northwest, empanadas *árabes* offer a Middle Eastern touch—chopped lamb with a touch of lemon. Whatever the filling, they're ideal for a long bus or car trip, or hike.

beyond which only climbers with ascent permits may continue on the **Ruta Noroeste** (Northwest Route). Experienced hikers do not really need guides, as the trails are clearly marked, but most climbers on this route—especially the inexperienced—hire guides for safety reasons and muleteers for logistical support. While not technically demanding, this is a strenuous climb and anyone intending to summit needs to spend several days at Plaza de Mulas (where

Pampa de Leñas, where there's a campground, and another four to five hours to the following campground at **Casa de Piedra.** From Casa de Piedra, it's about six hours to **Plaza Argentina,** the base camp for climbers at 13,780 feet (4,200 m).

Cristo Redentor

In 1904, during an era of good feeling in which Argentina and Chile settled territorial disputes dating from colonial times,

Cristo Redentor
 187 A3

Men and mules ride and walk beneath the hemisphere's highest peaks in Mendoza Province.

there is a hotel as well as a campground) for acclimatization. There are fatalities almost every year.

At Punta de Vacas, 10 miles (16 km) southeast of Puente del Inca, far fewer hikers and climbers approach the mountain via the **Ruta Glaciar de los Polacos** (Polish Glacier Route), which went unclimbed until 1934. It's a five-hour hike, and four-hour return, to the park entrance at

porters and mules lugged the bronze pieces of sculptor Mateo Alonso's four-ton (3.6 metric ton) **Christ the Redeemer statue** from the border post of Las Cuevas to the actual border at roughly 12,645 feet (3,854 m) above sea level. Until 1979, when the tunnel to Chile opened, this was the main highway across the Andes.

(continued on p. 204)

Drive: The Uco Valley Wineries

South of Mendoza and Luján de Cuyo, the Uco Valley drains the spectacular Cordón del Plata, a phalanx of snow-covered peaks. Their waters irrigate the fields of Mendoza's most fashionable new wine district, with its bodegas scattered over a wide area. Unlike in most of Luján, these wineries and their vineyards are almost inseparable, though most of them have outlying fields as well.

Vineyards of the Koch winery, Tupungato, Mendoza

Touring the wineries from Mendoza and returning via the Cordón del Plata is possible in a day, but an overnight stay is more desirable. From downtown **Mendoza ❶** (see pp. 188–192), southbound RN 40 is a four-lane highway that shrinks to two lanes north of the town of **Zapata ❷**, 43 miles (70 km) to the south. From here, RP 88 leads 10 miles (16 km) northwest to **Bodega y Viñedos Familia Giaquinta ❸** *(RP 88, Carril Zapata, La Arboleda, Tupungato, tel 2622/488-090, www.familiagiaquinta.com.ar)*—a family-run business whose rustic facilities don't quite fit the fashionability mold. Still, the winery gets high marks for its willingness to show visitors around the sometimes-cluttered quarters. Tastings, including the unusual white Pedro Ximénez, are generous.

NOT TO BE MISSED:
Bodega San Polo • Bodega O. Fournier • Bodegas Salentein

Returning to the junction, the highway heads 18 miles (30 km) south through the town of Tunuyán to **San Carlos ❹**, where Avenida San Martín leads 2 miles (3 km) west to **Bodega San Polo** *(San Martín, La Consulta, tel 2622/471-200, www.sanpolo.com.ar)* in the La Consulta area. Like Giaquinta, San Polo is a traditional winery, once operated by the Giol-Gargantini family that also ran Maipú's massive Bodega Giol (see p. 193), but it has expanded and modernized to produce export-quality

Malbec and other varietals and blends. The winery still preserves some antique machinery, including hydraulic presses.

Returning to the highway, pass through the center of San Carlos to República de Chile, a street that turns west and then immediately doglegs across a bridge to Los Indios street; after 3 miles (5 km) on a dusty road, you arrive at **Bodega y Viñedos O. Fournier** (*Los Indios, San Carlos, tel 02622/451-579, www.ofournier.com*), an ultrachic winery surrounded by 650 acres (263 ha) of vineyards. Around the winery, the pebbled xeriscape mimics the local riverbeds. At tour's end, visitors pass through the subterranean cellars, with their gallery of contemporary paintings, and finish with a tasting at the restaurant, which overlooks a bird-filled pond with the mountains in the background. The winery also offers overnight accommodations.

Backtracking to San Carlos, RP 92 and several other secondary roads pass through a series of

small towns for 24 miles (38 km) en route to **Bodegas Salentein ❺** (*Ruta 89, Los Arboles, tel 02622/429-500, closed Mon., www.bodega salentein.com*), which surpasses even Fournier for its views—the Andes seem close enough to touch—and facilities. With its **Galería Killka** representing Dutch and Argentine painters, a restaurant that's a branch of Mendoza's renowned La Marchigiana, and its own guest-house, this is the best stopover on the route.

From Salentein, RP 89 leads north for 12 miles (20 km) to **Tupungato ❻**, where it doglegs to the northwest along one of the province's most spectacular roads for 25 miles (41 km) to **Potrerillos** (see p. 197). There it intersects RN 7 and returns to Luján de Cuyo and Mendoza, another 43 miles (68 km) northeast. En route, RN 7 passes several Luján wineries, including the roadside **Bodega Séptima ❼** (see p. 196) and the boutique operation, **Bodega Ruca Malén** (see p. 196).

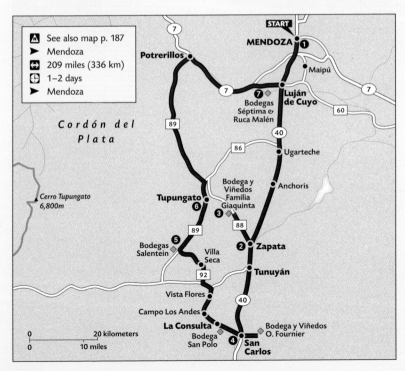

San Rafael

📍 187 B2

Visitor Information

✉ Avenida Hipólito
Yrigoyen 780

☎ 0260/442-4217

www.sanrafael
turismo.gov.ar

Finca y Bodega La Abeja

✉ Avenida Hipólito
Yrigoyen 1900,
San Rafael

☎ 0260/443-9804

🕐 Closed Sun.

www.bodegalaabeja
.com.ar

Bodega y Viñedos Jean Rivier e Hijos

📍 Avenida Hipólito
Yrigoyen 2385,
San Rafael

☎ 0260/443-2675

🕐 Closed Sun. &
holidays

www.jeanrivier.com

Casa Bianchi

✉ RN 143 &
Valentín Bianchi,
Las Paredes

☎ 0260/444-9600

🕐 Closed Sun.

www.vbianchi.com

Today, by contrast, private cars and minivans are the only vehicles that climb the zigzag route to see Alonso's 23-foot (7 m) tribute to peace between the two countries. For those who can withstand the wind and cold, there are views of the upper Río Mendoza drainage and the Chilean Andes to the west. Motor vehicles cannot proceed across the border here to Chile, but determined cyclists and hikers can (it's downhill all the way to the border post at Los Libertadores).

San Rafael & Around

In almost the precise center of the province, where the Atuel and Diamante Rivers almost converge, San Rafael is an orderly city of tree-lined avenues that's a base for kayaking, rafting, and visiting a cluster of wineries that are within staggering distance of each other.

Excursions are more frequent, and easier to arrange, on the **Río Atuel,** which has been tamed by hydroelectric dams except for a few accessible Class I–III stretches. The **Río Diamante,** by contrast, is a less accessible and more challenging Class IV–V river that also runs between two dams.

Rather lower than most of Mendoza's other wine regions, San Rafael is only about 2,460 feet (750 m) above sea level; its warm summers have an impact on the harvest. Its wineries range from mom-and-pop operations to state-of-the-art industrial facilities. The best example of the former is **Finca y Bodega La Abeja,** which started in the 1880s; in fact,

much of its original gear—wooden presses, for instance—is still in use. Set back slightly from the highway through town, it is increasing its fine wine productions such as a Bonarda/Tempranillo blend and offering informative guided tours.

Guarding the Vines of San Rafael

One of Argentina's lesser known wine districts, San Rafael is off the tourist track except for overland visitors en route to the ski resort of Las Leñas—and ski season is not the best time for visiting bodegas and vineyards. In fact, the proximity of the high Andes is a real risk for grapes—San Rafael gets hot in summer, but when the heat collides with cold Andean air, hailstorms can damage or even destroy the harvest. Many growers use netting to protect their crops.

Just a few blocks west, **Bodega y Viñedos Jean Rivier e Hijos** cultivates its grapes on about 150 acres (60 ha) outside town, some of them in the Uco Valley. It's also a family operation but, unlike La Abeja, it has upgraded its winery facilities to include the latest hoppers, crushers, and presses. It's also casual enough that drop-in visitors can take the tour with the owner and sample the uncommon white Tocai Friulano.

Casa Bianchi, meanwhile, is the area's highest profile winery, especially since its new industrial plant—on the western outskirts of town—opened to include a separate plant for sparkling wines. While it's still a family winery, its facilities produce far greater quantities of fine wines, in stainless-steel tanks, than its nearby competitors.

Malargüe & Around

Southwest of San Rafael, Malargüe is a high, cool town in a rugged volcanic landscape that, until recently, was known for its goatherds. Over the past couple of decades, though, the town has become a popular winter destination; skiers from around the country, the continent, and the world stay here because of the limited accommodations and because it's a less expensive alternative to the nearby Las Leñas resort (see p. 207).

Its volcanic backcountry to the south has the potential to become a destination in its own right. Paved but rough in parts, RN 40 continues south into the Patagonian province of Neuquén, but public transportation is rare. The recently improved access to the area may encourage travelers to explore an area that, at the moment, is for those willing to endure rough roads and limited services. It could also make the wild high Andean crossing southwest of Malargüe to the Chilean city of Talca more routine.

Malargüe hasn't lost its traditions, though. Goatherds are

Vines of the Koch winery, Tupungato, Mendoza Province

still a sight in the surrounding mountains. Its **Fiesta Nacional del Chivo** (National Goat Festival) brings big-name folklore performers into town for a week in early January, and *chivito* (kid goat) from Malargüe is a premium dish on menus around the province.

Malargüe's traditions are also on display at the **Museo Regional Malargüe,** a well-organized municipal museum stressing natural and local history, on the grounds of the **Parque del Ayer,** the city's largest green space, which is also home to the **Molino Histórico de Rufino Ortega,** a pioneer flour mill. Across the highway is **Observatorio Pierre Auger,** which has erected a network of 1,600 detectors over an

Malargüe
△ 187 A2
Visitor Information
✉ RN 40 N
☎ 0260/447-1659
🕐 Closed Jan. 1 & Dec. 25
www.malargue .gov.ar

Museo Regional Malargüe
✉ RN 40 N & Pasaje La Orteguina
☎ 0260/447-0154

Observatorio Pierre Auger
✉ Avenida San Martín Norte 304
☎ 0260/447-1562
🕐 Closed Sat.–Sun.
www.auger.org.ar

Skiers at Las Leñas, Mendoza Province

Monumento Natural Provincial Castillos de Pincheira

⚠ 187 A2

✉ Camino de las Canteras, 17 miles (27 km) W of Malargüe

💲 $$

Reserva Provincial Laguna de Llancanelo

⚠ 187 B2

✉ RP 186, 47 miles (75 km) SE of Malargüe

⊕ Guide required

💲 $$$$$

area of nearly 1,200 square miles (3,000 sq km) for research into ultra-high-energy cosmic rays.

East, south, and west of Malargüe, rough and often poorly marked roads thread through mostly volcanic badlands dotted with craters, cones, caves, and lava flows. Because logistics are awkward, hiring a local agency to visit at least some of them is a good idea; some sites require a guide.

West of town, the most accessible of these sights is the **Monumento Natural Provincial Castillos de Pincheira** (Castles of Pincheira Provincial Natural Monument) that, as its name might suggest, is a Tertiary series of sedimentary and volcanic bluffs, up to 197 feet (60 m) high, that resembles the battlements of a medieval castle. According to legend, the Chilean-born caudillo José Antonio Pincheira used them as a hideout in the early independence years.

Immediately east, by an especially confusing series of dirt roads

that can be impassable after rains, the **Reserva Provincial Laguna de Llancanelo** is a saline lake, surrounded by marshes, that's only a third of its original size because of the drying climate. Even so, it supports 175 species of birds, many of them aquatic, including black-necked swans and flamingos.

About 43 miles (70 km) south of Malargüe via RN 40, the **Monumento Natural Provincial Caverna de las Brujas** is a limestone anomaly in the midst of the dominant volcanic landscape. The cave's entrance is barred, but it is open to the public during daylight hours for guided tours.

The area's largest reserve, though, is the **Reserva Provincial La Payunia,** a massive region nearly 1,750 square miles (4,500 sq km) in size with hundreds of extinct—or at least dormant—volcanic cones, ashfalls, and sprawling lava flows. The wildlife here, most notably herds of guanacos, sprinting rheas, and hovering Andean condors, is easy to spot because of the open landscape, where even the scrub vegetation is discontinuous.

Las Leñas Ski Area

Since it opened in 1983, Las Leñas has become Argentina's premier ski resort because of its reliable snowpack and despite—or perhaps because of—its inaccessibility. At the end of a meandering mountain road that starts 19 miles (30 km) north of Malargüe, with no commercial airport closer than San Rafael, the exclusive resort draws Argentine, regional, and overseas skiers for pricey weeklong packages. At the same time, Las Leñas remains accessible to budget-minded skiers who stay in Malargüe and get 50 percent discounts off lift tickets, but the hour-plus trip from town means less time on the slopes.

With help from instructors, Las Leñas's beginners' runs are easy to navigate, with no turns, so that neophytes can usually handle them within a day, but that's only 5 percent of the total. The steeper intermediate, advanced, and especially expert slopes are more challenging in this treeless landscape. Some skiers say the steepest slopes are the best on the continent.

Because Argentines tend to sleep late—the resort's pubs and discos keep long hours—early risers can get a head start on the lifts and enjoy less-crowded runs. Some runs have lights for night skiing.

To make the best of their investment, Las Leñas's owners are making a concerted effort to attract summer visitors for hiking, mountain biking, and climbing. Despite the elevation, the sunny weather is ideal for outdoor activities, and prices are a fraction of those during ski season. ∎

INSIDER TIP:

Las Leñas has fantastic runs for free-riding. The best way to get there is heli-skiing. It's not expensive, and you'll marvel at the amazing Andes scenery.

—ELISEO MICIU
National Geographic photographer

Monumento Natural Provincial Caverna de las Brujas
- 🅰 187 A2
- ✉ 43 miles (70 km) SW of Malargüe. Access from RN 40
- 💲 $$$$$. Guide required; register in advance at visitor center in Malargüe

Reserva Provincial La Payunia
- 🅰 187 B1/B2
- ✉ Access via RN 40 & RP 186, 100 miles (160 km) S of Malargüe
- 💲 Fee included in tour price. Registered local guide required

Las Leñas
- 🅰 187 A2
- ✉ RP 222, 48 miles (78 km) NW of Malargüe
- ☎ 0260/447-1281
- www.laslenas.com

Caves & Cones & Marshes: Argentina's Empty Quarter

Some Malargüe residents argue that the area south of the city, via the legendary RN 40, is part of Patagonia. For most geographers, that's a stretch, but *malargüenses* have a point: Thinly populated southern Mendoza Province is a nearly roadless area whose native flora and fauna mark a transition from the central to the southern Andes. Much of the area is south of the Río Colorado headwaters, though north of the river that marks Patagonia's traditional boundary.

Still, it has things that Patagonia doesn't: limestone caves, suitable for spelunking; wildfowl-rich wetlands; and a vast, stunningly desolate landscape of broad volcanic cones unmatched anywhere else. With Patagonia's rising popularity, this could be the last frontier for adventurous travelers.

Northern Cuyo

Mendoza may be a desert, but the northern Cuyo provinces are, for the most part, hotter, drier, and far more desolate. That said, there's a breathtaking beauty to the desolation of their polychrome deserts, and intriguing offbeat sights are available in a region that sees a relative handful of foreign travelers. Given a chance, though, avoid the hottest summer months of January and February.

Badlands at Parque Nacional Talampaya, La Rioja Province

Province of San Luis

◭ 187 C2/C3

Visitor Information

✉ Avenida Arturo Illia & Junín, San Luis

☎ 0266/442-3479

www.turismo .sanluis.gov.ar

San Luis & Around

Primarily east of Mendoza, the province of San Luis bills itself as the Portal de Cuyo ("gateway to Cuyo"). Its namesake city is an easygoing provincial capital whose bustling downtown fills three full blocks between **Plaza Juan Pascual Pringles** (the commercial center) and **Plaza Independencia** (the civic center). The main dining and entertainment zone lies along **Avenida Arturo Illia,** a northwesterly diagonal off Plaza Pringles that links it to the former Estación de Ferrocarril, the train station.

Facing Plaza Pringles, the 19th-century **Iglesia Catedral** is noteworthy for its twin bell towers, central cupola, and the bas-reliefs of its richly decorated pediment above half a dozen Corinthian columns. It also holds the crypt of local independence hero Juan Pascual Pringles (1795–1831), whose equestrian statue stands in the center of the plaza.

Plaza Independencia holds the city's oldest surviving building, the 18th-century **Antiguo Templo de Santo Domingo,** on its south side. A newer section of the church, with a Moorish facade, is a 1930s reconstruction, but the carved algarrobo doors on the older portion are original. On the north side, dating from 1913, the **Casa de Gobierno** (Government House) is now occupied by Claudio Poggi, a protégé of the Rodríguez Saá dynasty—one of whom, the five-term governor Adolfo, served a week as Argentina's president in late 2001.

From San Luis, the finest excursion is the hill station of **Potrero de los Funes,** only 12 miles (19 km) northeast of town. It's the place where *puntanos* (natives of San Luis) go for hiking, cycling, horseback riding, and water sports on its artificial lake.

Villa de Merlo

In the northeasternmost part of the province, San Luis shares the Sierras de Comechingones with neighboring Córdoba, and the western face of the granitic and metamorphic mountains rises steeply behind the town of Merlo. Most visitors come in January and February, but the shoulder seasons of November–December and March–April are no less pleasant and much less crowded.

Merlo dates from colonial times, but only the central, sycamore-shaded **Plaza Marqués de Sobremonte,** with its 18th-century baroque **Iglesia Nuestra Señora del Rosario** at the base of the mountains, has any genuine colonial ambience. Most visitors choose to stay in **El Rincón,** the zone of summer homes and hotels that rises sharply up Avenida del Sol, two blocks south.

Municipal authorities assert that Merlo is among the world's three finest microclimates—at about 3,000 feet (900 m) above sea level, the weather here is almost invariably agreeable—but provide no evidence to support the claim. Merlo can justly claim easy access, by road, to the Comechingones divide, where adventure-travel operators offer hiking, climbing, horseback riding, rappelling, and even parasailing on the thermals that rise up the slopes. Mountain biking here is a real workout but, once you've reached the ridge above town, the terrain is relatively gentle.

INSIDER TIP:

Hike back from the sauropod tracks in Parque Nacional Sierra de las Quijadas around sundown. The sunset colors will amaze you.

—CHARLIE O'MALLEY
Travel writer

Parque Nacional Sierra de las Quijadas

In the northwestern corner of the province, in the running to be a UNESCO World Heritage site, the polychrome Sierra de las Quijadas is one of a series of sedimentary basins that stretches north to La Rioja. Along with San Juan's Ischigualasto and La Rioja's Talampaya, it's also the source of major fossil finds, including massive sauropod tracks and full skeletons of pterosaurs (flying reptiles).

Villa de Merlo
◭ 187 C3
Visitor Information
✉ Coronel Mercau 605
☎ 02656/475-155
www.villademerlo .gov.ar

Parque Nacional Sierra de las Quijadas
◭ 187 B3
✉ RN 147, 75 miles (120 km) NW of San Luis. Administrative office: Pedernera 1488, San Luis
☎ 0266/444-5141 (San Luis)
$ $$$$
www.parques nacionales.gov.ar

Only about 75 miles (120 km) from the provincial capital by paved RN 147, near the locality of Hualtarán, the park entrance marks the access to a 5-mile (8 km) gravel road that leads west past the pre-Columbian **Hornillos Huarpes,** a series of 25 earthen ovens used for cooking and for firing ceramics. First exposed by surface flow and then excavated by archaeologists, they date from about A.D. 1000.

From the ovens, the road winds west through a narrow scrub-filled canyon, passing the simple campground (the only accommodations) before opening onto the **Potrero de la Aguada,** a vast red sandstone amphitheater that stretches to the horizon. Surrounded by jaggedly weathered cliffs of horizontally bedded sentiments, it seems straight out of the Four Corners area in the southwestern U.S.

Where the road ends, a short nature trail leads through thickets of cactuses, the endemic *chica* (a small tree with a spiral trunk and dense, hard wood), and the resinous *jarilla* (a low-growing shrub often used in folk medicine). For the most part, though, the vegetative cover is spotty in a climate with high summer temperatures (upwards of 104°F/40°C) and low rainfall. Likewise, much of the wildlife—foxes, peccaries, pumas—is nocturnal to avoid the midday heat.

From road's end, a longer looping trail provides even better panoramas of the *potrero,* but descending into the complexity of the badlands trails requires a local guide—available at the park campground, where there are also limited refreshments—plus water

The Political Earthquake of 1944

The San Juan earthquake of January 15, 1944, was Argentina's Hurricane Katrina—perhaps the most notorious natural disaster in the country's history. With an estimated magnitude of 7.0, it killed at least 10,000 people and left half the province homeless, according to historian Mark Healey.

The humanitarian disaster, though, was a political opportunity and, unlike the Katrina example, Argentina had a government eager to legitimize itself. The year before, a military regime had overthrown the civilian government of President Ramón Castillo (who was only marginally more legitimate than the military regime that had installed him).

In a provincial capital that was sharply divided between wealthy winemakers and an urban middle class who inhabited the central city, and an impoverished working class beyond "the four avenues," the previously obscure Gen. Juan Domingo Perón saw a chance to "pay off our great debt to the suffering and virtuous masses: The era of Argentine social policy has begun." Perón rushed assistance to the provincial capital, where rich and poor suffered alike from the collapse of precarious adobe buildings.

Unfortunately for *sanjuaninos,* the follow-up was more like Katrina, and a drawn-out reconstruction was still ongoing when a new military regime overthrew Perón—by then an elected president—in 1955. It had one other dramatic impact though: At an earthquake relief benefit in Buenos Aires, an obscure soap opera actress named Eva Duarte maneuvered to meet Perón and, eventually, to become "Evita."

and snacks. In summer, the area is off-limits from midmorning through midafternoon because of the heat.

San Juan & Around

Only two hours north of Mendoza via RN 40, the smaller provincial capital of San Juan de la Frontera has played a key role in Argentine history. During the wars of independence (1810–1818), it sheltered national hero José de San Martín; it was the birthplace of President Domingo F. Sarmiento; and it suffered a massive 1944 earthquake—seismic movements are frequent here—that helped bring Juan Perón to prominence (see sidebar opposite).

Because of its earthquakes, San Juan has only a handful of surviving historic sites, but there's a pedestrian-friendly downtown shaded by sycamores, an abundance of museums, and a thriving wine industry on a much smaller landscaping scale than Mendoza's. The town center is **Plaza 25 de Mayo,** whose graceful fountains, palms, and statuary contrast dramatically with its **Iglesia Catedral,** a modern monolith that replaced a colonial cathedral damaged in the 1944 quake.

One block north and a block west, the **Convento de Santo Domingo** also suffered severe damage in the quake, but its **Celda Histórica de San Martín,** where the liberator planned his dramatic crossing of the Andes, still survives.

San Juan's best preserved historic site, though, is the **Museo y Biblioteca Casa Natal de Sarmiento,** the boyhood home

of the soldier, politician, diplomat, and educator who overcame his provincial origins to become one of the most eloquent spokesmen for the Unitarist cause. Damaged in the 1944 quake, it was one of few buildings that survived the rebuilding frenzy that robbed the city of its historic heritage.

INSIDER TIP:

The melons, peaches, and grapes of San Juan are especially tasty if tried in the orchards where they grow, in the shade of poplar trees.

—NICOLAS KUGLER
National Geographic contributor

In his memoir, *Recuerdos de Provincia (Provincial Memories),* Sarmiento recalled the fig tree—regrown from a sprout—beneath which his mother spread her weaver's loom. Today, the historic tree is under continual observation by an agronomist, and the loom stands in a separate salon. Other rooms include Sarmiento's actual birthplace, the restored kitchen with original implements, the library he built while governor of San Juan, and prized personal possessions in a private room and the office he used while governor.

Five blocks west and four blocks north, the Universidad Nacional de San Juan has integrated the **Museo de Ciencias Naturales** with its research into the dinosaur country of Parque Provincial Ischigualasto

(continued on p. 214)

Province of San Juan

- 🗺 187 A4/B4

Visitor Information

- ✉ Sarmiento 24 S, San Juan
- ☎ 0264/421-0004
- 🕐 Closed Jan. 1, May 1, & Dec. 25

www.turismo.sanjuan .gov.ar

Celda Histórica de San Martín

- ✉ Laprida 57 W, San Juan
- ☎ 0264/423-0291
- 🕐 Closed Sun. & most holidays
- 💲 $

www.celdahistorica .blogspot.com

Museo y Biblioteca Casa Natal de Sarmiento

- ✉ Sarmiento 21 Sur, San Juan
- ☎ 0264/422-4603
- ☎ Closed Jan. 1, May 1, & Dec. 25
- 💲 $

www.casanatal sarmiento.com.ar

Museo de Ciencias Naturales

- ✉ Predio Ferial, Avenida España Norte & Maipú, San Juan
- ☎ 0264/421-6774

The Fossils of Cuyo

Where the westernmost outliers of the Sierras Pampeanas meet the easternmost Andes, Argentina has some of the world's most important paleontological sites. In an ancient landscape, the Ischigualasto (see pp. 216–217), Talampaya (see pp. 217–218), and Las Quijadas (see pp. 209–211) parks form a triad that can boast some of the oldest, largest, and best preserved dinosaurs on Earth.

Herrerasaurus, Parque Provincial Ischigualasto, San Juan Province

Ischigualasto

After Harvard paleontologist A. S. Romer saw Ischigualasto in 1958, he called it "the most extraordinary fossil cemetery ever imagined. And all perfectly preserved." Considered the most undisturbed Triassic formation on Earth, its sediments preserved beneath a layer of volcanic ash, it covers 45 million years of a period that started around 245 million years ago.

Its prize finds have been the dinosaurs *Eoraptor lunensis,* a small swift predator that may have been omnivorous, and the larger

Herrerasaurus ischigualastensis, best described as a smaller version of *Tyrannosaurus rex.* Skeletons of both are on display at the visitor center.

Some paleontologists have questioned whether *Eoraptor* was even a dinosaur, suggesting it was instead a closely related archosaur; in either case, its size and other physical characteristics—only about a yard (1 m) in length, with a three-fingered hand—indicate that the earliest dinosaurs were bipedal predators. *Herrerasaurus,* about twice the size of *Eoraptor,* seems to mark a transition from the archosaurs to true dinosaurs (some individuals were so large that they were thought to belong to a different species).

Dinosaurs form only a small percentage of Ischigualasto's fossils. Most of them date from the earlier Permian period and include reptiles such as herbivorous rhynchosaurs and carnivorous cynodonts, early predecessors of mammals. At one time, Ischigualasto's environment was a forested floodplain, and petrified trees and ferns are abundant. The most imposing of the fauna were ancestors of today's crocodiles, which occupied both riverine and terrestrial ecological niches.

Talampaya

Geologically, Talampaya resembles Ischigualasto and its scenery is even more striking, but it lacks the diversity of fossil remains that Ischigualasto can boast. *Riojasaurus*, a plodding late Triassic herbivore that reached 33 feet (10 m) in length, was found here, but the most characteristic species were *Lagosuchus talampayensis*, a small dinosaur ancestor that died out in the middle Triassic, and the late Triassic turtle *Palaeochersis talampayensis*.

Las Quijadas

Las Quijadas, on the other hand, can boast tracks from late Jurassic sauropods and an abundance of Cretaceous pterosaurs, flying reptiles with wingspans over 8 feet (2.5 m). Three seasons of fieldwork by the Universidad Nacional de San Luis and New York's American Museum of Natural History yielded nearly a thousand specimens, and their varying ages—from juveniles to adults—has made it possible to study their growth patterns. Because their discoveries came from only a small part of the Lagarcito formation, the paleontologists involved expect to find much more material.

Some crocodiles may also be present here, though the evidence is incomplete. In addition, there are imprints of small invertebrates, as well as petrified wood from the time when this area was not the desert it is today. If, as anticipated, the park is declared a World Heritage site, this formal recognition would enhance the reputation of a remarkable regional paleontology circuit that, with more research, is likely to be the site of even greater finds.

Layers of geological history at Valle de la Luna, Parque Provincial Ischigualasto, San Juan Province

Water bottles are offerings to the folk saint Difunta Correa.

Museo de Bellas Artes Franklin Rawson

✉ Avenida Libertador 862 Oeste

☎ 0264/420-0958

🕐 Closed Mon.

💲 $

Antigua Bodega

✉ Salta 782 N, San Juan

☎ 0264/421-2722

🕐 Closed Sun.

www.antiguabodega.com

(see p. 216), and this facility makes a good introduction for park-bound travelers and even those who won't be able to make it. Its prize exhibit is a reconstructed skeleton of *Herrerasaurus*, a late Triassic predator that's one of the oldest dinosaurs ever discovered, but it also features a re-creation of the park's paleo-environment and a living laboratory where technicians prepare fossils for future display.

In addition to science, San Juan supports the arts through its **Museo de Bellas Artes Franklin Rawson,** now in new quarters in the southwestern part of town. Named for the son of

a Massachusetts-born pioneer, it includes 19th-century paintings by Rawson (1820–1871) himself, who never had commercial success. It also includes contemporary works by Berni, Raquel Forner, and others.

Compared with Mendoza, San Juan's fine-wine district is pretty modest—until recently it was known for bulk table wines—but the **Pocito** district south of town and the **Pie de Palo** district to the east are both worth visiting. A good starting point is **Antigua Bodega,** a winery with a museum and a tasting room, one block east and four blocks north of the natural history museum.

About 6 miles (10 km) south of San Juan, directly on the west side of RN 40, **Bodegas y Viñedos Fabril Alto Verde** is an organic winery that has added a modern tasting room to facilities that produce red and white wines, including blends and sparkling wines. West of the highway, but still accessible, **Viñas de Segisa** tailors its tours to the individual.

For the active, a side trip to **Dique Ullum,** 11 miles (18 km) west of San Juan, can earn hikers a panoramic view of the reservoir and the Andes, which are the source of the water that irrigates the district's vineyards. Inadvisable in really hot weather, the trail climbs steeply from the Stations of the Cross, near the dam outlet, before it takes a more undulating course to the 5,900-foot (1,800 m) summit of **Cerro Tres Marías.**

Difunta Correa Shrine

One of Argentina's most offbeat destinations, the Difunta Correa shrine owes its existence to a legend from the civil wars of the mid-19th century. According to this story, a nursing mother, María Antonia Deolinda Correa, was trailing her conscript husband but died in the waterless desert near the present-day village of Vallecito, 39 miles (63 km) east of San Juan. Her infant son, though, miraculously survived at her breast until found by roving muleteers.

However implausible, the story struck such a chord among *sanjuaninos* that the Difunta Correa ("dead Correa") became a folk saint whose cult has spread around the country, despite no conclusive evidence that she ever existed. Roadside shrines

INSIDER TIP:

At Easter, hundreds of thousands of pilgrims descend on the colorful shrine of the Difunta Correa, filled with an amazing collection of ex-votos [offerings] to this folk saint.

—MARIA LAURA MASSOLO
Anthropologist

with water bottles and other offerings can be found from the Bolivian border to the tip of Tierra del Fuego, but the shrine near Vallecito is the "mother church," so to speak, where working-class pilgrims bring their offerings—license plates that symbolize their journey, model cars and houses—that represent their good fortune thanks to their prayers

to the Difunta. Some visitors even scramble on their backs to the hillock grotto to see and touch the life-size image of her and her baby.

In terms of sheer numbers, the Difunta Correa shrine is the province's biggest tourist attraction—it draws upwards of 100,000 pilgrims to one of Argentina's starkest deserts at Easter—but it remains below the radar for foreign visitors. That's partly because of its remoteness, but also because its style of popular—or populist—religion differs so dramatically from conventional religious landmarks like cathedrals. Even the Church has had to come to terms with the Difunta's ineradicable appeal, but the on-site chapel is only a minor attraction.

At the same time, because of the crowds it draws, the shrine is an economic force, a complex with accommodations, restaurants, souvenir stands, and its own tourist office. Some brides even choose their wedding dresses from a huge inventory here. For foreign visitors, though, it's a surreal wonderland and a chance to appreciate an aspect of Argentina usually unseen by those whose image of the country is tango and the gaucho.

San Agustín de Valle Fértil

About three hours northeast of San Juan by a roundabout road, the oasis of San Agustín de Valle Fértil is an ideal getaway from the provincial capital. For overseas visitors, though, it's become the gateway to the twin World Heritage sites of Ischigualasto and Talampaya (La Rioja Province), the fossil-rich badlands that, together with San Luis's

Bodegas y Viñedos Fabril Alto Verde
✉ RN 40 bet. Calles 13 & 14, Pocito, San Juan
☎ 0261/492-1905
www.fabril-altoverde.com.ar

Viñas de Segisa
✉ Aberastain & Calle 15, La Rinconada, Pocito
☎ 0264/492-2000
www.saxsegisa.com.ar

Difunta Correa Shrine
🅰 187 B4
✉ RN 141, 39 miles (63 km) E of San Juan
☎ 0264/496-1018 (Caucete)
www.visitedifuntacorrea.com.ar

San Agustín de Valle Fértil
🅰 187 B4
Visitor Information
✉ General Acha 52
☎ 0264/642-0104

Parque Natural Valle Fértil

🏔 187 B4

✉ Ruta 510, 31 miles (50 km) W of San Agustín de Valle Fértil

Parque Provincial Ischigualasto

🏔 187 B4

✉ 45 miles (73 km) NW of San Agustín via RP 510 & RN 150

☎ 0264/422-7372

💲 $$$$$

Las Quijadas, form a scenic paleontological wonderland.

San Agustín has attractions of its own, in addition to its placid village atmosphere. These include the **Piedra Pintada,** a splash of petroglyphs among the fractured, aloe-studded rocks across the Río Seco; the pre-Columbian **Morteros Indígenas** (Indian Mortars), a short distance beyond; and the **Meseta Ritual** (Ritual Mesa), near the agricultural school. In the sierras to the west, the **Parque Natural Valle Fértil** is a separate provincial reserve that gets only a handful of visitors. Best explored by horseback, it differs greatly from the other parks because of its heavier rainfall.

Parque Provincial Ischigualasto

With improved roads, a World Heritage site designation shared with nearby Talampaya, and a sparkling new museum, no single Argentine park has seen greater progress than the Valle de la Luna ("valley of the moon") of Ischigualasto over the last several years. Only an hour north of Valle Fértil and the site of major paleontological discoveries in a lunar landscape, Ischigualasto is both a scenic and scientific wonderland.

Ischigualasto's **Centro de Interpretación Museo de Ciencias Naturales Sede Ischigualasto** is the starting point for guided tours of the park, whether by private car or minivan tour from San Agustín or San Juan (most tours also visit Talampaya). In a cavernous warehouse, paleontology students from the Universidad Nacional de San Juan lead their guests through sophisticated dinosaur displays. Unfortunately, the displays lack English translations, and the students themselves only rarely handle the language.

Students also accompany tourists on the three-hour, 26-mile

Naturally formed stones in the Cancha de Bochas, Parque Provincial Ischigualasto

(42 km) **Circuito Vehicular,** which loops past the red sandstone parapets of **Barrancas Coloradas** and unique landforms such as the **Cancha de Bochas** ("ball court"), **La Catedral** ("the cathedral"), **El Gusano** ("the worm"), **El Hongo** ("the mushroom"), and **El Submarino** ("the submarine"). Bicycle tours take place when weather permits, and there are monthly full-moon tours as well.

INSIDER TIP:

In Villa Unión, have a barbecue goat dinner at La Palmera. Try *cayote* (a kind of pumpkin) and *quesillo* (goat cheese) for dessert.

—SERGIO A. MARENSSI
National Geographic field scientist

Because most of the park's wildlife is nocturnal, the full-moon tours may be the best time to see animals such as foxes, hares, pumas, reptiles, and rodents. It's also possible to spot wildlife, and get some exercise, on the hike up **Cerro Morado,** an isolated 5,700-foot (1,750 m) summit with 360-degree views. Local guides, contracted at the visitor center, are obligatory and, because of the heat, hikers need to start early.

Parque Nacional Talampaya

Talampaya's red sandstone canyons often draw local comparisons with Arizona's Grand Canyon of the Colorado, but there's one enormous difference—the dry riverbed of the Tala rarely holds any surface water. Nor is it as deep as the Grand Canyon, but that has its advantages—on vehicle tours, visitors can get up close and view the sheer-sided canyon walls, pre-Columbian petroglyphs, and evocative landforms that have made it, with nearby Ischigualasto, a UNESCO World Heritage site. Like Ischigualasto, it's a fossil field for research paleontologists.

Less than an hour north of Ischigualasto, often visited in the same day, Talampaya is just across the provincial border in La Rioja. Unlike Ischigualasto, certain parts of the park enjoy a high water table that sustains larger trees such as the algarrobo (related to the common mesquite) and Peruvian pepper, but much of the two parks' vegetation is similar.

Nearly all park visits start at the **Parador Turístico,** near RN 76; private cars must be left at the parador (inn), which has a restaurant and campground. It's possible to arrange minivan excursions on the spot, but many travelers contract day trips from San Agustín to visit both Ischigualasto and Talampaya in the same day. Leaving at least four times daily from the inn, the excursions proceed eastward on a sandy track to the **Puerta de Talampaya** ("gate of Talampaya") for short hikes to pre-Columbian **Petroglifos** (petroglyphs) and mortars, and through the **Jardín Botánico,** a native forest that survives on groundwater, to the popular **Chimenea del Eco,** a natural echo chamber. It also stops at **La Catedral** along the nearly

La Palmera
- RN 76, near intersection with Ruta 40

Parque Nacional Talampaya
- 187 B4/B5
- RN 76, 34 miles (55 km) SE of Villa Unión. Administrative office: San Martín, Villa Unión
- 03825/470-356 in Villa Unión
- $$$$$
www.talampaya.gov.ar

Parque Nacional Talampaya
Visitor Information
- Rolling Travel, Parque Nacional Talampaya
- 0351/570-9905 in Córdoba
- Cooperativa de Transporte Talampaya, Parque Nacional Talampaya
- 03825/155-12367
www.talampaya.com

Province of La Rioja

🗺 187 B4

Visitor Information

✉ Avenida Ortiz de Campo & Avenida Félix de la Colina

☎ 0380/442-6345

🕐 Closed Sat.–Sun. & holidays

www.turismolarioja.gov.ar

Museo Folclórico de La Rioja

✉ Pelagio B. Luna 811, La Rioja

☎ 03822/442-8500

🕐 Closed Mon.

---

vertical sandstone walls that provide secure nesting sites for condors and raptors. It continues to **El Monje,** an isolated landform that, from some angles, appears to be a Catholic friar, before returning to the Parador.

Before returning, some excursions continue to **Los Cajones,** where in a few places, the canyon narrows to about 20 feet (7 m) and the river sometimes breaks through the surface. The park is subject to summer thunderstorms, and an excursion may be canceled.

La Rioja City

La Rioja is a colonial city of caudillo traditions, though part of its ambience is faux colonial,

---

The Olives of Anillaco

One of Argentina's least likely landmarks is outside the La Rioja village of Anillaco—probably no other settlement of fewer than a thousand inhabitants can boast an airfield capable of handling commercial jets or, in Anillaco's case, former president Carlos Menem's "Tango 02." Anillaco was Menem's birthplace and getaway (where he also built an 18-hole golf course).

Menem, now despised elsewhere in the country, ordered the facility built in the 1990s with the justification that, after his presidency ended, it could be used to export the produce from nearby olive orchards.

---

because repeated earthquakes have flattened venerable buildings over the centuries since its founding in 1591. Despite political intrigue and mismanagement by everyone from the legendary Facundo Quiroga (1788–1835) to former provincial governor Carlos Menem, the city has managed to preserve its traditions while rebuilding its central core around **Plaza 25 de Mayo.** Many current residents are, like the Syrian Menems, descendants of Middle Eastern immigrants.

On the plaza's south side, the Byzantine **Basílica Menor y Santuario de San Nicolás de Bari** dates from 1899. It holds the image of San Nicolás de Bari, the city's patron saint, renowned for his missionary activities in what is now Turkey. One block north, the **Iglesia y Convento de San Francisco** has the image of the Niño Alcalde (Christ Child Mayor), beloved of the Diaguitas. Their legacy is the **Tinkunako,** a New Year's Eve ceremony in which San Nicolás acknowledges the authority of the Niño in front of the plaza's **Casa de Gobierno** (Government House).

One block east, a stone-studded exterior and carved algarrobo lintel (dated 1623) were the only parts of the **Convento de Santo Domingo** to survive an 1894 earthquake. Built by Diaguita labor, this is Argentina's oldest surviving convent.

Two blocks west of the plaza, occupying a late colonial house, the **Museo Folclórico de La Rioja** is really a hybrid institution that holds half a dozen exhibit halls on everyday artifacts ranging

The hills of Chilecito, La Rioja Province

from kitchen goods to silverwork. At the same time, it offers quality reproductions of its original exhibits for sale; with frequent community events, the institution is as much a cultural center as a museum.

Chilecito & Around

Across the Sierra de Velasco from La Rioja, by a roundabout highway route, Chilecito is a one-time mining town that acquired its name from the Chileans who labored in the nearby Famatina gold mines. Higher and cooler than the provincial capital, it sits at the base of the 20,500-foot (6,250 m) **Nevado del Famatina,** whose runoff helps to irrigate a little-known vineyard zone that produces some of the country's best Torrontés.

Traffic moves slower on Chilecito's narrow colonial streets than in most other Argentine cities. Four blocks west of the central **Plaza Caudillos Federales,** the **Museo de Chilecito–Molino San Francisco** is a colonial flour mill that, its exterior restored and its

interior refurbished, has become a museum stressing pre-Columbian archaeology and, especially, the mining industry that transformed the town in the late 19th century.

Most of Chilecito's wineries are in the surrounding countryside, but **Bodegas La Riojana Coop.**—a cooperative of small and midsize growers specializing in Torrontés but also reds such as Malbec, Cabernet Sauvignon, Tempranillo, Bonarda, and blends—is only a block beyond the museum. Tours and tastings, which include their dried fruits as well, take place throughout the day.

The most entertaining sight, though, is the **Cable Carril Chilecito–La Mejicana,** an aerial tramway that once linked the southern outskirts of town with the Santa Florentina smelter and the mine at more than 14,400 feet (4,400 m) above sea level. Carrying miners to work and ore to the smelter, the tramway had nine stations; **Estación No. 2** is accessible by taxi, with a working power plant and great views of the valley. ■

Chilecito
🗺 187 B5
Visitor Information
✉ Castro y Bazán 52
☎ 03825/422-688
www.emutur.com.ar

Museo de Chilecito–Molino San Francisco
✉ Jamín Ocampo 50
🕐 Closed Sat.–Sun.
💲 $

Bodegas La Riojana Coop.
✉ La Plata 646, Chilecito
☎ 03825/423-150
🕐 Closed Sun.
www.lariojana.com.ar

Cable Carril Chilecito–La Mejicana
✉ Avenida Presidente Perón 1300
🕐 Closed Sat.–Sun.
💲 $

Bordered by the Andes and the Atlantic and stretching far
to the south, renowned for its wildlife and wild scenery

Patagonia

An extreme skier slides over the edge at Chapelco, San Martín de los Andes, Neuquén Province.

Patagonia

Patagonia, the Texas-size territory south of the Río Colorado, has been a land of legend ever since Magellan's Spanish sailors stepped onto the South Atlantic shoreline in 1520. Today, it is famous around the world for its magnificent blend of mountains, lakes, grasslands, and wild ocean shores.

In political terms, Argentine Patagonia consists of the provinces of Neuquén, Río Negro, Chubut, and Santa Cruz (the archipelago of Tierra del Fuego, across the Strait of Magellan, is an insular extension of the region). In geographical terms, it consists of a long Atlantic coast, vast steppe grasslands, rolling foothills, and forested uplands that culminate in the Andean cordillera, one of the world's great mountain ranges, along the Chilean border. From the Atlantic to the Andes, it is endowed with magnificent national parks and reserves and filled with wildlife, ranging from penguins and whales to guanacos, rheas, and the Andean condor. For hikers, cyclists, climbers, rafters, kayakers, and all sorts of other outdoor recreationists, the options are almost unlimited.

Land of Legend

Internationally, Argentine Patagonia's best known asset is the "lakes district" in and around the Río Negro city of San Carlos de Bariloche, where a series of national parks forms an almost unbroken ribbon along the Andes. The most famous is Parque Nacional Nahuel Huapi, where hikers can go hut-hopping through mountainous backcountry barely half an hour beyond the city limits or sailing on its namesake lake. In winter, the snow brings skiers and snowboarders. To the north, around the resort of San Martín de los Andes, an equally scenic chain of lakes, endemic Araucaria (monkey-puzzle) forests, and the snow-topped cone of Volcán Lanín are the highlights of Parque Nacional Lanín.

To the south, snuggled between the taller Andes and a lower range to the east, the town of El Bolsón is a low-key getaway where farmers and artisans offer their wares at the region's most entertaining street fair. Like Bariloche, it enjoys easy access to a well-integrated trail network in the surrounding mountains.

Only a little farther south, the city of Esquel is the terminus of the narrow-gauge train made famous as the "Old Patagonian Express," even if Argentines prefer the term "La Trochita"—the little railroad. It's the gateway to Parque Nacional Los Alerces, named after the coniferous endemic "redwood of the south."

On the Atlantic coast, the Chubut provincial reserves of Península Valdés and Punta Tombo

NOT TO BE MISSED:

Parque Nacional Nahuel Huapi, the Argentine Switzerland **227–230**

El Bolsón, Argentina's counter-culture capital **231–233**

Parque Nacional Los Alerces, land of the Patagonian "redwood" **240**

The volcanoes, lakes, and forests of Parque Nacional Lanín **243–244**

Península Valdés, whale-watch central **250–252**

Parque Nacional Monte León's dramatic Atlantic headlands **256–257**

The Moreno Glacier and more at Parque Nacional Los Glaciares **258–261**

are the realm of right whales, elephant seals, sea lions, and Magellanic penguins. At Parque Nacional Monte León, in Santa Cruz Province, much of the same wildlife inhabits scenic headlands with far fewer visitors.

In the southwest corner of Santa Cruz Province, in Parque Nacional Los Glaciares, the grinding Moreno Glacier is one of Argentina's top three sights, but trails in the park's northern Fitz Roy sector offer the country's wildest landscapes. To the north, en route to the lakes district, legendary Ruta 40 passes the UNESCO World Heritage site of Cueva de las Manos, the continent's oldest rock-art site. ∎

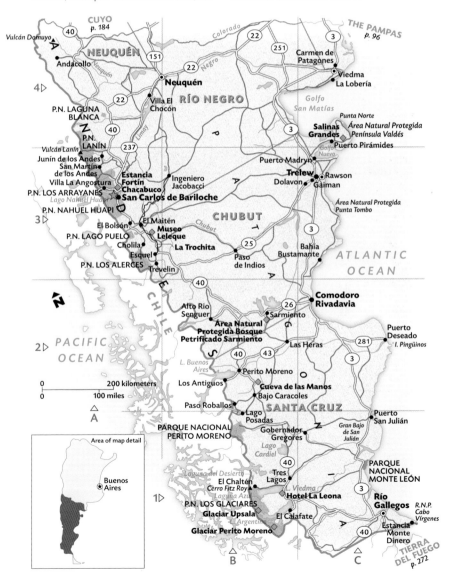

Bariloche & Around

Along the Andes, northern Argentine Patagonia has for many years enjoyed a reputation as a European-style lakes district. In the words of Patagonian pioneer Francisco P. Moreno, the area around Lago Nahuel Huapi—where Moreno received a land grant for his services to the Argentine government—was "a beautiful piece of Argentine Switzerland." The city of San Carlos de Bariloche is the bustling hub of this scenic area.

San Carlos de Bariloche from the air

San Carlos de Bariloche

  223 A3

Visitor Information

 Centro Cívico

 0294/442-9850

Closed Jan. 1, May 1, Nov. 8, & Dec. 25

www.bariloche turismo.gob.ar

San Carlos de Bariloche

Overlooking Nahuel Huapi's north shore, San Carlos de Bariloche, founded in 1902, has grown from a humble lakeside village to be the metropolis of the lakes—or at least its foremost tourist destination, transportation hub, and commercial center. Its population now exceeds 100,000, it grew only slowly until the 1930s, when the railroad began to provide easy access to the lake, Parque Nacional Nahuel Huapi, and a scenic backcountry that today is only minutes beyond the city limits.

Growth has brought problems, though, as the densely built city center has blocked lakeshore views, souvenir shops have cluttered many streets, and outlying neighborhoods have developed without zoning controls. Student graduation trips can also make it notoriously rowdy in winter. Still, only towns like North America's Jackson

Hole and South Lake Tahoe can match this setting and convenience to recreational resources, including winter skiing.

Bariloche's best survives in the **Centro Cívico,** a central open space bounded on three sides by Euro-Andean buildings. The structures' hewn granite blocks and roughly cut but polished cypress trunks symbolize a dialogue with nature and preserve the view to the lake. Architect Ernesto de Estrada conceived the project, executed under national parks director Exequiel Bustillo and inaugurated in 1940. Even if its frequently defaced statue of the brutal Gen. Julio Argentino Roca spends part of the day shaded by a sore-thumb high-rise, the complex's architectural harmony shines through.

Several of Estrada's individual buildings are noteworthy. The tallest is the municipality's **Torre Reloj,** a south-side clock tower from which, at noon and 6 p.m., symbolic figures of Indians, priests, soldiers, and pioneer farmers emerge to mark the hour. Immediately west, the colonnades of the former **Correo** (post office) now shelter chain saw sculptures and house the municipal tourist office. On the east side of the complex stands a museum that honors the naturalist and surveyor who donated his land grant to start Argentina's first national park.

Museo de la Patagonia Francisco P. Moreno:

Moreno (1852–1919), an internationally respected figure

Museo de la Patagonia Francisco P. Moreno

☒ Centro Cívico
☎ 0294/442-2309
🕐 Closed Sun. & holidays
🟢 $$
www.bariloche.com.ar/museo

Defining Patagonia

Though there's widespread agreement that Patagonia is the southernmost sector of South America's Southern Cone—so-called because of its shape on the map—it means different things in different contexts. Both Argentina and Chile possess Patagonian territory, but Argentina's share, east of the Andean divide, is far larger. In fact, it's larger than the state of Texas.

Magellan apparently named the area after a fictional savage, and the region's native peoples—who remained beyond European domination until the late 19th century—became a large part of its identity. These included the mounted Mapuche, whose vigorous resistance helped keep European and Argentine forces north of the Río Colorado for more than three centuries.

Discharging its waters into the Atlantic Ocean in Buenos Aires Province, the Río Colorado became Argentine Patagonia's geographical boundary. It also served as a biological boundary, where lush Pampas grasslands gradually gave way to sub-Antarctic moors, glaciers, and snowfields.

With the 19th-century defeat of the Mapuche, in a dispossession known in Argentina as the "Campaign of the Desert," Patagonia acquired a political geography. The Río Colorado remained the traditional boundary, but the new territories—later provinces—of Neuquén, Río Negro, Chubut, and Santa Cruz came to comprise modern Argentine Patagonia. Many would add Tierra del Fuego, but that archipelago (also shared with Chile) has its own distinctive identity.

who hosted Theodore Roosevelt here when Bariloche was only a frontier village, did more than any other Argentine to bring Patagonia to the attention of the country and of the wider world.

In its **Sala de Historia Aborigen,** the museum provides comprehensive coverage of Patagonia's first peoples, from the northern Mapuche to the nomadic southern Tehuelche and the hunter-gatherers of Tierra del Fuego—integrating displays on natural history, economic

the Mapuche, the museum is unsparing about Roca's ruthlessness, quoting him to the effect that "in my judgment, the best way to finish off the Indians, either wiping them out or pushing them across the Río Negro, is an offensive." One of his generals reported toward the end of the campaign that his opponents were "on the run, poor, miserable, and hopeless," and the accompanying photographs bear out this sorry description of the Mapuche.

Roca's success opened the region to a settled European

EXPERIENCE: To Chile & Back

For more than a century now—ever since Theodore Roosevelt rode it in 1913—the bus-boat-bus-boat shuttle from Bariloche to the Chilean port of Puerto Varas on Lago Llanquihue has been a highlight of the Patagonian lakes district.

Today's passengers can enjoy the grand Andean scenery aboard catamarans that depart from Nahuel Huapi's Puerto Pañuelo, west of Bariloche, and on comfortable buses that carry them between lakes along the route.

Chile-bound passengers have a choice of accommodations at the hamlets of

Peulla and **Petrohué,** at opposite ends of Lago Todos los Santos, or in the city of **Puerto Varas,** where it's possible to catch a bus back to Bariloche.

Those who don't care to cross the Andes, though, can take the catamaran just to the west end of Nahuel Huapi and then double back—with a different perspective on one of the lakes district's classic excursions.

Tickets for excursions with Cruce Andino, the local company that operates the bus-boat shuttle, are available online (www.cruceandino.com) or through any Bariloche travel agency.

organization, social structure, and religion. It makes a smooth transition from early European contacts to the push against the indigenous frontier by dictator Juan Manuel de Rosas and then, in particular, covers General Roca in the **Sala Conquista del Desierto.**

In its coverage of Roca's campaign (1878–1885) against

presence, chronicled in the **Sala San Carlos de Bariloche,** which portrays the region's development after the war ended. The room includes border surveys by Moreno and land-use surveys by Stanford geologist Bailey Willis (whose name graces a peak outside Bariloche). The arrival of the railroad, which reoriented the economy away from Chile, and brought tourists to Moreno's Parque Nacional del Sud—a relatively small unit that became today's sprawling Nahuel Huapi and its neighbor Lanín to the north—is detailed. So are explorations such as Moreno's 1880 expedition, in which he had to escape the Mapuche on a precarious raft down the Río Limay. (After Roca's war ended, Moreno invited some of the defeated Mapuche to live with him in La Plata.)

Other Landmarks: Two buildings in the style of the Centro Cívico deserve special mention. One block north of the museum and designed to match it is the **Intendencia del Parque Nacional Nahuel Huapi** (Nahuel Huapi National Park Administration; *San Martín 24, Bariloche*), created by Exequiel Bustillo's brother Alejandro Bustillo (1889–1982), one of Argentina's greatest architects. Five blocks east of the museum, on a rise above the lakeshore, Bustillo also created the **Catedral Nuestra Señora del Nahuel Huapi** (*Calles Almirante O'Connor & Beschtedt*), a neo-Gothic church whose needle tower evokes the Andean peaks visible in the distance. Its stained-glass windows represent figures such as the Jesuit missionary Nicolás Mascardi, the popular Mapuche saint Ceferino Namuncurá (a lay Salesian candidate for sainthood), and ironically, General Roca.

The Architect of Patagonia

No Argentine did more than architect Alejandro Bustillo (1889–1982) to create, from Patagonia's natural landscape, a cultural landscape that has become the benchmark for the region. Using local materials—quarried stone and native timber—he created a hybrid Euro-Andean style that survives in national park headquarters in Bariloche and San Martín de los Andes, the cathedral in Bariloche, the Hostería Futalaufquen in Parque Nacional Los Alerces near Esquel, and most impressively in his masterpiece, Hotel Llao Llao, west of Bariloche.

Bustillo lived long enough to be proud of that legacy, widely emulated throughout the lakes district, but some of the tributes border on kitsch. What would he have thought of public phone booths built in his rustically sophisticated style?

Parque Nacional Nahuel Huapi

When Francisco P. Moreno donated his land grant at the west end of Lago Nahuel Huapi to create the Parque Nacional del Sud in 1903, he envisioned a "natural public park" where "visitors from around the world would mingle."

Part of his prophecy has come true; the successor park Nahuel Huapi draws plenty of overseas visitors. It's unlikely that Moreno ever foresaw how San Carlos de Bariloche, founded only a year earlier, would spread along the lake and onto the mountainsides to create, in part, an urban park, despite his desire for "no additional constructions other

Parque Nacional Nahuel Huapi

 223 A3

Visitor Information

✉ Intendencia, San Martín 24, Bariloche

☎ 0294/442-3111

$ $$$$$ for access to Cerro Tronador, Cascada Los Alerces, & boat excursions

www.nahuelhuapi .gov.ar

than those that facilitate the comforts of the cultured visitor." That said, today's Nahuel Huapi (established in 1934) encompasses far more wild country than Moreno ever anticipated: 2,900 square miles eastward into the Río Limay; the park nearly surrounds the lake. Connected to several smaller lakes as well, Nahuel Huapi offers easy walks along the waterfront, sailing (Bariloche has a small yacht harbor), trout fishing, and swimming

Lago Nahuel Huapi and its *teleférico*

(7,500 sq km) that include Patagonian steppe, deep blue waters, forested mountainsides, and snow-topped peaks. While much of it is accessible by road, the park also enjoys a good network of backcountry trails and shelters that make a hike comparable to hut-hopping in the Alps. Mountain biking, climbing, horseback riding, and white-water rafting and kayaking are summertime favorites; in winter it has some of Argentina's best skiing.

The park's centerpiece, and jewel, is its namesake **Lago Nahuel Huapi.** This glacial finger lake covers 216 square miles (560 sq km) before draining

and sunbathing (more common west of the city).

In Nahuel Huapi's north arm, **Isla Victoria** was once the site of the park service's ranger school. Today it's home to a luxury lodge, but it's also catamaran-accessible for day trips from Bariloche, with routes to **Parque Nacional Los Arrayanes** (see p. 241), near Villa La Angostura.

Excursions in the Park:

From the hills of residential Barrio Belgrano, immediately southwest of Bariloche's Centro Cívico, Avenida de los Pioneros becomes a gravel road that switchbacks to the top of

4,600-foot (1,405 m) **Cerro Otto,** 5 miles (8 km) to the west. At Km 5 on the paved road, the gondolas of the **Teleférico Cerro Otto,** accessible by public transportation, provide an option for non-hikers or mountain bikers.

The park's most popular excursion, though, is the overland **Circuito Chico,** an afternoon excursion, by car, public bus, or bicycle, that leads west out along Avenida Bustillo to Península Llao Llao and loops back via the tiny community of Colonia Suiza. En route, several stops offer possibilities for sightseeing and shorter or longer hikes. At about the 5-mile (8 km) point, a paved road leads south for a further

INSIDER TIP:

Skip Tierra del Fuego's overhyped trout and salmon runs to fly-fish hundreds of accessible rivers and lakes in the north near Bariloche.

—PORTER FOX
National Geographic writer

6 miles (10 km) taking you to **Cerro Catedral,** Bariloche's top ski area, where the **Cable Carril y Telesilla Doble Lynch** takes passengers to the **Refugio Lynch** alpine hut *(closed intermittently; check for availability)*; trekkers and climbers can also overnight at the **Refugio Emilio Frey.**

Another common stop, some 11 miles (17.5 km) west of town via Avenida Bustillo, is the **Aerosilla Campanario,** the chairlift that climbs to the 3,445-foot (1,050 m) summit of **Cerro Campanario.** The road follows the shoreline northwest for about 5 miles (8 km) to **Puerto Pañuelo,** the port of departure for excursions to Isla Victoria and Los Arrayanes, and for the legendary boat-bus shuttle to Chile (see sidebar p. 226).

Immediately across the road, dating from 1940, Alejandro Bustillo's hilltop **Llao Llao Hotel & Resort** (see Travelwise p. 317) is an architectural landmark—Patagonia's first grand hotel, in the stone-and-wood style pioneered in the Centro Cívico. Overlooking the smaller Lago Perito Moreno, it's open for free guided tours on Wednesdays *(tel 0294/444-8530).*

Barely a mile (1.5 km) farther west, **Parque Municipal Llao Llao** *(Avenida Ezequiel Bustillo Km 27.5)* contains a series of short but scenic hiking trails to the Nahuel Huapi lakeshore and to an *arrayán* (false myrtle) forest on the western edge of Lago Perito Moreno. The road then loops 4 miles (6 km) to a junction where the main paved road turns north and returns to Cerro Campanario; a gravel alternative leads east for 2.5 miles (4 km) to **Colonia Suiza.**

At the junction of the road, a forested trail climbs steeply along the Arroyo López for about 2.5 hours to **Refugio López.** About 1.3 miles (2 km) farther east along the road, a dirt road

Teleférico Cerro Otto

- ✉ Avenida de los Pioneros Km 5
- ☎ 0294/444-1031
- 🕐 Closed Jan. 1, May 1, & Dec. 25
- 💲 $$$$$

www.catedralalta patagonia.com

Cable Carril y Telesilla Doble Lynch

- ✉ Base Cerro Catedral
- ☎ 0294/440-9000
- 🕐 Check for availability
- 💲 $$$$$

www.catedralalta patagonia.com

Aerosilla Campanario

- ✉ Avenida Bustillo Km 17.5
- ☎ 0294/442-7274
- 💲 $$$

Club Andino

- ☎ 0294/442-2266

REFUGIOS: For information on the refugios of Parque Nacional Nahuel Huapi, call 0294/452-7966 or visit www.clubandino .com.ar.

suitable for mountain bikes but marginal even for 4WD vehicles switchbacks up the mountainside almost to the hut. From the hut, it's possible to scale 6,800-foot (2,076 m) **Cerro López** or to continue hut-hopping south by trail into more remote parts of the park.

The only other part of the park readily accessible by road is the extinct volcano **Monte Tronador,** the ice-covered 11,411-foot (3,478 m) "Thunderer" on the Chilean border. About 52 miles (83 km) southwest of Bariloche via RN 40 and a gravel road that heads toward the border from **Lago Mascardi,** Tronador's most impressive sight is the **Ventisquero Negro,** a mass of flowing ice dirtied by sand and other sediments. From **Pampa Linda,** just before road's end, trekkers can reach Club Andino's **Refugio Otto Meiling** and even continue to Lago Nahuel Huapi's **Puerto Blest,** catching the boat back to Puerto Pañuelo. Technical climbers can stay at the **Refugio Viejo Tronador** before challenging the summit.

The road, RN 40, leads south for 19 miles (31 km) to a checkpoint at Río Villegas, where westbound RP 83 goes to the upper **Río Manso,** considered Argentina's top white-water river. Bariloche agencies operate rafting and kayaking trips here and on the tamer lower Manso. ∎

EXPERIENCE:
The Endless Winter: Skiing in Patagonia

For many visitors to the Northern Hemisphere, Argentina means enjoying two summers in the same year. A smaller but committed cohort of skiers and snowboarders, though, looks forward to two winters.

Mendoza's Las Leñas (see p. 207) may be acknowledged as Argentina's top ski resort, but the Patagonian lakes, from San Martín de los Andes south to Esquel, provide the greatest choice of sites and conditions.

At San Martín's **Cerro Chapelco** *(Mariano Moreno & Roca, San Martín de los Andes, tel 02972/427-845, www .cerrochapelco.com)* skiers find fast lifts with easy access to expert, uncrowded backcountry runs. Little-visited **Cerro Bayo** *(Las Fucsias 121, Villa la Angostura, tel 0294/449-4189, www.cerrobayoweb .com),* near fashionable Villa La Angostura, has just gotten new investors who intend to make it a boutique resort. That may take time—so its first-rate forest runs will still be an underappreciated bargain for a time.

Dating from 1938, Bariloche's **Cerro Catedral** *(Base Cerro Catedral, San Carlos de Bariloche, tel 0294/440-9000, www.catedralaltapatagonia.com)* is the closest place for skiers from snow-starved Brazil to find soft, deep powder (they're responsible for the city's sardonic nickname, "Brasiloche"). Underrated **La Hoya** *(Avenida Fontana & Avenida Ameghino, Esquel, tel 02945/453-018, www.cerro lahoya.com),* near Esquel, draws praise for its natural bowl and backcountry, recently modernized lifts, and soft powder.

At all resorts, foreigners may find that the mornings are the best time to avoid the crowds.

The Southern Lakes

Less than 20 years ago, beyond Lago Mascardi, southbound RN 40 was a dusty artery with deep loose gravel and fist-size stones. Now the highway is smoothly paved but, amazingly, crowds haven't really deluged destinations like counter-cultural El Bolsón, the sprawling steppes, or other dramatic backcountry scenes of the lakes district.

Enjoying Lago Puelo, south of El Bolsón

The visitors that often over-run Bariloche have barely touched the eastern edge of "Big Sky" lands, where sprawling sheep ranches dominated the economy and Butch Cassidy and the Sundance Kid once homesteaded. And while the crowds may ride the "Old Patagonian Express" at the city of Esquel, they pay only passing visits to the picturesque enclave of Welsh colonists at Trevelin. Even the unique endemic false

larch forests of Parque Nacional Los Alerces, along the Chilean border, get only a fraction of Nahuel Huapi's visitors.

El Bolsón & Around

Only an hour and a half south of Bariloche, in the valley of the Río Quemquemtreu, El Bolsón is a different world. In fact, given its proclivity for political activism—in 1984, municipal authorities declared it a "non-nuclear zone" and, in 1991, an

El Bolsón
✉ 223 A3
Visitor Information
✉ Avenida San Martín & Roca
☎ 0294/449-2604
www.elbolson.gov.ar

A windsurfer tests the breezes on Lago Puelo.

thrice-weekly street fair that showcases skilled crafts workers and the products from the small *chacras* (fields) and orchards that surround the town. From about 10 a.m. Tuesday, Thursday, and Saturday, when the scaffolding for its stands starts going up, it's a snacker's extravaganza of baked goods, fresh and preserved fruits, jams and jellies, juices, and, of course, local beers on tap. In summer, it also takes place on Sundays.

But it's far from just food and produce. There's impromptu entertainment—perhaps a solo bandoneonist playing a wistful tango, or a clown or a puppeteer for the kids. Strolling back and forth around the ellipse, souvenir hunters can find detailed wood carvings, handmade jewelry, clothing and leather goods, musical instruments, and intricate flower arrangements. In its informality and unpretentiousness, the Feria summarizes Bolsón's countercultural, libertarian ethos—and its ability to enjoy a good time!

Like Bariloche, El Bolsón enjoys easy access to the mountains, on both the east and west sides of the valley. Unlike Bariloche, these lands are not part of any national park, but they do contain backcountry huts and an improving trail network. Some of the hikes are short, others longer and better for an overnight; as trailhead access is often by back roads, it's simplest to take a taxi to them.

West of town, it's about 3.5 miles (6 km) to the trailhead for the **Cabeza del Indio,** a natural rock formation that looks like an almost stereotypical "noble

"ecological municipality"—and disregard for crass commercialism, it's something of an anti-Bariloche. In a sheltered, wooded basin between sharp-crested granite mountain ranges where remarkable recreation possibilities are only minutes away, it favors small-scale accommodations, and its artisans make unique products from local materials, including some of the country's best beers and sweets.

All of this comes together in the elliptical **Plaza Adalberto Pagano,** where the **Feria Regional de El Bolsón** is a casual, savage." About the same distance to the north, a half-mile (800 m) loop trail in the municipal **Reserva Forestal Loma del Medio y Río Azul** is spectacular when there's enough water for the **Cascada Escondida** (Hidden Falls) to plunge out of its fault-line drainage and into the canyon below.

About 9 miles (15 km) northwest of town, a 4WD road drops into the Río Azul drainage and its confluence with the Río Blanco for an undulating hike to the **Cajón del Azul,** a narrow gorge spanned by a log bridge. Just across the bridge, the **Refugio Cajón del Azul** has communal accommodations, simple meals, and welcomes day hikers with coffee, tea, or mate. Before the climb to the gorge, a new southbound trail climbs and then drops into the Arroyo del Teno canyon and **Refugio Hielo Azul,** an alternative loop for overnighters returning to El Bolsón.

To the east, the trailhead for the igneous ridge of the 7,500-foot (2,284 m) **Cerro Piltriquitrón** is only 8 miles (13 km) from Plaza Pagano. From the 3,937-foot (1,200 m) level, the starting point for an afternoon's summiteering, is the **Bosque Tallado,** where carvers from Patagonia and around the country have taken their chain saws, chisels, and files to the trunks of singed southern beeches, and then polished them, to create an outdoor sculpture garden on the mountainside. Initiated by local artist Marcelo López, with varied themes, the initial 25 sculptures have been supplemented by an additional 25.

Only a few hundred yards above the sculpture garden, the **Refugio Piltriquitrón** provides basic bunks and meals for summit-bound hikers. From here, the trail becomes steeper through the former ski area and then levels off before reaching the tree line and crossing open fell fields to the top. The reward for the two-hour hike, in clear weather at least, is uninterrupted views of the Río Azul drainage and Andean divide along the Chilean border. If it's really clear, Chile's stunningly symmetrical Volcán Osorno is visible beyond the darker summit of Tronador.

INSIDER TIP:

Take the road up to Piltriquitrón, leave your vehicle, and hike up the trail to the Piltriquitrón mountain hut. A friendly host will offer you his home brew, best enjoyed at dusk, with the spectacular view of the Patagonian Andes beyond.

—DIEGO ALLOLIO
Director, Magellanica Journey of Exploration Expeditions

Parque Nacional Lago Puelo

Only about 11 miles (18 km) south of El Bolsón, across the Chubut line, Lago Puelo is a Tahoe clone without the casinos and rampant overdevelopment that's blighted the California-Nevada

Reserva Forestal Loma del Medio y Río Azul
✉ 2 miles (3 km) NW of El Bolsón, via gravel road off highway

Parque Nacional Lago Puelo
✉ 223 A3

Visitor Information
✉ RP 16, 11 miles (18 km) S of El Bolsón
☎ 0294/449-9232
$ $$–$$$$$
www.parques nacionales.gov.ar

REFUGIOS: For information on the refugios in the El Bolsón region, contact the **Club Andino Piltriquitrón** *(tel 0294/449-2600, www.capiltriquitron .com.ar).*

El Maitén

Ⓜ 223 A3

Visitor Information

✉ Av. San Martín s/n

☎ 02945/495-016

www.elmaiten .com.ar

La Trochita, Estación El Maitén

Ⓜ 223 A3/B3

✉ Rivadavia & Beruti

☎ 02945/495-190

🕐 Closed April– Sept. except Holy Week & winter school holidays

💲 $$$$

border. Fed by three rivers, it's only about 650 feet (200 m) above sea level, but the forested mountainsides and surrounding snowy peaks—which reach nearly 6,500 feet (2,000 m)— provide a setting that, if not quite matchless, deserves a visit. Unusually for Argentina, Lago Puelo itself drains toward the Pacific rather than the Atlantic.

On the north lakeshore—the only part of the park easily accessible by road—several trailheads begin near the visitor center. The easiest is the half-mile (1 km) **Sendero al Mirador del Lago,** which merely climbs to a 425-foot (130 m) platform for views to the west. To the west, though, a more adventurous trek on the **Senda a Los Hitos** fords the shallow (in summer) Río Azul and leads 3 miles (5 km) to the Argentine border post at Arroyo Las Lágrimas, where hikers can continue to the Chilean town of Puelo.

A road may soon supersede the trail, however.

From the lakeshore jetty near the visitor center, passenger launches such as the *Juana de Arco* and *Popeye 2000* take half-hour sightseeing trips on the lake, as well as to the Chilean border. On some days, they cross the lake to remote roadless settlements where truly off-the-beaten-path camping and hiking are possible, and sightings of the *huemul* (southern Andean deer) and *pudú* (the spaniel-size cervid) are likelier. For most visitors, though, this is a day trip despite a campground near the visitor center.

El Maitén

For better or worse, Paul Theroux made the "Old Patagonian Express" a household word with his best-selling travelogue of trains through Central and South America in the mid-1970s. The narrow-gauge line that gave his book its title then ran for 250 miles (402 km) over the steppe from Ingeniero Jacobacci (Río Negro) to the end of the line at Esquel (Chubut), the town most identified with **"La Trochita"** (as Argentines know the line). Today—unless you can afford to charter it for the distance—the only options for boarding are Esquel and the dusty backwater of El Maitén.

Thirty-five miles (57 km) southeast of El Bolsón via gravel RP 6, or via a 43-mile (69 km) combination of paved RN 40 and RP 70, El Maitén was the line's midpoint. Serious train enthusiasts prefer it to Esquel, because

---

EXPERIENCE:
Border Boat Crossing

One of the most beautiful boat journeys you can take explores Lago Puelo toward the Chilean border, a luscious land of verdurous mountains and glacier-blue waters. InterPatagonia offers two-hour cruises, as well as a one-hour hiking excursion with a knowledgable park ranger, who will tell you everything you need to know about the unique flora and fauna of the Valdivian forest. You'll also visit the rapids along the Río Puelo. Tours depart daily. Contact **InterPatagonia** *(tel 02972/429-267, www.interpatagonia .com)* for further information.

this is where the workshops and turntables, with an abundance of steam locomotives and railcars in conditions that range from rusted to polished, still survive. In summer, its 1922 U.S. Baldwin locomotive still pulls passengers across the steppe on 2.5-hour excursions that can be booked in El Bolsón—and even when there's no service, the

transformed the landscape. In 1999, eight years after Italian fashion mogul Carlo Benetton purchased the Compañía de Tierras Sud Argentino (Southern Argentine Land Company), Benetton transformed the historic hotel, school, and general store of Estancia Leleque—a ranch where rams, ewes, wethers, and

Museo Leleque

🗺 223 A3

✉ RN 40 Km 1440 (55 miles/90 km N of Esquel)

☎ 02945/455-151

🕐 Closed Wed., holidays, & May–June

💲 $

www.elmaiten.com.ar/ museo.htm

"La Trochita," Argentina's famous narrow-gauge railway, at Estación El Maitén

railyard at El Maitén is a photographer's paradise. In February, the **Fiesta Nacional del Tren a Vapor** celebrates the line's survival.

Museo Leleque

Southbound from El Bolsón, RN 40 veers east out of the mountains and onto the steppe where, ever since General Roca drove out the Tehuelche and Mapuche in the 1880s, sprawling sheep stations have dominated the economy and

lambs grazed more than 700 square miles (1,830 sq km)—into a long-awaited but nevertheless controversial museum.

Benetton's efforts helped organize the life's work of Ukrainian immigrant Pablo S. Korschenewski (1925–2000), who had gathered thousands of indigenous and historical artifacts over half a century's residence in Chubut and Santa Cruz Provinces. Upgraded in 2004, the museum treats regional development from the beginning,

Cholila

🗺 223 A3

Visitor Information

✉ Casa de
Informes, RP 71
at RP 16

☎ 02945/498-040

**www.turismocholila
.gov.ar**

with an entire room devoted to the pre-Columbian Tehuelche and their material culture—*boleadoras* (weighted balls on leather thongs), stone mortars, and weavings, for instance. It proceeds, in a separate room, to the encounter between cultures, with particular attention to the impact of the horse, which made the indigenes far more mobile than ever before.

A third room, though, depicts the Tehuelches' inevitable transition to a settled life, and a fourth deals with the immigration—by both Europeans and the Mapuche—that marked their absorption into contemporary society. Separately, Leleque's *boliche* (general store and boardinghouse) re-creates its historic role, but also sells drinks, light meals, and indigenous weavings.

Despite its achievements, Leleque remains controversial, as nearby Mapuche communities have claimed part of the Benetton properties, and the museum itself has been criticized as Eurocentric. The museum is only a short distance off RN 40, but the narrow-gauge train from El Maitén also stops here on some excursions.

Cholila

When Patagonia was a frontier, it had its share of bandits—Argentine singer León Gieco once dedicated an entire album to the theme of *bandidos rurales*—but ever since Paul Newman, Robert Redford, and Katherine Ross sailed to South America on screen in 1969, Butch Cassidy and the Sundance Kid have been celebrities on two American continents. From 1901 to 1905, their real-life counterparts Robert Leroy Parker, Harry Longabaugh, and Etta Place settled into a simple log cabin just outside this Chubut hamlet.

Skiers at La Hoya, near the city of Esquel, Chubut Province

U.S. author Anne Meadows and her partner Dan Buck managed to identify the Butch and Sundance cabin, then occupied by an aging gaucho, in the 1990s (just W of RP 71 at Km 21). Even as the gaucho's heirs argued over the property, the province of Chubut finally managed to undertake repairs and, today,

INSIDER TIP:

Cholila organizes the Fiesta Nacional del Asado [National Barbecue Festival; *www.bolsonweb.com/asado.html*] early in February— several days of barbecues, rodeos, horse races called *cuaderas*, folklore, music, and more.

—CAROL PASSERA
Director of Causana Viajes

plenty of Argentines and foreigners find their way down a gravel road and across an open meadow to the reroofed cabin and its adjacent shed. The floors also have been restored, and a few sheepskins hang from the ceiling. Though there's little to suggest who lived here or why the site is important, it's become an almost obligatory stop on the gringo trail, and equally important to Argentines.

Esquel & Around

The southernmost city in the Patagonian lakes district, Esquel is a ranching and mining service center that was the terminus for

Theroux's "Patagonian Express"— a happenstance that helped invigorate a moribund travel and tourism sector, even if Esquel's status as the gateway to nearby Parque Nacional Los Alerces is more significant. Esquel also has a small, quality ski area.

Esquel was the end of the narrow-gauge spur from Ingeniero Jacobacci for the Ferrocarril Roca, which took its name from the general responsible for the "conquest of the desert." Excursions on the train, "**La Trochita**," are more frequent than those at El Maitén—in high summer, sometimes twice daily. Drawn by an antique steam locomotive, the narrow wooden railcars, with their hard bench seats, roll north to the applause of city residents who feel a genuine affection for "El Trencito," as it's also known.

The little train takes only an hour to reach the station of **Nahuel Pan,** where its passengers spend an hour or so among the Mapuche for eats, drinks, crafts, and horseback rides before returning to town. The **Museo de Culturas Originarias Patagónicas,** covering the Mapuche legacy, is also at Nahuel Pan.

Only 8 miles (13 km) north of town, **La Hoya** is a small but underrated ski area that gets international groups in the know because of its fine powder (storms that have come this far over the Andes have dropped most of their moisture). Its main shortcoming is limited lift capacity; in summer, the lifts carry hikers into the high country.

(continued on p. 240)

Esquel
✉ 223 A3
Visitor Information
✉ Avenida Alvear & Sarmiento
☎ 02945/451-927
www.esquel.gov.ar/turismo

La Trochita, Estación Esquel
✉ Dr. Roggero & A.P. Justo
☎ 02945/451-403
💲 $$$$
www.latrochitaeweb.com.ar

Museo de Culturas Originarias Patagónicas
✉ Belgrano 330
🕐 Closed Sun. in summer, Sun.–Thurs. rest of year
💲 Donation

Centro de Actividades de Montaña La Hoya
✉ Sarmiento 784
☎ 02945/450-505
www.skilahoya.com

Drive: The Alerces & the Ashes

Starting in Bariloche, this three-day (or more) drive leads south past the lakes of Parque Nacional Nahuel Huapi to the bohemian burg of El Bolsón before veering onto the steppe for a glimpse of life on a Patagonian sheep farm. It continues to the terminus of the "Old Patagonian Express," loops through Parque Nacional Los Alerces, and visits the cabin of Butch Cassidy before returning north.

From **San Carlos de Bariloche ❶** (see pp. 224–227), southbound RN 40 trends southwest along the finger lakes of **Lago Gutiérrez, Lago Mascardi,** and **Lago Guillelmo** before winding through the **Cañadón de la Mosca.** After 76 miles (123 km), it descends into the Río Quemquemtreu Valley, where the village of **El Bolsón ❷** (see pp. 231–233) lies between parallel longitudinal mountain ranges. For its famous street market, hiking in its nearby mountains, and the **Lago Puelo** lakeshore, it's the best overnight stop north of Esquel.

From El Bolsón, RN 40 climbs southeast past the settlements of **El Hoyo** and **Epuyén ❸,** where local farmers raise the soft fruits (raspberries, strawberries), tree fruits (apples, pears, etc.), and hops that flavor the sweets and beers of El Bolsón's market. After 30 miles (49 km), the route doglegs southeast onto the steppe,

NOT TO BE MISSED:

El Bolsón • Esquel • Trevelin • Parque Nacional Los Alerces

and, in another 17 miles (27 km), it reaches the entrance of **Estancia Leleque ❹** (see pp. 235–236), where the Benetton empire has refurbished its farm buildings to create a unique archaeological and historical museum.

From Leleque, roughly following the route of the legendary narrow-gauge railway, RN 40 strikes south for another 49 miles (79 km) to intersect westbound RN 259. The road drops into **Esquel ❺** (see p. 237), where the "Old Patagonian Express"—"La Trochita" to Argentines—still steams out of the valley and onto the steppe to thrill trainspotters from around the world. Esquel, the best base for arranging excursions into the western cordillera, also has a nearby ski area with good summer hiking available, as well as the drive's best services (along with the city of El Bolsón).

From Esquel, the paved southbound highway leads for 15 miles (24 km) to **Trevelin ❻** (see p. 240), interior Chubut's most demonstrably Welsh settlement, with its brick buildings, teahouses, and chapels. In mid-2008, Esquel and Trevelin were in the path of massive ash falls from the Chaitén volcano on the Chilean side of the border. The eruptions forced the evacuation of the volcano's namesake town, killing plant life and livestock and polluting some of the world's most pristine rivers. The eruptions have diminished and life is

"La Trochita" steams out of Esquel.

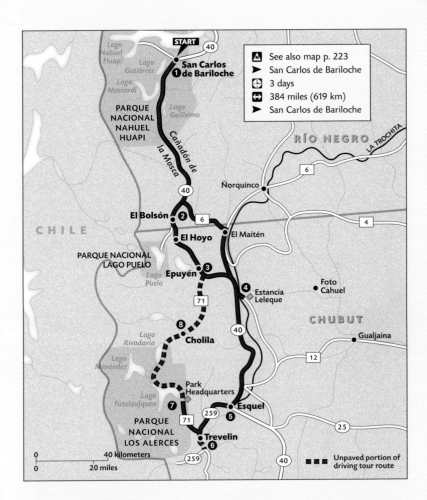

START 40

1 San Carlos de Bariloche

Lago Nahuel Huapi
Lago Gutiérrez
Lago Mascardi
Lago Guillelmo

PARQUE NACIONAL NAHUEL HUAPI

Cañadón de la Mosca

40

RÍO NEGRO
LA TROCHITA

6

Ñorquinco

4

CHILE

El Bolsón 2 6

El Hoyo
El Maitén

PARQUE NACIONAL LAGO PUELO

Lago Puelo

Epuyén 3

71

4 Estancia Leleque

Foto Cahuel

CHUBUT

8

Lago Rivadavia

Cholila

Lago Menéndez

40

Gualjaina

12

Lago Futalaufquen

Park Headquarters

7

Esquel

71 259 5

PARQUE NACIONAL LOS ALERCES

Trevelin 6

259

40

25

See also map p. 223
San Carlos de Bariloche
3 days
384 miles (619 km)
San Carlos de Bariloche

0   40 kilometers
0   20 miles

Unpaved portion of driving tour route

gradually recovering, but roadside evidence of the disaster will persist for years here and in the nearby national park of Los Alerces.

From Trevelin, a parallel gravel road leads northwest for 8 miles (13 km) to intersect paved RP 71, which continues another 13 miles (21 km) through the portals of **Parque Nacional Los Alerces 7** (see p. 240) to the park headquarters at **Villa Futalaufquen** on the lake of the same name. The park has short nature trails for day hikes, longer ones for overnight treks, and numerous finger lakes along the main road and in the backcountry. Its traditional highlight, though, is the **Lago Menéndez**

excursion, by boat and foot, to the false larch forests from which the park takes its name.

From park headquarters, an architectural landmark, northbound RP 71 becomes a dusty gravel road that narrows as it approaches **Lago Rivadavia,** on the park's northeast boundary. It's 44 miles (71 km) to the town of **Cholila 8** (see pp. 236–237), where a modest, recently restored log cabin was once the home of Robert Leroy Parker and Harry Longabaugh—Butch Cassidy and the Sundance Kid. From Cholila, the road continues northeast to intersect RN 40, returning to El Bolsón—well worth an additional layover—and Bariloche.

Trevelin

✉ 223 A3

Visitor Information

✉ Rotonda 28 de Julio, Plaza Coronel Jorge Luis Fontana

☎ 02945/480-120

www.trevelin.gob.ar

Museo Histórico Regional

✉ Molino Viejo 488

☎ 02945/480-189

$ $

Parque Nacional Los Alerces

▲ 223 A3

✉ RP 71, 21 miles (33 km) SW of Esquel

$ $$$$$

Visitor Information

✉ Villa Futalaufquen

☎ 02945/471-015, ext. 23

www.parques nacionales.gov.ar

Hostería Futalaufquen

✉ Parque Nacional Los Alerces 1

☎ 02945/471-008

Trevelin

Half an hour south of Esquel, distinguished by its oddball octangular **Plaza Coronel Jorge Luis Fontana,** Trevelin is the innermost outpost of the Welsh colonization that worked its way up the Río Chubut from the 1860s. Like Gaiman, it has Welsh teahouses that make it an excursion destination for travelers staying in Esquel and visiting Parque Nacional Los Alerces. (Trevelin itself has few accommodations.)

In addition to a summer artisans' market on the plaza, Trevelin honors its history in the **Museo Histórico Regional,** the four-story brick flour mill that operated here between 1922 and 1953. Its contents, appropriately, eschew the epic to focus on commonplace objects such as furniture and farm implements. Maps, photographs, and documents focus on the Welsh community but also on the indigenous Tehuelche and Mapuche.

Parque Nacional Los Alerces

Hugging the border west of Esquel, Los Alerces owes its name and national park status to *Fitzroya cupressoides*, the Patagonia cypress or false larch. The trees, in turn, owe their existence to the Pacific storms that cross the Andes and drop enough moisture to support the kinds of forests that mostly thrive on the wetter Chilean side. The coniferous *alerce* resembles the California redwood in size (up to 200 feet/60 m) and longevity (up to 4,000 years), as well as in the color and texture of the wood that have made it the

target of timber cutters since the 17th century. It is now a protected species.

Los Alerces is a land of lakes and rivers whose classic excursion is the **Safari Lacustre,** an all-day boat tour (water levels permitting) from **Lago Futalaufquen** via several other lakes to **El Alerzal.** This cathedral grove includes **El Abuelo,** the park's iconic alerce specimen. Some 2,600 years old, the reddish barked "Grandfather" is 187 feet (57 m) tall and measures more than 7 feet (2.2 m) in diameter.

INSIDER TIP:

Take care when journeying the Patagonian roads, especially by motorcycle; loose rock, dirt, and gravel can be very dangerous.

—ROGELIO DANIEL ACEVEDO
National Geographic field scientist

The park's **Hostería Futalaufquen** is a cultural landmark, the work of architect Alejandro Bustillo (see sidebar p. 227), who is also responsible for Bariloche's Llao Llao Hotel & Resort (see Travelwise p. 317) and other signature Patagonian buildings. It has surprisingly few challenging trails: The 6,286-foot (1,916 m) **Cerro Alto El Dedal** is a strenuous day hike, while the **Sendero Lago Krüger** is an overnighter along the shore of Lago Futalaufquen to a smaller lake that provides accommodations and camping. ■

Neuquén Province

Patagonia's northernmost province, Neuquén is a roughly triangular territory bordered by the Río Colorado on the north, the Río Limay on the south, and the Andean divide to the west. Its boundaries encompass most of Parque Nacional Nahuel Huapi, but also include Parque Nacional Lanín, with its iconic volcano and monkey-puzzle forests, some of South America's top trout streams and dinosaur grounds—and even a surprise wine district.

Poplars show their fall colors at Lago Correntoso, Neuquén Province.

Villa La Angostura & Around

Around Lake Nahuel Huapi from Bariloche, Villa La Angostura is an upmarket shoreline community that, despite its location on the highway to Chile, manages to maintain a slower pace than its better known neighbor. Its ready access to national parklands, winter sports, and the scenic Siete Lagos (Seven Lakes) route to San Martín de los Andes make it one of the region's elite destinations.

On Península Quetrihué, which juts south into the lake, **Parque**

Nacional Los Arrayanes is a forested enclave known primarily for 50 acres (20 ha) of the red-barked evergreen *Myrceugenella apiculata*, a myrtle relative with bright white flowers. Catamaran excursions leave regularly for the peninsula's southern tip, where the *arrayán* woods occupy a fraction of the park's lake-studded woodlands; from there, the undulating footpath back to town will get you back by mid-afternoon.

Villa La Angostura is also home to the **Centro de Ski Boutique Cerro Bayo** (RP 66 Km 6, tel 0294/ 449-4189, www.cerrobayoweb.com),

Villa La Angostura
🅰 223 A3
Visitor Information
✉ Avenida Arrayanes 7, El Cruce
☎ 0294/449-4124
🕐 Closed May 1
www.villalaango sturaturismo .blogspot.com

A fly fisherman casts a line at Lago Huechulafquen.

San Martín de los Andes

Nestled in a valley at the east end of Lago Lácar, between the Andean crest and the Cordón de Chapelco, the resort of San Martín de los Andes is Bariloche without the clutter. Founded in 1898, it's the gateway to the lakes and trout streams of Parque Nacional Lanín, which nudges the city's western edge, as well as a winter sports center.

Like Bariloche, the town boasts a distinguished **Centro Cívico**, the legacy of architect Alejandro Bustillo, around its **Plaza San Martín.** The masterwork here is Luis Bottini's **Intendencia del Parque Nacional Lanín,** the park's visitor center, resembling Nahuel Huapi's block-and-beams building. Across the plaza, the **Museo Primeros Pobladores** *(Rosas 758, tel 02972/428-676, closed Mon., $)* chronicles the region's cultural evolution.

From the lakeside pier, there are excursions on Lago Lácar to **Quila Quina,** on the south shore, and to the Chilean border at **Paso Hua Hum; Lago Lolog,** to the north, is a prime windsurfing site.

Barely beyond the outskirts of town, **Cerro Chapelco** *(www .cerrochapelco.com)* is one of Argentina's top ski and snowboard areas, suitable for everyone from beginners to experts.

Junín de los Andes & Around

Only 25 miles (41 km) northeast of San Martín, Junín de los Andes is an affordable alternative to its more exclusive neighbor. For fishermen, Neuquén's

Parque Nacional Los Arrayanes

🅰 223 A3

✉ Bulevar Nahuel Huapi, La Villa

☎ 0294/449-4152

💲 $$$$$

www.parques nacionales.gov.ar

San Martín de los Andes

🅰 223 A3

Visitor Information

✉ Avenida San Martín & Rosas

☎ 02972/491-160

www.sanmartin delosandes.gov.ar/ turismo

a small but excellent winter sports complex 6 miles (10 km) southeast of town. Immediately north of town by a 2.5-mile (4 km) road, a 2-mile (3.2 km) trail leads to the 6,535-foot (1,992 m) summit of **Cerro Belvedere.**

Villa La Angostura is the starting point for the recently rerouted 68-mile (109 km) **Ruta de los Siete Lagos,** a scenic highway to San Martín de los Andes through the northernmost sector of Parque Nacional Nahuel Huapi and the southernmost sector of Parque Nacional Lanín. As the name suggests, the road passes seven major lakes, traveling through an underdeveloped area that's likely to see increased visitation.

"trout capital" is even more enticing for its proximity to the Río Chimehuín, which runs right through town. The Chimehuín's pools and riffles have an international reputation, but Junín is also the best access point for the backcountry sights of Parque Nacional Lanín.

Founded in 1883 and Neuquén's oldest town, Junín values its indigenous and devotional heritage through the **Museo Mapuche** and the **Santuario Nuestra Señora de las Nieves y Beata Laura Vicuña** *(Ginés Ponte e Don Bosco)*, a chapel that blends Mapuche elements with traditional Catholicism. On the western outskirts of town, the **Vía Crucis** is a zigzag trail among stations of the cross to the top of Cerro de la Cruz.

Junín also has a gaucho tradition, reflected in February's **Fiesta del Puestero.** Serious fly-fishers will find a good base for their expeditions at **Estancia Huechahue** *(www.huechahue.com)*, an Anglo-Argentine ranch some 18 miles (30 km) east of Junín. On 25 square miles (66 sq km) of rolling steppe, Huechahue boasts volcanic caverns, pre-Columbian rock art, and bluffs of nesting condors.

Parque Nacional Lanín

Wilder than Nahuel Huapi, Parque Nacional Lanín encompasses nearly 1,600 square miles (4,120 sq km) of grassy steppes, crystalline finger lakes, verdant forests, and snowcapped volcanoes. Two special features distinguish it from Nahuel Huapi: the stunning white sentinel of **Volcán**

Lanín, shared with Chile; and the flourishing forests of *Araucaria araucana*, the monkey-puzzle tree known to the Mapuche as the *pehuén* (see sidebar below).

At 12,388 feet (3,776 m) above sea level, Lanín dwarfs every other peak in the area. For Andeanists, its summit is the district's gold standard, approached either from **Lago Huechulafquen** (to the south) or, more commonly, **Lago Tromen** (to the north).

For the most part, Lanín lacks the integrated trail network of Nahuel Huapi, but the area northwest of Junín de los Andes offers

---

Harvesting the Pehuén

Throughout the mountainous North American west, indigenous peoples such as the Shoshone were renowned for their diet of pine nuts, a durable resource that they gathered every autumn. South America has no native pines, but the narrow endemic *pehuén*—the Araucaria or monkey-puzzle tree—served the same purpose for the indigenous Pehuenche of the Andean lakes region.

Throughout the *pehuén*'s limited range, in places such as Parque Nacional Lanín, hikers in March or April will find a wealth of "pine nuts" scattered along trails and even by the highway. Don't hesitate to gather a few to add to your trail mix.

Intendencia del Parque Nacional Lanín

◪ 223 A4

✉ Perito Moreno e Elordi, San Martín de los Andes

☎ 02972/427-233

Junín de los Andes

◪ 223 A3

Visitor Information

✉ Padre Milanesio 596

☎ 02972/491-160

Museo Mapuche

✉ Ginés Ponte 540

🕑 Closed Sun. e holidays

💲 $

Centro de Visitantes y Museo del Parque Nacional Lanín

◪ 223 A4

Visitor Information

✉ Emilio Frey 749

☎ 02972/420-884

🕑 Park open year-round; visitor center closed holidays in off-season

💲 $$$$

Parque Nacional Laguna Blanca

A 223 A4

Visitor Information

✉ RP 46, 21 miles (33 km) SW of Zapala

☎ 02942/431-982 in Zapala

🕐 Park open daily; visitor center closed March–mid-Dec. except Sat.–Sun. & holidays

www.pnlagunablanca.com.ar

the best options—and opportunities to see the park's highlights—for hikers and for everyone else.

About 2.5 miles (4 km) north of town, RP 61 is a gravel road that climbs the Río Chimehuín Valley to its outlet with Lago Huechulafquen and continues to **Lago Paimún,** where the road ends after 34 miles (54 km). At Paimún, hikers can cross the narrows that separates it from Huechulafquen on a cable raft or by rowboat to hike among forests of araucarias. The southwesterly trail eventually meets the gravel

midway between Junín de los Andes and the city of Neuquén, it's a shallow, interior drainage lake where birders can also find up to a hundred different species that include the odd flamingo and the flightless rhea (along its edges).

Laguna Blanca has an informative visitor center but no other services except a basic campground; the nearest accommodations and food are in the nondescript town of **Zapala,** about 21 miles (33 km) to the northeast.

Wines of Patagonia

In a region renowned for ferocious winds and grinding glaciers, fine wines might seem out of place, but the northernmost Patagonian steppe's irrigated valleys, in the vicinity of Neuquén, have long been a garden spot for temperate-climate fruits such as apples, pears, and grapes—along with secondary products such as cider and wine.

The world wine boom, meanwhile,

has led producers such as Río Negro's Bodega Humberto Canale (see p. 245) to focus on whites and up-and-coming reds such as Pinot Noir that are suitable to the region's cool climate. Neuquén's Familia Schroeder winery (*Calle 7 Norte, San Patricio del Chañar, tel 0229/489-9600, www.familiaschroeder.com*) markets itself under the label Saurus, echoing the province's impressive dinosaur discoveries.

Province of Neuquén

A 223 A4

Visitor Information

✉ Félix San Martín 182, Neuquén

☎ 0299/442-4089

www.neuquentur.gov.ar

Museo Nacional de Bellas Artes Neuquén

✉ Mitre & Santa Cruz, Neuquén

☎ 0299/443-6268

🕐 Closed Mon.

www.mnbaneuquen.gov.ar

RP 62, which loops back to Junín, at the **Baños de Epulafquen** hot springs. This route requires an overnight stay at a Mapuche-run campground at the approximate midway point.

Parque Nacional Laguna Blanca

Where the unrelenting wind blows across rugged volcanic terrain in the virtual center of the province, Laguna Blanca is a critical wetland nesting site for the black-necked swan. On a detour off RN 40, roughly

Neuquén (City) & Around

Where the Río Limay and the Río Neuquén join to form the Río Negro, Neuquén is the commercial center for a prosperous fruit-growing area and a gateway to the Patagonian lakes. At the same time, it's home to noteworthy museums, a base for visiting some of the world's most dramatic dinosaur discoveries on the surrounding steppe, and even part of a wine district.

Over the past decade, Neuquén has transformed its former

Park your car facing the wind. Patagonian gusts get so strong that they can bend car doors backward, or even tear them off.

—PETER MCBRIDE
National Geographic photographer

railyards into the **Parque Central,** an open urban space whose **Museo Nacional de Bellas Artes Neuquén** is a provincial branch of the national fine arts museum. Its permanent collections, part of the national heritage, include works by painters such as Antonio Berni, Xul Solar, and Joaquín Torres-García.

There are several wineries around Neuquén, the most accessible of which is **Bodega Humberto Canale,** in the Río Negro locality of General Roca.

Patagonia's most venerable bodega has an engaging wine museum, the starting point for tours, doubling as a tasting room.

A fossil wonderland, Neuquén has several dinosaur sites within easy driving distance. At the oil town of **Plaza Huincul,** 66 miles (106 km) west of Neuquén on the road to Zapala and Laguna Blanca, paleontologist Rodolfo Coria has transformed the **Museo Municipal Carmen Funes** into a cavernous space big enough for *Argentinosaurus huinculensis,* the world largest dinosaur, and for many others.

At the damside site of **Villa El Chocón,** 47 miles (76 km) southwest of Neuquén via RN 237, the **Museo Paleontológico Municipal Ernesto Bachmann** can boast of *Giganotosaurus carolinii,* the world's largest carnivorous dinosaur, other carnivorous dinosaurs, and dinosaur tracks in the vicinity. ∎

Bodega Humberto Canale

- ✉ Chacra 186, General Roca, Neuquén
- ☎ 02941/430-415
- 🕐 Tours Thurs. & Sat.; closed Sun.– Mon. & holidays
- 💲 $$$

www.bodegahcanale.com

Museo Municipal Carmen Funes

- ✉ Avenida Córdoba 55, Plaza Huincul, Neuquén
- ☎ 0299/496-5486
- 🕐 Closed Nov. 8
- 💲 $

Museo Paleontológico Municipal Ernesto Bachmann

- ✉ Centro Cívico, Villa El Chocón
- ☎ 0299/490-1230, ext. 280
- 💲 $

Mountain bikers ride through southern beech forests, San Martín de los Andes.

The Dinosaurs of Patagonia

From its endless shoreline to the vast steppe and the high Andes, everything in Patagonia is larger than life—or at least as large as life once was. Patagonia may have its share of tall tales, dating from the first European explorers' fables of human giants, but there's no need to exaggerate the riches, and achievements, of Patagonian paleontology.

The dinosaur experience at Villa El Chocón

Most of today's Patagonia is desert, but in the early Mesozoic era about 250 million years ago, before South America separated from the supercontinent of Pangaea, its climate was warmer and wetter than it is today. The first dinosaurs appeared in the Triassic, up to about 230 million years ago, but the creation of the Andes by tectonic uplift and volcanism gradually altered the climate. Dinosaurs survived only until the late Cretaceous, about 65 million years ago, but sediments and volcanic ash fossilized their remains. In the newly arid climate—a function of the Andean rain shadow—natural erosion and human activities, such as mining and drilling for oil, gradually exposed them.

Patagonia's first dinosaur finds date from 1882, when a Comandante Buratovich found bones near the confluence of the Limay and Neuquén Rivers and sent them to pioneer paleontologist Florentino Ameghino (1854–1911). Succeeding researchers, such as the German Friedrich von Huene (1875–1969), established

the significance of Patagonian dinosaurs in the 1920s, but it was José Bonaparte (1928–) who really put Patagonia on the map. Bonaparte has named more than two dozen dinosaur species, and his disciples have given Argentine paleontology an international reputation.

Most of these Patagonian finds have taken place near Neuquén, and some are truly monumental. With Rodolfo Coria, for instance, Bonaparte discovered the massive Cretaceous herbivore *Argentinosaurus huinculensis*, 115 feet (35 m) long and 59 feet (18 m) in height, possibly the world's largest dinosaur. *Puertasaurus reuili* may have been even larger—perhaps 131 feet (40 m) long—but no complete skeleton has yet been found.

Land of the Giants

Patagonia can also boast one of the world's largest carnivorous dinosaurs. When *Giganotosaurus carolinii* appeared on the scene in the 1990s, Coria and Leonardo Salgado measured it at 43 feet (13.2 m) tall—larger than *Tyrannosaurus rex*. At the time, a message board commentator remarked, "It figures the world's largest carnivore would be an Argentine!"

It wasn't long, though, before Coria and Phillip Currie of the University of Alberta uncovered the late Cretaceous *Mapusaurus roseae*, embedded in sandstone, only 15 miles (25 km) from Plaza Huincul. Equally large, or perhaps even a bit larger than *Giganotosaurus*, *Mapusaurus* may have hunted in packs for herbivores like *Argentinosaurus*—whose sheer size made it difficult for a single predator to attack.

Mapusaurus might also have gone after a more recent discovery in the titanosaur family.

An in situ representation of a dinosaur find at the Museo Paleontológico Municipal Ernesto Bachmann

At Lago Barreales, northwest of Neuquén, Jorge Calvo found the tongue-twisting *Futalognkosaurus dukei*—"big chief" in the Mapuche language—at 111 feet (34 m) long, only slightly smaller than *Argentinosaurus*.

One of the remarkable discoveries of the last decade-plus, though, has been the unearthing of huge caches of titanosaur eggs in Neuquén Province. While searching for fossil birds, Coria, Luis Chiappe (an Argentine now at the Los Angeles County Museum of Natural History), and others stumbled upon the Auca Mahuevo site north of Barreales. Even more importantly, they found well-preserved embryos within those caches—a rarity that could provide even greater clues to dinosaur evolution.

Coastal Patagonia

Where the Atlantic surf strikes an arid coastline that stretches south for thousands of miles, the thinly populated provinces of Río Negro, Chubut, and Santa Cruz are a cornucopia of marine, amphibian, and terrestrial wildlife. Along with an abundance of penguins, whales, elephant seals, sea lions, and other beasts is a surprising cultural diversity. Only in Patagonia can you end a day of penguin-watching with high tea in a Welsh village.

Headlands at Punta Ninfas, Chubut Province

Carmen de Patagones

 223 C4

Visitor Information

 Mitre 84

☎ 02920/464-819

🕑 Closed holidays

www.patagones.gov.ar

Traditionally, the Río Colorado in southern Buenos Aires Province marks the northern limit of Patagonia. To the south some 95 miles (152 km) via RN 3 is the town of **Carmen de Patagones.** Facing the Río Negro provincial capital of Viedma, linked to it by bridges and boat shuttles, Carmen dates from 1779 and its narrow riverfront streets have a distinct colonial feel.

Despite the colonial ambience,

the only remaining colonial structure is the **Torre del Fuerte** (1780), the fortified tower alongside the **Iglesia Parroquial Nuestra Señora del Carmen** (1885) on the high ground of Plaza 7 de Marzo. On the flood-prone riverfront, the **Museo Histórico Regional Emma Nozzi** is notable for the so-called **Cueva Maragata**—one of several grottos that the first Spaniards dug into the riverbank for shelter.

Viedma & Around

Across the river from Carmen, Río Negro's provincial capital is a bustling city whose 15 minutes of fame came in the mid-1980s, when President Raúl Alfonsín proposed moving the federal capital here from Buenos Aires. The river parklands, with their paddlers and swimmers, are the big attraction for locals.

Unlike Carmen, it has no colonial remains, but **Plaza Alsina** and its **Vicariato Apostólico de la Patagonia Septentrional y Central** (Vicarage of Northern and Central Patagonia), established to evangelize the region

INSIDER TIP:

At Doradillo, ten minutes from Puerto Madryn, lie on the beach in winter and watch right whales breaching and getting so close to shore you can feel their breath.

—PABLO GARCIA
BORBOROGLU
National Geographic writer

in the 1880s, form a historic complex that includes two good museums: the **Museo Salesiano Cardenal Cagliero,** promoting the order's missionary efforts; and the **Museo Tecnológico del Agua y Suelo Ingeniero Osvaldo Casamiquela,** dealing with water use and conservation.

From Viedma, it's about half an hour southeast via RP 1 to the

Atlantic beaches of the **Golfo San Matías,** and another half hour to **La Lobería** *(RP 1, 36 miles/58 km SW of Viedma, $$$),* where thousands of southern sea lions breed on the beach in summer, visible from the bluff above. For travelers with their own vehicles, the road continues northwest to rejoin RN 3 at several locations.

Puerto Madryn & Around

On the sheltered Golfo Nuevo, 274 miles (440 km) southwest of Viedma via RN 3, Puerto Madryn was the first Welsh outpost in Patagonia in the 19th century. Little remains of that heritage, and today it's a beach resort for summer tourism, a port of call for South Atlantic cruise ships, and, most important, the gateway to some of the world's most spectacular coastal wildlife sites at Península Valdés and Punta Tombo.

Facing the Golfo Nuevo, Puerto Madryn is a tidy modern city whose sandy waterfront is good for sunbathing, swimming, diving, and windsurfing, all organized at a series of beachside *balnearios* that have cafés, bars, and rental gear. It has only a handful of historic buildings, most notably the restored **Chalet Pujol,** which houses the **Museo Oceanográfico y de Ciencias Naturales.** Capped by a cupola, dating from 1917, the "castle" delves into the city's Welsh heritage and summarizes the region's maritime ecology in bright new display cases.

Madryn's pride, though, is the **Ecocentro Puerto Madryn,**

Museo Histórico Regional Emma Nozzi
- J.J. Biedma 64, Carmen de Patagones
- 02920/462-729
- Closed Sun. & holidays

Viedma
- 223 C4

Visitor Information
- Avenida Francisco de Viedma 51
- 02920/427-171
- www.viedma.gov.ar

Museo Salesiano Cardenal Cagliero
- Rivadavia 34, Viedma
- 02920/15-613-355
- Closed Sat.–Sun. & holidays
- Donation

Museo Tecnológico del Agua y Suelo Ingeniero Osvaldo Casamiquela
- Colón 498, 1st floor, Viedma
- 02920/426-096
- Closed Sat.–Sun. & holidays

Puerto Madryn
- 223 C3

Visitor Information
- Avenida Julio A. Roca 223, Puerto Madryn
- 0280/445-3504
- www.madryn.gov.ar/turismo

Museo Oceanográfico y de Ciencias Naturales

- ✉ Domecq García & Menéndez
- ☎ 0280/445-1139
- 🕐 Closed Sun.
- 💲 $$

Ecocentro Puerto Madryn

- ✉ Julio Verne 3784
- ☎ 0280/445-7470
- 🕐 Closed Tues. March & July– Sept.; Mon.–Tues. April–June; & Jan. 1, Dec. 25, & Dec. 31
- 💲 $$$$$

www.ecocentro.org.ar

Área Natural Protegida Península Valdés

- 🗺 223 C4
- ✉ RP 2, 28 miles (45 km) NE of Puerto Madryn at El Desempeño
- 💲 $$$$$

Visitor Information

- ✉ RP 2, 41 miles (66 km) NE of Puerto Madryn at Istmo Carlos Ameghino
- ☎ 0280/445-0489

www.peninsulavaldes .org.ar

a stunning environmental and cultural center, in a traditional "Magellanic" style with Victorian touches, on the southeastern out- skirts of town. On a bluff above the Golfo Nuevo, surrounded by native shrubs and bunchgrasses, its atrium and mezzanine offer sophisticated exhibits on maritime ecology and a three-story tower provides views to Península Valdés. In winter, right whales swim just offshore. In addition to its perma- nent collections, the Ecocentro has frequently changing fine-arts exhibitions, usually on environ- mental themes, and a theater for lectures and concerts. Few cities of Madryn's size—population about 82,000—can match the Ecocen- tro's sophisticated facilities.

For wintertime visitors who want a good chance of seeing whales without daily trips to Penín- sula Valdés, the beasts come close to shore at **Playa El Doradillo,** an easy bike ride only 10 miles (17 km) north of town via gravel RP 42. About 9 miles (15 km) southeast of town, the **Área Nat- ural Protegida Punta Loma** (*tel 0280/448-5271, $$$$$*) is known for its southern sea lion colonies but also has many birds, including giant petrels.

Área Natural Protegida Península Valdés

Shaped like a medieval battle axe jutting into the South Atlantic, Península Valdés is a wasteland of saline sinks and scrub-covered hills, but its bor- dering beaches and seas support a cornucopia of marine wildlife that has earned it UNESCO

World Heritage site status. Connected to the continent by a panhandle isthmus, it's the top attraction along the Atlantic shore for foreigners and Argentines alike. Among the sights are southern right whales, orcas, elephant seals, sea lions, Magellanic penguins, and many other bird species. Not all of them stick around all year—the whales, for instance, are winter visitors while the penguins waddle ashore in spring to breed in the austral summer.

Valdés's wildlife is not con- fined to the coasts. The camel- like guanaco forages on the inland shrubs and, on occasion, even on shoreline seaweed, while the ostrich-like rhea dashes along

INSIDER TIP:

Don't miss the chance to kayak with sea lions in Puerto Madryn. The silence of the paddling is unthreatening, but always be aware that you are on the territory of these wild animals.

—ALISON INCE
National Geographic contributor

and across the dirt roads that line the landscape. At the **Istmo Car- los Ameghino,** which connects the peninsula to the mainland, the park's visitor center provides an introduction to the reserve's natural and cultural history— the Tehuelche hunted and gath- ered there before Columbus, the Spaniards and Argentines collected salt, and many sheep stations still survive.

On the isthmus's north side, just offshore in the Golfo San José, **Isla de los Pájaros** is home to nesting cormorants, gulls, herons, and, in summer, burrowing Magellanic penguins.

wildlife-watchers. Here, in summer, you may even find yourself swimming alongside a penguin as the waves approach the shore.

One of the lowest points on land, 138 feet (42 m) below sea level, the **Salinas Grandes** and other interior depressions were a source of salt for pioneers on

A bull elephant seal roars at Punta Delgada, Península Valdés, Chubut Province.

Most easily reached from the hamlet of **Puerto Pirámides,** the peninsula's only town, the shallow waters of the **Golfo Nuevo** are the nursery for the southern right whale, *Eubalaena australis,* and its calves in the winter and spring months. In season, whale-watching boats leave frequently from Pirámides, which is also a summer seaside destination for Argentine tourists and foreign

the sheep farms that still dot the peninsula. Above the peninsula's southeastern tip, the **Punta Delgada** headlands hold a hotel (see Travelwise p. 312) and a landmark lighthouse. There, a steep trail descends to tidal pools and sandy beaches where elephant seals haul ashore in summer and sea lions stay all year.

At **Punta Norte,** the peninsula's northeastern tip, mixed

Trelew

△ 223 C3

Visitor Information

✉ Mitre 387

☎ 0280/442-0139

🕒 Closed Jan. 1, May 1, & Dec. 25

www.trelew patagonia.gov.ar

Museo Regional Pueblo de Luis

✉ Avenida Fontana & Lewis Jones, Trelew

☎ 0280/442-4062

🕒 Closed Jan. 1, May 1, & Dec. 25

$ $

Hotel Touring Club

✉ Avenida Fontana 240, Trelew

☎ 0280/443-3997

www.touring patagonia.com.ar

colonies of elephant seals and sea lions resemble those at Punta Delgada, but the most stunning sights are the orcas ("killer whales") that lunge to grab sea lion pups off the beach and drag them into the ocean. Near **Punta Norte,** a dirt road through the isolated sheep station of Estancia San Lorenzo drops to a beach where tens of thousands of Magellanic penguins hatch every summer.

Península Valdés is a popular but long day trip from Puerto Madryn, which is 28 miles (45 km) from the

The Bryn Gwyn Fossil Walk

Trelew's Museo Paleontológico Egidio Feruglio is more than a building— this museum also oversees a paleontological trail on the southern *bardas* (cliffs) of the Río Chubut Valley. What is now desert was, between 40 million and 10 million years ago, savanna and an inland sea.

That time span is too recent for dinosaurs, but hikers can see 38-million-year-old wasp nests, pre-Pleistocene megafauna fossils such as the elephantine *Astrapothericulus* (25 million years old), penguins (15 million years old), and river dolphins (15 million years old). At the top of the cliffs, the younger formations show more recent fossils and a view back into the Chubut Valley—and through time.

natural area's entrance and 59 miles (95 km) from Puerto Pirámides. Minivan tours leave frequently from Madryn, but many visitors prefer the convenience of an automobile.

INSIDER TIP:

Follow in the footsteps of Butch Cassidy and visit Trelew's Hotel Touring Club. This lovely old bar is lined with bottles and mirrors, and you can practice Spanish with the locals over a beer.

—ALISON INCE
National Geographic contributor

Trelew & Around

Only 40 miles (65 km) south of Puerto Madryn, the wool and factory town of Trelew has managed to maintain its Welsh heritage through landmarks, like the **Salón San David** and **Capilla Tabernacl,** and events, like the annual Eisteddfod of Gaelic music and poetry. It summarizes that historical heritage in the **Museo Regional Pueblo de Luis,** the former station (1889) for the railway that climbed the Río Chubut Valley.

While it's undergoing improvements, the historical museum lags far behind the state-of-the-art **Museo Paleontológico Egidio Feruglio (MEF),** a paleontological museum that outshines the museums of Neuquén in style, if not always in content. In distant times, the

EXPERIENCE: Teatime in Patagonia

When a boatload of Welsh colonists left the United Kingdom in 1865 with the idea of preserving their language and religion, they settled in the unlikely destination of the Río Chubut Valley, then a thinly settled frontier. No longer a frontier, it's still thinly settled; even if immigrants from elsewhere in Argentina far outnumber the Welsh, place-names such as Madryn, Trelew, and Bryn Gwyn are prominent on the landscape. City streets often bear names such as Berwin, Evans, Matthews, and Roberts.

If the Welsh language has been making a comeback in villages such as **Gaiman** (the most self-consciously Welsh settlement), Welshness is also conspicuous in the brick-faced teahouses where

Argentine and foreign clients alike flock throughout the year. Their most famous visitor was Diana, Princess of Wales, who feasted on freshly baked bread, cookies, pies, and scones, and sipped tea from a bottomless pot, at **Ty Te Caerdydd** *(Finca 202, Gaiman, tel 0280/449-1510)* in 1995.

Many tour operators from Puerto Madryn take their clients to Gaiman after a day at the Punta Tombo penguin colony, but plenty of travelers make Gaiman a day trip—or an overnight at a local B&B. Those whose travel plans don't include coastal Patagonia can find equally good choices in the lakes district town of **Trevelin** (see p. 240), near the city of Esquel. Most teahouses open around 2 or 3 p.m. and stay open until 7 or 8 p.m.

---

steppe to the west of Trelew was home to carnivores such as the Cretaceous *Carnotaurus sastrei*—made famous in *The Lost World* sequel to *Jurassic Park*—and the Jurassic *Pianitzkysaurus floresi*, both of which are re-created here. The museum also honors pioneer Patagonian paleontologists such as the Italian petroleum geologist (1897–1954) whose name it bears and Alejandro Pianitzky, and it has a lab whose activities are visible to the public.

Only 16 miles (25 km) east of Trelew, the beach town of Playa Unión is a suburb of **Rawson,** the nondescript provincial capital. At the town's south end, launch tours navigate among leaping *toninas,* or Commerson's dolphins.

Gaiman & Around

Trelew may have preserved some of its Welshness, but Gaiman, with its ivy-covered

teahouses, looks and *feels* Welsh. Only 11 miles (17 km) west of Trelew, with street names like Evans, Jones, and Matthews, landmarks like the **Amgueddfa Hannesydol** (the former railway station, now a historical museum) and the **Twnnel yr Hen Reilfford** (where the train chugged through a hill en route to Dolavon), Gaiman is unique.

Another 12 miles (19 km) up the Río Chubut Valley, the village of **Dolavon,** with its almost uniformly brick houses and waterwheel-fed orchards and fields, feels even more Welsh than Gaiman, but unlike the latter, lacks services for out-of-town visitors.

Área Natural Protegida Punta Tombo

On a desolate shoreline at the end of a partially paved road, 76 miles (122 km) south of

Museo Paleontológico Egidio Feruglio (MEF)
- ✉ Avenida Fontana 140, Trelew
- ☏ 0280/443-2100
- 🕐 Closed Jan. 1 & Dec. 25
- 💲 $$$$
- www.mef.org.ar

Gaiman
- 🗺 223 C3

Visitor Information
- ✉ Belgrano 574
- ☏ 0280/449-1571
- www.gaiman.gov.ar

Amgueddfa Hanesyddol
- ✉ Sarmiento & 28 de Julio
- ☏ 0280/449-1007
- 💲 $

Área Natural Protegida Punta Tombo

🗺 223 C3

✉ 76 miles (122 km) S of Trelew via RN 3, RP 75 & RP 1

☎ 0280/448-5271

www.puntatombo.com

Trelew via RN 3, RP 75, and RP 1, tens of thousands of visitors flock to view hundreds of thousands of Magellanic penguins between mid-September and early April at Punta Tombo (closed mid-April–Aug, $$$$$). Waddling onto the shore and

> ## Penguin Etiquette
>
> Along Argentina's Patagonian coast, colonies of Magellanic penguins number in the hundreds of thousands at Punta Tombo (Chubut) and Cabo Vírgenes (Santa Cruz). And every year they get more and more human visitors who, enamored of the penguins' undeniable charm, want to get close to them.
>
> That's not a good idea, and it's unnecessary. At Punta Tombo, for instance, narrow fenced paths and elevated boardwalks restrict humans, but penguins pass freely beneath. As the birds are always scurrying to and from their nesting sites, it's only necessary to stand still and wait to snap that unforgettable photo without disturbing them. And you'll avoid a bloody, painful peck from the bird's sharp beak.

Bahía Bustamante

🗺 223 C3

✉ RN 3 Km 1674

☎ 0297/480-1000

www.bahiabustamante.com

Comodoro Rivadavia

🗺 223 C2

Visitor Information

✉ Avenida Hipólito Yrigoyen & Moreno

☎ 0297/444-0664

🕐 Closed Sat.–Sun. & holidays

www.comodoroturismo.gob.ar

burrowing beneath the coastal scrub, breeding penguins make frequent trips to bring back food—which they regurgitate to the chicks—until the molting young are ready to go to sea themselves.

The continent's largest penguin colony, Punta Tombo has much more to see: Giant petrels glide along the shore, flightless steamer ducks scoot through the surf, cormorants alight on rocky breeding sites, and oystercatchers pick their way along the rocks. That said, the Magellanics are in

trouble because of the overfished Patagonian anchovy—a major part of their diet—and oil spills along the South American coast.

Minivan tours from both Puerto Madryn and Trelew visit Punta Tombo daily during the season, and rental cars are an option. There are now accommodations nearby at Estancia La Antonieta (www.laantonieta.com) and food is available at a small café.

Parque Nacional Marino Patagonia Austral

On the Atlantic, about 155 miles (250 km) south of Trelew and 112 miles (180 km) north of Comodoro Rivadavia, the tiny company town of **Bahía Bustamante** is the gateway to Parque Interjurisdiccional Marino Costero Patagonia Austral, the first Argentine reserve to encompass offshore as well as onshore territory. Its street named for the algae that provide part of its livelihood, Bustamante also offers more than comfortable guest accommodations with elaborate meals and tours of wildlife-rich islands and a remarkable petrified forest just a short distance inland.

Comodoro Rivadavia & Around

Some 234 miles (377 km) southwest of Trelew, Comodoro Rivadavia is an oil town that has some of the only accommodations along RN 3 this side of Puerto San Julián, another 264 miles (425 km) south. However, a night spent here need not be wasted—in the suburb of

General Mosconi, Comodoro's **Museo Nacional del Petróleo** is a thoughtful exploration of the Argentine petroleum industry. Alternative-energy activists will approve of the windmills atop Cerro Chenque.

The best excursion, well worth a detour for motorists, is the late Mesozoic fossil forest at the **Área Natural Protegida Bosque Petrificado Sarmiento,** via RN 26 and RP 20 to the town Sarmiento, 92 miles (149 km) west, and another 19 miles (30 km) south on a gravel road. About 65 million years ago, this was a subtropical woodland, but today a nature trail leads through 1.2 miles (2 km) of petrified stumps, logs, chips, and bark near the red desert outcrop of **Cerro Colorado.**

Puerto Deseado & Around

Southbound RN 3 goes nowhere close to Puerto Deseado, which lies at the east end of the paved RN 281 spur, 183 miles (295 km) from Comodoro Rivadavia, but it's arguably the most worthwhile detour along the entire Patagonian coast. Once the port for a failed railway intended to reach Bariloche, its **Ex Estación del Ferrocarril Patagónico** *(Eufrasia Arias, open 4–7 p.m.)* looks like a Union Pacific station out of the Great Plains; ex-railmen staff the current museum here.

First seen by privateer Thomas Cavendish, who named it for his vessel *Desire* in 1586, Deseado has seen a succession of famous visitors including Darwin ("I do not think I ever saw a spot ... more secluded from the rest of the world") and Perito Moreno ("the most picturesque place on the eastern Patagonian coast").

Puerto Deseado has other historic sites, such as the **Vagón Histórico** *(San Martín y Almirante*

Museo Nacional del Petróleo

✉ San Lorenzo 250, Barrio General Mosconi Km 3
☎ 0297/455-9558
🕐 Closed Sat.–Sun. & holidays.
💲 $

Área Natural Protegida Bosque Petrificado Sarmiento

🅐 223 B2
☎ 0297/489-8282
💲 $$$$

Puerto Deseado

🅐 223 C2
Visitor Information
✉ Avenida San Martín 1525
☎ 0297/487-0220
www.deseado.gov .ar/dire_turismo

A right whale breaches for whale-watchers off Puerto Pirámides, Península Valdés.

Puerto San Julián

🅼 223 C1

Visitor Information

✉ Avenida San
Martín *&*
Rivadavia

☎ 02962/452-009

www.sanjulian.gov.ar

Brown), a railcar that was Col. Héctor Benigno Varela's headquarters during the anarchist rebellion of 1921. Its outstanding asset, though, is the **Reserva Natural Provincial Ría Deseado,** a wildlife-rich estuary where local operators run launches to the beachfront Magellanic penguin colony of **Isla Chaffers** and to the cormorant perches of **Barranca de los Cormoranes.**

Glossy black-and-white Commerson's dolphins are companions on any trip up the *ría,* but the most distinctive sight here is the **Isla Pingüino,** where the South Atlantic surf slams the short-crested rockhopper penguins against steep cliffs as they climb to summer nesting sites. The species' northernmost nesting site, the island is also home to elephant seals.

Puerto San Julián & Around

Like Puerto Deseado, Puerto San Julián is a historic port where Magellan, Sir Francis Drake, and Darwin all spent time. The Spaniards established their first Patagonian settlement at nearby **Floridablanca,** now an archaeological site. Some 264 miles (425 km) south of Comodoro Rivadavia via RN 3, San Julián is a service center for nearby sheep stations but also notable for excursions to **Banco Cormorán,** which has a penguin colony, and **Reserva Provincial Islas Cormorán y Justicia,** a king cormorant nesting site. On rigid inflatables, often accompanied by Commerson's dolphins, the excursions last about two hours.

About 31 miles (50 km) south of town, west of the highway, **Gran Bajo de San Julián** is the lowest point in the Americas—345 feet (105 m) below sea level.

Parque Nacional Monte León

About midway between Puerto San Julián and Río Gallegos, in one of Patagonia's most thinly populated places, RP 63 is a gravel road—gates are locked in wet weather—that leads southeast to Parque Nacional Monte León, a land of broad sandy beaches, dramatic headlands,

Magellanic penguins, Parque Nacional Monte León

INSIDER TIP:

The Patagonia myth was born in the cheerful town of San Julián when Magellan's cartographer, Antonio Pigafetta, put the word on the world's first map of the region. Not to be missed.

—SIMON WORRALL
National Geographic contributor

and prolific wildlife that's one of only three coastal national parks in Argentina. The former estancia was donated to the park service by Doug Tompkins and Kris McDivitt, who are also the owners of extensive subtropical wetlands at Iberá, in Corrientes Province (see pp. 134–135).

Approaching the 25-mile (40 km) sedimentary coastline, watch for grazing guanacos and sprinting rheas on the coastal steppe. Along the coast, the 1.5-mile (2.5 km) **Sendero de la Pingüinera** leads to a breeding colony of 75,000 pairs of Magellanic penguins, while the **Pasarela de la Cabeza del León** is a boardwalk up the side of a coastal mountain that resembles a maned African lion; from its summit, look for a southern sea lion colony. Cormorants and gulls nest atop the offshore stack of **Isla Monte León.**

Río Gallegos & Around

The last city before the Chilean border, Río Gallegos is a windswept town that, for overland travelers to Tierra del Fuego and El Calafate, can be an unavoidable overnight. Some 221 miles (355 km) south of Puerto San Julián via RN 3, it still sports metal-clad "Magellanic" houses, and its **Museo de los Pioneros** tells the story of the first British settlers, who created the sheep stations on which the city's wealth depended. One of those sheep stations, the Fenton family's **Estancia Monte Dinero,** 75 miles (120 km) southeast of Gallegos

Low Tide Only!

Though it collapsed in 2006, the remains of the stunning grotto known as La Olla remain a worthwhile hike along the beach at Monte León. At high tide, though, La Olla is inaccessible. Ask at the visitor center on RN 3 for tide tables, try to descend just before low tide, and walk cautiously on the slippery surface left by the receding waters. The tide returns rapidly and forcefully— don't get stranded.

via RN 3 and gravel RP 1, hosts "day in the country" visits and also has overnight accommodations.

Another 9 miles (15 km) down the road, the **Reserva Natural Provincial Cabo Vírgenes** contains a huge Magellanic penguin colony—only Punta Tombo exceeds its 160,000 birds—and marks the southern tip of the continent. Travel agencies in Gallegos arrange day trips. ∎

Parque Nacional Monte León
- 223 C1
- RN 3 Km 2,358
- 02962/498-184 in Puerto Santa Cruz
- Closed May–Oct. & after rain
www.pnmonteleon.com.ar

Province of Santa Cruz
- 223 B2/C2
Visitor Information
- Avenida Avenida Presidente Néstor Kirchner 863, Río Gallegos
- 02966/437-412
www.epatagonia.gov.ar

Río Gallegos
- 223 C1

Museo de los Pioneros
- Elcano & Alberdi, Río Gallegos
- 02966/437-763

Estancia Monte Dinero
- Cabo Virgenes, Rio Gallegos, Santa Cruz
- 02966/428-922
www.montedinero.com.ar

Reserva Natural Provincial Cabo Vírgenes
- 223 C1

The Southern Andes

In westernmost Santa Cruz Province, the area in and around Parque Nacional Los Glaciares is one of the country's top attractions. The sight that makes it so is the awe-inspiring
Moreno Glacier, drawing even city dwellers to its groaning river of ice. Its northern Fitz
Roy sector is a prime destination for hikers into its wooded lowlands and exhilarating high
country and for climbers challenging some of the world's most intimidating rock and ice.

A tourist launch cruises Lago Argentino along the face of the Moreno Glacier.

Parque Nacional
Los Glaciares

In westernmost Santa Cruz Province, hugging the Chilean border,
Los Glaciares is a UNESCO
World Heritage site encompassing 2,795 square miles (7,240 sq
km). Startlingly beautiful granite
needles rise above the Southern

Patagonian Ice Field, which
discharges indigo icebergs into
the vast glacial troughs of Lago
Argentino and Lago Viedma, and
emerald green southern beech
forests stand beneath Andean
fell fields. Its icon is the Moreno
Glacier, one of few glaciers on
the globe that, despite all the

evidence of global warming and receding glaciers elsewhere, continues to advance. At the same time, the park's northern Fitz Roy sector is a magnet for hikers and extreme climbers from around the world.

Glaciar Moreno: In a sense, the Moreno Glacier is a paradox. Though ice covers nearly a third of the park's surface, most of its glaciers are receding; however, this particular glacier continues to advance. It's both extraordinary—a dazzling natural spectacle at the center of a global concern over climate change—and commonplace, as the single most frequent excursion for visitors to southern Argentine Patagonia.

Every day, dozens of tour buses, minivans, and private cars motor to the end of RP 11, about 48 miles (77 km) west of El Calafate, where the glacier steadily advances across the **Brazo Rico** (Rico Arm) of Lago Argentino. From a parking area on the Península de Magallanes, visitors descend a zigzag series of catwalks, with occasional broad platforms at strategic viewpoints, toward the lakeshore—but not too close to it, as shards from calving icebergs off the glacier's nearly 200-foot (60 m) face move at bullet speed and backwash can sweep unsuspecting spectators into the water.

Observing the glacier is rarely a solitary experience, especially in summer, as the hordes of visitors ascending and descending the catwalks can reach gridlock levels. But the crackle of the advancing ice, the sight of ice chunks tumbling toward

the **Canal de los Témpanos** (Iceberg Channel), and the high splash as they crash into the water are unforgettable even when spectators are elbow to elbow. It's possible to sit for hours, barely moving and often with eyes closed, in contemplation of the glacier's majesty.

The glacier often makes its own weather, but even when the clouds close in and powerful westerlies bring horizontal snow flurries, its unrelenting noises make the trip worthwhile. In some years, relentless Pacific storms dump their loads on its upper reaches until, eventually, the ice blocks the outlet from the Brazo Rico. The water level gradually rises until

INSIDER TIP:

When shooting photos of glaciers and ice fields, given their vast size, try to include additional elements that provide scale.

—JASON EDWARDS
National Geographic photographer

the ice can no longer support its weight. At that point, it ruptures in a rush of ice and water toward the main body of Lago Argentino—an event that occurred most recently in March 2012. When the glacier's at no risk of rupture, which is most of the time, visitors can get a relatively close-up view from water level on a small catamaran or, more actively, hike onto the ice with experienced guides.

Parque Nacional Los Glaciares

🅰 223 B1

✉ Entrances via El Calafate & El Chaltén

💲 $$$$$ (charged at park entrance on RP 11 & before boat tours). No charge at El Chaltén.

Visitor Information

✉ Avenida del Libertador and Coronel Rosales, El Calafate

☎ 02902/491-755

✉ RP 23, El Chaltén

☎ 02962/493-004

www.parques nacionales.gov.ar

TOUR OPERATORS:
To tour the glaciers, contact **Solo Patagonia excursions** (Avenida del Libertador General José de San Martín 867, El Calafate, tel 02902/491-155 or 02902/491-428, www.solopatagonia .com) or **Hielo y Aventura Tours** (Avenida del Libertador 935, El Calafate, tel 02902/492-205, www .hieloyaventura.com).

Glaciar Upsala: From Punta Bandera, 28 miles (45 km) west of El Calafate on the north shore of the Península de Magallanes, frequent full-day catamaran excursions carry spectators through the iceberg-filled northwestern arms of Lago Argentino to view **Glaciar Spegazzini, Glaciar Upsala**—larger than the Moreno Glacier—and even make a landing at Bahía Onelli for a short hike to **Lago Onelli.** While scenic, more spontaneous travelers may chafe at the rigidly organized itinerary, its tight schedule, and the sheer number of passengers.

Lago Roca: Across the Brazo Rico from the Península de Magallanes, Lago Roca sits at the base of the Cordón de los Cristales, 34 miles (55 km) from El Calafate via graveled RP 15. Far less visited than the rest of the park, its standout attraction is 4,206-foot (1,282 m) **Cerro Cristal,** a cross-country hike offering boundless panoramas to the west, north, and east. After one of the Moreno Glacier's ruptures, the conspicuous ring around the shores of the Brazo Rico makes it look like a drained hydroelectric reservoir at summer's end.

Sector Fitz Roy: At the north end of the park, where the meandering Río de las Vueltas flows toward **Lago Viedma** and the granite pinnacles of the Fitz Roy range soar above the steppe, footpaths into the backcountry start barely beyond the

doorways of **El Chaltén**'s (see pp. 263–264) hostels, hotels, and B&Bs. Several of the paths are loops that permit hikers to start at one trailhead and exit at another; the trails are well signed and good maps are readily available in town.

From the park visitor center, at the south end of town, hikers are fewest on the trail to the **Loma del Pliegue Tumbado,** a gradual four-hour climb that provides the best overall views of the Fitz Roy range. For those with less time, it's only 45 minutes from the same trailhead to **Mirador de los Cóndores** (Condor's View), looking back toward El Chaltén and the Río de las Vueltas.

INSIDER TIP:

Walk on the Moreno Glacier with Hielo y Aventura Tours. They provide crampons, a fascinating two-hour walk on the ice, and chocolate and whiskey—served over glacier ice cubes—at the end of the hike.

—ALISON INCE
National Geographic contributor

It's trails like the 7-mile (11 km) **Sendero Laguna Torre,** though, that provide up-close perspectives on the vertiginously steep **Cerro Torre,** a 10,177-foot (3,102 m) needle where climbers may wait weeks for the weather to clear.

Hikers can reach the lake, **Laguna Torre,** in less than four hours.

At the north end of town, the **Sendero Río Blanco** zigzags steeply through southern beech woodlands before reaching the river and then switchbacking even more steeply to the **Laguna de los Tres** for close-ups of 11,170-foot (3,405 m) **Cerro Fitz Roy,** the granite sentinel from which the range takes its name. When the winds are high—which is often—it's easy to slip and fall along this highly exposed route.

Like Laguna Torre, Laguna de los Tres is a doable day hike, but there's a backpacker's campground at **Laguna Capri,** a southerly midpoint detour along the trail, for those who care to overnight. Alternatively, a short distance southeast of Poincenot campground, a southbound trail passes little-visited **Laguna Madre** and **Laguna Hija** before intersecting the Laguna Torre trail back to town.

From the climbers-only Río Blanco campground, another trail leads north along the river to **Laguna Piedras Blancas,** an icy (and ice-filled) tarn. Day hikers will need to return from Piedras Blancas to El Chaltén. Backpackers can continue beyond the park limits to the **Río Eléctrico,** an access point for the **Hielo Continental Patagónico Sur,** the Southern Patagonian Ice Field (which requires experience and expedition preparation). Those not continuing to the ice fields can walk down the valley to the road between El Chaltén, to the south, and **Laguna del Desierto,** to the north.

El Chaltén is also the place to arrange catamaran excursions to

---

EXPERIENCE:
Hiking Laguna Azul

Starting on Lago Viedma's south shore, at the end of the westbound RP 21 turn-off from RN 40, the summertime hike to Laguna Azul is usually a privilege of overnighters at **Hostería Helsingfors** *(tel 011/5277-0195 or 02966/15-675-753, www.helsingfors.com.ar),* one of Patagonia's elite estancias. It's part of Parque Nacional Los Glaciares, though, and Helsingfors's proprietors cannot claim exclusive rights to the footpath that starts on steppe grasslands and climbs through southern beech forest to a cirque lake beneath a hanging glacier.

Travelers with their own cars—tours do not come here yet—can handle this half-day hike and make it to El Chaltén with time to spare. It is courteous to inform Helsingfors personnel before starting.

Glaciar Viedma, the deceptively large glacier reached from **Bahía Túnel,** a sheltered harbor on Lago Viedma, only 11 miles (18 km) south of town. While its lakeside tongue is small, this receding ice sheet is Argentina's largest, and full-day excursions disembark on the shore for an optional guided trek. Equipped with crampons, visitors walk across the ice and into frigid indigo caverns where meltwater drips from the ceiling before streaming toward the lake. The reward is whiskey or Bailey's on glacial ice cubes before returning to the boat.

El Calafate & Around

On the south shore of Lago Argentino, El Calafate is a one-time wool town and stage stop that takes its name from the

El Calafate

▲ 223 B1

Visitor Information

✉ Coronel Rosales
☎ 02902/491-090
www.elcalafate.tur.ar

thorny shrub, with bright blue edible berries, that covers so much of the Patagonian landscape. Because of its proximity to the famed Moreno Glacier, the town has boomed with Argentine and international tourist traffic. Despite a population of less than 22,000, it has an international profile and a state-of-the-art international airport thanks, at least in part, to former governor and Argentine president Néstor Kirchner and his

wife, Cristina Fernández, Argentina's current president. Over the past decade, the town has seen a storm of hotel construction that, metaphorically speaking, almost matches the Pacific fronts of snow and sleet that cross the Andes to feed the glacier; it has even acquired an incongruous new casino.

Unlike almost all other Argentine cities and towns, El Calafate has no central plaza, few open spaces, and few buildings of any antiquity. The liveliest part of town is **Avenida del Libertador General José de San Martín,** commonly known as Avenida Libertador or San Martín, between Perito Moreno and Ezequiel Bustillo. On those four pedestrian-friendly blocks, with broad sidewalks and a pine-lined median, chic restaurants and bars, cafés, travel agencies, clothiers, and souvenir shops are almost wall-to-wall. Except for the glacier trips and other excursions, the experience is not so different from the Florida pedestrian mall in Buenos Aires—except for the slower holiday pace.

At the private **Centro de Interpretación Histórica,** a time line establishes the natural history and cultural evolution of southern Patagonia through vivid paintings and illustrations that start with its Pleistocene megafauna, proceed through pre-Columbian peoples and their rock-art legacy, and cover the Tehuelche presence and the town's inauspicious beginnings as the stage stop. It does a far better job of covering the anarchist rebellion than the regional museum; its café, with a

The pedestrian-friendly heart of El Calafate

Patagonian-themed library, makes an ideal breather.

El Calafate's center is set back some distance from the **Lago Argentino** lakeshore, which is not readily visible except from the hills behind Avenida Libertador. Only a short distance from the Centro de Interpretación Histórica, though, is the grassy wetland of **Laguna Nímez** *(check for opening dates)*, a reclaimed sewage pond that's home to a host of birds—more than a hundred species—including Chilean flamingos, buff-necked

INSIDER TIP:

Cross the Baguales Range by horse with local guides. Expeditions usually connect El Calafate with Río Turbio in the south, or with Torres del Paine National Park, Chile.

—LUIS BORRERO
National Geographic field scientist

ibises, Andean ruddy ducks, red-gartered coots, and others. A series of footpaths winds through the site, with wooden supports through some soggy areas.

On the western outskirts of town, new in 2011, the **Glaciarium** is a striking new building whose façade mimics the face of a calving glacier. Within, it's an encyclopedic museum of the Patagonian ice fields, and their natural and cultural history, intended to raise consciousness of the global warming crisis. It also has a 3-D

theater to offer virtual tours of the region's glaciers, a café, a souvenir shop, and even an ice bar (for which there is a separate admission charge).

West of town, on the route to the Moreno Glacier and directly on the lake, **Estancia Alice** is a day-in-the-country getaway whose 2 miles (3.5 km) of shoreline are also ideal for birding. Alice offers overnight accommodations, horseback riding, mountain biking, fishing, and farm activities, including gathering and shearing sheep.

El Chaltén & Around

Thirty years ago, only a handful of hard-core climbers made it out of El Calafate, to drive around the north side of Lago Viedma and up the valley of the Río de las Vueltas—a 137-mile (220 km) trip taking at least six hours on dusty gravel roads that regularly shattered windshields—to the forlorn outpost of El Chaltén. At that time, just a few gendarmes upheld Argentina sovereignty in a vaguely defined border zone. These days smoothly paved roads whisk climbers and hikers to some of the continent's finest outdoor recreation.

No place in Argentina has superior scenery; its southern beech forests line the riverbanks and climb the foothills beneath the dramatic peaks of the Fitz Roy range. Parque Nacional Los Glaciares is literally in Chaltén's backyard.

The village has acquired an air of permanence, if not quite fashionability. (The streets are

Centro de Interpretación Histórica
- Almirante Brown 1050i
- 02902/492-799
- Closed Tues. April–July
- $$$
www.museocalafate.com.ar

Glaciarium
- RP 11 Km 6
- 02902/497-912
- $$$$$
www.glaciarium.com

Estancia Alice–El Galpón del Glaciar
- RP 11 Km 22
- 02902/497-793
www.estanciaalice.com.ar

El Chaltén
- 223 B1
Visitor Information
- Terminal de Ómnibus, Perito Moreno 28
- 02962/493-370
- Closed Sat.–Sun. & holidays June–Sept.
www.elchalten.com

Laguna del Desierto

🄼 223 B1

TOUR OPERATORS:
For tours, contact
Patagonia Aventura
*(Avenida San Martín,
El Chaltén, tel
02962/493-110,
www.patagonia
-aventura.com)* or
**Villa O'Higgins
Expediciones** *(Camino
Austral Km 1,240,
Villa O'Higgins, Region
de Aysén, Chile, tel
05667/491-293,
www.villaohiggins.com).*

currently being paved to keep down the dust raised by the ferocious winds that blow off the Southern Patagonian Ice Field.) Parkas and hiking boots are the universal style. At the end of the day, though, the town provides all the necessary comforts after a hard day's hiking, but few extravagances. Those could come, as the paved highway brings some of the

---

The Death of Lieutenant Merino

For several years now, backpackers have been crossing the border by a rugged boat, foot, and bus shuttle to the Chilean outpost of Villa O'Higgins, the southernmost point on Chile's Carretera Austral (Southern Highway). In 1965, though, this was a disputed border area, and when Chilean Lieutenant Hernán Merino led a police patrol there, he died in a firefight with the Argentine border guards. Lieutenant Merino remains a powerful symbol to Chilean nationalists, but the Argentines have also erected a small monument in his honor—and to goodwill between neighbors.

---

speculators who have transformed El Calafate, but Chaltén's highlights will always remain just beyond the town limits, in the national park of Los Glaciares.

Chaltén has no museums as such, but the Parque Nacional Los

Glaciares **visitor center,** in a recycled hotel, has fine natural-history exhibits and an auditorium where rangers hold lectures and slide shows on the park's attractions.

Laguna del Desierto

North of El Chaltén, RP 23 is a narrow gravel road that climbs the Río de las Vueltas Valley through a steep-sided canyon that, 23 miles (37 km) later, opens onto the south shore of Laguna del Desierto, a slim finger lake that stretches north for 7 nautical miles (13 km) toward the Chilean border. Bordered by dense southern beech forests, and also known as Lago del Desierto to Argentines, it is not part of the national park. It was, however, the subject of a border dispute that, several times, brought Chile and Argentina close to armed conflict. In fact, in 1965, a shootout with Argentine border guards resulted in the death of a Chilean policeman (see sidebar left).

Where the road ends, a short trail leads to **Laguna Huemul,** where a hanging glacier nearly reaches the shore of the aquamarine lake. On Laguna del Desierto itself, scheduled launches shuttle day-trippers as well as backpackers and mountain bikers to the Argentine border post at the north end of the lake. Here the truly adventurous can now cross the Chilean border in safety and continue to the hamlet of Villa O'Higgins via a bus-boat shuttle *(closed May–Sept.).* Alternatively, a rugged 12-mile (20 km) trail through dense beech forest follows the eastern shore of the lake to the border. ∎

Ruta 40

North of El Calafate, RN 40 to Esquel is one of the loneliest segments of Argentina's longest highway—a legendary road that runs from the Bolivian border to Río Gallegos on the South Atlantic. The Santa Cruz segment can offer cloudless blue skies where exotic wildlife ranges over seemingly endless steppe, a remote national park, a spectacular rock-art site with UNESCO recognition, and even a fruit-growing "banana belt."

A gaucho gallops across the steppe near Paso Roballos.

Lago Cardiel & Around

About 20 miles (32 km) west of El Calafate, freshly paved RN 40 leads north along the Río La Leona and, after the RP 23 turnoff to El Chaltén, turns east toward mysteriously named **Tres Lagos,** 80 miles (129 km) away (there is no lake within at least 20 miles/32 km). Tres Lagos has one important reason to stop: the last gas station on RN 40 for 210 miles (336 km).

At Tres Lagos, the pavement ends, but RN 40 continues northeast and, after 52 miles (83 km), it starts to skirt the scrub-filled shore of **Lago Cardiel,** a closed-basin lake nearly 250 feet (76 m) deep, covering 143 square miles (370 sq km). According to studies by Argentine and international climatologists, it was far deeper—nearly 400 feet (120 m)—during the early Holocene. It has since stabilized, but its relict shorelines and

Lago Cardiel
223 B1

Sorting sheep at Estancia Sol de Mayo, Paso Roballos

Parque Nacional Perito Moreno

🏔 223 B1

✉ RP 37, 56 miles (90 km) off RN 40

Visitor Information

✉ San Martín 882, Gobernador Gregores

☎ 02962/491-477

🕐 Access to park April–Sept. conditional on weather

www.parques nacionales.gov.ar

lake-bottom cores have allowed them to track precipitation for the last 21,000 years.

Lago Cardiel is popular with sportfishermen who, because of the lake's isolation, find little competition. A handful of ranches in the vicinity take paying guests; the town of **Gobernador Gregores** 37 miles (60 km) east has more services, including gasoline, but fuel occasionally runs out.

Parque Nacional Perito Moreno

From Gobernador Gregores, RN 40 leads northwest for 76 miles (123 km) to meet RP 37, which in turn leads northwest for another 56 miles (90 km) to Parque Nacional Perito Moreno. This land of wild high mountains, lakes, streams, and forests gets only a tiny fraction of the visitors that go to Los Glaciares. Tourism is increasing, though, since safaris from El Calafate to Bariloche have begun to overnight here.

The park's sights include frigid fjord-like finger lakes such as **Lago Burmeister** and **Lago Belgrano,** where **Península Belgrano** is

home to herds of guanacos and a nature trail. The best short hike, though, climbs from Estancia La Oriental to the 4,700-foot (1,434 m) summit of **Cerro León,** where condor chicks get airborne at the volcanic outcrop called **Cerro de los Cóndores.** Hikers need to be aware that the weather here is unpredictable and, at the high altitudes, sometimes extreme.

Perito Moreno has guest ranch accommodations at **Estancia La Oriental** (see Travelwise p. 317), which enjoys a convenient, central location for visitors to the park. The estancia has a campground as well, but campers need to bring all supplies.

Bajo Caracoles & Around

If it only had a train, the lonely crossroads of Bajo Caracoles would be a whistle-stop. At the dusty junction of four highways— RN 40, RP 39, RP 41, and RP 97— it has acquired a certain notoriety not only because it has the only gas station in more than 62 miles (100 km)—but also because it often runs out of fuel. That means motorists often have to spend a night or more, for better or worse, at the landmark **Hotel Bajo Caracoles** (1943), a basic-plus roadhouse distinguished by a handsome stone block facade. Because of these unique circumstances, it's become a de facto meeting place for travelers from around the country and the world.

Bajo Caracoles, 80 miles (128 km) south of the town of **Perito Moreno,** is the main gateway to the UNESCO World Heritage site of Cueva de Las Manos (see below) via RP 97. RP 39 leads

INSIDER TIP:

At Cueva de las Manos, you'll go back 9,000 years to primitive man trying to express himself in rock paintings—and fall in love with a wild, beautiful canyon that speaks to the soul.

—JOAN "PETTY" NAUTA
Former local sheep farm owner for more than 60 years

southwest for 55 miles (89 km) to **Lago Posadas,** a startlingly turquoise lake with guest ranch accommodations, while RP 41 goes west for 62 miles (100 km) to **Paso Roballos,** an adventurous border crossing into Chile. Alternatively, from Paso Roballos, RP 41 turns north through even more wildly scenic country to the fruit-basket town of **Los Antiguos.**

Cueva de las Manos

From Bajo Caracoles, graveled RP 97 leads northeast for 27 miles (44 km) to the scenic valley of the Río Pinturas, a stream that, in the course of its history, cut through the steppe to form a series of *aleros* (overhangs) occupied by humans as many as 10,000 years ago. Since then, occupants have left a legacy of more than 800 polychrome stencils of humans and game animals that shed light on the lives of hunter-gatherers in the continent's earliest rock-art site.

Last occupied about 700 years ago, probably by the ancestors of (continued on p. 271)

Hotel Bajo Caracoles
- RN 40 & RP 39
- 02963/490-100

Cueva de las Manos
- 223 B2
- RP 97, 27 miles (44 km) N of Bajo Caracoles
- Access with local registered guides only
- $$$$$

A Patagonian Roadhouse

Nineteenth-century Patagonia was pioneer country, where the only accommodations were the nearest estancia. No payment was offered or accepted, with the understanding that hospitality was always reciprocal for residents and the norm for strangers. Dating from 1894, one of the first buildings in Patagonia specifically designed to be a hotel was **Hotel La Leona** (*RN 40 Km 110 N of El Calafate, tel 011/5032-3415, www.hoteldecampola leona.com.ar*), a basic roadhouse where riders—horses were the sole means of transport—could get a bunk for the night and a hot meal.

Today travelers in their automobiles can take RN 40 to La Leona, which offers upgraded, if less than luxurious, accommodations. The kitchen has certainly adapted to the times and the presence of the highway. Its biggest sellers are pies and bread, and tea and espresso, for the buses that stop here on their way from El Calafate to El Chaltén.

Big Sky Country: Patagonia's Steppe & Its Wildlife

When Charles Darwin reflected on the voyage of H.M.S. *Beagle*, he observed that the plains of Patagonia "can be described only by negative characteristics: without habitations, without trees, without mountains." Yet he also asked himself "Why ... have these arid wastes taken so firm a hold on my memory?" He concluded that "it must be partly owing to the free scope given to the imagination" in lands "where there appears to be no limit to their duration during future times."

Guanacos stroll across the Patagonian steppe.

In reality, the Patagonian steppe still appears much as it did during Darwin's day, with its sparse bunchgrasses and dwarf shrubs. It's true that scattered sheep ranches have impoverished the flora, gravel roads raise dust on the horizon, and towns, cities, and even the occasional mine have transformed parts of the landscape. The endless clear skies, though, have remained, and with them the wildlife that Darwin saw while developing his theory of natural selection.

Today, many of Patagonia's signature species are common sights along the highways—most notably the haughty, elegant guanaco that leaps with ease over wire fences. A relative of the domestic llama and alpaca, and a more distant relative of the Old World camels, the rust-colored *Lama guanicoe* stands about 4 feet (1.2 m) at the shoulder and weighs perhaps 200 pounds (90 kg).

The guanaco ranges from northern Peru to the tip of the continent, and from sea level to more than 13,000 feet (4,000 m) above sea level. Led by a dominant male, each troop consists of about ten females plus their young, known as *chulengos*. "Bachelor" males travel in a separate troop until they are ready to form a family herd. In both cases, a solitary male usually keeps lookout for predators; at one time, these were human—Tehuelche Indians dressed themselves in guanaco skins and European settlers shot the animals to make room for sheep—but today it's the puma that's the alpha predator. In protected areas such as Chile's Parque Nacional Torres del Paine, guanacos are now so tame as to hardly flinch at humans.

Sprinters on the Steppe

The other real attention-grabber on the steppe is the flightless *ñandú petiso,* or lesser rhea, the New World counterpart to the ostrich, which sprints almost as fast as automobiles can motor across some stretches

INSIDER TIP:

The dusty desert plains of the Patagonian steppe and Península Valdés appear drab and monotonous. Leave your car, walk out onto the plain, and sit quietly. In no time, the sounds of birds and small mammals will return.

—JASON EDWARDS
National Geographic photographer

of RN 40. Sometimes also known as the *choique, Rhea pennata* is, like the guanaco, polygamous, with harems of up to a dozen females. The male builds the nest in the ground and incubates up to 60 eggs. A separate species, *Rhea americana,* and several subspecies exist north of the Río Negro and in other parts of South America.

Less conspicuous, but still of an impressive size, the Patagonia *mara,* or cavy, is a stocky, long-legged, short-eared rodent related to the guinea pig. Among rodents, only the capybara, porcupine, and beaver are larger. The cavy, *Dolichotis patagonum,* reaches 18 inches (46 cm) high and weighs up to 25 pounds (11 kg), but can still sprint up to 18 miles (30 km) an hour and spring like a mini-kangaroo. Unlike the guanaco and the rhea, the burrowing cavy is monogamous.

Sometimes the cavy has to share its burrow with the *piche,* the dwarf armadillo that occasionally scurries across the highways of the steppe. Barely a foot (30 cm) long, *Zaedyus pichiy* is one of the smallest of its kind.

The rhea is one of Patagonia's notable inhabitants.

EXPERIENCE: Argentina's Loneliest Road

Argentina's longest highway, RN 40 (La Cuarenta), runs from the Bolivian border at La Quiaca, to just beyond the southern city of Río Gallegos—a distance of nearly 3,091 miles (4,973 km). Segments of it are smoothly paved and connect provincial capitals, such as Mendoza and San Juan, but most of it runs through desolate country such as the altiplano of Jujuy and Salta and the Patagonian piedmont steppe of Chubut and Santa Cruz. Driving it—or cycling it, as a handful of rugged riders do every year—is an unforgettable experience.

That's not just because the powerful Patagonian westerlies can impede an automobile, sideswipe a motorcyclist, or stop a cyclist in his or her tracks. Services are limited to a handful of hotels, restaurants, and a few gas stations—which can run out of fuel—though the countryside is also home to some of the country's elite estancia accommodations. Some bus companies have begun summer services between El Calafate and the town of Perito Moreno, but it's still rare to see more than a dozen vehicles per day in the nearly 323 miles (520 km) between the hamlet of Tres Lagos and Perito Moreno.

Explorers in search of a frontier highway experience can still find segments of the rugged gravel route, but the administrations of Presidents Néstor Kirchner and Cristina Fernández have advanced their ambitious project to pave "La Cuarenta."

Even as the pavement advances, the 210-mile (336 km) stretch between Tres Lagos and the hamlet of Bajo Caracoles will continue to offer the thrills of a road so remote that, when the author first explored it in 1991, he saw only three other vehicles in four days. Still, in those remaining areas with loose gravel and sloping sides, drivers tend to drive in

the middle of the road and, while the desert landscape lacks blind curves, it does have blind rolling hilltops—vehicles may be few but, for safety's sake, sound the horn and move to the right as you advance. Even then, low-clearance vehicles may scrape the gravel, and the gusting wind can make staying on the road a challenge.

The rewards, though, are worth it. In few other places on Earth will you find the ostrich-like *ñandú petiso* (lesser rhea)—or a flock of them—sprinting ahead of or alongside your car before veering to safety. Sheep may huddle by fences along the road, but the graceful guanaco leaps them with ease.

Even if, at the end of the stretch, you find yourself awaiting the arrival of the fuel truck at Bajo Caracoles along with other adventurers, you won't lack material for conversation about the legendary La Cuarenta.

For excursions, see:

Chaltén Travel (*Avenida Libertador 1174, El Calafate, tel 02902/492-212, www .chaltentravel.com*)

Taqsa (*Terminal de Ómnibus, Local 3, El Calafate, tel 02902/491-843, www .taqsa.com.ar*)

Soon, Patagonia's loneliest road will be completely paved, but for now it offers an adventurous backroads experience.

Who's in a Name? The Ubiquitous Perito Moreno

Argentines' penchant for honoring their most illustrious citizens in place-names has also led to these names appearing almost ad infinitum—Gen. José de San Martín being the most notorious case. The main street of almost every Argentine city or town is, in one form or another, "San Martín."

Francisco Pascasio Moreno (1852–1919) isn't quite so ubiquitous, but the Patagonian explorer and naturalist—who founded the Museo de La Plata in Buenos Aires Province and gave a jump start to the national park system—has lent his name to such a series of sights and places in Santa Cruz Province that first-time visitors often come away confused. It's ironic that Moreno, usually known as "Perito" (expert) for the surveying and mapping skills that helped settle border disputes with Chile, should be the source of their uncertainty.

The most famous of Perito Moreno's Santa Cruz namesakes is, of course, the iconic Moreno Glacier. Much less visited, in a remote location along the Chilean border, the backcountry of Parque Nacional Perito Moreno is higher and wilder. Even farther north, where RN 40 meets the highway east to Comodoro Rivadavia, the nondescript wool town of Perito Moreno marks a return to civilization.

---

the few surviving Tehuelche, the site stretches for nearly 750 yards (680 m) above the river; from the information center, visitors descend a trail into the "caves," protected by bars to prevent vandalism.

Most of the art is of human hands, but some also shows individual hunters attacking animals, such as guanacos and rheas, with *boleadoras*, and groups of hunters trapping them in ambushes. Figures from several periods, some of which are more abstract, may be mixed and even superimposed.

While the road from Bajo Caracoles is the main access point, there is also a road and trail from **Estancia Casa de Piedra**, 26 miles (42 km) north, and another from **Estancia Cueva de las Manos,** 13 miles (21 km) farther north.

Los Antiguos & Around

At the town of **Perito Moreno,** northbound RN 40 meets RP 43, the paved international highway, which turns west to the town of Los Antiguos. Here, in a favored microclimate on **Lago Buenos Aires,** farmers grow quality orchard crops—apples, apricots, cherries, peaches, pears, plums—and soft fruits like raspberries and strawberries. With its lakeside location, poplar windscreens, and vivid flower gardens, Los Antiguos is an agreeable town but, in the absence of major infrastructure, it's primarily an off-the-beaten-path destination where fishermen and hikers have to find their own way along the lakeshore and in the mountains.

Los Antiguos is only a few miles east of the Chilean border town of **Chile Chico,** on **Lago General Carrera** (as the lake is known across the line). In 1991, massive ashfalls from the eruption of Chile's Volcán Hudson devastated both towns and depressed the economy for years. ∎

Los Antiguos
🅜 223 B2
Visitor Information
✉ Lago Buenos Aires 59
☎ 02963/491-261
www.losantiguos .tur.ar

A remote and historic archipelago, the gateway to Antarctica and a haven for seabirds along the Beagle Channel

Tierra del Fuego

The "Lighthouse at the End of the World" in the Beagle Channel, Ushuaia

Tierra del Fuego

In some ways it's an extension of Patagonia, but the archipelago of Tierra del Fuego has an identity of its own as the "uttermost part of the Earth"—in the words of early settler Lucas Bridges. At the chilly southern tip of the continent, cut off from the rest of the Southern Cone by the Strait of Magellan, Tierra del Fuego is divided between a relatively populous Argentine side and a thinly peopled Chilean side.

In the 19th century, when "rounding the Horn" meant challenging ferocious gales that left scores of shipwrecks along its shores, famous figures such as Charles Darwin and Richard Henry Dana helped evoke the danger and grandeur of a land where a few indigenous foragers—"canoe Indians"—lived off fish, shellfish, and the fires that kept them warm. Those fires, seen from the sea by the earliest European explorers, gave the archipelago its name—"land of fire."

Relations between the two countries occupying Tierra del Fuego have been rocky at times.

In 1978, Chile and Argentina nearly went to war over three small islands in the celebrated Beagle Channel on the south side of the Argentine portion. Things have been peaceful since, but connections are not as good as they could be.

The archipelago's Isla Grande ("big island") is the only one with any significant infrastructure in Argentine territory. Nearly all visitors arrive at the provincial capital of Ushuaia, the world's southernmost city. Many fly in, while others arrive on cruise ships; those who come overland need to pass through Chilean territory.

But for its location between the Beagle Channel and the spires of the Montes Martial, Ushuaia is a nondescript city that, nevertheless, has one exceptional museum and two good ones. It's also the point of departure for cruises to Antarctica and "around the Horn" to the Chilean port of Punta Arenas and back. Primarily, though, it's the base for excursions to nearby destinations such as the Martial Glacier trail, the Beagle Channel itself, historic Estancia Harberton, and the shores, forests, and summits of Parque Nacional Tierra del Fuego. Nearby Cerro Castor is the world's southernmost ski area.

Just north of Ushuaia, on the cusp between the steppe and the sierras, the fault-line shore of Lago Fagnano—the world's southernmost ice-free lake—extends nearly 60 miles (100 km) onto the Chilean side of Isla Grande. While the southern part of Isla Grande is mountainous, the northern part is mostly windswept steppe whose major city, Río Grande, is a base for fly-fishing excursions. The city is also home to the historic Salesian mission that catechized the now nearly extinct Selk'nam Indians, a worthwhile stop for overland travelers. ■

Area of map detail

Buenos Aires

PATAGONIA
p. 220

3▷

San Sebastián

3

Río Grande

Estancia
Viamonte

Grande

2▷

CHILE

Isla Grande

ATLANTIC
OCEAN

San Pablo

P.N. TIERRA
DEL FUEGO

Lago
Fagnano

Tolhuin

TIERRA
DEL FUEGO

Policarpo

Cabo
San Diego

Glaciar
Martial

Cerro
Castor

3

Estancia
Harberton

Isla de los
Estados

Ushuaia

Beagle Channel

Isla Martillo

Isla de los Lobos

Isla de Pájaros

1▷

0   80 kilometers
0   40 miles

△
A

△
B

△
C

Darwin in Tierra del Fuego

Charles Darwin's famous voyage was not the *Beagle*'s first to Tierra del Fuego, but his presence made things different. On a previous voyage, with a missionary fanaticism, Capt. Robert Fitz Roy had abducted several "canoe Indians" and taken them to England, catechizing the "savages" before returning them to their homeland.

In 1832–33, Darwin observed Fitz Roy's reintroduction of the Fuegians to their homeland and, with an ethnographer's skill, noted the superficiality of their conversion. While he shared some of Fitz Roy's prejudices, Darwin could also note that their British captivity made returning to a hunter-gatherer life difficult. Jemmy Button—the most famous

of the Fuegians—was a case in point.

A year after being returned to his homeland, Jemmy was found to be a "thin, haggard savage, with long disordered hair ... We did not recognize him till he was close to us, for he was ashamed of himself, and turned his back to the ship."

At the same time that Darwin left this invaluable account of early contacts with the Fuegians, he also provided benchmark descriptions of the desolate Fuegian wildlands—"a broken mass of wild rocks, lofty hills, and useless forests"—at a time when a city the size of Ushuaia was unthinkable. The expedition's legacy, though, survives, and the Beagle Channel remains one of the world's most recognizable place-names.

Ushuaia

Few cities anywhere in the world can match Ushuaia's startlingly beautiful setting facing the wind-whipped whitecaps of the Beagle Channel, beneath the backdrop of the glacial horns of the Montes Martial. Few can compete with its epic history from the European age of exploration—which hasn't completely ended. And none can equal its antipodean location, where the world's roads end and the Antarctic frontier, in a sense, begins.

From the Sierra Martial, hikers can see the city of Ushuaia and the Beagle Channel.

Ushuaia
🗺 275 A1
Visitor Information
✉ San Martín 674
☎ 02901/424-550
www.e-ushuaia.com

Unfortunately, though Ushuaia's waterfront is becoming more presentable every day, a beautiful setting does not mean a beautiful city. A tourism boom has had many positive effects, but, along with fishing and duty-free manufacturing, it has also brought a population boom. The resulting unruly sprawl has spread along the shores of the Beagle Channel to the east and up the steep hillsides beyond the central city. Ushuaia's main commercial street, San Martín, is a tourist-trap jumble of mostly lackluster restaurants, souvenir stands, travel agencies,

and plastic signage. That said, the city's easy access to its scenic surroundings makes it easier to overlook some of its shortcomings.

Ushuaia's handful of historic "Magellanic" buildings are easy to miss in the torrent of new construction that has inundated the city in the past two decades. Still, two outstanding museums in town help remedy the lack of context in a remote area where native people fished and foraged, Anglican missionaries starved to death at isolated outposts, ships sank on unseen reefs, and political prisoners of all stripes languished in their sub-Antarctic lockups.

Facing the harbor, the **Museo del Fin del Mundo** is a solid block building, originally intended as a private residence, that housed the Banco de la Nación from 1912 until 1977. Its glassed porch, easing the transition from the often blustery weather, gives entry to half a dozen thematically arranged exhibit halls, starting with Yámana artifacts and accounts of the early European explorers up until Ushuaia's formal founding, in 1884, as a penal colony. Another room re-creates an Almacén de Época, an early general store, and yet another documents the presidio and its most notorious inmates, though the maritime museum covers this better. The bank, of course, is covered by its own exhibit, and another room is used for special displays.

INSIDER TIP:

One of Ushuaia's oldest restaurants, Tía Elvira, is still one of the best.

—NATALIE P. GOODALL
National Geographic field scientist

Visitors to the museum may add, with no extra fee, a visit to the **Antigua Casa de Gobierno** (first House of Government and governor's residence), built in the 1890s, three blocks away.

On the eastern edge of downtown, the **Museo Marítimo de Ushuaia** occupies the old presidio, a building of five two-story pavilions that actually consists of four separate museums. Under the rubric of the maritime museum, it also includes the **Museo del Presidio** (prison museum), the **Museo Antártico Ushuaia Dr. José María Sobral** (Antarctic museum), and the **Museo de Arte Marino Ushuaia** (Ushuaia Museum of Marine Art). The one that absorbs most visitors, though, is the prison museum, its cells inhabited by mannequins outfitted as serial killers like Santos Godino (a little man nicknamed "El Petiso Orejudo" for his enormous ears) and Russian-born anarchist Simón Radowitzky, who assassinated Buenos Aires police chief Ramón Falcón in 1909. More mainstream politicians, such as Honorio Pueyrredón and Mario Guido of the Radical Party, were also incarcerated here under military dictatorships in the 1930s—one of the reasons that the curators like to compare Ushuaia with South Africa's Robben Island (where Nelson Mandela was imprisoned) as well as California's Alcatraz.

That said, the rest of the museum lives up to its billing, with extensive exhibits on historic ships, including models of Magellan's *Trinidad*, Fitz Roy's *Beagle*, and the Norwegian Antarctic explorer Roald Amundsen's *Fram,* in the Antarctic museum. That museum focuses on Argentina's presence on the frozen continent, starting with the 1902 Swedish expedition that included Gualeguaychú-born José María Sobral. The art museum deals not just with the far south, but also with sea- and ship-themed paintings from around the country. ∎

Museo del Fin del Mundo
- Avenida Maipú 173
- 02901/421-863
- Closed May–Sept. & Jan. 1, May 1, & Dec. 25
- $$$$ (including entrance to Antigua Casa de Gobierno)

Antigua Casa de Gobierno
- Avenida Maipú 465
- 02901/422-551
- Closed Sun. May–Sept. & Jan. 1, May 1, & Dec. 25
- Included in entrance to Museo del fin del Mundo

Museo Marítimo de Ushuaia
- Yaganes & Gobernador Paz
- 02901/437-481
- Closed Jan. 1 & Dec. 25
- $$$$
- www.museo maritimo.com

Tía Elvira
- Av. Maipú 349
- 02901/424-725
- Closed Sun. & July

Antarctica's Home Port

In 1978, Tierra del Fuego's Ushuaia was a hamlet of about 7,000 people on a war footing, as Argentine and Chilean military dictatorships feuded over three small islands in the Beagle Channel. Now the city is booming, having been transformed into the world's main embarkation point for voyages to the Antarctic across the stormy waters of the Drake Passage.

Ushuaia, the world's most southerly city and departure central for Antarctica-bound cruise ships

A few decades ago, Ushuaia had a substandard airport, a small naval base—established in the late 1940s to help support Argentina's claim to Antarctica—and a handful of tourists, many of them "gringo trail" backpackers. Some may have dreamed of continuing across the Drake Passage to the Antarctic Peninsula, but, in those years, only the Finnish-built, Liberian-flagged Lindblad Explorer regularly covered the route. Today, matters are dramatically different.

Argentina has had an Antarctic presence since 1902, when the Swedish Nordenskjöld expedition, including Argentine geologist José

María Sobral, fueled in Ushuaia and wintered on the peninsula. Tourism began informally in 1933, when Capt. Ángel Rodríguez of the naval vessel Pampa invited several Ushuaia-bound passengers to continue to the South Orkneys. It started formally in 1958, when the naval vessel Les Eclaireurs took about a hundred tourists in two separate summer trips. The following year, the state company Empresas Líneas Marítimas Argentinas (ELMA) carried 260 passengers south on the Yapeyú.

National and international political events fueled a tourism boom after the 1980s. A diplomatic settlement helped avoid war over the

Beagle Channel, and the Argentine dictatorship's disastrous invasion of the Falkland Islands in 1982 actually helped tourism by bringing a return to constitutional government that made Argentina more appealing to foreigners. Even more important, the Soviet Union's 1991 collapse liberated former research vessels to hire themselves out to international tourism companies other than Lindblad.

Gateway to Antarctica

Since the 1990s, traffic from Ushuaia has blossomed, largely because the city is at least a day's sail closer to Antarctica than any other southern-oceans port, even if the trip still involves a two-day crossing of the Drake Passage's savage seas.

The statistics support Ushuaia's case. Excluding Chile's tiny Puerto Williams across the Beagle, it's the closest port to Antarctica, at latitude 54° 56′ S. The next closest is the Chilean city of Punta Arenas (latitude 53° 10′ S), a full day's sail away. New Zealand, Australian, and South African ports are much farther north. In fact, at present, upward of 90 percent of all Antarctica-bound travelers leave from Ushuaia. It helps,

of course, that the city now has an improved airport with nonstops from Buenos Aires. Every southern summer, tens of thousands of passengers depart on hundreds of cruises carrying as few as a dozen passengers or upwards of 2,000.

Politics has influenced growth. For much of its existence, Ushuaia was a territorial capital, but in 1991, Tierra del Fuego became a full-fledged province and, to Argentines at least, also the seat of Antarctic political power. Argentina claims a slice of Antarctica between latitude 25° W and 74° W, from latitude 60° S to the South Pole, although these coordinates overlap British and Chilean claims.

All such claims are on hold by international treaty, but that doesn't mean the countries in question don't take them seriously. Tierra del Fuego's governor, the Gobernador de Tierra del Fuego, Antártida, e Islas del Atlántico Sur (Governor of Tierra del Fuego, Antarctica, and South Atlantic Islands), appoints his or her own Antarctica-based representative to enforce civil authority. The governor's writ holds only on Argentina's bases but, combined with its economic influence, that's enough to make Ushuaia Antarctica's de facto home port.

EXPERIENCE: Journey to the White Continent

The notion of Antarctica has enchanted the human psyche since ancient Greeks first envisioned a great southern land they surmised that must exist to provide a balance to those in the north. Capt. James Cook fearlessly pursued this continent, finally crossing the Antarctic Circle in 1773, and American sealer John Davis became the first person to visit Antarctica, in 1821.

For those curious about this mysterious land, an assortment of different cruises leave from Ushuaia. How about a 14-day penguin safari? Or a 12- to 20-day adventure trip that combines kayaking, mountaineering, and camping? If comfort

is more your thing, explore Antarctica's natural beauty on a slower-paced tour. Contact **Quark Expeditions** (tel 888/ 978-7380, www.quarkexpeditions) for further information.

For a different type of adventure, **National Geographic Expeditions** (tel 866/966-8687, www.nationalgeographic expeditions.com) offers 15- to 25-day, all-inclusive trips, accompanied by renowned photographers and fellows. You'll be transported from the United States to Argentina and Chile, with stops including the Valdés Peninsula, historic Port Lockroy, Puerto Deseado, and Paradise Bay.

Around Ushuaia

The city's surroundings are a primary reason to make a stop in Ushuaia. Local attractions include the historic ranch, Estancia Harberton, and Argentina's first coastal national park, Parque Nacional Tierra del Fuego.

Wind-flagged *Nothofagus* (false beech) at Estancia Harberton

Estancia Harberton

🏛 275 B1
✉ Ruta C-J
💲 $$$$$

www.estancia
harberton.com

Cerro Castor

✉ Ruta 3 Km 26
from Ushuaia
City
☎ 02901/499-301
(ski lodge)

www.cerrocastor
.com

Visitors need travel no farther than the **Muelle Turístico,** on Ushuaia's waterfront by the commercial port, to arrange half-day boat trips along the **Beagle Channel.** Most of these are on large catamarans, so you may want to choose a smaller boat that carries fewer passengers and makes a closer approach to sites such as **Isla de los Lobos,** where both southern sea lions and southern fur seals reside, and **Isla de los Pájaros,** where cormorants and other seabirds nest. Some of the smallest boats

can land on **Isla Bridges** to get close to the cormorants and, on occasion, a penguin or two.

It's not much in summer, but **Cerro Castor,** about 17 miles (27 km) east of Ushuaia via RN 3, offers downhill-skiing facilities. Other nearby areas are for cross-country skiers.

Estancia Harberton

Some boat trips from Ushuaia go all the way to Estancia Harberton, Tierra del Fuego's most historic ranch. Here, Anglican missionary pioneer Thomas

INSIDER TIP:

For an excellent afternoon side trip, to witness the beauty of the Beagle Channel, go down a short gravel road east of Ushuaia in time to watch the sun set.

—JORGE CRISCI
National Geographic field scientist

Bridges created his own little England, although with Yámana laborers, on the shores of the Beagle Channel. (The ranch and surroundings are described in *The Uttermost Part of the Earth*, a 1947 memoir by Thomas Bridges's son Lucas.) Today great-grandson Tommy Goodall and his American wife Rae Natalie Prosser de Goodall still graze sheep and cattle, but Harberton has become a destination in its own right for its history and natural appeal.

Boat tours calling at Harberton from Ushuaia usually visit **Isla Martillo,** an offshore island with Magellanic penguins and the odd gentoo penguin, which may leave the visitor limited time to see the rest of the farm. Minivan tours from Ushuaia, which is 53 miles (85 km) west via paved RN 3 and the gravel spur RC-J, spend almost the whole day at Harberton, but individuals are also welcome. Guided tours, in either English or Spanish, take in part of the family homestead—a 19th-century kit house that now includes a tearoom—and its gardens, along with outbuildings such as the boathouse, woodshop, and woolshed. A separate native botanical garden contains ethnographically precise reconstructions of Yámana lean-to shelters.

With help from the National Geographic Society and others, Natalie Goodall, who is a biologist, has also organized the **Museo Acatushún de Aves y Mamíferos Marinos Australes,** a cavernous warehouse-style building displaying marine mammal skeletons salvaged from around the region. The specimens include enormous blue, white, and humpback whales, smaller beaked whales, dolphins, and porpoises, as well as seals and sea lions. In addition, the collections include some 80 species of native birds.

In addition to its teahouse, Harberton has guest ranch accommodations and permits camping, with written permission.

Museo Acatushún de Aves y Mamíferos Marinos Australes

✉ Estancia Harberton

🕐 Closed May– Sept.

💲 $$$

www.acatushun.com

To the End of the Road

Every year, by car, motorcycle, or even bicycle, intrepid adventurers leave Arctic Alaska's North Slope to travel the Panamerican Highway from Prudhoe Bay to Bahía Lapataia in Argentine Tierra del Fuego. At least 16,000 miles (25,750 km) long, depending on the roads you take, the last segment of the route, RN 3, covers about 2,014 miles (exactly 3,242 km) from Buenos Aires's Plaza del Congreso, ending at an unassuming parking lot.

Though motorized travelers take months or longer to drive the route, which means an aerial or maritime crossing from Panama to Colombia, cyclists need at least a year. Tim Cahill's manic travelogue *Road Fever*, though, tells how to drive it in fewer than 24 days!

Parque Nacional Tierra del Fuego

**Parque Nacional
Tierra del Fuego**
- 275 A1/A2
- RN 3, 7 miles
  (11 km) W of
  Ushuaia

Visitor Information
- San Martín 1395,
  Ushuaia
- 02901/421-315
  in Ushuaia
- $$$$$

www.parques
nacionales.gov.ar

West of Ushuaia, it's only 7 miles (11 km) along RN 3 to the main gate of Argentina's first coastal national park, which rises from sea level through boggy wetlands and beech-covered hillsides to the glaciated spires of the Montes Martial. Along the Beagle Channel, its shoreline is a cornucopia of birdlife—not only ordinary gulls, but also oystercatchers, steamer ducks,

a half-mile (900 m) boardwalk loop through peat bogs where ferns, wildflowers, and insectivorous plants flourish. The nearby **Paseo a la Castorera** meanders through a quarter mile (400 m) of southern beech forest killed by Canadian beaver, fauna foolishly introduced in the 1940s.

For more active hikers, the 3-mile (5 km) **Senda al Hito XXIV** follows the forested northeastern shore of **Lago Roca** to dead-end at the Chilean border.

Introducing ... the Beaver!

One of Parque Nacional Tierra del Fuego's most conspicuous mammals has no business being there. Hikers who marvel at the beaver on the Paseo a la Castorera are rarely aware that *Castor canadensis* is an exotic plague dating from the 1940s, well before the park's creation in 1960.

When the military government brought 50 beaver to Ushuaia, pelts were still a valuable commodity, but no longer. Meanwhile, lacking natural predators, the beaver has proliferated to perhaps 100,000, felling trees that, unlike some in Arctic boreal forests, do not sprout when toppled by gnawing rodents. To prevent the beaver's spread off Isla Grande, authorities hope to eradicate them—a difficult task.

---

and, gliding over the water, the black-browed albatross.

From downtown Ushuaia, it's only a short bus or taxi ride to the **Aerosilla del Glaciar,** a chairlift that marks the start of a trail to the **Glaciar Martial,** a steep two-hour climb over mostly barren ground; at trail's end, the reward is spectacular views across the Beagle Channel to Chile's Isla Navarino. Taking the chairlift cuts the hiking time in half.

The main sector of the park has no trails suitable for overnight backpacking—only short nature trails and longer day hikes. Near Bahía Lapataia, at road's end, the **Paseo a la Laguna Negra** is

About 0.6 mile (one km) up the trail, the northeast lateral **Senda Cerro Guanaco** is a more strenuous climb up its 3,182-foot (970 m) namesake peak.

When Ushuaia was a penal colony, convict labor laid the tracks for the world's southernmost railway, a narrow-gauge line that, from 1909 to 1952, carried timber from the forests of today's park. Its roadbed restored in 1994, it's now the **Tren del Fin del Mundo** (www.trendelfindelmundo.com.ar), a tourist train that sanitizes this dark history while climbing the Río Pipo Valley into the eastern sector of the park. The station is 5 miles (8 km) west of town. ■

Northern Tierra del Fuego

In contrast to the mountainous south, most of Tierra del Fuego's northern sector is a wind-swept grassy steppe, with occasional rolling hills and patches of southern beech forest, plus a plethora of trout-rich lakes and rivers that attract fishermen from around the world. It has the island's only other city in Río Grande, a bird-rich shoreline, and one of the country's most beautiful bodies of water in Lago Fagnano, just over the mountains from Ushuaia.

The village of Tolhuin sits at the eastern end of Lago Fagnano.

Río Grande & Around

The wind blows relentlessly along the Atlantic shoreline of Río Grande, the self-proclaimed Capital Internacional de la Trucha (International Trout Capital), 132 miles (212 km) northeast of Ushuaia by paved RN 3 and 57 miles (92 km) southeast of the Chilean border post of San Sebastián. The only real city on the island's northern steppe, it's often an obligatory stopover for overland travelers because of

public transportation schedules from the mainland cities of Río Gallegos or Punta Arenas (Chile).

Founded in 1921 to serve surrounding sheep estancias, Río Grande has few historic landmarks, but its **Museo Municipal de la Ciudad de Río Grande Virginia Choquintel** (*Alberdi 555, tel 02964/430-647, closed holidays*) provides an insightful, respectful account of the island's ethno-history. This is especially notable in an area where, wrote pioneer Lucas

Río Grande

⚐ 275 A2

Visitor Information

✉ Rosales 350

☎ 02964/431-324

🕐 Closed Sat.–Sun. & holidays

www.riogrande.gob.ar

Misión Salesiana Nuestra Señora de la Candelaria

✉ RN 3 Km 2,980

☎ 02964/421-642

💲 $ (includes chapel, cemetery, & museum)

www.misionrg.com.ar

Bridges, many farmers saw the indigenous Fuegians as a "horde of dangerous, untamed natives, to be wiped out as speedily as possible"—sometimes by hunting parties.

The museum takes its name from the last surviving Selk'nam or Ona Indian, who died in 1999 but was born at the **Misión Salesiana Nuestra Señora de la Candelaria,** the Salesian mission 7 miles

INSIDER TIP:

For ornithologists: The bare, sandy, and windy beaches from Río Grande northward to Bahía San Sebastián are the southern summer home of thousands of small shorebirds that have flown south from the Canadian winter.

—NATALIE P. GOODALL
National Geographic field scientist

(11 km) north of the city. Lucas Bridges, who thought the Salesians were in league with sheep farmers, criticized them harshly for trying to settle and organize the nomadic Ona: "I always encouraged my Ona friends to change back into their robes and paint when the day's work was done."

Founded in 1893, the mission moved three times before settling at the present site four years later. The complex of "Magellanic" buildings, with their wooden frames and corrugated metal cladding, includes the **Capilla Histórica de Nuestra**

Señora de la Candelaria, a chapel where the Ona received baptism, communion, and religious instruction. When the Ona died out, however—due to persecution by farmers, new diseases, and alcoholism—the Salesian fathers schooled settlers' children.

Across the highway from the chapel, the **Cementerio Aborigen** contains the remains of more than 150 Ona who, the Salesian website admits, "lived mostly short lives." Some of them had learned weaving at the **Taller de las Hermanas,** which is preserved as it was in 1897. The original **Casa de la Misión,** where Italian-born founder Monseñor José Fagnano (1844–1916) occupied the ground floor and the first Ona neophytes lived upstairs, is undergoing restoration. The cemetery and the original buildings form part of the **Museo de Historia, Antropología y Ciencias Naturales Monseñor Fagnano,** which includes an open-air sector with horse carts and farm machinery and an interior with well-preserved specimens of condors, guanacos, and other fauna.

Living birds can be seen at the **Reserva Provincial Costa Atlántica de Tierra del Fuego** (tel 02901/432-807), a bird sanctuary that extends from Cabo Nombre in the north to the Río Ewan in the south, a distance of roughly 140 miles (220 km). The South Atlantic here has a huge tidal range, so the receding waters open up a vast territory for foraging shorebirds—but the advancing tide comes in fast. Beginning in early September, look for the American golden plover, which migrates from the Canadian Arctic.

Estancia Viamonte

About half an hour south of Río Grande via RN 3, Viamonte may be Tierra del Fuego's second most historic estancia after Harberton, and it's all in the family—Lucas Bridges and two of his brothers founded the farm in 1902. Today, Simon and Carolina Goodall offer room and board at their **Sea View Guest House,** where Bridges himself lived. Safe from the more unsavory sheep farmers, Bridges's Ona friends built their lean-tos in the vicinity.

On 15 miles (27 km) of shoreline, Viamonte is still a working

and the gateway to Lago Fagnano, named for the Salesian missionary but also known by its Ona name of Kami.

The world's southernmost ice-free lake, Lago Fagnano lies along a fault and extends westward into Chile, where it drains into Seno Almirantazgo (Admiralty Fjord). It is also the island's largest lake, 61 miles (98 km) long, more than 650 feet (200 m) deep, and covering 261 square miles (676 sq km). Along the border, both sides are part of Parque Nacional Tierra del Fuego, inaccessible except by private boats.

Estancia Viamonte

- 275 A2
- RN 3, 26 miles (42 km) SE of Río Grande
- 2964/430-861 or 2964/15-500-025
- Closed April–Oct., Jan. 1, & Dec. 25

www.estancia viamonte.com

Sheepshearing at Estancia Viamonte, one of Tierra del Fuego's most historic sheep farms

sheep farm, but it also offers good birding, along with hiking in the low beech forests behind the farm buildings and along the shore.

Lago Fagnano (Kami)

From Río Grande, it's 68 miles (109 km) south via paved RN 3 to the village of **Tolhuin,** the island's third largest settlement

At Tolhuin, the **Panadería La Unión** (www.panaderialaunion.com) is a landmark bakery that has become an obligatory stop for every Argentine celebrity en route to Ushuaia. Have fun trying to guess the identities of the rich and famous in the photographs that cover the walls. The bread and pastries are good, too. ∎

TRAVELWISE

Rafting on the Río Juramento, Salta Province

PLANNING YOUR TRIP

When to Go

In a country that stretches from tropical latitudes on the Bolivian border to sub-Antarctic environments on Tierra del Fuego, there's no single time that's best for a visit. Remember, of course, that the seasons are reversed from those in the Northern Hemisphere—January and February are midsummer, July and August midwinter. Most Argentines take vacations at these times, when tourist destinations throughout the country can be crowded.

Buenos Aires is lively at any time of year and has mild winters. Its summers are hot and humid, though; many museums close, and high-profile cultural activities are fewer. Spring and fall have almost ideal weather and a vigorous

cultural calendar. The Pampas, like the capital, can be an all-year destination, though the Atlantic beach resorts clear out in winter.

Like Buenos Aires and the Pampas, the Mesopotamian provinces and the Chaco can be stiflingly hot in summer, but sights like Iguazú Falls draw visitors in all seasons. Still, they're better in autumn, winter, and spring.

In the high red-rock deserts of the Andean northwest, summers can get hot but not unbearable, and elevations are high enough that it almost always cools off at night. Summer is also the rainy season, and flash floods can limit or eliminate access to some of the most appealing destinations. Winter, by contrast, is the dry season and, while the days are shorter and nights can get cold at the highest elevations, it's probably

the best season for touring.

Cuyo also gets hot summers, dangerously so in some desert areas, but at the loftiest Andean elevations Mendoza Province is a perfect summer getaway—especially for climbers who want to challenge the summit of Aconcagua, the highest peak in the Americas. Mendoza's wine country is most appealing in March and April, during the autumn grape harvest, but spring is nearly as good. In winter, the region has Argentina's best skiing at Las Leñas, near Malargüe.

Patagonia is a special case. Many of its sights, such as the Moreno Glacier, are best in summer, when long days permit outdoor activities. For wildlife-watchers, though, destinations like Península Valdés vary seasonally—penguins in summer, whales in winter, etc., so visitors must prioritize. Hikers and fishermen will want to visit the Patagonian lakes district in summer, but skiers will flock there in winter.

Tierra del Fuego is a summer destination, as the "uttermost part of the Earth" and the home port for Antarctica. At the same time, it has a winter ski season as well.

What to Take
Because of Argentina's size and diverse terrain, what to take can vary as dramatically as the climate and the geography. At high Andean elevations, even summer weather can be chilly or downright cold—perhaps necessitating a warm sweater, parka, and wet-weather gear. In Buenos Aires, attending the opera or symphony demands formal attire; yet many of the chic new restaurants in Palermo are surprisingly casual.

Compact, lightweight, but sturdy luggage is best as it often gets thrown about on airplanes and buses. Equally sturdy locks are desirable, though theft is not epidemic. A leg pouch or money belt is good for carrying cash and passports. Lightweight binoculars are also useful for birders and wildlife-watchers.

Insurance
Travel insurance is a wise investment. Companies that provide insurance for Argentina include: **Allianz Travel Insurance** *(tel 866/884-3556, www.allianz travelinsurance.com)* **Assistcard** *(tel 877/369-2774, www.assist-card.com).* Based in Florida, it has an assistance center in Buenos Aires. **Travel Guard** *(tel 800/826-4919, www.travelguard.com)*

Entry Formalities
Citizens of the U.S., Australia and Canada need a valid passport and must pay an online "reciprocity fee" *(http://virtual.provinciapagos .com.ar/ArgentineTaxes)*; Europeans need not do so. Tourists are permitted stays of 90 days; tourist cards are issued on arrival and can be extended for AR$300 at the Dirección Nacional de Migraciones *(Avenida Antártida Argentina 1355, Buenos Aires, tel 011/4317-2067 or 0800/333-728-742, www .migraciones.gov.ar)* or at provincial delegations of the Policía Federal.

FURTHER READING
Argentina 1516–1987: From Spanish Colonization to the Falklands War and Alfonsín (1987) by David Rock. Comprehensive history from the earliest days through the "Proceso" dictatorship and return to democracy.

The Argentina Reader (2002) by Gabriela Nouzeilles and Graciela Montaldo, eds. A primer on Argentine history, culture, and politics, with excerpts from early chronicles and contributions from mostly Argentine literary figures and scholars.

Buenos Aires: A Cultural and Literary Companion (2000) by Jason Wilson. A synopsis of fiction and nonfiction on the Argentine capital, by Argentine and foreign authors.

Chasing Che: a Motorcycle Journey in Search of the Guevara Legend (2000) by Patrick Symmes. Nearly half a century later, Symmes re-creates the 1952 journey of Che Guevara through Argentina, Chile, Peru, and beyond, with nearly as many mechanical breakdowns.

Cowboys of the Americas (1990) by Richard Slatta. Lavishly illustrated account of horsemen throughout the hemisphere, with abundant material on the Argentine gaucho.

Freud in the Pampas (2001) by Mariano Ben Plotkin. A history of the Buenos Aires psychoanalytical culture on a par with Vienna.

The Life, Music, and Times of Carlos Gardel (1986) by Simon Collier. An analysis of Argentina's signature music and dance, and of its greatest popularizer.

The Motorcycle Diaries: a Journey Around South America (1995) by Ernesto Guevara. The epic journey by the youthful medical student who became an icon of the Cuban revolution; the template for the award-winning movie.

On Heroes and Tombs (1981) by Ernesto Sábato. Hallucinatory psychological novel of Buenos Aires, by the author of the *Nunca Más* report on the "disappeared" of the Dirty War.

The Perón Novel (1988) by Tomás Eloy Martínez. A fictional biography, but based on the author's real-life interviews with the quintessential caudillo.

The Return of Eva Perón (1980) by V. S. Naipaul. Sardonic, candid take on Argentine society in the dark days of military dictatorship.

Santa Evita (1996) by Tomás Eloy Martínez. Fictional version of Eva Perón's life and afterlife—which her body spent traveling from Buenos Aires to Italy, Spain, and back again.

The Voyage of the Beagle (1839) by Charles Darwin. Available in many editions, perhaps the greatest travelogue ever. Filled with observations on people, plants, animals, and even politics in Buenos Aires, the Pampas, Patagonia, and Tierra del Fuego.

HOW TO GET TO ARGENTINA
By Air
The majority of flights arrive at Aeropuerto Internacional Ministro Pistarini *(tel 011/5480-2500),* commonly known as "Ezeiza," after its namesake suburb, 22 miles (35 km) southwest of Buenos Aires. Most flights from Uruguay arrive at Aeroparque Jorge Newbery *(tel 011/5480-6111)* in the Palermo neighborhood.

The nationalized carrier **Aerolíneas Argentinas** *(tel 800/333-0276, or 0810/2228-6527 in Argentina, www.aerolineas.com.ar)* flies to Miami, Australia, Spain, and Italy. **LAN Argentina** *(tel 866/435-9526, or 0810/999-9526 in Argentina, www.lan.com)* flies to Miami.

The following U.S. airlines offer regular flights to Buenos Aires: **American Airlines** *(tel 800/433-7300, www.aa.com)* **Delta Airlines** *(tel 800/221-1212, www.delta.com)* **United Airlines** *(tel 800/864-8331, www.united.com)*

By Sea

Many cruise lines now include Argentina on their itineraries, often on "around the Horn" voyages that start in Brazil or Buenos Aires and continue to Chile. Contact the Cruise Lines International Association *(tel 754/224-2200, www.cruising.org)*.

Group Tours

Most packaged tours focus on the big three of Buenos Aires, Iguazú Falls, and the Moreno Glacier, or on outdoors activities in Patagonia. There are also thematic tours on tango, wine, and other topics. One good option for general tours is PanAmerican Travel Services *(320 E. 900 S., Salt Lake City, UT 84111, tel 800/364-4359, www.panam-tours.com)*. Members of the Adventure Travel Trade Association *(tel 360/805-3131, www.adventure.travel)* often provide environmentally oriented packages.

GETTING AROUND
In Buenos Aires

A new system called Sistema Único de Boleto Electrónico, or SUBE *(tel 0810/777-7823, www.sube.gob.ar.)*, is being introduced for Buenos Aires that will require a single rechargeable card for all public transportation. The card is not yet obligatory, but fares are half-price, so it's worth getting.

By Bus

Colectivos—city buses—operate throughout the city and its suburbs day and night. Fares vary slightly but most trips cost about AR$1.50. Available at newsstands,

Guía Lumi and *Guía T* contain route maps and itineraries. Airport buses to Ezeiza cost about AR$14 using the Manuel Tienda León company *(tel 0810/888-5366, www.tiendaleon.com.ar)*.

By Subway

Buenos Aires is expanding its almost century-old subway system throughout the city under the concessionaire Metrovías *(www.metrovias.com.ar)*. Fares are slightly lower than bus tickets, but services end around 11 p.m., resuming 6 a.m. the next day.

By Taxi

Black-and-yellow taxis are a staple form of transportation in town. For safety purposes, take a radio taxi even if flagging one down in the street; robberies are unlikely, but not unheard of. Most hotels and restaurants will call you a cab. The basic fare is about U.S.$1.75 plus roughly 17 U.S. cents for every 200 meters.

Unmetered taxis known as *remises* also respond to phone requests, operating on fixed fares arranged in advance. Both taxis and remises will take passengers from downtown Buenos Aires to Ezeiza airport for about U.S.$34, but from Ezeiza the price is around U.S.$44.

Around Argentina
By Air

Flights depart Aeroparque Jorge Newbery *(tel 011/5840-6111)* for destinations around the country. The domestic flag carrier **Aerolíneas Argentinas** *(tel 0810/2228-6527, www.aerolineas.com.ar)* has many flights but a reputation for erratic service. **LAN Argentina** *(tel 0810/999-9526, www.lan.com)* has fewer flights and is more reliable. **Andes Líneas Aéreas** *(tel 0810/7772-6337, www.andesonline.com)* serves northwestern Argentina and Puerto Madryn, while **Sol Líneas Aéreas**

(tel 0810/444-4765, www.sol.com.ar) now has a growing roster of destinations, including Bariloche, Trelew, and Ushuaia.

Líneas Aéreas del Estado *(tel 011/5353-2387, www.lade.com.ar)*, the air force's notoriously unreliable commercial wing, serves mostly Patagonian destinations.

By Bus

Buses to destinations throughout Argentina depart from Retiro's Estación Terminal de Ómnibus *(Avenida Ramos Mejía 1680, tel 4310-0707, www.tebasa.com.ar)*. Many private companies compete along most routes, offering four-across Pullman, or *semicama*, seats or three-across, *coche cama* sleepers, which are only slightly more expensive. All the seats recline, but coche cama seats become nearly horizontal and are more comfortable on long trips. Reservations are rarely needed except on busy routes during holidays.

By Car

To rent a car you should be 21 years or older and hold a passport and driver's license (theoretically an International Driving Permit should supplement a foreign license, but agencies and police rarely care). You will also need a credit card and insurance, and even then you may be liable for a deductible of several hundred dollars. For off-road driving, some visitors prefer four-wheel drive *(doble tracción or cuatro por cuatro)*, but this is only rarely necessary. Rental cars may be taken into Chile, but only with express notarial permission from the agency, and this may entail additional charges.

Car rental is pointless in Buenos Aires, which has excellent public transportation, ferocious traffic, and little parking. It makes more sense in the provinces, especially on back roads, where public transportation is less frequent.

Main roads are mostly in good condition, but back roads are often unpaved, and loose gravel can make them dangerous. In some areas, particularly Patagonia, livestock and wildlife may cross the highways. Many Argentine drivers are aggressive and reckless—the traffic fatality rate is the continent's highest, nearly twice that of the U.S. Argentine highways are either Rutas Nacionales (abbreviated as RN) or Rutas Provinciales (abbreviated as RP). Speed limits are 68 miles an hour (110 kph) on most highways but 81 miles an hour (130 kph) on four-lane divided roads. Those limits are frequently ignored, as are motorcycle-helmet laws.

Camper and RV rentals are possible through Austral RV *(Avenida San Martín 2254, Oficina 3, Vicente López, Buenos Aires Province, tel 011/5368-1544, www.australrv.com).*

By Train

The only rail line really worth considering for anyone other than fanatical trainspotters is the Ferrobaires *(tel 011/4304-0028, www.ferrobaires.gba.gov.ar)* service to Mar del Plata from Estación Constitución, in the southern part of Buenos Aires; even then, buses are faster and more comfortable (though not cheaper). There are tentative plans to extend rail services to Bariloche.

Adventure Travel

Argentina has many reputable tour agencies, several of them activities oriented, including: **Aymará Travel** *(tel 0261/ 424-4773; U.S. tel 619/573- 4062, www.aymara.com.ar).* Known for backcountry trips to Aconcagua but also to the wineries of Cuyo. **Meridies** *(tel 0294/451-2073, www.meridies.com.ar).* Hard and soft adventure in and around Bariloche, but also in regions. **Sendero Sur** *(tel 011/4343-1571,*

www.senderosur.com.ar). Cycling and hiking, plus guest-ranch stays, in Patagonia.

PRACTICAL ADVICE
Communications
Post Offices
It costs U.S.$2.50 to mail a letter or postcard to North America; slightly more to Europe or other overseas destinations. Never mail anything of obvious value, as theft is common. Figure up to 12 days to reach North America or 15 days to Europe. Express mail is unreliable, and many Argentines prefer FedEx or similar international express services for critically important documents.

Telephones
Public telephones have nearly disappeared, but it's still possible to make calls from *locutorios* (private call centers that are often Internet outlets as well). Or you can use prepaid phone cards—available at many corner kiosks—on private telephones. These scratch-off cards, with fixed values, have a code that you must enter before making any call. You can also purchase SIM cards for cell phones.

Making Calls
Local calls cost about AR$0.23 for every two minutes. Hotels often charge a high fee for calls from in-rooms phones. For long-distance calls, locutorios are abundant and offer the best rates.

For direct-dial international calls from Argentina, dial 00, the country code (U.S. is 1, U.K. is 44) and area code, then the number. For operator-assisted calls within Argentina, dial 19; for operator-assisted calls outside Argentina, dial 000. For directory assistance, dial 110.

Calling Argentina from the U.S., dial 011 plus the country code, 54, and the number. From the U.K.,

dial 00 plus 54 and the number. If calling a different area from within Argentina, you must dial the 0 of the area code (such as 011); from outside the country, omit the zero.

All cellular phone numbers in Argentina begin with the prefix 15. They have eight digits in Buenos Aires but fewer in provincial cities. When dialing a cell phone from a different area within Argentina, you must dial the area code, the prefix, and the number. Calling a cell phone from abroad, dial 54 + 9 + the area code (no 0) and the number (no prefix 15).

International calls are easiest from locutorios, which may allow VOIP calls. Credit-card calls are expensive; cheaper prepaid phone cards (available at locutorios) can be used at public telephones, which are less abundant with the proliferation of cellular communications. Almost all accommodations have phones for guest use, but these calls are expensive. Using a foreign cell phone requires an Argentine SIM card, but inexpensive prepaid phone cards are also available. For international calls, dial 00, then the country code, area code (minus any initial zero), and the number.

E-mail & Internet
Almost every city, town, and village has Internet and e-mail access at locutorios or cafés, and Wi-Fi is also commonplace. Rates are cheap—usually less than US$1 per hour—but at upscale tourist hotels, there may be charges for Internet access (which budget hostels often provide free).

Conversions
Argentina uses the metric system. Useful conversions are:

1 mile = 1.61 kilometers
1 kilometer = 0.62 mile
1 meter = 39.37 inches
1 liter = 0.26 U.S. gallon

1 kilogram = 2.2 pounds
1 pound = 0.45 kilogram

Weather reports use Celsius:
0°C = 32°F
10°C = 50°F
20°C = 68°F
30°C = 86°F

Electricity

Argentina operates on 220-volt AC (50 cycles) nationwide. Traditional outlets have two rounded plugs, but more recent ones have three flat blades that form a triangle; some outlets accept both. Cheap adapters are available in Buenos Aires, but may be harder to find in the provinces; it's best to purchase an international adapter kit before traveling here. Some appliances may need converters, which are harder to find.

Etiquette & Customs

Argentina's reputation is that of a Europeanized society. It would be truer to call it a New World immigrant country, like the U.S., with growing populations from all over the world. There are also indigenous populations in the Andean northwest, Mesopotamia and the Chaco, and Patagonia, whose customs differ dramatically from those of urban Argentines.

Argentines are normally courteous to strangers, using the formal *usted* form of "you," but they are also gregarious and often, in a very short time, they will use the familiar form *vos* (in lieu of the *tú* used in most of the rest of Latin America). Among other Latin Americans, they are often considered arrogant, and *porteños* (residents of Buenos Aires) have a reputation for rudeness that only New Yorkers can match. At the same time, they are capable of self-deprecating humor.

The normal greeting is *buenos días* (good morning), *buenas tardes* (good afternoon), or *buenas noches* (good evening). *Hola* (hello or hi) is much less common except on the

telephone. Unfamiliar adults are addressed as Señor (Mr.), Señora (Mrs.), or Señorita (Miss). The honorifics Don (for men) and Doña (for women) are unusual in Buenos Aires, but frequently used as terms of respect in provincial capitals and rural areas. Argentines relate especially well to families with children.

Argentina is traditionally a macho society, but women are making headway in politics and the professions—current president Cristina Fernández de Kirchner is the prime example. However, women are still subject to harassment through inappropriate touching and verbal aggression through *piropos* (sexist comments).

At the same time, Argentines are increasingly accepting of homosexuals, and Buenos Aires has become one of the world's most gay-friendly cities. It was the first Latin American city to adopt domestic partner legislation. In 2010, Argentina became the first Latin American country to approve same-sex marriage.

Most Argentines are camera-friendly, but among the Kolla of northwestern Argentina, the Mapuche of Patagonia, and other indigenous peoples, an in-your-face approach is definitely inappropriate. Photographers should also be circumspect in shooting around political protests, as demonstrators may believe—often with good reason—that the police are compiling data on them. When in doubt, refrain from snapping photos.

Outside the main tourist areas and business centers, you may not be understood in English, so it is advisable to learn at least a few Spanish phrases. Many, but not all, restaurants in Buenos Aires, larger cities, and tourist areas have bilingual menus.

Formality rules in the business sector, where etiquette here requires social as well as commercial skills. Topics such as family are an important means of getting to know a potential business partner. The

summer months of January and February, when most Argentines take their family vacations, are less than ideal for conducting business.

Holidays

In addition to Christmas, New Year's, and Good Friday, Argentina observes the following national holidays:
May 1—Labor Day
March 24—National Day of Memory for Truth and Justice
April 2—Day of the Falklands/Malvinas War Veterans and Fallen
May 25—Revolution of 1810
June 20 (or third Monday)—Flag Day
July 9—Independence Day
August 17 (or third Monday)—Death of San Martín
October 12 (or nearby Monday)—Columbus Day
December 8—Immaculate Conception

Most tourist sites and services stay open on most of these holidays, but banks and government offices close.

Liquor Laws

Drinking alcoholic beverages is legal at 18 in Argentina. Driving under the influence of alcohol is illegal, but enforcement is lax.

Media

Newspapers & Magazines

Dating from 1876, the venerable English-language daily *Buenos Aires Herald* provides a good summary of Argentine events. It has a useful Friday entertainment section, and Sunday's expanded edition often includes reports and opinion from the *New York Times* and Britain's *Guardian*.

The daily *Clarín* is a centrist, non-sensationalist tabloid. *La Nación* is right of center, but its political orientation does not affect its reporting or, especially, its outstanding cultural coverage. In the tabloid *Página 12*, reporting plays second fiddle to lengthy left-of-center opinion pieces. *Crítica*, also a tabloid, is a recent independent newspaper that stresses reporting over opinion. *Noticias* is a counterpart of *Time* or *Newsweek*.

Television & Radio
Television reaches everywhere in Argentina, and all major cities have dozens of AM and FM radio stations as well. Coverage of international news is good. Cable TV usually includes English-language channels such as CNN and the BBC.

Money Matters
Currency
Argentina's official currency is the peso ($), composed of 100 centavos, but the smallest coin is five centavos. In Buenos Aires and many other tourist areas, U.S. dollars—but not coins—are widely accepted for purchases.

Buenos Aires and some other cities have *casas de cambio* (exchange houses), but most banks will exchange dollars as well. Recent currency controls have led to an active "blue dollar" market in which sellers can obtain nearly twice the official rate for US currency. Traveler's checks are not advisable.

When traveling in remote areas such as Patagonia and parts of the Andean northwest, carry a cash reserve, as it may be difficult to find either banks or ATMs.

Automated Teller Machines
Most banks have 24-hour automated teller machines (ATMs). Using ATMs during regular banking hours is advisable in case of problems. Avoid using ATMs, which pay only the disadvantageous official rate, in dark locations where crime may common.

Credit Cards
Credit cards (*tarjetas de crédito*) are widely accepted. Visa and

MasterCard, followed by American Express, are the most commonly accepted. In some remote areas, though, cash is the only option.

Opening Times
In Buenos Aires, government offices typically keep a 10 a.m.–6 p.m. schedule, while most retail businesses open by 9 or 10 a.m. and close around 8 p.m. or so. Banks are open from 10 a.m.–3 p.m., while malls, supermarkets, and souvenir stores will stay open later in the evening. In the provinces, businesses often close for several hours at midday and reopen until 8 or 9 p.m. Travel agencies keep regular business hours and sometimes Saturday mornings as well.

Places of Worship/ Religion
Most communities have at least one Roman Catholic church but, except in Buenos Aires and other large cities, Protestant churches are mostly fundamentalist evangelicals. Buenos Aires also has a large mosque and synagogue. Tourist offices and leading hotels can suggest places of worship.

Restrooms
There are few public *baños* (restroom facilities), but restaurants, bars, and bus stations usually have them even if clean liness varies. Toilet paper can run out, so it's good to carry some of your own.

Smoking
Many Argentines are heavy smokers but, in 2006, the city of Buenos Aires introduced an antitobacco ordinance that has proved remarkably effective—despite the occasional scofflaw—in restaurants, bars, and public buildings. The rules permit

smoking on patios and sidewalk seats, so that indoor air quality is better. Many provinces are following suit with similar regulations.

Time Differences
Argentine time is three hours behind Greenwich Mean Time (GMT), but Argentina no longer observes daylight savings time. Normally Argentina is two hours ahead of Eastern Standard Time but, when the U.S. observes daylight savings, the difference is only an hour.

Tipping
Custom suggests a 10 percent tip for restaurant service, but if service is poor do not feel obliged. In small family-run places and budget eateries it's unusual. Cabbies do not expect tips and may even round *down* to avoid having to make change. It is appropriate to tip tour guides.

Travelers with Disabilities
With its narrow, broken sidewalks and aggressive drivers, Buenos Aires can be cruel to the wheelchair-bound, and other cities aren't much better. That said, many street corners are being dropped to facilitate wheelchairs to cross the streets—at least when drivers respect the crosswalks. A few buses are adapted for wheelchairs and some subway stations have elevators. Many upscale and boutique hotels, though, have rooms suitable for the disabled, including special suites. The following agencies provide information for visitors with disabilities:
  Gimp on the Go (*www.gimponthego.com*). An Internet-based newsletter and forum for disabled travelers.
  Society for Accessible Travel & Hospitality (*347 Fifth Ave., New York, NY 10016, tel 212/447-7284, www.sath.org*)

Visitor Information

The federal government tourism authority is the Secretaría de Turismo de la Nación (*Avenida Santa Fe 883, Buenos Aires, tel 011/4312-2232 or 0800/555-0016, www.turismo.gov.ar*). It also has a U.S. office (*1101 Brickell Avenue, North Tower, Suite 900, Miami FL 33131, tel 305/373-1889*).

The Administración de Parques Nacionales (*Avenida Santa Fe 690, Buenos Aires, tel 011/4311-0303, www.parquesnacionales.gov.ar*) manages Argentina's national parks and provides information about them. Individual park administrators in the provinces offer current information about their own units.

EMERGENCIES
Crime & Police

Argentina is a relatively safe destination; violent crime against tourists is rare and guns are far less common in Argentina than in the U.S. However, visitors should be cautious in impoverished parts of Buenos Aires, such as La Boca. Do not carry or wear conspicuous valuables and keep cameras out of sight. In towns and cities, where there is a danger of pickpockets and snatch-and-grab theft, be especially wary in crowded areas.

Keep your possessions in a locked suitcase in hotels, though theft is not widespread, and avoid leaving valuables or visible luggage, at least, in cars. Do not carry large amounts of cash, and keep passports and credit cards out of sight. If anything is stolen, report it immediately to the police and/or your hotel; you may need a police report for insurance purposes.

Unfortunately, both the Policía Federal and provincial police forces are notorious for corruption; at best, they're often uninterested in performing their duties. Buenos Aires does have a police station dedicated to tourist assistance, the Comisaría del Turista (*Avenida*

Corrientes 436, tel 011/4346-5748 or 0800/999-5000, e-mail: turista @policiafederal.gov.ar).

Embassies & Consulates in Buenos Aires

United States Embassy (*Avenida Colombia 4300, Palermo, tel 011/5777-4533, http://argentina .usembassy.gov*)
British Embassy (*Dr. Luis Agote 2412, Recoleta, tel 011/4808-2200, www.ukinargentina.fco.gov.uk*)
Canadian Embassy (*Tagle 2828, Palermo, tel 011/4808-1000, www .canadainternational.gc.ca/argen tina-argentine*)

Emergency Telephone Numbers

Most communities are served by these emergency numbers:
Fire (*bomberos*), tel 100
Police (*policía*), tel 101 and 911
Medical, tel 107
Directory assistance, tel 110

In Buenos Aires, ambulance service is provided through the Servicio de Atención Médica de Emergencia or SAME (*tel 011/4923-1051*). Provincial cities have similar services. Emergency care is free or inexpensive in public hospitals, but service is often slow.

What To Do in a Car Accident

In the event of an accident, don't move the vehicle or let the other vehicle be moved. Take down the license plate numbers and *cédula* (legal identification card) number of any witnesses. Call the police and await their arrival, and insist on their providing a report. If someone is seriously injured or killed, contact your embassy.

Health

Most cities and towns have hospitals or clinics, and in Buenos Aires and the largest cities they are up to international standards. Specialist clinics are abundant,

and most have English-speaking personnel. The Instituto Fleni (*Montañeses 2325, Belgrano, tel 011/5777-3200, www.fleni.org.ar*), for instance, focuses on neurology, orthopedics, and pediatrics. The Fundación Favaloro (*Avenida Belgrano 1746, tel 011/4378-1200, www.fundacionfavaloro.org*) concentrates on cardiology.

Full travel insurance will cover all emergency or acute care costs. A medical evacuation clause is vital should you need to return home.

Most hotels keep a list of doctors and medical centers, and many of them have their own emergency coverage. Keep any receipts or paperwork for insurance claims.

Tap water is safe to drink almost everywhere but, for those on short trips, bottled water may help avoid exotic bugs. In some backcountry areas, Giardia can be a problem, so boiling or otherwise treating stream water is a good idea. Salads and fresh fruits are generally safe to eat.

Be liberal with sunscreen. In northern Argentina, the subtropical sun's rays are more direct, while the Patagonian "ozone hole" makes exposure to the southernmost sun almost equally risky. Drink plenty of water to guard against dehydration, especially in the northern deserts and highlands, and in humid areas where you can sweat a lot.

Biting insects, primarily mosquitoes, are abundant throughout the country. Only a few truly remote northern areas, which tourists are unlikely to visit, are prone to malaria, but yellow fever and dengue fever have returned even if they are not a major threat. Visitors to Iguazú Falls and other lower northern areas may wish to get a yellow fever vaccination. Use an insect repellent if the pests are numerous.

Various species of the pit viper *yarará* extend from the subtropics even into northernmost Patagonia. Use care when hiking in subtropical forest or savanna grasses, and if you are bitten, seek immediate help.

Hotels & Restaurants

Accommodations in Argentina are abundant, diverse, and range from acceptable to outstanding in all price categories, with great differences among the facilities available. Remember that many areas of the country are remote, and the availability of accommodations is limited; more desirable rooms can fill quickly during busy months and especially during special events such as the Buenos Aires Tango festival. Eating out can be a great pleasure in Buenos Aires, which offers some world-class options. Even provincial capitals and resort areas have rapidly improving food scenes, not to mention Argentina's outstanding wines, but in some rural areas the options may be limited to the standard *parrillada* (mixed grill) and pasta dishes.

Accommodations

There are many kinds of accommodations. As a world capital, Buenos Aires has an abundance of top-of-the-mark hotels up to international standards. These range from small, family-run boutique hotels that combine intimacy and charm to high-rise international chains, usually with convention facilities. Some chains have toll-free numbers:

Intercontinental Hotels & Resorts *(tel 800/424-6835, www.intercontinental.com)*
Marriott International *(tel 888/424-6835, www.marriott.com)*
NH Hotels *(tel 888/726-0528, www.nh-hotels.com)*
Sofitel Luxury Hotels *(tel 800/763-4835, www.sofitel.com)*
Starwood Hotels & Resorts *(tel 800/328-6242, www.starwoodhotels.com)*

The Cuyo, Salta, Bariloche, El Calafate, and Ushuaia areas have some of the country's best accommodations, including intimate bed-and-breakfasts, boutique winery hotels, and design landmarks. Large-scale beach resorts, such as Mar del Plata, are primarily for the Argentine public. Mid-range hotels are abundant, but standards vary. In some areas, hostels have good private rooms at low prices.

Throughout the country, there are many estancias (guest ranches) that vary from simple country inns to luxurious lodges with gourmet meals. Some specialize in fishing or horseback riding. Camping is possible along many beaches and in most national parks, and even some large cities offer that option for visitors with their own vehicles.

Vacation rentals and long-term properties—everything from Buenos Aires apartments to lakeside houses in Patagonia—are another option. Try, for example, **B y T Argentina** *(tel 011/4876-5000, www.bytargentina.com.ar)* or **Bariloche Vacation Rental** *(tel 54-9-294-460-4613 in the U.S., tel 0294/15-460-4613 in Argentina, www.barilochevacationrental.com)*.

In budget hotels, maintenance may not be up to snuff, with lumpy mattresses, peeling paint, and balky plumbing. Ensure windows and doors are secure. Avoid *hoteles alojamiento*, also known as *albergues transitorios* or *telos*, which are primarily for sexual encounters. If the desk clerk does a double take for a single guest, that's a pretty good indicator what the place is.

Unless otherwise stated, all hotels listed here have dining rooms and private baths and are open year-round. Except in Buenos Aires, where rates can drop slightly in January and February, rates rise in summer, sometime substantially. Rates also rise for long weekends, such as Easter, and during winter holidays in late July. In mid-range and budget hotels, ask to see several rooms, as the same price often applies to vastly different rooms.

A 21 percent IVA (value added tax) applies to all hotel rooms.

Making Reservations:

Giving a credit card number is often the only way to reserve rooms in upscale hotels. Some places add a *recargo* (surcharge) of up to 10 percent for credit card payment; some will offer a discount for cash payments.

Although we have tried to give comprehensive information, please check details before booking. This applies particularly to facilities for disabled guests or nonsmoking rooms, acceptance of credit cards, and rates. Do not rely on booking by mail; fax or e-mail your hotel reservation, and take your written confirmation with you. If an Argentine tour operator informs you that the hotel of your choice is full, check directly with the hotel; even the most reputable operators have been known to steer clients toward hotels that pay preferential commissions.

For disabled access, it is recommended that you check with the establishment to verify the extent of their facilities.

Restaurants

Beef is the Argentine staple, usually as part of the *parrillada* (mixed grill) that includes some items foreign diners might prefer not to know of. Pastas, though, come a close second given the Italian origins of many Argentines. However, for most Argentines *cordero* (lamb), *pollo* (chicken), and *cerdo* (pork) belong to a separate food group that is not *carne*, or meat. Fish and seafood are less common, but can be very good along the Río Paraná and along the Patagonian shoreline. Vegetarian options are becoming more common.

Restaurants are usually open noon to 3 or 4 p.m., and again from 7 or 8 p.m. until at least midnight. Most Argentines wouldn't dream of dining out before 9 p.m., and many prefer much later—it's not hard to find a good restaurant open at 2 a.m. in Buenos Aires. Make reservations for exclusive restaurants or those with limited seating. Service varies in quality and speed, even in top restaurants.

Local fare can be enjoyed for U.S.$10 or less, with a good *menú ejecutivo* (businessman's lunch) at top restaurants running only around U.S.$15. This will usually include a starter, an entrée with a side dish, and either a soft drink, a beer, or a glass of wine.

Buenos Aires has a spectacular dining scene, especially in the "gourmet ghetto" of Palermo and some other areas. Even in the provinces, quality international cuisine has become common; in Cuyo, for instance, many wineries now have their own restaurants.

A selection of the best restaurants for each area is given below, but don't hesitate to experiment if something looks interesting. All things being equal, a restaurant with ample crowds is probably worth consideration.

Organization

The hotels and restaurants listed below have been grouped first according to their region (by chapter), then listed alphabetically by price category.

L = Lunch
D = Dinner

Credit Cards

Abbreviations used are: AE (American Express), DC (Diner's Club), MC (MasterCard), V (Visa).

■ BUENOS AIRES & THE DELTA

BELGRANO

🍽 CONTIGO PERÚ
$$$–$$$$
ECHEVERRÍA 1627
011/4780-3960
Contigo Perú has a frills-free ambience but fills fast with a Peruvian public in search of Andean comfort food, such as *lomo saltado* (stir-fried beef and vegetables) and *arroz chaufa* (fried rice). Its ample ceviche makes a lunch in itself.
🪑 120 🕐 Closed Sun.
🅢 🅢 Cash only

CENTRO/ SAN NICOLÁS

🏨 EL CONQUISTADOR HOTEL
$$$$$
SUIPACHA 948
TEL 011/4328-3012
www.elconquistador.com.ar
Located near Calle Florida and lots of shopping, bars, and nightlife, this clean, perfunctory hotel is a good choice if you want to be centrally located. Very friendly service.
🛏 110 plus 23 suites
🅢 🅢 🅢 🅢 All major cards

🏨 HOTEL A&B INTERNATIONAL
$$$–$$$$
MONTEVIDEO 248
TEL 011/4384-9516
www.hotelayb.com
Centrally located in a recycled building that's combined some relatively small rooms into more spacious lofts, the A&B has done a lot with a little while maintaining modest prices. The best rooms have Jacuzzis and even small patios.
🛏 40 🅢 🅢 🅢 MC, V

🍽 SABOT
$$$$–$$$$$
25 DE MAYO 756
TEL 011/4313-6587
In an inconspicuous location just off Avenida Córdoba, Sabot is a lunch-only spot where politicians and stockbrokers can take a weekday breather. But anyone is welcome to enjoy Italo-Argentine dishes like chicken and pumpkin ravioli and baked Patagonian lamb.
🪑 70 🕐 Closed D & Sat.– Sun. 🅢 🅢 🅢 All major cards

🍽 LA ESTANCIA
$$$–$$$$
LAVALLE 941
TEL 011/4326-0330
The gauchos who tend the grills in its picture window are a stereotype, but countless tourists parade into the cavernous restaurant for their first taste of succulent Argentine beef.
🪑 400 🅢 🅢
🅢 All major cards

🍴 PIZZERÍA GÜERRÍN

$$–$$$

AVENIDA CORRIENTES 1372

TEL 011/4371-8141

In these days of chains, Güerrín is an independent throwback that sells slices to eat at stand-up streetside counters; it also has a large but crowded dining room. Its specialties are the sweet-onion *fugazza* (without cheese) and *fugazzeta* (with cheese, sometimes with ham). Some locals think this is the city's best pizza.

🍴 150 🚫 ❄️ 🏦 All major cards

LA BOCA

🍴 EL OBRERO

$$$–$$$$

AGUSTÍN CAFFARENA 64

TEL 011/4362-9912

Despite the run-down industrial neighborhood, El Obrero draws a celebrity crowd of soccer stars and showbiz icons. Beef is the main dish, but its Spanish fish dishes also deserve consideration. Given the dodgy surroundings, almost everyone arrives by taxi or remise.

🍴 90 🕐 Closed Sun. & holidays 🚫 🏦 Cash only

MONSERRAT

🏨 AXEL HOTEL

$$$$–$$$$$

VENEZUELA 649

TEL 011/4372-0466

www.axelhotels.com

The Axel is a gay-oriented but "hetero-friendly" hotel. It welcomes visitors of any orientation to its midsize, contemporary rooms.

🛏 48 ❄️ 🚫 ❄️ 🏊 🏦 All major cards

🏨 HOTEL INTERCONTINENTAL

$$$$–$$$$$

MORENO 809

TEL 011/4340-7100

FAX 011/4340-7199

www.buenos-aires.inter
continental.com

This 17-story high-rise in one of the city's oldest neighborhoods is popular with business customers. It evinces a contemporary elegance, with spacious and well-equipped rooms.

🛏 319 🅿️ ❄️ 🚫 ❄️ 🏊 🏥
🏦 All major cards

🏨 CASTELAR HOTEL & SPA

$$$$

AVENIDA DE MAYO 1152

TEL 011/4383-5000

FAX 011/4383-8388

www.castelarhotel.com.ar

In the heart of Buenos Aires's historic center, a landmark lodging since 1929, the Castelar's Academicist facade, Carrara marble floors, subterranean spa, and tastefully modernized rooms have solidified its niche among the city's accommodations.

🛏 151 ❄️ 🚫 ❄️ 🏥
🏦 All major cards

🍴 CAFÉ TORTONI

$$–$$$

AVENIDA DE MAYO 825

TEL 011/4342-4328

Tortoni's historic ambience and live entertainment bring the crowds; the coffee, sandwiches, and *tablas* of cured meats and cheese are ideal for breakfast, lunch, and teatime. It can get uncomfortable when full.

🍴 400 🚫 ❄️
🏦 All major cards

🍴 STATUS

$$

VIRREY CEVALLOS 178

TEL 011/4382-8531

Just south of Plaza del Congreso, the no-frills Status packs in hungry diners for Peruvian standards, such as ceviche, *ají de gallina* (chicken in walnut sauce), and *lomo saltado* (stir-fried beef with vegetables).

🍴 100 🚫 ❄️
🏦 All major cards

PALERMO

🏨 LEGADO MÍTICO BUENOS AIRES

$$$$$

GURRUCHAGA 1848

TEL/FAX 011/4833-1300

www.legadomitico.com

Palermo Soho's Legado Mítico is a boutique hotel whose theme is larger-than-life Argentines such as tango singer Carlos Gardel, but it steers clear of kitsch.

🛏 11 ❄️ 🚫 ❄️
🏦 All major cards

🏨 FIVE COOL ROOMS BUENOS AIRES

$$$$–$$$$$

HONDURAS 4742

TEL 011/5235-5555

www.fivehotelbuenosaires
.com

Most of the rooms in this sleek boutique hotel are compact "smalls." Appealing common areas include a terrace with a shared hot tub. Though close to Palermo Soho's nightlife, it's remarkably quiet.

🛏 17 ❄️ 🚫 ❄️ 🏥
🏦 All major cards

🏨 VAIN BOUTIQUE HOTEL

$$$$–$$$$$

THAMES 2226

TEL 011/4776-8246

www.vainuniverse.com

Palermo Soho's Vain Boutique Hotel hides a redesigned interior behind a traditional facade. The name is a facetious acronym for the categories of rooms that range from beautifully outfitted doubles to elaborate suites.

🛏 15 ❄️ 🚫 ❄️
🏦 All major cards

🏨 CHE LULÚ GUEST HOUSE

$$–$$$$

EMILIO ZOLÁ 5185

TEL 011/4772-0289

www.chelulu.com

🚫 Nonsmoking ❄️ Air-conditioning 🏊 Indoor Pool 🏊 Outdoor Pool 🏥 Health Club 🏦 Credit Cards

Che Lulú occupies a three-story house tucked away on a block-long street. On a once marginal block, it appeals to budget-conscious travelers who seek accommodations with easy access to Palermo. Only two rooms have private baths and air-conditioning.

🛏 10 🔲 🔳 📺 🔲 Cash only

🍴 AZÉMA EXOTIC BISTRÓ
$$$$$
CARRANZA 1875
TEL 011/4774-4191
At Azéma, Buenos Aires is not the "Paris of the South" but, arguably, the "Indochina of the West" for its French colonial cuisine that also subsumes the South Pacific. Here, when Jean Paul Azéma says the curry's spicy—he oversees the kitchen and the dining room—many Argentines can't handle it, but the flavors are rich indeed. The dessert mousses are sufficient for two in richness, if not necessarily size.

🍽 40 🔲 🔳 🕐 Closed Sun.–Mon. L, Sun. D. 🔲 All major cards

🍴 BARDOT
$$$$$
HONDURAS 5237
TEL 011/4831-1112
Despite the misleading name, Bardot is part of Palermo's Peruvian gastronomic boom, serving sophisticated versions of standards like lomo saltado (stir-fried beef with vegetables) and ceviche, plus pisco sours and other Central Andean items. The ambiance is an offbeat blend of belle epoque chandeliers and sofas, and more contemporary bar and place settings.

🍽 50 🔲 🔳 🕐 Closed Mon. 🔲 All major cards

🍴 TEGUI
$$$$$
COSTA RICA 5852
TEL 011/5291-3333
Viewing its streetside facade, a solid wall saturated with stickers and graffiti, it's hard to tell that Tegui is one of Buenos Aires's elite dining experiences, in elegant contemporary surroundings. The menu is hard to pin down, despite Francophile appetizers like rabbit terrine and main dishes like roasted quail, since there are also Argentine standards like lomo con chimichurri (tenderloin with a garlic garnish). The nightly six-course tasting menu, with champagne, will satisfy your taste buds but stress your wallet.

🍽 80 🕐 Closed Sun.–Mon. 🔳 🔲 All major cards

🍴 NEMO
$$$$–$$$$$
CABELLO 3672
TEL 011/4803-5878
Nemo may be the capital's best seafood restaurant. The tapeo mare appetizer, in various sizes, provides a sampling of shellfish that are often used to garnish the pastas as well. It can get crowded; reservations are advisable on weekends.

🍽 40 🔲 🔳 🔲 All major cards

SOMETHING SPECIAL

🍴 ØLSEN
$$$$–$$$$$
GORRITI 5870
TEL 011/4776-7677
Celebrity chef Germán Martitegui's Scandinavian-Patagonian restaurant has become a gastronomic landmark for smoked bondiola (pork shoulder), trout, kippers, and game dishes with raspberry and other soft fruit sauces. Behind a high streetside wall, it hides a Zen-like garden dotted with sculptures.

🍽 100 🕐 Closed Mon. 🔲 🔳 🔲 All major cards

🍴 GRAPPA CANTINA
$$$$
EL SALVADOR 5802
TEL 011/4899-2577
In fashionable Palermo Hollywood, Grappa is an unpretentious upgrade on the traditional but unfashionable bodegón where workingmen went for their meals. This one is more family friendly, the ambiance is more spacious and luminous, and the menu of pizza, pasta, and comfortfood standards like milanesa (chicken-fried steak) is more than a step above the traditional quality.

🍽 120 🔳 🔲 MC, V

🍴 SUDESTADA
$$$–$$$$$
GUATEMALA 5602
TEL 011/4776-3777
Sudestada serves a mostly Vietnamese menu—curries, rolls, etc.—but also Thai noodles and the like. The weekday menú ejecutivo is an outstanding value.

🍽 30 🕐 Closed Sun. 🔲 🔳 🔲 AE, V

🍴 LOBBY
$$$
NICARAGUA 5944
TEL 011/4770-9335
Lobby's wine bar has a light menu of salads, sandwiches, and vegetarian options. For wine enthusiasts, it offers a diversity of by-the-glass wines and sells full bottles straight off its retail shelves. On Sundays and Mondays it closes at 8 p.m.

🍽 40 🔲 🔳 🔲 AE, V

🍴 BELLA ITALIA CAFÉ
$$–$$$
REPÚBLICA ÁRABE SIRIA 3330
TEL 011/4807-5120
Bella Italia is the budget café version of, and a better value than, its nearby namesake restaurant. In a Mediterranean style, with sidewalk as well as interior seating, it serves

light but flavorful variations on traditional panini, pastas, and salads.

🔢 50 🕹 🅕 🅢 Cash only

PUERTO MADERO

SOMETHING SPECIAL

🏨 FAENA HOTEL & UNIVERSE
$$$$$

MARTA SALOTTI 445
TEL 011/4010-9000
FAX 011/4010-9191
www.faenahotelanduniverse.com
Situated in a recycled Puerto Madero granary, the Faena has a renovated interior by architect Philippe Starck. Celebrities feel at home here, but once you're in the door, its informality is welcome.

ⓘ 110 🅿 🕹 🅢 🅕 🈯 🎽
🅢 All major cards

🏨 HILTON BUENOS AIRES
$$$$$

AVENIDA MACACHA GÜEMES 351
TEL 011/4891-0000
www.hiltonbuenosaireshotel.com
A luminous seven-story atrium is the entrée to a gleaming modern hotel in the capital's rejuvenated docklands. Guests on the upper floors have views of the yacht basins.

ⓘ 414 🅿 🕹 🅢 🅕 🈯 🎽
🅢 All major cards

🏨 HOTEL HOME BUENOS AIRES
$$$$-$$$$$

HONDURAS 5860
TEL 011/4778-1008
FAX 011/4779-1006
www.homebuenosaires.com
Home Buenos Aires gets celebrity clientele, but on its grounds, there's a casual egalitarianism. With sophisticated rooms, it's easy walking distance to some of the city's best dining and shopping.

ⓘ 17 🕹 🅢 🅕 🈯 🎽
🅢 All major cards

SOMETHING SPECIAL

🍽 CABAÑA LAS LILAS
$$$$$

AVENIDA ALICIA MOREAU DE JUSTO 516
TEL 011/4313-1336
In a country known for its beef, Cabaña Las Lilas is one of a few restaurants whose quality matches its upscale prices. Reservations are advisable after 7 p.m.

🔢 130 🅢 🅕 🅢 AE, V

🍽 HELADOS JAUJA
$$

CERVIÑO 3901
TEL 011/4801-8126
Jauja has pastries and coffee, but the real reason to come here is to indulge in some of the richest ice cream, and most unusual flavors, that Argentina has to offer—try the *calafate con leche de oveja* (sheep's milk with calafate berries) or *mate cocido* (Argentina's favorite infusion). It produces dozens of others, trucked here from its Patagonian base at El Bolsón. Dessert here can be dinner in itself. It delivers in Palermo and Belgrano.

🔢 40 🅢 🅕 🅢 MC, V

RECOLETA

SOMETHING SPECIAL

🏨 ALVEAR PALACE HOTEL
$$$$$

AVENIDA ALVEAR 1891
TEL 011/4808-2100
FAX 011/4804-0034
www.alvearpalace.com
The Alvear Palace has been the uncontested doyen of Buenos Aires ever since it opened in 1928. While it has maintained its belle epoque mystique in the city's most prestigious neighborhood, it has also

upgraded its facilities with every contemporary convenience. This is the standard to which other *porteño* hotels aspire.

ⓘ 195 🅿 🕹 🅢 🅕 🈯 🎽
🅢 All major cards

🏨 PALACIO DUHAU–PARK HYATT BUENOS AIRES
$$$$$

AVENIDA ALVEAR 1661
TEL 011/5171-1234
FAX 011/5171-1235
www.buenosaires.park.hyatt.com
The Hyatt has integrated new and old buildings seamlessly—terraced gardens unite rather than separate them. It's a worthy competitor for the Alvear Palace.

ⓘ 165 🅿 🕹 🅢 🅕 🈯 🎽
🅢 All major cards

🍽 BULLER BREWING COMPANY
$$$-$$$$

PRESIDENTE ROBERTO M. ORTIZ 1827
TEL 011/4808-9061
Brewpubs are few in Buenos Aires, but Buller's provides at least half a dozen beers on tap, with a pub grub menu of panini, pizza, and even a few simple Mexican dishes. On warm days, the streetside patio is shady.

🔢 300 🅢 🅕
🅢 All major cards

SOMETHING SPECIAL

🍽 LA BIELA
$$-$$$

AVENIDA QUINTANA 596/600
TEL 011/4804-0449
La Biela is one of the city's best sites for people-watching. Though it costs more to eat outside, the spot is ideal for a break from grave-spotting at the nearby celebrity cemetery.

🔢 200 🅢 🅕 🅢 V

🅢 Nonsmoking 🅕 Air-conditioning 🈯 Indoor Pool 🎽 Outdoor Pool 🎽 Health Club 🅢 Credit Cards

RETIRO

CAESAR PARK HOTEL
$$$$$
POSADAS 1232
TEL 011/4819-1100
FAX 011/4819-1121
www.accorhotels.com
One of the capital's top business and luxury hotels, the high-rise Caesar Park's vast common spaces and spacious rooms ensure that it keeps its patrons.

🛈 175 🔌 🆂 ♿ 🏊 📺
🆂 All major cards

FOUR SEASONS HOTEL BUENOS AIRES
$$$$$
POSADAS 1086
TEL 011/4321-1200
FAX 011/4321-1201
www.fourseasons.com/buenosaires
The Four Seasons' 1990s high-rise tower is an elegant complement to the Francophile mansion that holds its suites. Like the Caesar Park, it's close to, but not in, the Recoleta neighborhood.

🛈 165 🔌 🆂 ♿ 🏊 📺
🆂 All major cards

MARRIOTT PLAZA HOTEL
$$$$$
FLORIDA 1005
TEL 011/4318-3000
FAX 011/4318-3008
www.marriott.com
The century-old German baroque Plaza Hotel has become a Plaza San Martín monument in its own right. In terms of venerable elegance, only Recoleta's Alvear Palace belongs in the same league.

🛈 318 🔌 🆂 ♿ 🏊
🆂 All major cards

SOFITEL BUENOS AIRES
$$$$$
ARROYO 841
TEL 011/4131-0000
FAX 011/4131-0001
www.sofitel.com
The Sofitel occupies a site on one of Retiro's most elegant blocks. Its self-consciously Francophile ambience is seen in both its deco-style rooms and particularly the marble-floored lobby. The restaurant Le Sud is French Mediterranean.

🛈 169 🅿 🔌 🆂 ♿ 🏊 📺
🆂 All major cards

SHERATON BUENOS AIRES HOTEL
$$$$$
SAN MARTÍN 1225
TEL 011/4318-9000
FAX 011/4318-9346
www.starwoodhotels.com
Overlooking the Torre de los Ingleses, the Sheraton is an institution among the capital's luxury hotels, even if it can't match the personalized service of some boutique hotels.

🛈 742 🔌 🆂 ♿ 🏊 📺
🆂 All major cards

NH HOTEL LANCASTER
$$$$-$$$$$
AVENIDA CÓRDOBA 405
TEL 011/4131-6464
FAX 011/4131-6450
www.nh-hotels.com
Featured in *The Honorary Consul*, this Georgian building has been renovated into a sleekly contemporary design, though it meant the loss of the original corner pub.

🛈 115 🔌 🆂 ♿ 📺
🆂 All major cards

GRAN BAR DANZÓN
$$$$-$$$$$
LIBERTAD 1161
TEL 011/4811-1108
Possibly the city's hippest wine bar, with more than 200 varietals, the Danzón is also a restaurant with variations on traditional dishes such as ravioli stuffed with sweet corn and mushrooms. Its specialty, though, is sushi.

🍴 60 🕐 Closed L 🆂 🆂
🆂 All major cards

FILO
$$$$
SAN MARTÍN 975
TEL 011/4311-0312
A self-consciously hip pizzeria in an upscale Retiro neighborhood. Its pizzas have toppings like mixed fish and shellfish, in addition to the usual Mediterranean standards. Pastas and panini are also on the menu.

🍴 170 🆂 🆂
🆂 All major cards

MILIÓN
$$$-$$$$
PARANÁ 1048
TEL 011/4815-9925
Serving tapas, stir-fried vegetables, risotto, and relatively light beef dishes, Milión is primarily an informal bar that fills three floors of a mansard-topped building. Its weekday businessman's lunch is an outstanding value. Garden seats are at a premium.

🍴 200 🕐 Closed L Sat.-Sun
🆂 🆂 🆂 All major cards

SAN TELMO

SOMETHING SPECIAL

HOTEL MANSIÓN DANDI ROYAL
$$$$-$$$$$
PIEDRAS 922
TEL 011/4361-3537
FAX 011/4307-7623
www.mansiondandiroyal.com
In the heart of San Telmo, Dandi Royal is a boutique theme hotel dedicated to the tango. With period décor from the 1920s and 1930s, the hotel has bilingual personnel who know every *milonga* in

town—in fact, it even hosts its own next door. The rooms vary considerably, but all are good.

🚪 30 🚭 ⓢ ⓢ ⓐ 🇻
🅰 All major cards

🍴 EL BAQUEANO
$$$$$
CHILE 495
TEL 011/4342-0802
Unique in the city, El Baqueano offers changing six-course tasting menus of game dishes such as *carpincho* (capybara), *yacaré* (caiman), *vizcacha* (a chinchilla relative), plus river fish and the domesticated llama.
🍴 55 🕐 Closed Sun.–Mon.
🚭 ⓢ 🅰 All major cards

🍴 1880
$$$–$$$$
DEFENSA 1665
TEL 011/4307-2746
Opposite Parque Lezama's national history museum, 1880 has fine beef and pork. Vegetarians will find pastas on the menu. Its main drawback is the lack of space between tables.
🍴 80 🕐 Closed Mon. 🚭 ⓢ
🅰 All major cards

🍴 DESNIVEL
$$$–$$$$
DEFENSA 855
TEL 011/4300-9081
For visitors who can't indulge themselves at Cabaña las Lilas, DesNivel is a budget alternative with a less sophisticated mixed grill. Close to the Plaza Dorrego flea market, it gets scores of tourists on Sundays.
🍴 300 🕐 Closed Mon. L
🚭 ⓢ 🅰 Cash only

🍴 TANCAT
$$$
PARAGUAY 645
TEL 011/4312-5442
One of the most reliable restaurants in the downtown area, Tancat is a Spanish tapas bar that also serves fresh

seafood and appetizers like *jamón serrano*, similar to prosciutto. It's especially popular at lunchtime, when there's a fixed price *menú ejecutivo*.
🍴 80 🕐 Closed Sun.
🚭 ⓢ 🅰 All major cards

🍴 BAR EL FEDERAL
$$–$$$
CARLOS CALVO 399
TEL 011/4300-4313
This classic corner bar deserves a visit for a draft beer or hard cider, but also for excellent but inexpensive pastas and *picadas* (snack plates).
🍴 90 🚭 ⓢ 🅰 All major cards

TIGRE

🏨 CASONA LA RUCHI
$$$
LAVALLE 557
TEL 011/4749-2499
www.casonalaruchi.com.ar
This family-run Tudor-style B&B, with its lush gardens, is an ideal base for exploring the historic town and the delta. The four doubles and one triple share three baths among them.
🚪 5 🚭 ⓢ ⓐ 🅰 Cash only

🍴 IL NOVO MARÍA DEL LUJÁN
$$$–$$$$
PASEO VICTORICA 611
TEL 011/4731-9613
www.ilnovomariadellujan.com
María del Luján is an attractive riverside restaurant that sometimes serves big crowds but still maintains high quality in its diverse homemade pastas, Spanish-style fish and seafood, and Argentine *minutas* (short orders) such as *milanesa* (breaded steak). On fine days, the sycamore-shaded terrace is the best place for lunch.
🍴 300 🚭 ⓢ
🅰 All major cards

■ THE PAMPAS

ALTA GRACIA

🏨 SIERRAS HOTEL CASINO
$$$$$
VÉLEZ SARSFIELD 198
TEL 03547/431-200
www.hojoar.com
During Ernesto Guevara's boyhood, the Sierras Hotel was the center of Alta Gracia's social scene, but the hotel declined until, a few years ago, the Howard Johnson chain took over its management after an impressive restoration.
🚪 26 🅿 🚭 ⓢ ⓐ 🇻
🅰 All major cards

BAHÍA BLANCA

🏨 HOTEL VICTORIA
$$$
GENERAL PAZ 84
TEL/FAX 0291/452-0522
www.hotelvictoriabb.com.ar
Dating from 1930, in a pedestrian-friendly downtown location four blocks from Plaza Rivadavia, the Victoria has a period ambiance with a few unfortunately modernized details. Air-conditioning costs extra, and there's a surcharge for credit cards.
🚪 30 🅿 🚭 ⓢ 🅰 V

🍴 GAMBRINUS
$$–$$$
ARRIBEÑOS 174
TEL 0291/456-2750
Dating from 1890, Gambrinus is a Bahía Blanca classic, a European beer hall whose origins reflect the city's polyglot ethnic heritage. Tucked into an alleyway, it's notable for its informality, pub grub, and Teutonic lagers.
🍴 150 🚭 ⓢ
🅰 All major cards

CÓRDOBA

🏨 INTERPLAZA HOTEL
$$$$-$$$$$

SAN JERÓNIMO 137
TEL/FAX 0351/426-8900
www.interplazahotel.com.ar
The Interplaza is a centrally located, contemporary high-rise hotel with spacious rooms and suites. For business travelers who've had a frustrating day, the fitness center even includes a boxing ring.

🛏 110 🅿 🚫 🍴 🏊 🎾
🃏 All major cards

🏨 NH PANORAMA HOTEL
$$$$

MARCELO T DE ALVEAR 251
TEL 0351/410-3900
www.nh-hotels.com
The Panorama is a design-conscious contemporary hotel with amenities suitable for both business travelers and tourists. In the wooded La Cañada area, streetside rooms have pleasing views.

🛏 144 🅿 🍴 🚫 🍴 🏊
🃏 All major cards

🍴 LA LINDA
$$$$

CASEROS 84
TEL 0351/429-0045
On the pedestrian mall perpendicular to the historic Manzana Jesuítica, La Linda stresses regional specialties from the northwestern province of Salta, specifically the spicier empanadas typical of that region, but also corn-filled *humitas* and *tamales* (similar to their Mexican namesakes). Pastas and meats are also on the menu, along with the spicy stew known as *locro* in winter.

🍴 120 🚫 🍴 🃏 Cash only

🍴 SAN HONORATO
$$$-$$$$

25 DE MAYO & PRINGLES
TEL 0351/453-5252

East of the river, in the rapidly improving Barrio General Paz, San Honorato is a stylish tapas-oriented restaurant and wine bar.

🍴 80 🕐 Closed D Sun. & L Sat.–Mon. 🚫 🍴
🃏 All major cards

LA PLATA

🏨 HOTEL BENEVENTO
$$$$

CALLE 2 NO. 645
TEL 0221/423-7721
www.hotelbenevento.com.ar
Some of Benevento's high-ceilinged rooms are small, but all have sparkling wooden floors, small balconies, modern baths, and personality.

🛏 21 🛗 🚫 🍴
🃏 All major cards

🍴 CERVECERÍA EL MODELO
$$$-$$$$

CALLE 5 & CALLE 54
TEL 0221/421-1321
El Modelo is a historic site, dating from 1892, that's the place to go for sandwiches, a cold brew or hard cider, and home-baked bread.

🍴 215 🚫 🍴 🃏 Cash only

LUJÁN

🏨 HOTEL HOXÓN
$$$$-$$$$$

9 DE JULIO 760
TEL 02323/429-970
www.hotelhoxon.com.ar
The three-story motel-style Hoxón is the best choice in Luján. It's modern, central, and everything is immaculate. It's Luján's only hotel with a swimming pool.

🛏 51 🅿 🚫 🛗 🍴 🃏 MC, V

🏨 ESTANCIA DE LA TRADICIÓN
$$$$

RP 47 KM 19
TEL 011/4343-2366

www.estanciasargentinas
.com.ar
On Luján's outskirts, Los Talas is a working cattle estancia and historic guest ranch that hasn't changed dramatically since the 19th century, but that's what gives it its charm. It also houses a 40,000-volume library and archive of early Argentine history. It lacks luxuries such as private baths and air-conditioning. Rates include full board.

🛏 4 🅿 🚫 🏊
🃏 Advance bank transfer

🍴 1800 RESTAURANT
$$$

RIVADAVIA 705
TEL 02323/433-080
Its 1800s brickwork is sagging, but that adds to the mystique of a restaurant that has the most traditional décor and diverse menu in town. Options include squid rings and garlic prawns at moderate prices, plus good wines by the glass.

🍴 120 🕐 Closed Sun. & hol. D
🚫 🍴 🃏 All major cards

MAR DEL PLATA

🏨 HERMITAGE HOTEL
$$$$–$$$$$
BULEVAR PATRICIO PERALTA
RAMOS 2657
TEL 0223/451-9081
www.hermitagehotel.com.ar
Facing the waterfront promenade, the Hermitage has preserved its classic facade but refurbished its classic interior. Sea-view rooms draw premium prices.

🛏 330 🅿 🚫 ❄ 🏊 🎽
🍴 All major cards

🏨 HOTEL IMPERIO
$$$$
AVENIDA COLÓN 1186
TEL./FAX 0223/486-3993
www.imperiohotel.com.ar
In a prime location two blocks from the beach and barely a block from the restaurant scene on Calle Güemes, the Imperio is a classic hotel with ample rooms, some with balconies.

🛏 30 🅿 🚫 ❄ 🍴 AE, MC, V

🍴 EL ANTICUARIO
$$$$–$$$$$
BERNARDO DE IRIGOYEN 3819
TEL 0223/451-6309
Its very name—The Antiquarian—suggests a traditional approach to the Spanish seafood menu, but most dishes have a creative touch. The wine list is diverse and the service professional; reservations are advisable.

🪑 90 🕐 Closed L & Sun.
🚫 ❄ 🍴 All major cards

🍴 ZOE
$$$–$$$$
BERNARDO DE IRIGOYEN 3947
TEL 0223/486-5355
Barely a block from El Anticuario, Zoe is younger and hipper, with a savory but low-end pasta menu and showier upper-end dishes based on beef and fish.

🪑 70 🕐 Closed L Mon.–Sat. &
D Sun. 🚫 ❄ 🍴 AE, V

PINAMAR

🏨 HOTEL NITRA
$$$$
AVENIDA JUAN DE GARAY 229
TEL 02254/486-680
www.hotelesnitra.com.ar
Pinamar grades into Ostende, a more residential area where this placid beachfront hotel is a family-friendly facility with moderate high-season prices. Amenities include pools for adults and kids, a gym, and a game room.

🛏 50 🅿 🚫 🍴 V

🍴 ESTILO CRIOLLO
$$$$–$$$$$
AVENIDA BUNGE 768
TEL 02254/495-246
Six blocks from the beach, Estilo Criollo goes beyond the standard beef, pork, and chicken grills to specialize in *chivito* (goat). The ambience is sociable but often noisy.

🪑 300 🚫 ❄
🍴 All major cards

ROSARIO

🏨 HOTEL PLAZA REAL
$$$$–$$$$$
SANTA FE 1632
TEL./FAX 0341/440-8800
www.plazarealhotel.com
The 13-story Plaza Real has a contemporary elegance. The rooms come in four styles—standard, executive, special, and luxury—with corresponding amenities.

🛏 139 🅿 🚫 ❄ 🏊 🎽
🍴 All major cards

SAN ANTONIO DE ARECO

Also see "Guest Ranches of the Pampas," p. 109.

🏨 ESTANCIA LA BAMBA
$$$$$
RN 31
TEL 02326/454-895
www.labambadeareco.com
A former stage stop on the colonial Camino Real, La Bamba is one of the Pampas's most distinctive guest ranches, with a casual country ambience. Activities include horseback riding, birding, and fishing.

🛏 11 🅿 🚫 ❄ 🏊
🍴 AE, MC

🏨 HOTEL PATIO DE MORENO
$$$$
MORENO 251
TEL 02326/455-197
www.patiodemoreno.com
The Patio de Moreno is San Antonio's first boutique hotel. Despite its gaucho style, it displays an urban sophistication in its public wine bar, art collection, and bilingual staff. Activities such as horseback riding and golf are also on the agenda.

🛏 11 🅿 🚫 ❄ 🏊
🍴 All major cards

🏨 PARADORES DRAGHI
$$$$
MATHEU 380
TEL 02326/455-583
www.paradoresdraghi.com.ar
Located behind the Draghi silversmith's museum, studded with antiques, this striking B&B looks like a traditional Pampas house. Guests enjoy free access to the museum and a room-service breakfast.

🛏 5 🅿 🚫 ❄ 🏊
🍴 All major cards

🍴 DON FERRO
$$$$
AVENIDA ESPAÑA &
RÍO PARANÁ
TEL 0341/421-1927
Primarily a grill restaurant, in a recycled 19th-century complex that was once a major train

station, Don Ferro also serves river fish, with river views. Its size and vast interior, though, make it a mass experience rather than a place for an intimate meal.

🍴 200 🅢 🅢
🅢 All major cards

🍴 ALMACÉN DE RAMOS GENERALES
$$$
ZAPIOLA 143
TEL 02326/456-376
In a mid-19th-century house embellished with rustic relics, Ramos Generales is a cozy *parrilla* that also serves homemade pasta—spaghetti, gnocchi, ravioli. Duck, rabbit, trout, and seafood stand out from the rest.

🍴 100 🅢 🅢
🅢 All major cards

SANTA FE

🏨 CASTELAR HOTEL
$$$$
25 DE MAYO 2349
TEL 0342/456-0999
www.castelarsantafe.com.ar
A hotel with history, the Castelar retains its classic deco facade and traditional lobby, but the rooms themselves—despite upgrades—are small and utilitarian.

🛏 108 🅿 🛒 🅢 All major cards

🍴 EL QUINCHO DE CHIQUITO
$$$–$$$$
ULERICHE 50
TEL 0342/460-2608
On Santa Fe's northern outskirts, overlooking the river, Chiquito has a vast dining room beneath a thatched roof, serving large portions of grilled freshwater fish such as *boga, pacú,* and *surubí.* The food can seem generic, but it's a genuine Santa Fe experience.

🍴 180 🅢 🅢 Cash only

SANTA ROSA & AROUND

🏨 LA CAMPIÑA CLUB HOTEL
$$$$$
RN 5 KM 604
TEL 02954/426-714
www.lacampina.com
On Santa Rosa's eastern outskirts, La Campiña is a colonial-clone resort hotel. It's a good full-service alternative to accommodations in the bustling downtown, and none of those can match the verdant gardens here.

🛏 41 🅿 🅢 🅢 🛒 🏴
🅢 All major cards

🍴 CANTINA RUMI
$$$–$$$$
PUEYRREDÓN 9
TEL 02954/411-666
In both decor and dining, Rumi has more to offer than most Santa Rosa restaurants—a diversity of pastas supplements above-average meats in a spacious venue.

🍴 100 🅢 🅢 🅢 Cash only

SIERRA DE LA VENTANA & AROUND

🏨 LA ANGELITA
$$$
AVENIDA PILLAHUINCÓ 383
TEL 0291/491-5396
In the Villa Arcadia neighborhood, Angelita is a snug teahouse serving homemade breads, scones, and pastries until around 1 or 2 p.m.; then it reopens around 5 p.m. Lunch and dinner options include crepes, smoked meats and cheeses, and the house specialty, fondue.

🛏 50 🅢 🅢 🅢 Cash only

🏨 PILLAHUINCÓ PARQUE HOTEL
$$$
AVENIDA RAÍCES 161
TEL 0291/491-5423
www.hotelpillahuinco.com.ar

In the residential zone of Villa Arcadia, the Pillahuincó has simple rooms in a Normandy-style country inn on sprawling wooded grounds. Rates include breakfast, and it also provides excursions in the nearby Sierras.

🛏 31 🅿 🅢 🛒 🅢 Cash only

TANDIL

🏨 HOSTERÍA AVE MARÍA
$$$$–$$$$$
PARAJE LA PORTEÑA
TEL 0249/442-2843
www.avemariatandil.com.ar
On Tandil's outskirts, Ave María is a former estancia with more than 100 acres (40 ha) of woodlands surrounding its Normandy-style farmhouse and gardens. All the rooms have fireplaces and walk-in closets; rates include half board. The outdoor pool is not heated, but activities such as cycling and horseback riding are readily arranged.

🛏 8 🅿 🛒 🅢 AE, V

🍴 TRAUUN
$$$–$$$$
FUERTE INDEPENDENCIA 26
TEL 0249/443-4212
Occupying a handsome old house near Plaza Independencia, Trauun offers *tablas* of local cheeses and cured meats, a diversity of salads, and appetizers (such as bruschetta) to complement creative versions of the standards.

🍴 40 🕐 Closed Sun.–Wed.
🅢 🅢 🅢

VILLA CARLOS PAZ

🏨 HOTEL PORTAL DEL LAGO
$$$$$
GOBERNADOR ÁLVAREZ &
AVENIDA J. L. DE CABRERA
TEL/FAX 03541/424-931
www.portaldelago.com.ar
On the shore of Lago San

🏨 Hotel   🍴 Restaurant   🛏 No. of Guest Rooms   🍴 No. of Seats   🅿 Parking   🕐 Closed   🛒 Elevator

Roque, Portal del Lago is a resort hotel set among extensive grounds and gardens, with several swimming pools, tennis courts, and a terrace. The standard rooms are smallish and relatively dark.

ⓘ 110 🅿 🚭 🅰 🛋 🏊
🔲 All major cards

🍴 VILLAPAZ
$$$–$$$$
GENERAL PAZ 152
TEL 03541/433-230
Despite its size, the cavernous Villapaz manages to turn out fine appetizers, beef dishes, pastas, and desserts.

ⓘ 400 🚭 🅰
🔲 All major cards

VILLA GESELL

🏨 HOTEL BAHÍA
$$$$$
AVENIDA 1 NO. 855
TEL 02255/462-838
www.hotelbahiavg.com.ar
Just minutes from the beach, the Bahía is a high-rise whose sea-view rooms have balconies; the rooftop has a *confitería* (tearoom with pastries). It also offers spa services.

ⓘ 32 🅿 🚭 🅰 🛋 🏋
🔲 AE, V

🍴 LA JIRAFA AZUL
$$
AVENIDA 3 BET. PASEO 102 &
AVENIDA BUENOS AIRES
TEL 02255/468-968
For 40 years now, the Blue Giraffe has been serving a standard Argentine menu of meats, pastas, poultry, plus fish and seafood, to families from around the country. It's reliable but unremarkable.

➕ 150 🚭 🅰
🔲 All major cards

MESOPOTAMIA & THE CHACO

CORRIENTES

🏨 CORRIENTES PLAZA HOTEL
$$$$
JUNÍN 1549
TEL 0379/446-6500
www.hotel-corrientes.com.ar
Facing Plaza Cabral, the Corrientes Plaza is a sprawling contemporary hotel with a secluded pool and gym. The well-lighted, carpeted rooms have up-to-date baths.

ⓘ 110 🅿 🚭 🅰 🏋
🔲 AE, MC, V

ESTEROS DEL IBERÁ

SOMETHING SPECIAL

🏨 HOSTERÍA RINCÓN DEL SOCORRO
$$$$$
RP 40 KM 90
TEL 03782/497-073
TEL BUENOS AIRES
011/5272-0344
www.rincondelsocorro.com
Capybaras and rheas roam the grounds of Rincón del Socorro, environmental philanthropist Doug Tompkins's Argentine flagship. Decorated with regional flourishes, with half a dozen guest rooms and three separate bungalows, it also features a restaurant open to nonguests *(by reservation only)*. It also takes charge of activities such as horseback riding, fly-fishing, and of course excursions into the wildlife-rich marshes. Rates include full board and one day of excursions for two people.

ⓘ 9 🅿 🚭 🛋 🔲 V

🏨 POSADA AGUAPÉ
$$$$$
RP 40, COLONIA CARLOS
PELLEGRINI

TEL/FAX 03773/499-412
www.iberaesteros.com.ar
Posada Aguapé's sprawling grounds and rural colonial style (dating from 1997) resemble a typical Mesopotamian estancia with broad lawns, scattered palms, and shady colonnades. It's open for minimum two-night packages with full board and one day of excursions included.

ⓘ 12 🅿 🚭 🛋 🔲 Cash only

🏨 POSADAE YPA SAPUKAI
$$$$$
RP 40, COLONIA CARLOS
PELLEGRINI
TEL 011/15-3704-2288
www.ypasapukai.com.ar
With its own jetty on Laguna Iberá, Ypa Sapukai offers excursions into the floating islands of the marshes. Prices are low for such good (if simple) accommodations and knowledgeable guide service. Rates include full board and one day of excursions.

ⓘ 5 🅿 🚭 🛋 🔲 Cash or bank transfer

GUALEGUAYCHÚ

🏨 HOTEL PUERTO SOL
$$$$
SAN LORENZO 477
TEL 03446/434-017
www.hotelpuertosol.com.ar
Only a short walk from the riverfront, the Puerto Sol is a modern hotel with midsize rooms, mid-range prices, and conscientious service. The interior rooms, which face the gardens, are quieter than the streetside rooms.

ⓘ 20 🚭 🅰 🔲 All major cards

🏨 HOTEL AGUAY
$$$–$$$$
AVENIDA COSTANERA 130
TEL 03446/422-099
www.hotelaguay.com.ar
The riverside rooms at the

Aguay enjoy waterfront views, but all guests can enjoy similar views from its rooftop pool. The rooms themselves are unexpectedly small.

☐ 30 P ⊟ ◉ ⊠ ⊠ ⊽
⊠ All major cards

🍴 **DACAL**
$$$–$$$$
AVENIDA COSTANERA &
ANDRADE
TEL 03446/427-602
Along the waterfront, Dacal is a traditional restaurant that draws big crowds, day and night, for parrillada and especially for fresh fish from the Río Uruguay.
⊞ 150 🕒 Closed Tues.
◉ ◉ ⊠ All major cards

MERCEDES

🏨 **LA CASITA DE ANA**
$$$$
MITRE 924
TEL 03773/422-671
This cozy Anglo-Argentine B&B, set among verdant subtropical gardens, is a gem. Because it has so few rooms, reservations are necessary. The breakfast is above the Argentine standard, with cereal, fresh fruit, and pastries.
☐ 3 ◉ ◉ ⊠ Cash only

PARANÁ & AROUND

🏨 **HOTEL SAN JORGE**
$$$
BELGRANO 368
TEL 0343/422-1685
www.sanjorgehotel.com.ar
Offering great value for the money, the San Jorge occupies a century-old building with updated amenities. The modernized rooms surround a lush central patio.
☐ 30 P ◉ ⊠ MC, V

🍴 **LA FOURCHETTE**
$$$
URQUIZA 976

TEL 0343/422-3900
Within the Gran Hotel Paraná, La Fourchette is a formal Mediterranean-style restaurant that incorporates local products—most notably river fish—into its offerings. So small that reservations are imperative, it has a good reputation for creative desserts.
⊞ 30 ◉ ◉ ⊠ All major card

POSADAS & AROUND

🏨 **HOTEL JULIO CÉSAR**
$$$$
ENTRE RÍOS 1951
TEL 0376/442-7930
Posadas's top hotel, the high-rise Julio César has sparsely furnished but bright rooms and a plethora of amenities that include an outdoor pool in lush subtropical landscaping. It's most popular with Argentine business travelers.
☐ 98 P ◉ ⊠ ⊽
⊠ All major cards

🍴 **CAVAS**
$$$$
BOLÍVAR 1729
TEL 0376/443-5514
Cavas is an elegant formal locale whose brick walls, soft lighting, and dark wooden bar presage a sophisticated menu, with wines to pair with dishes such as *pacu Bolívar* (river fish with onion, garlic, prosciutto, and a touch of cream).
⊞ 90 🕒 Closed Sat. L
◉ ◉ ⊠ All major cards

PRESIDENCIA ROQUE SÁENZ PEÑA

🏨 **HOTEL ATRIUM GUALOK**
$$$$
SAN MARTÍN 1198
TEL 0364/442-0500
This hot springs hotel may bring on a 1970s nostalgia—all steel and glass, with no real style, but reasonable comfort at modest prices. Its access to

the baths is its greatest asset. After a recent renovation, though, the Gualok has also upgraded its restaurant and bar
☐ 106 P ⊟ ◉ ◉ ⊠
⊠ All major cards

PUERTO IGUAZÚ & AROUND

🏨 **IGUAZÚ GRAND HOTEL RESORT & CASINO**
$$$$$
RUTA 12 KM 1640
TEL 03757/498-050
www.iguazugrandhotel.com
On the road to the falls, the Iguazú Grand boasts an elegant lobby and beautifully appointed suites (even the smaller "junior" suite has 431 square feet/40 sq m!). The beautifully landscaped grounds incorporate three swimming pools.
☐ 134 P ⊟ ◉ ◉ ⊠
⊠ All major cards

🏨 **SHERATON IGUAZÚ RESORT & SPA**
$$$$$
PARQUE NACIONAL IGUAZÚ
TEL 03757/491-800
www.sheraton.com/iguazu
Close enough to see and hear the falls, the Sheraton is a three-story behemoth out of synch with its subtropical rainforest setting, but its accommodations and services are up to the highest standards. Staying here allows its guests to get an early start on the trails and falls.
☐ 176 P ◉ ◉ ⊠ ⊽
⊠ All major cards

🏨 **SECRET GARDEN IGUAZÚ**
$$$$
LOS LAPACHOS 623
TEL 03757/423-099
www.secretgardeniguazu.com
In a residential zone south of Avenida Aguirre, the Secret Garden has only three intimate rooms set among gardens. Its

owner serves his guests sunset caipirinhas on the deck.

(i) 3 **P** (S) (A) (V)
(A) Cash only

¶¶ AQVA
$$$–$$$$
AVENIDA CÓRDOBA &
CARLOS THAYS
TEL 03757/422-064
In a striking building crafted from local wood, Aqva specializes in river fish but also creative variants on Italo-Argentine cuisine. More formal than most Iguazú restaurants, it has an intimate mezzanine.

(+) 120 (S) (A)
(A) All major cards

¶¶ DOÑA MARÍA
$$$–$$$$
AVENIDA CÓRDOBA 148
TEL 03757/425-778
Part of Hotel St. George, Doña María offers a diverse menu ranging from international dishes to Argentine standard beef and pastas. Its most distinctive dishes, though, are regional—especially grilled river fish such as *surubí*.

(+) 110 (S) (A)
(A) All major cards

¶¶ LA VITRINA
$$$–$$$$
AVENIDA VICTORIA AGUIRRE 773
TEL 03757/422-165
It plays for the cliché with its *gauchesco* décor, but La Vitrina aspires to something beyond the usual Argentine grill. In addition to the standard slabs of *bife de chorizo*, sausages, and innards, it also puts suckling pig and *surubí* over the coals, and has a more than credible salad bar.

(+) 250 (S) (A) (A) MC, V

RESISTENCIA

🏠 ATRIUM HOTEL
$$$
HERNANDARIAS 249
TEL 0362/442-9094
Only a few years old, the centrally located Atrium is a glistening multistory hotel with amenities, such as a gym and tennis courts, uncommon for a hotel in its price range.

(i) 44 **P** (S) (A) (A) (V)
(A) All major cards

¶¶ KEBÓN
$$$$
DON BOSCO 120
TEL 0362/442-2385
Reservations are advisable at Kebón, which executes its menu exceptionally well, though it consists only of standard beef dishes and the occasional river fish.

(+) 250 (S) (A)
(A) All major cards

THE ANDEAN NORTHWEST

BELÉN & AROUND

🏠 HOTEL BELÉN
$$$
BELGRANO & CUBAS
TEL 03835/461-501
www.belencat.com.ar
Bounded by gardens in the center of town, the Hotel Belén resembles an Andean fortress. It's recently been restored and it's a reasonable choice in a scenic area.

(i) 25 **P** (A) (A) Cash only

CACHI

🏠 EL CORTIJO HOTEL BOUTIQUE
$$$$
AUTOMÓVIL CLUB ARGENTINO S/N
TEL 03868/491-034
www.elcortijohotel.com

Behind El Cortijo's adobe facade, all the rooms at this stylishly renovated, U-shaped, two-story farmhouse face onto a patio. The rooms combine contemporary amenities with colonial style.

(i) 12 **P** (A) AE, MC, V

CAFAYATE

🏠 HOTEL KILLA
$$$$$
COLÓN 47
TEL 03868/422-254
www.killacafayate.com.ar
At Hotel Killa, a narrow vestibule opens onto a central patio with a gallery of handsome rooms in a traditional adobe; beyond that, several newly built suites overlook a garden oasis with a pool.

(i) 14 **P** (S) (A) (A) (A) MC, V

SOMETHING SPECIAL

🏠 PATIOS DE CAFAYATE
¶¶ HOTEL & SPA
$$$$$
RP 68 & RN 40
TEL 03868/422-229
www.patiosdecafayate.com
Just north of town, Patios de Cafayate is a luxury lodging on the edge of El Esteco winery and also a wine spa. Five of its rooms are part of a renovated 19th-century residence; the remainder are recent. Nonguests can lunch or dine by reservation.

(i) 32 **P** (S) (A) (A)
(A) All major cards

🏠 VILLA VICUÑA
$$$$–$$$$$
BELGRANO 76
TEL 03868/422-145
www.villavicuna.com.ar
Villa Vicuña is a boutique hotel in a two-story colonial building, furnished according to regional tradition.

(i) 12 **P** (S) (A)
(A) All major cards

🍴 LA CASA DE LAS EMPANADAS

$$

MITRE 24
TEL 0368/15-454-111

It can't get much more authentic than the "house of empanadas," which offers at least eight different varieties of Argentina's favorite fast food, plus additional regional specialties like *locro* (a corn and squash stew popular in winter) and *cazuela de cabrito* (a goat stew). Scribble your own review on the walls. It's added a larger branch half a block south of the plaza.

🪑 30 🕐 Closed Mon.
🚫 ✦ 🈵 V

HUMAHUACA

🏨 HOSTAL AZUL

$$$

BARRIO MEDALLA MILAGROSA
TEL 03887/421-107

Beyond the town center, east of the river, Hostal Azul has a bright blue block exterior and a soothing interior, distinguished with traditional cane and *cardón* cactus furniture.

🚪 8 🅿 🚫 🈵 MC, V

🍴 LA CACHARPAYA

$$$

JUJUY 295
TEL 03887/421-016

La Cacharpaya offers no-frills versions of Andean standards such as empanadas, maize-based *humitas* and tamales, and goat-based *locro* (stew). At the same time, it's also a cavernous venue for live folkoric entertainment.

🪑 220 🕐 Closed D March–June & Aug.–Dec.
🈵 Cash only

IRUYA

🏨 HOTEL IRUYA

🍴 $$$$–$$$$$

TEL 03887/482-002
www.hoteliruya.com

On a scenic site above the town, the Hostería de Iruya has spacious, light-filled rooms; those facing the village have spectacular views. Its restaurant stresses regional cuisine.

🚪 15 🅿 🚫 ✦ AE, V (in advance only) or bank transfer

MOLINOS

🏨 HACIENDA DE MOLINOS

$$$$–$$$$$

RN 40
TEL 03868/494-094
www.haciendademolinos
.com.ar

Rooms in this 18th-century adobe surround a pepper-shaded main patio; the larger superior rooms have more elaborate décor.

🚪 18 🅿 🚫 ✈ 🈵 MC, V

PURMAMARCA

🏨 HOSTAL POSTA DE PURMAMARCA

$$$$

SANTA ROSA
TEL 0388/490-8029
www.postadepurmamarca
.com.ar

La Posta de Purmamarca's moderately priced rooms evince a plausible neo-colonial style at a fraction of prices elsewhere. All the rooms have high ceilings and good natural light, but they lack views.

🚪 9 🅿 🈵 Cash or bank transfer only

🏨 HOTEL EL MANANTIAL DEL SILENCIO

$$$$

RN 52 KM 3.5

TEL 0388/490-8080
www.hotelmanantial.com.ar

On the north side of the highway to the altiplano, Manantial del Silencio is a low-slung adobe with impeccable colonial style. The baths, though, are thoroughly contemporary, and the subtropical gardens—with a pool—are a delight.

🚪 21 🅿 🚫 ✈
🈵 All major cards

🍴 RINCÓN DE CLAUDIA VILTE

$$$

LIBERTAD S/N
TEL 0388/490-8088

Purmamarca's best restaurants are hotel-based, but Claudia Vilte's is a simple B&B whose separate dining room serves regional comfort food such as grilled llama, empanadas, and *humitas* at modest prices. On occasion there's live folkloric entertainment.

🪑 30 🚫 🈵 Cash only

SALTA

🏨 HOTEL SOLAR DE LA PLAZA
$$$$$
J.M. LEGUIZAMÓN 669
TEL/FAX 0387/431-5111
www.solardelaplaza.com.ar
Facing Plaza Güemes, Solar de la Plaza is an architectural hybrid that links a low-slung colonial-style house with a small new tower. All the rooms have artisanal northwestern décor.
🛏 30 🅿 🔄 🚭 🅰 🍃 🏋
🛅 All major cards

🏨 SHERATON SALTA HOTEL
$$$$$
AVENIDA EJÉRCITO DEL NORTE 330
TEL 0387/432-3000
FAX 0387/432-3010
www.sheraton.com/salta
The Sheraton Salta is easy walking distance to the city's sights, but tucked into a lush hillside location. The modern building's hard right angles contrast with the city's colonial heritage.
🛏 145 🅿 🔄 🚭 🅰 🏊 🏋
🛅 All major cards

🏨 HOTEL ALMERÍA
$$$$–$$$$$
VICENTE LÓPEZ 146
TEL 0387/431-4848
www.hotelalmeria.com.ar
A charming hotel on a quiet street not too far from the city center, with Spanish Andalucian-style décor. The Jacuzzi is a plus after a day of sightseeing; the breakfast buffet is decent.
🛏 67 🅿 🔄 🚭 🅰 🏋
🛅 All major cards

🏨 HOTEL DEL ANTIGUO CONVENTO
$$$$
CASEROS 113
TEL 0387/422-7267

www.hoteldelconvento.com.ar
Prices have risen at this colonial-style hotel, but its bright rooms, filled with wrought-iron furniture, are still one of the city's best values. Despite the busy location, the rooms are quiet as they face inward toward the garden and pool.
🛏 17 🅿 🚭 🏊 🛅 Cash only

🏨 HOTEL DEL VIRREY
$$$$
20 DE FEBRERO 420
TEL/FAX 0387/422-8000
www.hoteldelvirrey.com.ar
A few blocks north of the colonial core, the Hotel del Virrey is an inviting boutique hotel with burnished wooden floors and tastefully modernized baths. It's close to the restaurant and nightlife area, but quiet.
🛏 8 🅿 🚭 🅰 🏊
🛅 All major cards

🍴 FIAMBRERÍA LA CORDOBESA
$$
J.M. LEGUIZAMÓN 1502
TEL 0387/422-2794
Well beyond the Balcarce dining district, La Cordobesa is a cluttered deli that sees oenophiles fill the handful of tables for *tablas* of cheeses and cured meats accompanied by their favorite red.
🍽 16 🕐 Closed L & Sun.
🚭 🅰 🛅 All major cards

🍴 LA VIEJA ESTACIÓN
$$
BALCARCE 885
TEL 0387/421-7727
In the heart of the Balcarce dining and entertainment district, La Vieja Estación offers regional specialties that include empanadas, *humitas*, *locro*, and kid goat. After the meal, it's the city's liveliest venue for folkloric music and dance.

🍽 200 🕐 Closed L & Sun.– Mon. 🚭 🅰
🛅 All major cards

SAN FERNANDO DEL VALLE DE CATAMARCA

🏨 AMERIAN CATAMARCA
🍴 PARK HOTEL
$$$$
REPÚBLICA 347
TEL 03833/425-444
www.amerian.com
This sleek business-oriented tower opened a few years ago in sleepy Catamarca. The restaurant patterns itself after a British-style pub, but offers a diversity of dishes.
🛏 60 🅿 🔄 🚭 🅰 🏊 🏋
🛅 All major cards

SAN MIGUEL DE TUCUMÁN

🏨 SWISS HOTEL METROPOL
$$$$
24 DE SEPTIEMBRE 524
TEL 0381/431-1180
www.swisshotelmetropol.com.ar
Only half a block off Plaza Independencia, the high-rise Metropol has a Central European formality from which only the rooftop pool feels exempt.
🛏 75 🅿 🔄 🚭 🅰 🏊
🛅 All major cards

🏨 HOTEL PREMIER
$$$–$$$$
CRISÓSTOMO ALVAREZ 510
TEL 0381/431-0381
www.hotelpremier.com.ar
After the 2002 crisis, a makeover modernized the Premier's common areas and guest rooms. Though not luxurious, the rooms are cheerful, comfortable, and fairly priced.
🛏 97 🅿 🔄 🚭 🅰
🛅 All major cards

🍴 LA CORZUELA
$$$–$$$$

LAPRIDA 866
TEL 0381/421-6402
In an aging but well-kept building with *gauchesco* décor, La Corzuela serves the usual *parrillada* but also salads, fish (including trout) and other seafood, and the regional specialties of empanadas and *locro*. The ambience is subdued and the service exemplary.

🔲 120 🅐 🅑
🅑 All major cards

🍴 SETIMIO
$$$–$$$$

SANTA FE 512
TEL 0381/431-2792
In Tucumán's Barrio Norte, Setimio is a wine merchant by day, but at night, after 6 p.m., it becomes a fashionable wine bar and restaurant where clients can sample reds and whites. Later in the evening, they can dine on garlic lamb, the house specialty.

🔲 70 🕐 Closed L & Sun.
🅐 🅑 🅑 All major cards

SAN SALVADOR DE JUJUY

🏨 HOWARD JOHNSON PLAZA HOTEL
$$$$$

GÜEMES 864
TEL 0388/424-9800
www.hojoar.com
The HoJo's brick tower is a full-service hotel, with gym and spa facilities, in the middle of the downtown business district. The rooms are spacious and the common areas attractive.

ⓘ 65 🅟 🅐 🅑 🅐 🅦
🅑 All major cards

🏨 HOSTERÍA MUNAY
$$$

ALVEAR 1230
TEL 0388/422-8435
www.munayhotel.com.ar

The Munay more closely resembles a B&B than a hotel proper. A block off the main commercial thoroughfare, its rooms vary, and the only real amenity is cable TV, but they're spotless.

ⓘ 21 🅑 Cash only

🍴 MANOS JUJEÑAS
$$$

AVENIDA SENADOR PÉREZ 379
TEL 0388/424-3270
Manos Jujeñas serves authentic regional cuisine at a high level. Here, for instance, the empanadas are genuinely spicy, the tamales are made of creamy Andean maize, and the llama steaks come fresh from the puna.

🔲 60 🅐 🅑 Cash only

SANTIAGO DEL ESTERO

🏨 HOTEL CARLOS V
$$$$–$$$$$

INDEPENDENCIA 110
TEL 0385/424-0303
www.carlosvhotel.com
Modern and central Carlos V is the most complete of all Santiago's accommodations and, for what it offers—including a full-scale spa—the best value. It also holds a casino, though, which means it's the focus of the city's nightlife.

ⓘ 97 🅟 🅑 🅐 🅑 🅐 🅦
🅑 All major cards

🍴 LA CASA DEL FOLCLORISTA
$$

POZO DE VARGAS 140
TEL 0385/421-8558
Several blocks northeast of Plaza Libertad, Parque Aguirre's cavernous restaurant offers beef empanadas, barbecued beef, and the occasional goat or suckling pig. Along with the dinner comes folkloric music and dance.

🔲 200 🕐 Closed L & Mon.–Wed. 🅐 🅑 AE, MC, V

TAFÍ DEL VALLE

🏨 LAS TACANAS
$$$$$

AVENIDA PERÓN 372
TEL 03867/421-821
www.estancialastacanas.com
The town of Tafí del Valle has surrounded Las Tacanas, but the former Jesuit estancia still has a rural colonial ambience. Its rooms vary, but no other place in town can provide even an iota of its historical charm.

ⓘ 9 🅟 🅑 V

🍴 EL PORTAL DE LA VILLA
$$$–$$$$

AVENIDA PERÓN 221
TEL 03867/421-065
On the heights of Tafí del Valle, the traditional *locro* stew is literal comfort food, and El Portal de la Villa is the place to sample it. The usual empanadas, *humitas*, and *cabrito* (kid goat) are also on the menu.

🔲 80 🅐 🅑 Cash only

TERMAS DE RIO HONDO

🏨 HOTEL LOS PINOS
$$$$$

MAIPÚ 201
TEL 03858/421-043
www.lospinoshotel.com.ar
Genuine spa accommodations such as these are few in town. Rooms at the all-inclusive Los Pinos include a traditional "colonial sector" and a newer, more technologically sophisticated "American sector"; both enjoy the sprawling grounds and pools.

ⓘ 140 🅟 🅑 🅐 🅐 🅦
🅑 All major cards

🍴 SAN CAYETANO
$$$–$$$$

CASEROS 204
TEL 03858/421-872
Primarily a *parrilla*, San Cayetano specializes in kid goat. For non-carnivores, the pastas and northwestern Argentine

tamales are good enough, and fish-eaters will also find options such as dorado.

🔲 110 �€¢ 🔳 MC, V

TILCARA

🏨 POSADA DE LUZ
$$$$–$$$$$
AMBROSETTI & ALBERRO
TEL 0388/495-5017
www.posadadeluz.com.ar
Each of the half dozen rooms at Posada de Luz comes with its own patio and views down the Quebrada de Humahuaca.

ⓘ 6 🅿 🌊 🔳 AE, MC, V

🏨 HOSTEL MALKA
$$$–$$$$
SAN MARTÍN
TEL 0388/495-5197
www.malkahostel.com.ar
On a hillside shaded by pepper trees, with winding paths through its gardens, Malka is a hostel that gets backpackers in its dorms, but it also boasts a handful of beautifully appointed private rooms.

ⓘ 4 🅿 🔳 🔳 Cash only

SOMETHING SPECIAL

🏨 QUINTA LA PACEÑA
$$$–$$$$
PADILLA
TEL 0388/495-5098
www.quintalapacena.com.ar
For sheer charm, the Santa Fe–style Quinta La Paceña is in a class of its own. On a cobbled block, the 19th-century house sits in a lush garden; the rooms are not large but compensate with canopy beds, locally woven blankets, and finely carved furniture. For what it offers, La Paceña is dramatically underpriced.

ⓘ 6 🅿 🔳 🔳 🔳 MC, V

🍴 LA CHACANA
$$$$–$$$$$
BELGRANO 470
TEL 0388/15-414-0833

La Chacana's sophisticated "Andean fusion" menu includes pastas stuffed with spinach and rabbit, and standard Argentine dishes accented with quinoa and goat cheese—not to mention, of course, the ubiquitous llama.

🔲 30 🔳 🔳 MC

🍴 LOS PUESTOS
$$
BELGRANO & PADILLA
TEL 0388/495-5100
In an Andean-style *pirca*, Los Puestos is a grill with a difference: In addition to the usual beef cuts and baked empanadas, the kitchen prepares lamb and the llama dishes for which the region is becoming known. A shady patio is ideal for lunchgoers.

🔲 70 🕐 Closed Mon. 🔳 Cash only

▪ CUYO

CHACRAS DE CORIA & AROUND

SOMETHING SPECIAL

🏨 CAVAS WINE LODGE
🍴 $$$$$
COSTA FLORES, ALTO AGRELO
TEL 0261/410-6927
www.cavaswinelodge.com
Cavas is dedicated to the wine experience. Scattered among its own vineyards, the romantic "vignette" accommodations have their own plunge pools, while the main building has an art collection, a restaurant (open to nonguests by reservation), and a spa. Cavas has added three villas, one with two bedrooms, for a total of 18 rooms.

ⓘ 18 🅿 🔳 🔳 🌊 🍷 🔳 All major cards

🏨 CLUB TAPIZ
🍴 $$$$$
PEDRO MOLINA S/N
RP 60 KM 2.5, RUSSELL
TEL 0261/496-3433
www.club-tapiz.com.ar
In what was once a winery, Club Tapiz now operates a boutique hotel whose rooms have solidly handsome wooden furniture and up-to-date technology. Its outstanding restaurant has Andean views, and the wine cellar holds tastings every afternoon.

ⓘ 7 🅿 🔳 🔳 🌊 🍷 🔳 All major cards

🏨 FINCA ADALGISA
$$$$$
PUEYRREDÓN 2222
TEL 0261/496-0713
www.fincaadalgisa.com.ar
Finca Adalgisa's 5 acres (2 ha) of grapevines lie within view of the snowcapped Andes. The ample rooms are an outstanding value in this suburban hotel.

ⓘ 11 🅿 🔳 🔳 🌊 🔳 All major cards

🏨 PARADOR DEL ÁNGEL
$$$$–$$$$$
JORGE NEWBERY 5418
TEL 0261/496-2201
www.paradordelangel.com.ar
Parador del Ángel is a stylish B&B, with extensive gardens, in the midst of Chacras de Coria's gourmet neighborhood. Most of the common areas belong to a century-old adobe, but the accommodations themselves are modern, in the original style.

ⓘ 6 🅿 🔳 🔳 🌊 🔳 MC, V

🍴 BODEGA RUCA MALÉN
$$$$$
RN 7 KM 1059, AGRELO
TEL. 0261/562-8357
Along the highway to Chile, Ruca Malén is a modern boutique winery. Many visitors choose to stay for lunch—with paired wines—in

its earth-toned dining room. Reservations are advisable.

🛏 45 🕐 Closed D
💳 💳 💳 All major cards

CHILECITO

🏨 HOTEL ACA CHILECITO
$$$
TIMOTEO GORDILLO 101
TEL 03825/422-202
www.hotelchilecitoaca.com.ar
Belonging to the Automóvil Club, the frills-free Hotel Chilecito has an institutional feel. That said, given its wooded grounds and quiet location, plus a pool, it offers excellent value for the money.

🛏 28 P 💳 💳 🏊 💳 V

🍽 LA ROSA
$$
ALBERTO G. OCAMPO 149
TEL 03825/424-693
Visitors could do far worse than the standard Argentine menu and, especially, the quality pizza at La Rosa. The patio seating is agreeable.

🛏 50 🕐 Closed Mon.
💳 💳 💳 Cash only

LA RIOJA CITY

🏨 NAINDO PARK HOTEL
$$$$$
SAN NICOLÁS DE BARI 475
TEL 0380/447-0700
www.naindoparkhotel.com
Only half a block off Plaza 25 de Mayo, the Naindo is a sparkling high-rise oriented toward business clients. Bright, cheerful, and cool, the most contemporary hotel in town is also suitable for tourists.

🛏 102 P 💳 💳 💳 💳 🏊
💳 💳 All major cards

🍽 LA STANZA
$$$$
DORREGO 164
TEL 0380/443-0809
As might be expected, La Stanza specializes in pastas

but also fish (salmon, sole, and trout) and other seafood (shrimp and squid rings, for instance). The large wine list has provincial vintages, and the décor is simple but inviting.

🛏 70 🕐 Closed D Sun.
💳 💳 💳 All major cards

LAS LEÑAS (SKI AREA)

🏨 HOTEL PISCIS
$$$$$
LAS LEÑAS
TEL 02627/471-100
www.laslenas.com
The most elaborate of Las Leñas's ski hotels, Hotel Piscis has a restaurant, several bars, and library.

🛏 98 P 💳 💳 💳 🏊 💳
💳 All major cards

MALARGÜE & AROUND

🍽 EL BODEGÓN DE MARÍA
$$$
RUFINO ORTEGA 502 &
VILLEGAS
TEL 02627/471-655
El Bodegón de María does a lot with regional specialties such as goat. The baked empanadas, especially the *caprese* with mozzarella and basil, deserve special attention, and the décor is appealing.

🛏 40 💳 Cash only

MENDOZA CITY

🏨 B&B PLAZA ITALIA
$$$$$
MONTEVIDEO 685
TEL 0261/423-4219
www.plazaitalia.net
Few places in the country feel so much like a family home as the Plaza Italia. The ground floor common areas have a Francophile feel, except for the Spanish-style patio; the upstairs belongs to the guests. It's easy walking distance to downtown Mendoza.

🛏 4 💳 💳 💳 Cash only

🏨 HOTEL HUENTALA
$$$$$
PRIMITIVO DE LA RETA 1007
TEL 0261/420-0766
www.huentala.com
The Huentala is a high-rise that seems too big for the boutique hotel it claims to be. It does have luxury hotel services, plus a wine bar.

🛏 81 P 💳 💳 💳 🏊 💳
💳 All major cards

SOMETHING SPECIAL

🍽 1884
$$$$$
BELGRANO 1188, GODOY CRUZ
TEL 0261/424-2698
In a wing of the old Escorihuela winery, 1884 is the project of celebrity chef Francis Mallmann, who named it after the year of the winery's founding here, just a few blocks south of Mendoza proper. Preserving the winery's period details, but with contemporary furnishings, the restaurant offers a regionally oriented menu with dishes such as Andean kid goat paired, of course, with a spectacular wine list. While not cheap, it's not a budget-buster either.

🛏 120 💳 🕐 Closed L Sat.
💳 All major cards

🍽 MAR Y MONTE
$$$$
PERÚ 765
TEL 0261/425-3387
Mar y Monte's Chilean chef blends his country's fish and seafood heritage with Argentine regional traditions (goat from Malargüe) and wild game (Andean *viscacha*). The Chilean maize casserole *pastel de choclo* is a standard.

🛏 110 🕐 Closed L & Sun.
💳 💳 💳 Cash only

🍽 LA MARCHIGIANA
$$$–$$$$$

AVENIDA PATRICIAS
MENDOCINAS 1550
TEL 0261/429-1590
La Marchigiana is an Italo-
Argentine institution in Men-
doza. Its pastas are first-rate,
and the entire menu is surpris-
ingly affordable.
🏠 195 🚭 ❄️
🔘 All major cards

PUENTE DEL INCA

🏨 HOTEL AYELÉN
$$–$$$$
RN 7 KM 165,
VILLA LOS PENITENTES
TEL 0261/425-3443
Built with skiers in mind, the
Ayelén gets an increasing sum-
mer trade from motorists and
tourists who come to explore
Parque Provincial Aconcagua.
The rooms are large, but a
little dark.
🛏 48 🅿 🚭 🔘AE, MC, V

SAN AGUSTÍN DE VALLE FÉRTIL

🏨 HOTEL VALLE FÉRTIL
$$$
RIVADAVIA 1510
TEL 0264/642-0015
www.hosteriavallefertil.com
On a promontory overlooking
the Río Embalse San Agustín,
Hostería Valle Fértil is far and
away the best accommodation
in town. It's well-maintained
but memorable only for the
surroundings.
🛏 38 🅿 🚭 ❄️
🔘 All major cards

SAN JUAN

🏨 HOTEL ALKÁZAR
$$$$
LAPRIDA 82 ESTE
TEL 0264/421-4965
www.alkazarhotel.com.ar
Barely a block from the main
plaza, the high-rise Alkázar has
relatively small rooms—except
for eight suites—but a host

of amenities in a business-
friendly hotel.
🛏 104 🅿 🚭 ❄️ 🏊 🎾
🔘 All major cards

🍴 DE SÁNCHEZ
$$$$
RIVADAVIA 61 OESTE
TEL 0264/420-3670
De Sánchez's sophisticated
international menu showcases
dishes such as pork medallions
in a plum sauce with caramelized onions. This intimate restaurant doubles as a bookstore
and music shop.
🏠 30 🕐 Closed Sun.
🚭 ❄️ 🔘 All major cards

🍴 PALITO CLUB SIRIO LIBANÉS
$$–$$$
ENTRE RÍOS 33 SUR
TEL 0264/422-3841
With its menu of dolmas
(stuffed grape leaves), kebbe
(minced lamb), and tabbou-
leh, Palito is part of the Club
Sirio Libanés and has long
fed the city's Syrian-Lebanese
population.
🏠 300 🕐 Closed D Sun.
🚭 ❄️ 🔘 All major cards

SAN LUIS

🏨 HOTEL QUINTANA
$$$$
AVENIDA ILLIA 546
TEL 0266/443-8400
www.hotelquintana.com.ar
The seven-story Hotel
Quintana has kept its slightly
superannuated rooms and
common areas in perfect
working order. The service is
flawless, and it's close to the
city's sights and restaurants.
🛏 96 🅿 🚭 ❄️ 🏊
🔘 All major cards

🍴 LA PORTEÑA
$$
JUNÍN 696
TEL 0266/443-1722
La Porteña is one of the city's
most traditional restaurants,

with basic décor and a profes-
sional staff. The menu is strong
on pizza, pasta, and parrilla,
along with empanadas.
🏠 110 🚭 🔘MC, V

SAN RAFAEL

🏨 ALGODÓN WINE
🍴 ESTATES
$$$$$
RN 144 KM 674
TEL 0260/442-9020
On San Rafael's western
outskirts, the only winery
hotel in the vicinity consists of
the three-suite Algodón Villa
(dating from 1921) and the
recently constructed five-suite
Wine & Golf Lodge. Open to
nonguests, Chez Gastón is the
clubhouse restaurant for the
complex, which also offers ten-
nis, winery tours and tasting,
and excursions to white water
on the Atuel and Diamante
rivers, and skiing at Las Leñas.
🛏 7 🅿 🚭 ❄️ 🏊
🔘 All major cards

🏨 TOWER INN & SUITES
$$$$$
AVENIDA HIPÓLITO
YRIGOYEN 774
TEL 0260/442-7190
www.towersanrafael.com
In low-rise San Rafael, the
ten-story Tower Inn is easily
the most complete accommo-
dation in town. The modern
building has a spa and casino.
🛏 96 🅿 🚭 🚭 ❄️ 🏊
🏊 🎾 🔘 All major cards

🏨 HOTEL JARDÍN
$$$
AVENIDA HIPÓLITO
YRIGOYEN 283
TEL 0260/443-4621
On the city's busiest avenue,
it's not much to look at, but
the rooms at Hotel Jardín are
quiet and comfortable, offering excellent value.
🛏 27 🅿 🚭 🔘 Cash or debit

USPALLATA

🏨 HOTEL USPALLATA
$$$$
RN 7 KM 1149
TEL/FAX 02624/420-066
www.granhoteluspallata
.com.ar
The Uspallata is a mountain lodge that began its days as a destination for Peronist unionists. Under private management, its rooms, parquet floors, and swimming pool—on meticulously kept grounds—once again shine.
🛏 74 🅿 ⬀ ⛱ ⛳
💳 All major cards

🍴 CAFÉ TIBET
$$–$$$
RN 7 & LAS HERAS
TEL 02624/420-267
Ever since the Andes stood in for the Central Asian highlands in *Seven Years in Tibet*, Uspallata has been the site of this cozy crossroads café where wayfarers snack on pizza, sandwiches, coffee, and stronger drinks.
🍽 50 🕐 Closed Mon.
🔇 💳 Cash only

VALLE DE UCO

🏨 POSADA SALENTEIN
🍴 **$$$$$**
RP 89, LOS ÁRBOLES, TUNUYÁN
TEL 02622/429-090
www.salenteinposada.com
Nestled into the Salentein vineyards, but set apart to insure privacy, the Posada consists of two houses with a total of eight double rooms with their own trout pond. Between the two houses, the dining room—not part of the winery restaurant—faces the company's plantings. Guests have access to bicycles, horses, and the winery's facilities.
🛏 16 🅿 🔇 ⛱
💳 All major cards

🍴 URBAN
$$$$$
LOS INDIOS, LA CONSULTA
02622/451-579
www.ofournier.com
On the grounds of O. Fournier's Uco Valley winery, the Urban is demonstrably rural—at least in its location facing the Andes. The five-course lunches come from a sophisticated menu of appetizers such as cold eggplant soup and main dishes such as marble tenderloin or vegetable risotto. All courses are paired with their own wines. By reservation only.
🍽 60 🔇 🔇 💳 All major cards

VILLA DE MERLO

🏨 HOSTERÍA CERRO AZUL
$$$
SATURNO & JUPITER
TEL 02656/478-648
www.hosteriacerroazul.com.ar
In a residential area off the main commercial drag, Cerro Azul has comfortable—if plain—guest rooms. The grounds offer expansive views of the valley; a large swimming pool is the main amenity.
🛏 7 🅿 🔇 ⛱ 💳 Cash only

🍴 EL ESTABLO
$$$–$$$$
AVENIDA DEL SOL 450
TEL 02656/475-352
El Establo's casual décor belies this urbane restaurant's creative preparations of its pastas, trout, and especially the grilled kid goat. It also has an extensive wine list.
🍽 120 🔇 🔇 💳 AE, MC, V

▰ PATAGONIA

ÁREA NATURAL PROTEGIDA PENÍNSULA VALDÉS

PRICES
HOTELS
The cost of a double room in the high season (in U.S. $) is indicated by **$** signs.

$$$$$	Over $126
$$$$	$76–$125
$$$	$51–$75
$$	$26–$50
$	Under $25

RESTAURANTS
The cost of a three-course meal without drinks (in U.S. $) is indicated by **$** signs.

$$$$$	Over $25
$$$$	$16–$25
$$$	$11–$15
$$	$6–$10
$	Under $5

SOMETHING SPECIAL

🏨 ESTANCIA RINCÓN CHICO
$$$$$
PUNTA DELGADA
TEL 0280/447-1733
www.rinconchico.com.ar
Near the Punta Delgada lighthouse, a dirt road leads southwest for 3 miles (5 km) to this traditional sheep farm with comfortable motel-style accommodations. Elephant seals flourish along its own uncrowded coastline.
🛏 8 🅿 🔇 💳 Cash or bank transfer

🏨 HOTEL FARO PUNTA
🍴 DELGADA
$$$$$
PUNTA DELGADA
TEL 0280/445-8444
www.puntadelgada.com
Comfortably renovated, the Faro Punta Delgada is the only local place where guests have easy access to the wildlife by a short hike down to the

beach. Its restaurant is open to nonguests.

ⓘ 27 🅿 🅂 🅲 🅰 MC, V

🏨 **HOSTERÍA PARADISE**
🍴 **$$$$**
SEGUNDA BAJADA AL MAR
TEL/FAX 0280/449-5030
www.hosteriatheparadise
.com.ar
Once a backpackers' refuge, the Paradise is now a solid seaside B&B on lushly landscaped grounds. The restaurant produces economical pizzas and sandwiches, along with fixed-price lunches and dinners.

ⓘ 12 🅿 🅂 🅲 🅰 MC, V

BAJO CARACOLES

🏨 **HOSTERÍA CUEVA**
🍴 **DE LAS MANOS**
$$$$$
RN 40
TEL 011/5237-4043 IN
BUENOS AIRES
www.cuevadelasmanos.net
At ex-Estancia Los Toldos, Hostería Cueva de las Manos is an ideal base for visiting its namesake rock-art site. There are four utilitarian but up-to-date private rooms and one six-bunk hostel-style cabin, which is cheaper per person. Meals and afternoon tea are available at the restaurant.

ⓘ 5 🅿 🅂 🅰 All major cards
(advance reservations only)

🏨 **HOTEL BAJO**
CARACOLES
$$$
RN 40 & RP 39
TEL 02963/490-100
Motorists who end up spending a night at Bajo Caracoles when its service station runs short of gasoline can take refuge at this plain stone landmark, where some rooms have shared baths. It has decent meals but notoriously grumpy management.

ⓘ 8 🅿 🅰 Cash only

COMODORO RIVADAVIA

🏨 **HOTEL AUSTRAL PLAZA**
🍴 **$$$$–$$$$$**
MORENO 725
TEL 0297/447-2200
www.australhotel.com.ar
The Austral Plaza is a two-for-one package: the older Austral Express Hotel, with plain but reliable accommodations, and its newer sibling, the Austral Plaza, with larger and more contemporary rooms. The two share common areas; the Austral Plaza's restaurant, Tunet, is highly regarded.

ⓘ 174 🅿 😊
🅰 All major cards

🍴 **PUERTO CANGREJO**
$$$–$$$$
AVENIDA COSTANERA 1051
TEL 0297/444-4590
The waterfront Puerto Cangrejo is the place to sample salmon and pelagic fish from the South Atlantic. It's one of Comodoro's best choices and good value for the price.

🍴 100 🅂 🅲
🅰 All major cards

EL BOLSÓN

🏨 **LA CASONA DE ODILE**
🍴 **$$–$$$**
BARRIO LUJÁN
TEL 0294/449-2753
www.odile.com.ar
About 3.5 miles (6 km) north of town, reached by a gravel road, Odile's is a French-run garden B&B where both guests and nonguests (with reservations) are welcome for elaborate dinners.

ⓘ 5 🅿 🅰 Cash only

SOMETHING SPECIAL

🍴 **JAUJA**
$$$–$$$$
SAN MARTÍN 2867
TEL 0294/442-2952
Jauja is one of Patagonia's

landmark restaurants, featuring a diverse menu that includes quality versions of hamburgers and pizzas, but also pastas, lamb, and wild game dishes. Lines form outside the adjacent ice creamery, with some 70 flavors.

🍴 52 🅂 🅰 AE, MC, V

EL CALAFATE

🏨 **DESIGN SUITES**
CALAFATE
$$$$$
CALLE 94 NO. 190
TEL 02902/494-525
www.designsuites.com
Few Calafate hotels can match the views of Lago Argentino from the glassy atrium of the four-story Design Suites. Only the suites have lake views; standard rooms face the steppe and Andean foothills.

ⓘ 60 🅿 😊 🅂 ⛱ 🛥 🏋
🅰 All major cards

🏨 **EOLO LODGE**
🍴 **$$$$$**
RP 11 KM 23
TEL 02902/492-042
www.eolo.com.ar
Eolo's style mimics the traditional Patagonian sheep estancia, but the rooms are larger and more comfortable than their 19th-century counterparts. The views are vast; nonguests can dine here by reservation.

ⓘ 17 🅿 🅂 ⛱
🅰 All major cards

🏨 **HOSTERÍA ALTA VISTA**
🍴 **$$$$$**
RP 15 KM 35
TEL 02902/491-247
www.hosteriaaltavista.com.ar
One of the first estancias to become a luxury lodge, Alta Vista is a full-service guest ranch with six rooms and one suite, plus a gourmet restaurant and bar, at the base of Cerro Freile. Guests have

the hotel and surroundings to themselves, except for the staff, the sheep, and their gaucho herders.

🎴7 🅿️ 🚫 🛗
🏧 All major cards

🏨 HOTEL KAU YATÚN
$$$$$
ESTANCIA 25 DE MAYO
TEL 02902/491-059
www.kauyatun.com
On 17 acres (7 ha) of gardens, the main guesthouse at Kau Yatún was once the big house at Estancia 25 de Mayo. The rooms are four-star all the way, and the hotel offers a full menu of activities and excursions.

🎴44 🅿️ 🚫
🏧 All major cards

🏨 PATAGONIA QUEEN
$$$$$
AVENIDA PADRE AGOSTINI 49
TEL 02902/496-701
www.patagoniaqueen.com
The Patagonia Queen is a sparkling boutique hotel with its own wine bar and amenities such as a game room and a gym. The rooms are just midsize.

🎴20 🅿️ 🚫 🏴
🏧 All major cards

🍽 CASIMIRO BIGUÁ
$$$–$$$$
AVENIDA LIBERTADOR 963
TEL 02902/492-590
One of three similarly named restaurants, Casimiro Biguá features a Patagonian and international menu in a building that doubles as a wine bar. The menu is Italian and Mediterranean, especially in its pastas, but with local ingredients.

🪑140 🚫 🏧 All major cards

🍽 PURA VIDA
$$$–$$$$
AVENIDA LIBERTADOR 1876
TEL 02902/493-356

A few blocks west of the most densely built section of the San Martín strip, this casual restaurant offers casseroles, pastas, and stews for a hearty meal after hours of glacier gazing. The mezzanine offers views of Laguna Nimes and Lago Argentino.

🪑40 🕐 Closed L & Wed.
🚫 🏧 Cash only

🍽 PIZZERÍA LA LECHUZA
$$$
AVENIDA LIBERTADOR 1301
TEL 02902/491-610
One of El Calafate's most popular eateries, La Lechuza combines moderate prices with one of the largest and most diverse pizza menus in the country. Other fast food favorites are also on the menu in an informal setting.

🪑110 🚫 🏧 All major cards

🍽 VIVA LA PEPA
$$–$$$
EMILIO AMADO 833, LOCAL 1
TEL 02902/491-880
The crepes—both savory entrees and desserts—at Viva La Pepa provide an alternative to the typical Patagonian diet, in cozy surroundings just off the main avenue. Salads, sandwiches, and soups are also on the menu.

🪑38 🕐 Closed Thurs.
🚫 🏧 Cash only

EL CHALTÉN

🏨 HOSTERÍA EL PUMA
🍽 $$$$$
LIONEL TERRAY 212
TEL 02962/493-095
www.hosteriaelpuma.com.ar
On sprawling lawns behind a rustic log fence, El Puma is a solid brick building with bay windows, a lounge with a large fireplace, and a restaurant/wine bar. Wi-Fi (unusual in town) is available in the spacious rooms.

🎴12 🅿️ 🚫 🏧 MC, V

🏨 HOSTERÍA EL PILAR
🍽 $$$$–$$$$$
RP 23 KM 17
TEL/FAX 02962/493-002
www.hosteriaelpilar.com.ar
Despite its traditional "Magellanic" style, the secluded El Pilar is barely a decade old and has modern comforts. Nonguests can dine in the restaurant.

🎴10 🅿️ 🚫 🏧 Cash or bank transfer

🏨 HOSTERÍA POSADA
🍽 LUNAJUIM
$$$$
TREVISÁN 45
TEL 02962/493-047
www.lunajuim.com
From its modest beginnings as a B&B, Lunajuim has added rooms and expanded to include a library and a bar/restaurant, as well as its own wine cellar.

🎴26 🅿️ 🚫 🏧 Cash only

🏨 NOTHOFAGUS BED & BREAKFAST
$$$–$$$$
HENSEN & RIQUELME
TEL 02962/493-087
www.nothofagusbb.com.ar
With nearly unobstructed views of Fitz Roy Monte, ample light-filled rooms, inviting common areas, and bargain prices, Nothofagus is the pick of El Chaltén's B&B accommodations. Four of the rooms have shared baths.

🎴7 🅿️ 🚫 🏧 Cash only

SOMETHING SPECIAL

🍽 RUCA MAHUIDA
$$$$–$$$$$
LIONEL TERRAY 104
TEL 02962/493-018
Open in summer, El Chaltén's first fine dining option is still one of the best. The rustically stylish dining room—customers sometimes have to share large tables—is the setting for

a menu that offers quinoa salad, soups, venison in a berry sauce, and even vegetarian choices such as moussaka.
⊞ 30 🕒 Closed May–Oct.
🚭 🏧 AE, MC, V

🍴 ESTEPA
$$$–$$$$
CERRO SOLO 86
TEL 02962/493-069
The signature dish at Estepa is Patagonian lamb with a *calafate* berry sauce. One of El Chaltén's finest restaurants, it's also one of the smallest, so reservations are imperative. In addition to meats and fish, it also prepares pizza and pastas and occasionally hosts live jazz.
⊞ 24 🕒 Closed Mon. 🚭
🏧 Cash only

🍴 FUEGIA
$$$–$$$$
SAN MARTÍN 342
TEL 02962/493-243
Run by the nearby Albergue Patagonia hostel, at midday and at night Fuegia becomes one of the town's better restaurants. Lamb anchors the Euro-Patagonian menu, along with trout, but the kitchen also produces soups and vegetarian dishes. Reservations recommended.
⊞ 40 🕒 Closed L 🚭
🏧 Cash only

🍴 PIZZERÍA PATAGONICUS
$$$–$$$$
GÜEMES 57
TEL 02962/493-025
At day's end, Patagonicus fills up fast with tired backpackers who come to sample the best pizza in town, along with draft beer; lamb is a specialty. It can get crowded and noisy, but its picture windows that look onto the soaring peaks are worth it.
⊞ 45 🕒 Closed May–Oct.
🚭 🏧 Cash only

ESQUEL

🏨 🍴 HOSTERÍA CUMBRES BLANCAS
$$$$$
AVENIDA AMEGHINO 1683
TEL 02945/455-100
www.cumbresblancas.com.ar
Except for its location on a busy avenue, the two-story Cumbres Blancas has much to offer: bright carpeted rooms and suites with wooden ceilings, a good restaurant, and even its own tiny golf course.
🛏 20 🅿 🚭 🌴
🏧 All major cards

🏨 HOSTERÍA CANELA
$$$$–$$$$$
LOS NOTROS & LOS RADALES, VILLA AYELÉN
TEL. 02945/453-890
www.canelaesquel.com
In a mostly residential neighborhood just south of downtown Esquel, the Hostería Canela has a handful of comfortable rooms that overlook sprawling lawns.
🛏 5 🅿 🚭 🏧 Cash only

🍴 DON CHIQUINO
$$$–$$$$
AVENIDA AMEGHINO 1641
TEL 02945/450-035
"Pastas with magic" is more than a slogan here, as the owner is, in fact, a magician who often performs tricks on the floor—particularly welcomed by families with kids—or else has a fill-in do so. A cluttered, informal décor reinforces the spontaneity for dishes such as *sorrentinos*—an Argentine stuffed pasta specialty—supplemented by *tablas* of cold cuts and cheeses.
⊞ 100 🚭 🏧 Cash only

GAIMAN & AROUND

🏨 HOSTERÍA TY GWYN
$$$$
9 DE JULIO 147
TEL 0280/449-1009
www.tygwyn.com.ar
Like Plas Y Coed, Ty Gwyn is a teahouse that has created several comfortable rooms with fine hardwood floors, balconies, and period details. All rooms face the river, but mosquitos are a factor.
🛏 4 🅿 🚭 🏧 Cash only

🏨 🍴 HOSTERÍA GWESTY PLAS Y COED
$$$
AVENIDA HIPÓLITO YRIGOYEN 320
TEL 0280/449-1133
www.plasycoed.com.ar
The teahouse Plas Y Coed has only three cozy guest rooms in a solid brick structure. Surrounded by extensive gardens, the building dates from 1887.
🛏 3 🅿 🚭 🏧 Cash only

🍴 TY TE CAERDYDD
$$$$
FINCA 202
TEL 0280/449-1510
Reached by a bridge near Parque El Desafío, on sprawling but manicured grounds, the town's biggest teahouse offers cakes, cookies, custards, bread, butter, and marmalade.
⊞ 180 🕒 Open from 2 p.m.
🚭 🏧 V

SOMETHING SPECIAL

🍴 TY NAIN
$$$–$$$$
AVENIDA HIPÓLITO YRIGOYEN 283
TEL 0280/449-1126
www.cpatagonia.com/gaiman/ty-nain
In the course of nearly 120 years, the British-looking Ty Nain teahouse has become a Gaiman institution. It serves a calorie-laden but irresistible assortment of cakes, scones, breads, and cheeses.
⊞ 60 🕒 Open from 4 p.m.
🏧 Cash only

JUNIN DE LOS ANDES

🏨 RÍO DORADO LODGE
$$$$–$$$$$
ILLERA 448
TEL 02972/492-451
www.riodorado.com.ar
With its cabin-style interior, the Río Dorado is self-consciously rustic. That said, it enjoys easy access to Parque Nacional Lanín and all the amenities in large rooms, on wooded grounds.

ⓘ 10 🅿 🅂 🏊 🅂 Cash only

🍴 CENTRO DE TURISMO
$$$–$$$$
PADRE MILANESIO 586
TEL 02972/492-555
The name may sound uninviting, but the kitchen at the Centro de Turismo does a good job with trout and other Argentine standards.

🪑 40 🅂 MC, V

LOS ANTIGUOS

🏨 HOSTERÍA ANTIGUA PATAGONIA
$$$$$
RP 43
TEL 02963/491-055
www.antiguapatagonia.net
At the eastern approach to town, Antigua Patagonia is a modern three-story hotel facing the lakeshore. While it lacks luxuries, it's the best choice in town.

ⓘ 16 🅿 🅃 🅂 MC, V

NEUQUÉN (CITY)

🏨 HOTEL ROYAL
$$$$
AVENIDA ARGENTINA 143
TEL/FAX 0299/448-8902
www.royalhotel.com.ar
Despite its busy location, the Royal deserves consideration for its impeccable common areas, large rooms, and up-to-date baths. It's easy walking distance to Neuquén's museums and restaurants.

ⓘ 40 🅿 🔌 🅂 🅂
🅂 All major cards

🍴 EL MUSEO DE LA PASTA
$$$–$$$$
LA RIOJA 424
TEL 0299/448-9472
Knowledgeable locals flock to the Museo de la Pasta for creative upmarket versions of Italian standards—think lamb ravioli in scarparo sauce—in a congenial setting.

🪑 40 🕐 Closed L & Sun.–Tues. 🅂 🅂 Cash only

PARQUE NACIONAL LOS ALERCES

🏨 🍴 HOSTERÍA FUTALAUFQUEN
$$$$$
VILLA FUTALAUFQUEN
TEL 02945/471-008
www.hosteriafutalaufquen
.com
Architect Alejandro Bustillo created the Futalaufquen on a cul-de-sac near park headquarters. The vast common areas of this Euro-Andean lodge include an enormous fireplace and a long wooden bar. Rooms are few, but nonguests can dine by reservation.

ⓘ 9 🕐 Closed May–Oct.
🅿 🅂 🅂 All major cards

PARQUE NACIONAL LOS GLACIARES

🏨 HOSTERÍA LOS NOTROS
$$$$$
PARQUE NACIONAL LOS GLACIARES
TEL 02902/499-510
www.losnotros.com
Few hotels in the world match the setting of Los Notros, with direct views of the Moreno Glacier. Multiday packages, with full board and excursions, are the default option at this handsome mountain lodge. The only accommodations with easy glacier access, it's notable for the *absence* of TV, cell phone signals, and similar distractions.

ⓘ 32 🅿 🅂 🅂 All major cards

PARQUE NACIONAL MARINO PATAGONIA AUSTRAL

🏨 BAHÍA BUSTAMANTE
$$$$–$$$$$
RN 3 KM 1674
TEL BUENOS AIRES
011/4156-7788
The owners of Bahía Bustamante have recycled several of the kelp village's administration houses as high-mid to upscale accommodations, plus a restaurant, for outdoors-oriented visitors who come to see the offshore and onshore wildlife, and go horseback riding or hiking in the nearby petrified forest.

ⓘ 17

PARQUE NACIONAL MONTE LEÓN

🏨 HOSTERÍA MONTE LEÓN
$$$$$
RN 3 KM 2385
TEL 011/4621-4780 IN
BUENOS AIRES
www.monteleon-patagonia
.com
This was the *casco* (big house) when Monte León was a sheep ranch; now fantasy wool barons can sleep in its soaring bedrooms and wander its antique-filled hallways in between excursions. Simpler accommodations are found in the former henhouse. All have shared baths.

ⓘ 4 🅿 🅂 🅂 Cash or bank transfer

PARQUE NACIONAL PERITO MORENO

🏨 ALDEBARÁN HOTEL & SPA

$$$$$

AVENIDA BUSTILLO KM 20.4,
PENÍNSULA SAN PEDRO
TEL 0294/444-8678
BUENOS AIRES
www.aldebaranpatagonia.com
On the wooded grounds
of a small peninsula jutting
into Lago Nahuel Huapi, the
Aldebarán is a distinctive contemporary hotel with just ten
outsized rooms, all with decks
or balconies looking across an
inlet toward Cerro Campa-
nario, Cerro López, and other
Andean peaks. As the name
suggests, the Aldebarán has
spa facilities and, in addition,
the fine Restaurante Sirius.

🛏 10 🅿 🗠 All major cards

🏨 ESTANCIA LA ORIENTAL

$$$$$

RP 37 KM 89
TEL 02962/452-196 IN
SAN JULIÁN
TEL 011/5237-4043 IN
TEL BUENOS AIRES
011/5237-4043
www.estanciasdesantacruz
.com
Within the limits of Parque
Nacional Perito Moreno, 55
miles (89 km) northwest of
the RN 40 junction, La Oriental is a rambling ranch-style
house in an incomparable setting. The accommodations are
nothing spectacular; there is
also a campground. Hiking and
other activities are exceptional.

🛏 7 🅿 🗠 🗠 All major cards
(advance reservations only)

PUERTO DESEADO

🏨 HOTEL ISLA CHAFFERS

$$$

AVENIDA SAN MARTÍN &
MORENO
TEL 0297/487-2246

www.hotelislachaffers.com.ar
The nondescript but tidy
Isla Chaffers has reasonably
spacious rooms, attractive
common areas, and attentive
personnel. The modern build-
ing is walking distance to every
point of interest.

🛏 17 🅿 🗠 All major cards

🍴 PUERTO CRISTAL

$$$–$$$$

ESPAÑA 1698
TEL 0297/487-0387
Overlooking a small lagoon,
Puerto Cristal is primarily a
seafood restaurant and a good
one. The pastas and Patago-
nian lamb are also excellent.

🍴 100 🕐 Closed Wed. L
🗠 🗠 MC, V

SAN CARLOS DE BARILOCHE

🏨 DESIGN SUITES BARILOCHE

$$$$$

AVENIDA BUSTILLO KM 2.5
TEL/FAX 0294/445-7000
www.designsuites.com
About 1.5 miles (2.5 km) west
of downtown, the Design
Suites has spectacular com-
mon areas including an indoor-
outdoor pool that seemingly
sits among the treetops. In
separate buildings, all the
rooms have lake views.

🛏 54 🅿 🗠 🗠 🗠
🗠 🗠 🗠 AE, MC, V

SOMETHING SPECIAL

🏨 LLAO LLAO HOTEL & RESORT

$$$$$

AVENIDA BUSTILLO KM 25
TEL 0294/444-8530
www.llaollao.com
The work of Alejandro
Bustillo, this 1940s construc-
tion may be Argentina's—and
perhaps the continent's—most
famous single hotel. Because
of its national monument
status, the original rooms are

relatively small and cannot be
expanded, but a newer annex
should satisfy anyone who
needs more space and greater
luxuries to accompany the ter-
rific views.

🛏 205 🅿 🗠 🗠 🗠 🗠
🗠 🗠 All major cards

🏨 HOSTERÍA LAS MARIANAS

$$$$–$$$$$

24 DE SEPTIEMBRE 218
TEL 0294/443-9876
www.hosterialasmarianas
.com.ar
In the hills of the Barrio
Belgrano, Las Marianas is an
urban Andean lodge with lake
views. Breakfasts are elaborate
in this family-run hotel.

🛏 16 🅿 🗠 🗠 Cash or
bank transfer

🏨 HOTEL TRES REYES

$$$$–$$$$$

AVENIDA 12 DE OCTUBRE 135
TEL 0294/442-6121
FAX 0294/442-4230
www.hotel3reyes.com.ar
Facing the lakefront, the refur-
bished Tres Reyes dates from
the 1950s, but it has a style
reminiscent of pioneering archi-
tect Alejandro Bustillo. Rates
vary by garden or lake views;
furnishings are conservative.

🛏 53 🅿 🗠 🗠
🗠 All major cards

🍴 ALMAZEN DE SABORES

$$$$$

LOS RADALES 667, DINA HUAPI
TEL 0294/452-1109
In new quarters on Bariloche's
eastern outskirts, the Alma-
zen has eclectic offerings of
Middle Eastern, South Asian,
Peruvian, and Argentine dishes
available à la carte or in a
six-course tasting menu that
also provides some choice.
The ingredients are local—
Moroccan meatballs made of
Patagonian lamb, for instance.

It's tiny, so make reservations.
Tasting menu costs U.S.$30.
🍴 16 🕐 Closed Tues.
🚫 Cash only

🍴 EL PATACÓN
$$$$–$$$$$

AVENIDA BUSTILLO KM 7
TEL 0294/444-2898
With its vast dining room, giant
stone fireplace where lamb
sizzles, and carved wooden bar
with a large wine selection, El
Patacón is a metaphor for Patagonia and its traditional diet.
🍴 220 🅂 🚫 D, V

🍴 KANDAHAR
$$$$–$$$$$

20 DE FEBRERO 698
TEL 0294/442-4702
Despite the misleading Central
Asian name, this is a distinctively Patagonian restaurant
stressing wild game dishes
such as trout, rabbit, and venison, plus the usual lamb and
salmon, often garnished with
locally gathered mushrooms.
🍴 40 🕐 Closed L 🅂 🚫 V

🍴 BAHÍA SERENA
$$$–$$$$

AVENIDA BUSTILLO 12275
TEL 0294/452-4614
On the Llao Llao road, Bahía
Serena specializes in pastas and
is one of the few Bariloche res-
taurants to enjoy a lakefront
location, with even a small
sandy beach. Game dishes are
also on the menu.
🍴 50 🕐 Closed Mon.
🅂 🚫 MC, V

🍴 CERVECERÍA BLEST
$$$–$$$$

AVENIDA BUSTILLO 11600
0294/446-1026
Blest is a brewery restaurant
with Germanic specialties such
as dumplings, goulash, and
strudel, as well as pizza and
draft beer. Its spacious locale
has an informal décor.
🍴 100 🅂 🚫 AE, MC, V

🍴 LA VIZCACHA
$$$–$$$$

EDUARDO O'CONNOR 630
TEL 0294/442-2109
Near the cathedral and the
lakefront, La Vizcacha is worth
seeking out for some of the
city's best, and best priced,
meat dishes.
🍴 80 🕐 Closed Tues.
🅂 🚫 All major cards

PUERTO MADRYN & AROUND

🏨 AUSTRALIS YENE HUE HOTEL & SPA
$$$$$

AVENIDA ROCA 33
TEL 0280/447-1496
www.hotelesaustralis.com.ar
On the waterfront, the high-
rise Yene Hue is one of the
city's tallest buildings and, for
that reason, the east-facing
rooms enjoy oceanic panora-
mas; others look onto the
distant steppe. All have clean
lines, good natural light, and
attractive wooden furniture.
The Acqua di Mare spa is
open to visitors as well as
hotel guests.
🛏 64 🅂 P 🛗 🅂 🚫 V
🚫 All major cards

🏨 HOTEL PENÍNSULA VALDÉS
$$$$–$$$$$

AVENIDA ROCA 155
TEL 0280/447-1292
www.hotelpeninsula.com.ar
Also overlooking the water-
front, the multistory Península
Valdés is a modern hotel with
bright cheerful rooms—but
the larger "panoramic" rooms,
which face the ocean, are the
best value. Its spa makes it a
good value for the money.
🛏 76 P 🛗 🅂 🚫 V
🚫 All major cards

🏨 HOTEL BAHÍA NUEVA
$$$$

AVENIDA ROCA 67
TEL 0280/445-1677
www.bahianueva.com.ar
Architecturally, the Bahía
Nueva reflects Welsh heritage.
The rooms are only midsize,
and several nearby hotels have
equally easy beach access, but
none of them has the same
ample gardens.
🛏 40 P 🛗
🚫 All major cards

🍴 EL ALMENDRO
$$$$–$$$$$

ALVEAR 409
TEL 0280/447-0525
Probably Madryn's best,
El Almendro takes its name
from the almond tree that
guards the entrance to a
sophisticated restaurant
that's more suitable for an
intimate meal than the
larger eateries that pack in
the diners here. The menu is
diverse, especially the fish
and seafood, but the ravioli
and lamb also deserve men-
tion. Sushi is available Fridays,

for dining here and take-out.
🍴 45 🚭 🕐 Closed Mon. D,
Sun. L 🍴 All major cards

🍴 PLÁCIDO
$$$$–$$$$$
AVENIDA ROCA 506
TEL 0280/445-5991
Plácido is easily Madryn's most
elegant restaurant, and its
signature dish of Patagonian
lamb, accompanied by sweet
potato puree, alone makes it
worth a visit. However, start-
ers, desserts, and wines are
overpriced.
🍴 120 🚭 🚭 🍴 AE, MC, V

🍴 MAR Y MESETA
$$$–$$$$
AVENIDA GALES 32
TEL 0280/445-8740
The Patagonian menu at this
waterfront boulevard restau-
rant provides such specialties
as *abadejo* (cod) with a honey
sauce and skewers of lamb,
bacon, onion, and red peppers.
The décor is bright and cheerful.
🍴 60 🚭 🚭 🍴 AE, MC, V

🍴 MARGARITA PUB
$$–$$$
ROQUE SÁENZ PEÑA 15
0280/447-2659
The Margarita Bar is the place
for good, cheap pub grub spe-
cials at lunch. Late at night, it's
a pub per se, and a good one.
🍴 70 🚭 🍴 AE, MC, V

PUERTO SAN JULIÁN

🏨 HOSTERÍA LA CASONA
$$$
AVENIDA HERNANDO DE
MAGALLANES 650
TEL 02962/452-434
Across from the beach,
La Casona is a classic
"Magellanic" house refur-
bished as a snug B&B. With
no on-site staff (they're
next door), guests prepare
their own breakfasts in the
kitchen. Still, for the price,

it's an outstanding value.
🕐 6 🍴 Cash only

🏨 POSADA DE DRAKE
$$$
MITRE & RIVADAVIA
TEL 02962/452-523
www.posadadedrake.com.ar
The Posada de Drake is a spar-
kling B&B that doubles as a
teahouse. While not luxurious,
its beamed ceilings and bright
white walls set it apart.
🕐 6 🍴 MC, V

🍴 LA RURAL
$$$
AMEGHINO 811
TEL 02962/454-066
Looking onto the bay,
La Rural's dining room fills
fast with diners in search of
pastas, often embellished
with seafood sauces. Beef,
fish, and Patagonian lamb
are also on the menu.
🍴 42 🕐 Closed Tues.
🍴 Cash only

RESERVA NATURAL PROVINCIAL CABO VÍRGENES

🏨 ESTANCIA MONTE DINERO
$$$$$
BRP 1
TEL./FAX 02966/428-922
www.montedinero.com.ar
Southwest of Río Gallegos,
Monte Dinero is a historic
guest ranch with easy access
to the penguin colony at Cabo
Vírgenes. The dining room is
open to guests only, and some
rooms have shared baths.
🕐 6 🅿 🚭 🍴 MC, V

RÍO GALLEGOS

🏨 HOTEL SEHUEN
$$$$
RAWSON 160
TEL 02966/425-683
www.hotelsehuen.com

The Sehuen is no luxury
choice, but its faultless execu-
tion makes it the best pick in
town. Rooms are plain but
comfortable. Reservations
are imperative.
🕐 34 🅿 🍴 AE, MC, V

🍴 BRITISH CLUB
$$$$
AVENIDA KIRCHNER 935
TEL 02966/432-668
For a sense of how the Anglo-
Argentine wool barons dominated southernmost Patagonia
in the early 20th century, a visit
to the British Club gives the
traveler a good feel for the era
when Britannia still ruled the
waves. The British Club isn't
quite what it was then, but history is still palpable even with a
more cosmopolitan menu than
the standard roast beef and
grilled lamb—even a Thai-style
seafood wok is no longer out
of place here.
🍴 100 🍴 All major cards

SAN MARTÍN DE LOS ANDES

🏨 HOTEL PATAGONIA PLAZA
$$$$$
SAN MARTÍN & RIVADAVIA
TEL/FAX 02972/422-280
www.hotelpatagoniaplaza
.com.ar
The Patagonia boasts a
luminous ground floor,
interior atrium, and plentiful
windows. The rooms vary
in size, but all have contemporary comforts. The central
location is a plus.
🕐 89 🅿 🚭 🚭 🏊 🍸
🍴 All major cards

🏨 HOSTERÍA LA POSTA DEL CAZADOR
$$$$
AVENIDA SAN MARTÍN 175
TEL/FAX 02972/427-802
www.lapostadelcazadoro
.com.ar

🚭 Nonsmoking 🚭 Air-conditioning 🏊 Indoor Pool 🏊 Outdoor Pool 🍸 Health Club 🍴 Credit Cards

On a densely planted lot near the lake, this Euro-style hotel's downstairs rooms are darkish and smallish—go for the upper floor instead. While it accepts credit cards, it inflicts a substantial surcharge on them.

(i) 20 **P** **S** ⛱
S All major cards

RESERVA MERLOT
$$$$
BELGRANO 940
TEL 02972/428-734
Reserva Merlot provides San Martín's most cosmopolitan menu on a base of Patagonian elements such as trout (in its stuffed ravioli) and lamb (skewered, with onions and peppers). The wine list is large, and there are also regional microbrews.

⛴ 65 **S** **S** AE, MC

COLORADO RESTAURANTE
$$$–$$$$
VILLEGAS 659 TEL 02972/427-585
Colorado specializes in a diversity of pastas but also offers salads and stir-frys, and game dishes such as venison; the trout is noteworthy. There's a good wine selection beyond the usual suspects, service is casually attentive, and the chef leaves the kitchen to engage clients in conversation.

⛴ 50 **S** V

TRELEW

HOTEL GALICIA
$$$$
9 DE JULIO 214
TEL 0280/443-3802
www.hotelgalicia.com.ar
Hotel Galicia has a glistening lobby and winding marble staircase but utilitarian rooms. A few blocks from the paleontological museum, it's the best value in town.

(i) 33 **P** **S** All major cards

MAJADERO
$$$$
AVENIDA GALES 250
TEL 0280/443-0548
Majadero has turned the city's historic flour mill into an appealing destination restaurant. Beef and lamb, roasted on the *parrilla,* are the standards, but it also offers pasta.

⛴ 120 **S** **S** **S** AE, MC, V

TREVELIN

NAIN MAGGIE
$$$$
PERITO MORENO 179
TEL 02945/480-232
Its quarters are contemporary, but one of Trevelin's oldest Welsh teahouses maintains the traditions of scones, apple tarts, cream tarts, and especially black cake.

⛴ 56 **Closed Tues. in winter **S** **S** MC, V

OREGON
$$$$
AVENIDA SAN MARTÍN &
JOHN MURRAY THOMAS
TEL 02945/480-408
Except for its teahouses, Trevelin's eating options are limited, but Oregon offers the usual beef dishes plus regional specialties such as Patagonian lamb and trout with a variety of sauces. The rustic décor veers toward kitsch, but doesn't quite get there.

⛴ 45 **S** **Closed Tues. **S** MC, V

VIEDMA

HOTEL AUSTRAL
$$$$
AVENIDA VILLARINO 292
TEL 02920/422-615
Overlooking the river and its parkland, the Hotel Austral is a modern multistory hotel with all the standard amenities and a bit more.

(i) 104 **P** **S** **S** ⛩
S All major cards

HOTEL NIJAR
$$$$
MITRE 490
TEL 02920/422-833
www.hotelnijar.com
Some of the rooms are small, but the Nijar is one of Viedma's best values. It's on a quiet block, the rooms are carpeted, and some have balconies.

(i) 39 **P** **S** **S**
S All major cards

SAHARA PIZZA & PASTA
$$$–$$$$
SAAVEDRA 336
TEL 02920/421-092
It's not special, but the Sahara is a reliable choice for a diversity of pizzas and pastas, plus the usual Patagonian meats and fish and seafood. Appealing to the family trade, it's not the choice for an intimate meal, but reliable at keeping both kids and adults happy.

⛴ 80 **S** **S** All major cards

VILLA LA ANGOSTURA

CORRENTOSO LAKE & RIVER HOTEL
$$$$$
RN 231 & RÍO CORRENTOSO
TEL 0294/15-461-9728
www.correntoso.com
A member of Small Luxury Hotels of the World, the Correntoso re-creates Bustillo's Euro-Andean style—but with the latest in amenities—on the lakeshore just 2 miles (3 km) north of Villa La Angostura. It prides itself on a lakeside fishing bar, spa facilities, and lake-view rooms.

(i) 27 **P** **S** ⛱ ⛩
S All major cards

SOMETHING SPECIAL

🏨 LAS BALSAS GOURMET
🍴 HOTEL & SPA
$$$$$
BAHÍA LAS BALSAS S/N
TEL 0294/449-4308
www.lasbalsas.com
One of only five Relais &
Chateaux affiliates in the
country, Las Balsas is the
champion among luxury
spa hotels on Nahuel Huapi's
north shore. All 12 rooms and
three suites have lake views in
a secluded location. Nonguests
may dine at its highly regarded
restaurant with reservations.

🚪 15 🅿 🚭 🌊 🍸
🔒 All major cards

🏨 HOSTERÍA VERENA'S
HAUS
$$$$
LOS TAIQUES 268
TEL 0294/449-4467
www.verenashaus.com.ar
On a quiet residential block
well off the highway, Verena's
is almost a stereotype of
Teutonic tidiness, a garden
variety B&B with a warm
welcome and cozy rooms. The
diverse breakfast is served to
you in a homey dining room.

🚪 6 🅿 🚭 🔒 Cash only

🍴 TINTO BISTRÓ
$$$$$
BULEVAR NAHUEL HUAPI 34
TEL 0294/449-4924
Using Patagonian products,
such as lamb, Tinto Bistró adds
Asian seasonings to create an
adventurous hybrid cuisine.
The wine list is large.

🍽 50 🕐 Closed Sun. 🚭
🔒 AE, MC, V

🍴 WALDHAUS
$$$$–$$$$$
AVENIDA ARRAYANES 6431,
PUERTO MANZANO
TEL 0294/447-5323
Along the highway east of
Villa La Angostura, Waldhaus

is a Hansel-and-Gretel house
in the woods that serves a
Central European menu of filet
mignon, fondue, German sausages, and goulash, plus some
fusion dishes and a sampling
of Patagonian game. Reservations recommended.

🍽 40 🕐 Closed L 🚭
🔒 All major cards

🍴 LA CABALLERIZA
$$$$
AVENIDA ARRAYANES 44
TEL 0294/449-4248
Under the same ownership
as Waldhaus, La Caballeriza
serves soups, trout, and Patagonian game dishes, alongside
more traditional Argentine
fare, and specializes in wood-
grilled meats.

🍽 30 🕐 Closed Mon.–Tues. L
& Wed. 🚭 🔒 AE, V

🍴 LA ENCANTADA
$$
CERRO BELVEDERE 69
TEL 0294/449-5515
Set on a side street, La Encan-
tada serves pizza, but also
pastas, trout-filled empanadas,
and appetizer platters of
smoked meats and cheeses.
Add in a small but well-chosen
wine list, and this is the town's
best everyday restaurant.

🍽 35 🕐 Closed Sun. D &
Mon. 🚭 🔒 Cash only

▨ TIERRA DEL FUEGO

RÍO GRANDE

🏨 ESTANCIA VIAMONTE
$$$$$
RN 3, 42 KM SOUTH OF
RÍO GRANDE
TEL 02964/430-861
www.estanciaviamonte.com
South of Río Grande,
Viamonte is a historic estancia,
on the cusp between the
steppe and the forests of the
island's northern half. All the

rooms at this comfortable
guest ranch share two baths;
full board is available.

🚪 3 🅿 🚭 🔒 Cash only

🏨 POSADA DE LOS
🍴 SAUCES
$$$$
ELCANO 839
TEL 02964/432-895
Almost facing the open
Atlantic, Posada de los Sauces
is Río Grande's top choice,
with a mix of standard and
VIP rooms, plus one ample
suite. Its restaurant, Comedor
de May, makes it a good self-
contained choice.

🚪 24 🅿 🚭
🔒 All major cards

USHUAIA

SOMETHING SPECIAL

🏨 ESTANCIA
HARBERTON
$$$$$
RUTA C-J
TEL 02901/422-742 IN USHUAIA
www.estanciaharberton.com
Overnighters can enjoy the
island's most historic estancia
in the remodeled cookhouse
(with shared bath) or the
former shepherds' house (with
private bath), though neither
is luxurious. Meals are taken in
the farm's teahouse.

🚪 4 🅿 🚭 🔒 Bank transfer
or cash only

🏨 HOTEL POSADA
FUEGUINA
$$$$$
LASSERRE 438
TEL 02901/423-467
www.posadafueguina.com.ar
Posada Fueguina enjoys unob-
structed panoramas of the
Beagle Channel. Its common
areas and rooms—some wood-
panelled—are comfortable.

🚪 28 🅿 🔒 All major cards

🏨 HOTEL Y RESORT LAS HAYAS
$$$$$
LUIS MARTEL 1650
TEL 02901/430-710
www.lashayashotel.com
Las Hayas is the 1990s version of a luxury hotel—a massive multistory structure with grand panoramas of the Beagle Channel. Its overdone Francophile interiors contrast dramatically with the wild landscape, but no other place in town can match the completeness of its amenities—if that's why you've come to the uttermost part of the Earth.
🛏 93 🅿 ❄ 🚫 🏊 🍴
👜 All major cards

🏨 HOTEL TIERRA 🍴 DE LEYENDAS
$$$$$
TIERRA DE VIENTOS 2448
TEL 02901/443-565
www.tierradeleyendas.com.ar
Once part of Estancia Río Pipo, the landscaping on the grounds is still maturing, but it should grow to match this appealing boutique hotel—whose gourmet restaurant dinners are open to nonguests by reservation—and its view.
🛏 5 🅿 🚫 👜 All major cards

🏨 PATAGONIA VILLA LODGE
$$$$$
BAHÍA BUEN SUCESO 563
TEL 02901/435-937
www.patagoniavilla.com
In a wooded residential area about a mile (1.6 km) east of downtown, Patagonia Villa is a B&B with gracious English-speaking ownership. It occupies two spacious duplexes plus one smaller semisubterranean room.
🛏 5 🅿 🚫 👜 All major cards

🏨 GALEAZZI-BASILY B&B
$$$–$$$$$
GOBERNADOR VALDÉZ 323
TEL 02901/423-213
www.avesdelsur.com.ar
Consisting of four semi-private rooms (sharing two baths) within the main house and three freestanding cabanas, the Galeazzi inhabits a verdant hillside neighborhood that's walking distance from downtown. The owners are longtime residents who know Tierra del Fuego extremely well and share their enthusiasm for it.
🛏 7 🅿 🚫 👜 All major cards

🏨 MARTÍN FIERRO B&B
$$$–$$$$
9 DE JULIO 175
TEL 02901/430-525
www.martinfierrobyb.com.ar
The four upstairs rooms in this small but stylish B&B have comfortable bunks and share two baths, while the two downstairs apartments have their own baths and kitchens. It's close to downtown dining and shopping.
🛏 6 🅿 🚫 👜 Cash only

🍴 CHEZ MANU
$$$$$
LUIS MARTIAL 2135
TEL 02901/432-253
Seafood with a view is the menu at Chez Manu, whose site on the road to the Martial Glacier yields panoramas of the Beagle Channel. It ranks among the city's top restaurants, with Fuegian lamb complementing king crab specialties. Reservations are recommended.
🪑 60 🚫 👜 All major cards

🍴 KAUPÉ
$$$$$
ROCA 470
TEL 02901/422-704
One of Ushuaia's prestige restaurants, the hillside Kaupé

specializes in seafood, particularly *centolla* (king crab), but also fish such as buttered *merluza* (hake) and *lomo* (tenderloin) in a plum sauce. It also features a sophisticated wine bar.
🪑 40 🕐 Closed L & Sun. 🚫 👜 All major cards

🍴 MARÍA LOLA
$$$$$
DELOQUI 1048
TEL 02901/421-185
One of Ushuaia's top restaurants, María Lola has a snug interior whose picture windows have views of the harbor and the Beagle Channel. The menu is strong on fish and seafood (overlapping with pasta dishes), along with Patagonian lamb fricassee. Reservations are recommended.
🪑 50 🕐 Closed Mon. 🚫 👜 All major cards

🍴 137 PIZZA & PASTA
$$$–$$$$
SAN MARTÍN 137
TEL/FAX 02901/435-005
In its specialty—pizzas and pastas, obviously—137 ranks far better than might be expected in a provincial city. The stuffed pastas and empanadas have a regional touch, with fillings such as king crab; the modern décor is comfortable.
🪑 60 🚫 👜 All major cards

🍴 RAMOS GENERALES
$$$
MAIPÚ 749
TEL 02901/424-317
New ownership has renovated a century-old building to create an atmospheric bar/restaurant with period artifacts. Besides wine and beer, the menu is limited to cheese boards, sandwiches, panini on their own fresh bread, and pastries.
🪑 70 🚫 👜 All major cards

Shopping in Argentina

Buenos Aires is Argentina's political capital and, simultaneously, its shopping and fashion capital, but other regions have their specialties, such as leather and silver from gaucho country, and weaving and crafts from the Andean northwest. In the northeastern provinces, carved animals from the aromatic *palo santo* are unique, while the obvious choice in the Cuyo provinces is wine. Lively street markets also abound in Buenos Aires and around the country.

Note that, in general, bargaining is not the everyday practice in Argentina that it is in Andean highland countries such as Bolivia and Peru. It may be more widespread in indigenous northwestern towns such as Humahuaca but, even there, it's less accepted than elsewhere in Latin America.

▦ BUENOS AIRES & THE DELTA

Buenos Aires has recycled many landmark buildings as shopping centers and, in some districts (particularly Palermo), as cutting-edge design and fashion stores. It boasts lively street markets and, in addition, a critical mass of antiques dealers, bookstores, music dealers, and wine shops.

Accessories

Almacén de Belleza *(Online only, tel 011/4723-8857, www.almacen debelleza.com)* For fashion, this virtual world of beauty is cutting-edge—even audacious—for cosmopolitan women anywhere in the world, but it also stocks variations on the classics. In addition, it carries artwork and household items in similarly unconventional styles.

López Taibo *(Avenida Alvear 1902, Recoleta, tel 011/4804-8585)* One of the city's most venerable leather shops, it's a men's footwear specialist, but that doesn't come close to suggesting its diversity of clothing and accessories.

Arts & Antiques

Churrinche Antigüedades *(Defensa 1031, San Telmo, tel 011/4362-7612, www.churrincheantiques.com.ar)* On

a street with wall-to-wall antiques dealers, Churrinche is the go-to place for furnishing your mansion in Recoleta with Limoges porcelain and Persian carpets, but its diversity of stock also includes glassware, gaucho silverwork, and guns.

Books & Maps

El Ateneo Grand Splendid *(Avenida Santa Fe 1860, Recoleta, tel 011/4813-6052,www.elateneo centenario.com)* The quality of the books, many of them in English on Argentine topics, matches the dramatic transformation of this former cinema, where the stage is now a café and readers browse floor-to-ceiling shelves on several levels.

Crafts & Jewelry

Arte Étnico Argentino *(El Salvador 4656, Palermo, tel 011/4832-0516, www.arteetnicoargentino.com)* For most visitors, Arte Étnico's rustically stylish furniture from northwestern Argentina will be too bulky for souvenirs, but its clothing and textiles (from the northern Patagonia Mapuche) will make the house more colorful.

El Boyero *(Florida 953, Retiro, tel 011/4312-3564, www.elboyero .com)* In the entire city, El Boyero has perhaps the most comprehensive selection of crafts from around the country, including clothing, leather, weaving, and gaucho gear (silverwork and jewelry).

Malls

Buenos Aires Design *(Avenida Pueyrredón 2501, Recoleta, tel 011/5777-6000, www.designrecoleta .com.ar)* One of the first, and most exclusive, of the city's shopping

malls, BA Design is home to some 70 different businesses specializing, mostly, in home design and decoration, but also art and clothing. Some have regional and even Patagonian touches.

Galerías Pacífico *(Florida & Avenida Córdoba, Centro/San Nicolás, tel 011/5555-5110, www.galerias pacifico.com.ar)* Originally built as a shopping mall, then neglected for decades as private and government railroad offices, Galerías Pacífico is the mall that even nonshoppers love, for the historic murals that grace its cupola.

Markets

Feria Plaza Belgrano *(Juramento & Vuelta de Obligado, Belgrano, www .feriaplazabelgrano.com)* On the plaza facing the landmark Iglesia La Redonda, a short walk from the Juramento underground station, Belgrano's weekend artisans' market is more manageable and less touristed than its counterparts in Recoleta and San Telmo. About 60 different craftspeople display their products here.

Feria de Artesanos de Plaza Francia *(Junín & Presidente Quintana, Recoleta, www.feriaplazafrancia .com)* With more than 150 stalls that start near Recoleta cemetery and wind around the corner to Avenida Libertador and Avenida Pueyrredón, this weekend and holiday street fair is the city's second most important, though kitschy.

Feria de San Pedro Telmo *(Defensa & Humberto Primo, San Telmo, www.feriasantelmo.com)* Every Sunday, the streets in and around Plaza Dorrego erupt with antiques and crafts stalls, not to mention street performers, in the city's most crowded and colorful outdoor market.

THE PAMPAS

The Pampas are gaucho country, and there's a silversmith on almost every corner in the "gaucho capital" of San Antonio de Areco, but other craftspeople also flourish there.

SAN ANTONIO DE ARECO

Cristina Giordano *(Sarmiento 112, San Antonio de Areco, tel 02326/452-829, www.telarcriollo ypampa.com.ar)* Giordano is a weaver of gaucho garments, including ponchos and sashes.

Primer Museo y Taller Abierto de Platería Criolla *(Lavalle 387, San Antonio de Areco, tel 02326/454-219, www.draghiplaterosorfebres.com)* At San Antonio's most famous silversmith, visitors can see the craftsmen at work on belt buckles, bridles, knives, and spurs, even if they can't afford the thousands of dollars that the most elaborate pieces cost.

THE ANDEAN NORTHWEST

The Andean northwest provinces, with the country's most conspicuous indigenous populations, are famous for their Aymara and Kolla crafts, especially weaving. Gaucho gear, with distinctive regional twists, is also popular—not to mention equally distinctive wines.

SALTA

Horacio Bertero *(Los Parrales 1002, tel 0387/439-9422, www.redsalta.com/hbertero)* The master silversmith Bertero is a protégé of the late Juan José Draghi, of San Antonio de Areco, and this is his workshop as well as his retail outlet.

Plaza de Almas *(Pueyrredón 6, tel 0387/422-8933, www.plazade*

almas.com) Not really a crafts store as such, this is an integrated cultural center with regional products for sale, as well as a pub/restaurant that displays regional art.

AMAICHA DEL VALLE

Museo Pachamama *(RP 307 Km 118, tel 03892/421-004, www.museo pachamama.com)* Héctor Cruz's huge Andean sculpture museum contains a large crafts shop.

PURMAMARCA

Mercado Artesanal On the picturesque town's central plaza, this delightful market panders to tour buses, but selective shoppers will find some memorable pieces.

TILCARA

Calabaza *(Quebrada Sarahuaico, La Banda, tel 0388/495-5169, www.calabazatilcara.com.ar)* The specialty of this workshop is carved, brightly painted gourds which, being lightweight, are easily carried as souvenirs. Also has accommodations.

TUCUMÁN

Museo Folclórico Manuel Belgrano *(24 de Septiembre 565, tel 0381/421-8250)* Neither a museum, in the traditional sense, nor an homage to General Belgrano, this high-end crafts outlet sells artisanal carvings, ceramics, gaucho gear, and leather, in a historic building.

CUYO

Cuyo's specialty is, of course, wine, but that's not everything.

MENDOZA

Las Viñas *(Avenida Las Heras 399, tel 0261/425-1520, www.lasvinas.com.ar)* The name implies wine, which it has in abundance, but this Mendoza institution

carries much more—weavings, leather, silverwork, and beyond, with a regional focus.

Plaza de las Artes On weekends, from 11 a.m. to 11 p.m., Mendoza's artisans line both sides of Plaza Independencia's broad sidewalks with a diversity of crafts, under awnings. The rest of the week, there are smaller numbers of semi-permanent booths.

Vines of Mendoza *(Avenida Belgrano 1194, tel 0261/438-1031, www.vinesofmendoza.com)* Sample the goods before you buy in this intimate wine bar.

PATAGONIA

The Patagonian lakes district is popular for its chocolates and, in the town of El Bolsón, one of the country's best street fairs. Most of Patagonia's finest crafts come from Mapuche Indians.

EL BOLSÓN

Feria Regional Plaza Pagano *(Avenida San Martín)* Every Tuesday, Thursday, and Saturday, this is the best street fair in the provinces.

SAN MARTÍN DE LOS ANDES

Artesanías Neuquinas *(Rosas 790, tel 02972/428-396, www.artesaniasneuquinas.com)* Under provincial administration, this is a cooperative of more than 700 craftspeople, most of them Mapuche women, who produce woolens, wood carvings, musical instruments, and pottery.

TIERRA DEL FUEGO

USHUAIA

Tierra de Humos *(San Martín 861, tel 02901/433-050, www.tierra dehumos.com)* Lots of kitschy souvenirs, but also regional woolens and leather goods.

Entertainment

Buenos Aires is the heart of Argentina's nightlife, a counterpart to New York City or Los Angeles, but in a country where hardly anyone eats dinner before 9 p.m., every city and town of any size has something to do into the early hours. Provincial capitals often have important festivals.

▦ BUENOS AIRES & THE DELTA

Buenos Aires has one of the best and most diverse arts and entertainment scenes in the country.

The Arts

Centro Cultural Borges *(Viamonte 525, tel 011/5555-5359, www.ccborges.org.ar)* Named for Argentina's most famous writer, the Borges hosts performing arts events, film cycles, fine arts exhibitions, and literary seminars.

Centro Cultural Ciudad de Buenos Aires *(Junín 1930, Recoleta, tel 011/4803-1040, www.centrocul turalrecoleta.org)* Alongside the barrio's world-famous cemetery, Recoleta's cultural center is a maze of galleries, museums, cinemas, and theaters, and a major venue for the annual city tango festival.

Teatro Avenida *(Avenida de Mayo 1222, Monserrat, tel 011/4381-0662, www.balirica.org.ar /teatro-avenida.php)* Restored in the 1990s after being gutted by fire, the Avenida hosted the Colón's opera and symphony as the other theater underwent its restoration.

Teatro Catalinas Sur *(Benito Pérez Galdós 93, La Boca, tel 011/4300-5707, www.catalinasur.com .ar)* This community theater group, with its left-of-center leanings and imaginative sets, offers alternative views of the Argentine experience.

Teatro Colón *(Tucumán 1171, tel 011/4378-7109, www.teatrocolon.org .ar)* This is the capital's, and the continent's, temple of opera and symphony.

Teatro General San Martín *(Avenida Corrientes 1530, Centro/San Nicolás, tel 011/4371-0111, www .teatrosanmartin.com.ar)* Architecturally undistinguished (though it has had a much-needed face-lift), the San Martín compensates with an active cultural calendar at several theaters and exhibit halls, and a repertory cinema. It's also the umbrella organization for several other theaters around town.

Festivals

Campeonato Abierto Argentino de Polo *(Campo Argentino de Polo, Avenida del Libertador & Dorrego, Palermo, tel 011/4777-8005, www .aapolo.com)* The mirror image of Argentina's rustic gaucho heritage is the annual polo championships, held mid-November to mid-December.

Exposición Internacional de Ganadería, Agricultura, e Industria Nacional Predio Ferial de la Sociedad Rural Argentina *(Avenida Sarmiento 2704, Palermo, tel 011/4777-5500, www.ruralarg.org.ar)* The nation's farmers and ranchers hold their traditional big event during July winter holidays.

Feria de Galerías Arte BA Predio Ferial de la Sociedad Rural Argentina *(Avenida Sarmiento 2704, Palermo, tel 011/4777-5500, www .sra.org.ar)* In mid- to late May, contemporary galleries from around the city showcase their clients for a week in Palermo, free of charge.

Feria del Libro Predio Ferial de la Sociedad Rural Argentina, *(Avenida Sarmiento 2704, Palermo, tel 011/4777-5500, www.el-libro.org .ar)* On the city fairgrounds, Latin America's biggest book fair draws literary figures of international stature from mid-April to mid-May.

Festival Buenos Aires Tango *(tel 0800/333-7848, www.festivalde tango.gov.ar)* The tango festival has become Buenos Aires's signature event, a ten-day extravaganza of music, song, and dance at multiple venues, usually in mid-August.

Nightlife

Most dance clubs don't get going until well past midnight.

Alsina Buenos Aires *(Alsina 940, Monserrat, tel 011/4334-0097, www.alsinabuenosaires.com.ar)* This enormous ballroom is the city's premier gay venue, with dancing to electronica on weekends.

Clásica y Moderna *(Avenida Callao 892, Recoleta, tel 011/4812-8707, www.clasicaymoderna.com)* The capital's live jazz institution, it's also a bookstore/café, ideal for breakfast and lunch.

La Trastienda *(Balcarce 460, Monserrat, tel 011/5533-5533, www.latrastienda.com)* Rock and electronica are the draws, but even the accordion-based *chamamé* of Mesopotamia is on the bill at this midsize venue.

Niceto Club *(Niceto Vega 5510, Palermo, tel 011/4779-9396, www .nicetoclub.com)* From Thursday through Saturday, Palermo's club of the moment has live bands around 9 p.m. and then, from midnight until daybreak, DJ dance parties.

Notorious *(Avenida Callao 966, Recoleta, tel 011/4813-6888, www .notorious.com.ar)* A jazz café with a contemporary sensibility.

The Roxy *(Niceto Vega 5542, Palermo, tel 011/4085-5274, www .roxylive.com.ar)* Big names in Argentine rock play the Roxy, in new Palermo Hollywood facilities, almost every night.

Spectator Sports

Argentines are sports fanatics, especially about soccer, but anything equestrian also draws enthusiastic attention.

Boca Juniors *(Brandsen 805,*

*tel 011/4309-4700, La Boca, www
.bocajuniors.com.ar)* The Brooklyn
Dodgers of Argentine soccer, in a
comparable neighborhood.
Horse Racing *(Hipódromo
Argentino, Avenida del Libertador
4101, Palermo, tel 011/4778-2800,
www.palermo.com.ar)* The country's
major racetrack.
River Plate *(Estadio Monumental,
Avenida Presidente Figueroa Alcorta
7597, Núñez, tel 011/4789-1200,
www.cariverplate.com.ar)* The New
York Yankees of Argentine soccer, in
an affluent northern neighborhood.

Tango
Confitería Ideal *(Suipacha 380,
Centro/San Nicolás, tel 011/4328-
7750, www.confiteriaideal.com)*
Inexpensive afternoon and evening
milongas in a classic environment.
**El Arranque Nuevo Salón La
Argentina** *(Bartolomé Mitre 1759,
Centro/San Nicolás, tel 011/4371-
6767)* Inexpensive but cliquish afternoon milonga on Monday, Tuesday,
Thursday, and Saturday, in a venue
designed for tango.
El Querandí *(Perú 302, Monserrat, tel 011/5199-1770, www
.querandi.com.ar)* Smaller and more
intimate than the Carlos Gardel.
Esquina Carlos Gardel
*(Carlos Gardel 3200, Balvanera, tel
011/4867-6363, www.esquina
carlosgardel.com.ar)* In the singer's
old neighborhood, this may be the
best of the tango floor shows.
Parakultural Salón Canning
*(Scalabrini Ortiz 1331, Palermo, tel
011/4832-6753, www.parakultural
.com.ar)* Less conventional milonga
with outstanding live music several
nights per week.
Torquato Tasso *(Defensa 1575,
San Telmo, tel 011/4307-6506, www
.torquatotasso.com.ar)* The best
venue for live tango music, with top
performers and reasonable prices.

■ THE PAMPAS
Festival Nacional del Folklore
*(Cosquín, Córdoba, tel 03541/450-
044, www.aquicosquin.org)*

Argentina's preeminent folkloric
music festival, held the last week
of January.
Fiesta de la Tradición *(San
Antonio de Areco)* Spanning two
weekends in mid-November, this is
Argentina's top gauchofest.
Teatro Argentino *(Avenida
51 bet. Calles 9 & 10, La Plata, tel
0221/4291700, www.teatroargentino
.gba.gov.ar)* Beyond Buenos Aires,
Argentina's most prestigious per-
forming arts venue.
**Teatro del Libertador San
Martín** *(Avenida Vélez Sarsfield 365,
Córdoba, tel 0351/433-2320, www
.teatrodellibertador.blogspot.com)*
Córdoba's counterpart to Rosario's
Teatro El Círculo.
Teatro El Círculo *(Laprida &
Mendoza, Rosario, tel 0341/424-5349,
www.teatro-elcirculo.com.ar)* Classical
music, ballet, and opera in the port
metropolis of the Río Paraná.

■ MESOPOTAMIA & THE CHACO
Carnaval del País *(Gualeguaychú,
Entre Ríos, tel 03446/438540,
www.carnavaldelpais.com.ar)* In
January through March, the
country's liveliest Carnaval.

■ THE ANDEAN NORTHWEST
Much of the entertainment in
northwestern Argentina consists
of folkloric shows with traditional
Andean music.
Carnaval Norteño *(Humahuaca,
Jujuy Province)* Though Carnaval takes place in many locales
throughout the Quebrada de
Humahuaca, this is the most accessible version.
Concierto en la Montaña
*(Quebrada de Cafayate, Salta Prov-
ince)* On the last Sunday of July, in
the canyon known as El Anfiteatro,
this is an open-air tribute to the
region's folkloric traditions.
El Boliche de Balderrama
*(San Martín 1126, Salta, tel
0387/421-1542, www.boliche-*

balderrama.com.ar) Salta's oldest
peña, the Boliche takes a floor show
approach to folkloric music.
Enero Tilcareño *(Tilcara, Jujuy
Province)* January is a month of
music, dance, art, and artisans in
Quebrada de Humahuaca's most
appealing town.
La Casona del Molino *(Luis
Burela 1, Salta, tel 0387/434-2835)*
Traditional folkloric music, in a
colonial-style house that also has a
first-rate menu of regional cuisine.

■ CUYO
**Degustación Anual Bodega
Familia Zuccardi** *(RP 33, Fray
Luis Beltrán, Maipú, Mendoza City,
tel 0261/441-0000, www.familia
zuccardi.com)* Every mid-
November, the Zuccardi winery
east of Mendoza City throws a
party, showcasing new vintages
and offering live music and
entertainment.
El Retortuño *(Dorrego 173,
Guaymallén, Mendoza City, tel 0261/
431-6300, www.intertournet.com.ar
/elretortuno)* Big names in national
music play at this suburban Mendoza restaurant.
Fiesta Nacional de la Vendimia
*(Mendoza City, tel 0261/425-1177,
www.vendimia.mendoza.gov.ar)* An
annual wine festival in sprawling
Parque San Martín, lasting four
days in early March.

■ PATAGONIA
Fiesta Nacional de la Nieve
*(San Carlos de Bariloche, Río Negro
Province)* For a week in mid-June,
this marks the start of Bariloche's
ski season.
Fiesta Nacional del Lúpulo
(El Bolsón, Río Negro Province) In
mid-February, El Bolsón's brewers
pour their best.
The Roxy Bariloche *(San
Martín 576, tel 0294/445-9950,
San Carlos de Bariloche, Río Negro
Province, www.theroxybsas.com.ar)*
The Patagonian branch of Buenos
Aires's premier rock venue.

Activities

With a wide range of environments, Argentina provides ample opportunities for outdoor activities. Climbers and hikers will find attractive trails around the country, but particularly in Mendoza Province, home to Cerro Aconcagua. The Pampas are ideal for horseback riding, while fans of extreme ice can hike onto the glaciers at the Southern Patagonian Ice Fields.

Adventure Trips

Aventura Andina *(Esmeralda 629, 7° H, Buenos Aires, tel 011/4322-1370, www.aventura-andina.com.ar)* Tour operator with regional offices in Salta and El Calafate, where it also covers Ushuaia and Chile's Torres del Paine.

Camino Abierto *(Maipú 42, 6th floor, Buenos Aires, tel 011/4342-4132, www.caminoabierto.com)* Operationally based in the Patagonian hamlet of El Chaltén, but offering adventure-oriented trips in all of Argentina's regions.

Cordillera del Sol *(25 de Mayo 43, El Calafate, Patagonia, tel 02902/492-822, www.cordilleradelsol.com)* Half-day and full-day excursions in and around El Calafate, including horseback riding and ice trekking, with longer trips into Chile.

Explorador Expediciones *(Perito Moreno 217, Puerto Iguazú, tel 03757/491-469, www.rainforest.iguazuargentina.com)* Three-day activities-oriented packages to Parque Nacional Iguazú and to Iberá, plus activity-based excursions to Iguazú.

Meridies *(tel 0294/451-2073, www.meridies.com.ar)* Meridies offers a diversity of activities-based programs that include rock climbing, hiking, sea kayaking, mountaineering, and combinations thereof. While Bariloche based, it covers the Andes from the altiplano of Jujuy south through Aconcagua and to the Patagonian Ice Fields.

NYCA Adventure *(Cabo García 122, El Chaltén, Patagonia, tel 02962/493-185, www.nyca-adventure.com.ar)* Rugged adventure trips onto the Southern Patagonian Ice Field, plus trekking, climbing, and kayaking on the Río Santa Cruz.

Rolling Travel *(tel 0351/570-9905, Córdoba, Cuyo, www.rollingtravel.com.ar)* It's the obligatory concessionaire for tours of Parque Nacional Talampaya, but it also arranges itineraries throughout the country.

Sendero Sur *(Perú 359, Oficina 608, Buenos Aires, tel 011/4343-1571, www.senderosur.com.ar)* Also Bariloche based, but with offices in Buenos Aires as well, it organizes mountain biking, hiking, horseback riding, sea kayaking, and multisport combinations in the Patagonian lakes district and the southern Patagonian Andes. Some include estancia stays.

Birding

In a country of Argentina's size and ecological diversity, birders—especially those visiting the Southern Hemisphere for the first time—will find plenty to add to their life lists. Prime sites include the subtropical Iberá marshes of Corrientes Province, the northwestern cloud forests and Andean uplands, the Patagonian coastline, and the northern Patagonian lakes district. Except perhaps on the Patagonian shore, where birds are abundant, a specialist guide is desirable.

Clark Expediciones *(Mariano Moreno 1950, Salta, tel 0387/497-1024, www.clarkexpediciones.com)* Committed and knowledgeable birding specialists in the *yungas* cloud forests and the Andean puna, with multiday safaris.

Estancia Monte Dinero *(RP 1, Patagonia, tel 02966/428-922, www.montedinero.com.ar)* Best base for visiting the huge penguin colony, with many other seabirds

and shorebirds, at Cabo Vírgenes, in Santa Cruz Province.

Rincón del Socorro *(RP 40, Km 83, Colonia Carlos Pellegrini, Corrientes, tel 011/5272-0344 in Buenos Aires, www.rincondelsocorro.com)* A birder's dream, with hundreds of species, plus mammals and reptiles in the Iberá marshes. Riding and hiking make it a multisport holiday.

Fishing

There are two major kinds of fishing in Argentina. One is big-game fishing in the Mesopotamian provinces, for species like *boga* and dorado. The other is trout fishing in the northern Patagonian provinces of Neuquén and Río Negro and, to a lesser degree, Chubut, Santa Cruz, and Tierra del Fuego.

Jerónimo Cantón *(tel 02945/534-311, patagoniatrout@gmail.com)*. Jerónimo Cantón is an independent English-speaking fishing guide.

Patagonia Adventures *(Pablo Hube 418, El Bolsón, Río Negro, tel 0294/449-2513, www.argentinachileflyfishing.com)* Patagonian fly-fishing specialist, in both Argentina and Chile.

Posada Paso de la Patria *(Avenida Santa Coloma & Dorado, Paso de la Patria, Corrientes, tel 03783/494-556, www.posadapasopatria.com.ar)* Only half an hour from the provincial capital, this lodge specializes in fishing big Paraná game such as the dorado.

Golf

Argentina has dozens of 18-hole courses, most of them in or around Buenos Aires, but with others scattered throughout the country. For details, contact the **Asociación Argentina de Golf** *(Avenida Corrientes 538, 11th floor, Buenos Aires, tel 011/4325-1113, www.aag.com.ar).*

Horseback Riding

For much of its history, Argentina has been a country on horseback, with the rugged gaucho style as the default option. English-style riding made major inroads with the upper classes, though, as did polo. For riders, the estancias of Buenos Aires Province offer a chance to gallop over endless pastures.

Club Alemán de Equitación *(Avenida Dorrego 4045, Palermo, Buenos Aires, tel 011/4778-7060, www.clubalemandeequitacion.com)* The German riding club is the best riding option within the city limits.

Estancia El Ombú de Areco *(RP 31, Cuartel VI, Villa Lía, San Antonio de Areco, Buenos Aires Province, tel 011/4737-0436 in Buenos Aires, www.estanciaelombu.com)* Riders here can even join the gauchos on the roundups and, if they're up to it, help brand the calves.

Estancia Huechahue *(RN 234, Junín de los Andes, Neuquén, www.huechahue.com)* Jane Williams is a Londoner who, adapting to the country through marriage and longtime residence, has made Huechahue the go-to place for hard gaucho-style riding on multiday trips into the Andes.

Estancia La Bamba *(RP 31, San Antonio de Areco, Buenos Aires Province, tel 011/4519-4996, www.labambadeareco.com)* If La Bamba seems cinematic, well, it is—director María Luis Bemberg used it for her historical epic *Camila.*

Estancia y Polo Club La Candelaria *(RN 215 Km 114.5, Lobos, Buenos Aires Province, tel 0227/494-132, www.estanciacandelaria.com)* A Norman-style castle is the backdrop for polo packages, but standard horseback riding is also possible.

La Martina Polo Ranch *(tel 0226/430772, Vicente Casares, Buenos Aires Province, www.lamartinapolo.com.ar)* At La Martina, the gaucho tradition influences the elegance of polo; aspiring riders can get lessons from world-class professionals such as Adolfo Cambiaso.

See also the sidebar "Guest Ranches of the Pampas," p. 109.

Mountain Biking

Argentina has almost unlimited potential for mountain biking, primarily in the Andes but also in the backcountry of Córdoba and in and around Tandil (Buenos Aires Province). The prime areas, though, are northwestern Argentina, Mendoza Province, the lakes district in and around San Carlos de Bariloche, and the southern Patagonian provinces of Chubut and Santa Cruz. Touring the country by mountain bike is an option (road bikes are not suitable for gravel routes, but are possible in areas with paved roads).

MTB Tours *(Maipú 26 2° G, Buenos Aires, tel 011/4288-1549, www.mtbtours.com)* MTB leads tours from Malargüe (Mendoza) across the Andes into Chile, and through northwestern destinations such as the Valles Calchaquíes and the altiplano of Salta and Jujuy Provinces.

Hiking & Mountaineering

With some of the world's highest, most scenic, and most challenging mountains, Argentina is prime hiking and climbing country, especially in the Patagonian lakes district and the far southern Andes. The biggest destination, literally, is Cerro Aconcagua, the "roof of the Americas" in Mendoza Province. National parks in the northern Patagonian district, such as Lanín and Nahuel Huapi, have fine trail networks, while the southern town of El Chaltén is the gateway to the country's finest hiking and iconic peaks such as Fitz Roy and Cerro Torre.

Aconcagua Trek *(Tel 0261/15-466-5825, www.rudyparra.com)* Trekking and mountaineering, with mule support, on Aconcagua.

Fernando Grajales Expediciones *(tel 800/516-6962 in the U.S., www.grajales.net)* The last four digits of the toll-free number match the height, in meters, of Aconcagua. Grajales also organizes climbs of lesser known but equally challenging Andean peaks.

FitzRoy Expediciones *(San Martín 56, El Chaltén, Patagonia, tel/fax 02962/493-178, www.fitzroyexpediciones.com.ar)* Specializes in trekking over the Southern Patagonia Ice Field, but also handles climbing and kayaking.

Rafting & Kayaking

For white-water rafting and kayaking, Argentina takes second place to its Andean neighbor Chile, but northern Patagonia's Río Manso is more than just a float. Other whitewater options include Salta and Mendoza Provinces.

Aguas Blancas *(Morales 564, San Carlos de Bariloche, Río Negro, tel 0294/443-2799, www.aguasblancas.com.ar)* Rafting and kayaking on the Río Manso, about an hour south of Bariloche.

Extremo Sur *(Morales 765, San Carlos de Bariloche, Río Negro, tel 0294/442-7301 www.extremosur.com)* Rafting and kayaking on the Río Manso.

Sendero Sur *(Perú 359, Oficina 608, Buenos Aires, tel 011/4343-1571)* One- and two-day sea kayak trips through the lush Paraná Delta, Buenos Aires Province.

Sailing & Cruising

Cruce Andino: Contact Turisur *(Mitre 219, tel. 0294/442-6109, www.turisur.com.ar or www.cruceandino.com).* The famous bus-boat shuttle from Bariloche across the Andes to Chile, experienced by luminaries ranging from Theodore Roosevelt to Ernesto (Che) Guevara.

Cruceros Australis *(4014 Chase Avenue, Suite 215, Miami, FL 33140, tel 305/695-9618, toll-free 877/ 678-3772, www.australis.com)* This Chilean company shuttles small cruise ships (about 100 passengers) between Ushuaia (Argentina) and the Chilean port of Punta Arenas, visiting Cape Horn and the fjords of Tierra del Fuego.

Tres Marías Excursiones *(tel 02901/436-416, Ushuaia, Tierra del Fuego, www.tresmariasweb .com)* Small boat alternative in the Beagle Channel, permitting closer approaches and landings in places where oversize tourist catamarans are less maneuverable. Also does scuba diving.

Scuba

Neither Argentina nor Patagonia jumps to mind immediately to divers, but the coastal city of Puerto Madryn has clear waters, natural and artificial reefs, and a bevy of diving operators. With luck, you may be swimming with penguins.

Lobo Larsen *(Avenida Roca 885, Puerto Madryn, Patagonia, tel 0280/447-0277, www.lobolarsen .com)* Diving among the natural and artificial reefs, and shipwrecks, at Argentina's most southerly beach resort.

Skiing

Argentina's prime skiing areas are Mendoza Province and the northern Patagonian lakes district from San Martín de los Andes south to San Carlos de Bariloche.

Chapelco Aventura *(Mariano Moreon 859, Río Negro, tel 02972/ 427-845, www.cerrochapelco.com)* Key skiing area in the northern Patagonian lakes district.

Las Leñas *(tel 011/4819-6060, www.laslenas.com)* Ski packages at a self-contained resort, widely considered to offer Argentina's finest powder, in Mendoza Province.

Surfing

Argentina's not known for its waves, but Mar del Plata and neighboring cities on the southern coast of Buenos Aires Province get their share of surfers.

Tango

Tango is a Buenos Aires brand. Some people visit the city for no other reason, and others move there to live it 24/7/365.

Mansión Dandi Royal *(Piedras 922, Buenos Aires, tel 011/4361-3537, www.mansiondandiroyal .com)* For those unable to move to Buenos Aires, this tango-themed hotel offers a limited-time, total immersion experience.

Tours With a Twist

Cicerones de Buenos Aires *(tel 011/5258-0909, www.cicerones.org .ar)* Nonprofit organization that arranges for knowledgeable but non-professional locals to escort visitors around Buenos Aires.

Eternautas *(Avenida Presidente Julio Roca 584, 7th floor, Monserrat, Buenos Aires, tel 011/5031-9916, www.eternautas.com)* Professional historians and other scholars are the guides on excursions in the Buenos Aires area that are more diverse, and intellectually challenging, than the norm.

La Bicicleta Naranja *(Pasaje Giuffra 308, San Telmo, tel 011/4362-1104, www.labicicletanaranja.com.ar)* Guided tours of Buenos Aires on one-speed bicycles.

Tangol *(Florida 971, Local 31, Retiro, Buenos Aires, tel 011/4312-7276, www.tangol.com)* Full-service travel agency that specializes in Argentina's twin passions—tango and soccer.

Other

MoviTrack *(Caseros 468, tel 0387/431-1223, Salta, www .movitrack.com.ar)* Monster-truck safaris through the high-altitude backcountry of Salta and Jujuy Provinces.

Yacutinga Lodge *(www.yacu tinga.com)* Multiday visits to a private nature reserve, with comfortable lodging, in a remote corner of Misiones Province. Contact via Internet only.

INDEX

Bold page numbers indicate illustrations.
CAPS indicates thematic categories.

ILLUSTRATIONS CREDITS

Front cover, Altrendo Images/Getty Images; spine, javarman3/iStockphoto. All interior photographs by Eliseo Miciu unless otherwise noted: 9, VikaValter/iStockphoto.com; 20, 3Fotografia/Getty Images; 24, wiedzma/Shutterstock; 35, James P. Blair; 38, Steven Wright/Shutterstock; 42, Claudio Villa/Getty Images; 53, Photofest; 58, blickwinkel/Alamy; 62, Gary Yim/Shutterstock; 66, Nikada/ iStockphoto.com; 71, Glowimages/Getty Images; 88, Stephen St. John/National Geographic/Getty Images; 91, David R. Frazier Photolibrary, Inc./Alamy; 109, Estancia El Rocio; 110, AP Photo/Pablo Aneli; 116, Juan Mabromata/AFP/Getty Images; 134, Jorge Uzon/ CORBIS; 141, Winfield Parks/National Geographic/Getty Images; 159, Lara Hata/Getty Images; 167, Barbara A. Noe, NGS; 173, Brooklyn Museum/CORBIS; 180, Leo La Valle/epa/CORBIS; 188, 3Fotografia/Getty Images; 191, Cristian Lazzari/iStockphoto.com; 198, James Brunker/Alamy; 201, George F. Mobley; 206, SambaPhoto/Sergio De Devittiis/Getty Images; 212, Louie Psihoyos/Science Faction/CORBIS; 224, Sebastien Cote/iStockphoto.com; 228, RFR/Alamy; 238, Kent Kobersteen, National Geographic Stock .com; 272, Adrian 507/Shutterstock; 278, Dan Kite/iStockphoto.com.

National Geographic
TRAVELER
ARGENTINA

Published by the National Geographic Society
Gary E. Knell, *President and Chief Executive Officer*
John M. Fahey, *Chairman of the Board*
Declan Moore, *Executive Vice President; President, Publishing and Travel*
Melina Gerosa Bellows, *Publisher and Chief Creative Officer, Books, Kids, and Family*
Lynn Cutter, *Executive Vice President, Travel*
Keith Bellows, *Senior Vice President and Editor in Chief, National Geographic Travel Media*

Prepared by the Book Division
Hector Sierra, *Senior Vice President and General Manager*
Janet Goldstein, *Senior Vice President and Editorial Director*
Jonathan Halling, *Creative Director*
Marianne R. Koszorus, *Design Director*
Barbara A. Noe, *Senior Editor, National Geographic Travel Books*
R. Gary Colbert, *Production Director*
Jennifer A. Thornton, *Director of Managing Editorial*
Susan S. Blair, *Director of Photography*
Meredith C. Wilcox, *Director, Administration and Rights Clearance*

Staff for This Book
Justin Kavanagh, *Project Editor*
Elisa Gibson, *Art Director*
Ruth Ann Thompson, *Designer*
Carl Mehler, *Director of Maps*
Mike McNey & Mapping Specialists, *Map Production*
Hannah Lauterback, *Contributor*
Marshall Kiker, *Associate Managing Editor*
Mike O'Connor, *Production Editor*
Galen Young, *Rights Clearance Specialist*

Production Services
Phillip L. Schlosser, *Senior Vice President*
Chris Brown, *Vice President, NG Book Manufacturing*
George Bounelis, *Vice President, Production Services*
Nicole Elliott, *Manager*
Rachel Faulise, *Manager*
Robert L. Barr, *Manager*

The information in this book has been carefully checked and to the best of our knowledge is accurate. However, details are subject to change, and the National Geographic Society cannot be responsible for such changes, or for errors or omissions. Assessments of sites, hotels, and restaurants are based on the author's subjective opinions, which do not necessarily reflect the publisher's opinion.

The National Geographic Society is one of the world's largest nonprofit scientific and educational organizations. Founded in 1888 to "increase and diffuse geographic knowledge," the member-supported Society works to inspire people to care about the planet. Through its online community, members can get closer to explorers and photographers, connect with other members around the world, and help make a difference. National Geographic reflects the world through its magazines, television programs, films, music and radio, books, DVDs, maps, exhibitions, live events, school publishing programs, interactive media, and merchandise. *National Geographic* magazine, the Society's official journal, published in English and 38 local-language editions, is read by more than 60 million people each month. The National Geographic Channel reaches 440 million households in 171 countries in 38 languages. National Geographic Digital Media receives more than 25 million visitors a month. National Geographic has funded more than 10,000 scientific research, conservation, and exploration projects and supports an education program promoting geography literacy. For more information, visit www.nationalgeographic.com.

For more information, please call 1-800-NGS LINE (647-5463) or write to the following address:

National Geographic Society
1145 17th Street N.W.
Washington, D.C. 20036-4688 U.S.A.

For information about special discounts for bulk purchases, please contact National Geographic Books Special Sales: ngspecsales@ngs.org

For rights or permissions inquiries, please contact National Geographic Books Subsidiary Rights: ngbookrights@ngs.org

National Geographic Traveler: Argentina
(Second edition)

ISBN: 978-1-4262-1361-8

Printed in Hong Kong
14/THK/1